Barbarossa to Berlin

A Chronology of the Campaigns
on the Eastern Front
1941 to 1945

Volume 1

The Long Drive East
22 June 1941 to 18 November 1942

BARBAROSSA TO BERLIN

A CHRONOLOGY OF THE CAMPAIGNS ON THE EASTERN FRONT 1941 TO 1945

Volume 1

The Long Drive East

22 June 1941 to 18 November 1942

by

Brian Taylor

SPELLMOUNT

British Library Cataloguing in Publication Data:
A catalogue record for this book is available
from the British Library

Copyright © Brian Taylor 2003, 2008
Maps copyright © Spellmount 2003, 2008

ISBN 978-1-86227-451-8

First published in the UK in 2003 by
Spellmount Limited
This paperback edition published in 2008 by
Spellmount Publishers, Cirencester Road,
Chalford, Stroud,
Gloucestershire, GL5 8PE

Tel: 01453 883300
Fax: 01453 883233
E-mail: enquiries@spellmount.com
Website: www.spellmount.com

1 3 5 7 9 8 6 4 2

Printed in Great Britain

Contents

List of Maps

Preface

Between June 1941 and May 1945 the largest conflict Europe had ever experienced raged across Russia and the East European States. *Barbarossa to Berlin* charts this conflict, detailing in chronological order the military events that extended across a combat front stretching from the Barents Sea in the north to the Black Sea in the south. The book does not seek to offer an interpretation of the great battles and manœuvres that took place, rather to give the facts.

By adopting a chronological style, the book aims to give the reader an understanding of the constraints time and space place upon military operations, their planners and commanders in the field. It aims to demonstrate how the actions of one sector of the front interacted with another.

As the account is divided into *sectors*, readers can if they wish, concentrate on the actions of a particular army group or front or follow the campaigns across all sectors simultaneously. There are three main sectors throughout the text, the *Northern Sector*, the *Central Sector* and the *Southern Sector*. Their areas of operation roughly follow the axes of the three main German army groups. The *Northern Sector* concentrates on operations in the Baltic States, and, as the campaign developed, the fighting around Leningrad, along the Volkhov and south of Lake Ilmen. Similarly, the *Central Sector* covers the theatre of operations of Army Group Centre, detailing the battles on the long road to Moscow and subsequent counter-offensives. The *Southern Sector* largely covers actions in the Ukraine and Caucasus regions. Each month end aims to give the reader a snapshot of the opposing forces. Under the headings such as Ostheer and Red Army, the deployment and commitments of the two combatant armies are detailed throughout the book in an effort to bring home the human cost of the war. Importantly, the perspective of the text is neither German nor Soviet but seeks to offer factual detail of the conflict by both armies. German orders of battle are given in divisional detail at the beginning of significant operations but the mainstay of the work concentrates on the actions of the German armies and korps. Similarly, Soviet deployment is given in army and corp detail at the beginning of major phases of operations, but remains largely at army level throughout the text. German divisional or Soviet corp accounts are only included in the detail of military operations when their actions are of significant importance.

Finally, while this book does not deal with the individual accounts of the war, it recognises the terrible human cost of the conflict. The horrendous atrocities committed by both regimes upon their enemies and their own people are not directly addressed but should always be remembered.

CHAPTER I
Historical Introduction

Why did war break out between Germany and the Soviet Union and how did time secret pacts between Weimar Germany and the new Bolshevik state end in the most bloody conflict ever to race on European soil? This chapter aims to give an out line of the masons behind the conflict, and its inevitability from the moment Adolf Hitler began his journey to power in Germany

Germany's Road to War

Adolf Hitler gained control of Germany in January 1933 after fifteen years of social and political turmoil. After joining the NSDAP[1], Hitler led an attempt to seize control of Bavaria by force of arms. The coup flopped under the fire of the Bavarian police and Hitler landed in jail, albeit with a remarkably light sentence handed down by a sympathetic judge. The setback did nothing to dampen the fledgling politician's ambition. From his prison cell he set out the aims of the Nazi Party, aims that called for the utter destruction of Jews and Bolshevism in Europe, coupled with the acquisition of living space for Germany at the expense of the Slavs in Eastern Europe. In 1933 the Nazi Party came to power, but Hitler's Chancellorship was not secure. Hindenburg reluctantly gave in to his demands. Despite his lowly origins, the man from Brannau, who had enlisted as an ordinary soldier in the Kaiser's army in 1914, had risen to the highest elected office in Germany.

With the death of Hindenburg in August 1934 Hitler gained complete control of the state, proclaiming himself Führer of the Third German Reich. From this day on, war with the Soviet Union was inevitable.

In 1935 the office of Minister of Defence, held by General von Blomberg, the Commander in Chief of the Armed Forces, became that of Minister for War, but Hitler was not satisfied with the *status quo*. With Goering conspiring to become Minister for War, Hitler forced Blomberg to resign

1

during 1938. However, Goering was cheated of his prize as Hitler had his eye on the Ministry. In February Hitler appointed himself Minister for War, and by default Commander in Chief of the Armed Forces. Goering was placated with control of the Luftwaffe. Shortly afterwards, the War Ministry was dissolved to become the Armed Forces High Command (Oberkommando der Wehrmacht, commonly abbreviated to OKW) with General Wilhelm Keitel appointed its head. This was a serious blow to the authority of the army, which was relegated to a branch of service instead of an office in its own right. With Blomberg gone, General Fritsch was appointed Commander in Chief of the Army and General Beck Chief of the Army General Staff. Neither would be in his post long. With Himmler's and Goering's aid, Hitler removed Fritsch in mid-1938 on the flimsiest of grounds, accusing the general of being a homosexual. Field Marshal Walther von Brauchitsch took over the vacant command and this time Hitler had his man. Brauchitsch was a firm supporter of Hitler, having recently married a fervent Nazi supporter. By the end of August, Beck had also gone, resigning in protest at the treatment of Fritsch. General Franz Halder was appointed Chief of the General Staff, bringing into position the final pawn in the game that was about to be played across Europe.

In 1939 Hitler turned his attention to the Polish question. Revoking the 1934 Non-Aggression Pact, Hitler demanded the return of Danzig and a guarantee of access through the Polish Corridor between Pomerania and East Prussia. The Poles refused and Hitler prepared to attack. On 1st September 1939 German forces crossed the border with Poland to resolve the issue by force of arms, a nervous Hitler gambling that Britain and France would refuse to go to war over the fate of the Polish state. However, he made his first serious error of udgement, and on 3rd September Britain and France declared war. The gamble had failed. For the second time in a quarter of a century, Germany was plunged into a European War against the British and the French.

Initially, however, it appeared that Hitler's gamble had paid off. Poland fell after a Iightening campaign lasting just twenty-eight days, indelibly marking the Blitzkrieg principle upon the world. But the German army had still not entirely appreciated the weapon it had at its disposal. Continuing General Staff misgivings would not be allayed until after the campaign in the west. In accordance with the secret Non-Aggression Pact signed with the Soviet Union in August 1939, the eastern provinces of Poland went to the Soviet Union, securing Germany's eastern border, for the short term at least. Throughout this critical period, with almost all of German armed strength committed to war with Poland, the British and French remained inactive. France was reluctant to leave the protection of the Maginot defences. Following the fall of Poland, Hitler turned west, contemplating the continuation of the war with Britain and France. Even before the attack upon Poland,

Hitler knew that if Germany was to be victorious in any European war, she could commit her resources to only one theatre. He therefore determined that if he was to avoid a two front war, one had to be secured through negotiation.

Before the invasion, Hitler had sought an alliance with his ideological opponent, the Soviet Union. Despite his overwhelming hatred of Bolshevism, at the end of May 1939 Hitler let it be known through the German Foreign Office, that Germany was willing to come to a settlement with the Soviet Union over the question of territorial ambitions in Eastern Europe. Negotiations followed and on 23 August 1939 the German Foreign Minister, Joachim von Ribbentrop, signed a Non-Aggression Pact with Molotov, his Soviet counterpart. Through this agreement Poland was partitioned between the Germans and the Soviets while Germany also recognised Soviet influence in Finland, Estonia and Latvia. Lithuania was to come under German influence. Ribbentrop, with an open manifesto authorised by Hitler, also agreed to sign away German ambitions in the Balkans, a clause of the agreement which was to cause Hitler a great deal of concern a year later as he sought to protect his supplies of oil from the Ploesti fields in Rumania. In addition to the political agreement that had been reached, there had also been a favourable trade agreement settled. In exchange for Soviet deliveries of raw materials to Germany, the Germans would export finished manufactured goods to the Soviet Union.

Germany came off substantially better from the agreement, receiving large quantities of foodstuffs, including grain and cattle along with oil, coal, lead and zinc, all fuel for the hungry German war machine. At the same time Hitler forbade the intelligence section of the OKW, a department known as Foreign Armies East (Fremde Heeren Ost, led by Colonel Kinzel), from gathering any information on the Soviet Union so as not to jeopardise the treaty. Kinzel had no real knowledge of Russia, her strengths or weaknesses and was unable to speak Russian.

On I0 May 1940 the Germans attacked in the West. Within six weeks France lay defeated. German armies smashed through the hastily established French defence lines and occupied all of France north of the Loire, including the entire Atlantic coast. The military might of France had been crushed in just six brief summer weeks.

With her main continental enemy beaten, all that stood between Germany and peace in the west was Britain. Hitler half-heartedly attempted to make peace, but then decided that Britain must be invaded. This led to the Battle of Britain in the skies above England, the Luftwaffe attempting to gain air supremacy over the RAF. The Germans failed to gain control of the skies and by early autumn the battle had wound itself down, Germany having suffered her first military reverse of the war. Hitler shelved his plans for an invasion, and had already turned his attentions to the east. The defeat of Germany in the skies over Britain was of major importance as it left a door open to a renewal of the conflict in the west. Despite his efforts over the previous year, Hitler had failed to bring the war in the west to a satisfactory conclusion.

By this stage of the conflict Hitler was thinking of a campaign in the east. Hardly had the battle of France ended than he spoke of German eyes being turned to the east. Less than a month later, on 21 July, he ordered Brauchitsch to conduct a study on the possibility of a campaign against the Soviet Union. By the end of the month Hitler announced to his generals that a reckoning with the Soviet Union was necessary to decide the course of the war in Europe. Initially wanting to proceed with the operation in the autumn of 1940, Hitler realised this was not feasible and decided that the offensive must begin by May 1941. However, the operation had to be swift to prevent the possibility of American or British intervention. Five months were allowed for the defeat of the Russian colossus.

On 1 August 1940 Halder tasked General Marcks with the planning of an offensive against the Soviet Union utilising two army groupings. Marcks set to work and on 5 August returned with a draft outline. It envisaged a primary attack against the Russian forces north of the Pripet Marshes on the Moscow axis with a secondary attack through the Baltic States towards Leningrad. The second prong would push towards Kiev to tie down Russian forces in the Ukraine. The primary strategic aim of the campaign was the capture of Moscow. Hitler considered the attack a preventative war, having convinced himself that the Soviets would attack Germany in the next year or two. Among other details the appreciation called for the occupation of Russian territory to a line running from Archangel, through Corki and on to Rostov. Moscow, Leningrad, the Ukraine and the Donbas (the mining and industrial region west of Rostov) were designated economic and political targets. Not all the German General Staff shared Hitler's enthusiasm for an attack into the Soviet Union. Halder had serious reservations, expressing his opinion that war with Russia would do nothing to help the struggle against Britain and in actual fact would worsen Germany's overall situation, substantially weakening her economic position as she struggled to fight on two fronts. He also stressed that if war with Russia was indeed inevitable, it must be total and the only theatre to which the German army was committed. Admiral Erich Raeder, commanding the Kriegsmarine (Navy) was also opposed to the plan and spoke out repeatedly against it. He proposed that Germany should pursue action against the British, seizing Gibraltar, Egypt and Palestine. Both Halder and Goering backed Raeder's proposal, but Hitler would not be swayed.

Even at this early planning stage, German intelligence on Russia was extremely poor. Hitler's earlier ban on intelligence gathering had seriously hindered an already inadequate knowledge of the gigantic eastern enemy. The maps available to Germans were extremely poor, being badly detailed and wildly inaccurate. Furthermore, Germany lacked detailed information on Soviet military strength or industrial and military potential, and had scant information about the Red Army officer caste. Only Stalin's closest compatriots from the Russian Civil War days were known, men like Voroshilov, Budenny and Timoshenko. No orders of battle were available for Soviet units in the west, except those deployed in the immediate border areas.

Not only was German knowledge of the military lacking, the economic potential of the Soviet Union was also virtually unknown. The existence of heavy industry east of the Urals was greatly underestimated not only by Germany but by the rest of the world. It is hard to understand that with such glaring deficiencies in even the most basic fields of data, operational planning should go any further. Remarkably it carried on unhindered, sponsored by Hitler's dreams of conquering the east. At the end of October 1940 planning was continued under General Friedrich Paulus, later commander of the ill-fated 6th Army. Paulus followed on from the basic principles established by General Marcks, envisaging the attack being made by three separate army groups, two north of the Pripet Marshes and one south. The primary aim remained the destruction of the Soviet field army and the prevention of escape into the interior. War games between 28 November and 3 December thrashed out the plan and revealed likely problems. The results were presented to Hitler along with a formal outline of the operation on 5 December. The army group staffs, independently of each other, expressed their concerns over the inevitable expansion of the German front as it moved east and the subsequent demands and strains this would place upon their manpower resources. There were also major concerns over the ability of the transport service to supply the 3,000,000 men and half a million horses of the invasion force, the lack of usable through railways forcing the Germans to transport the bulk of their freight by truck. The problem with the railways was that the Soviets used a wider rail gauge than the Germans. This meant that all captured railway lines had to be reset by engineers before freight could travel straight through to the advancing armies. The alternative was to truck everything from the borders or reload it at the border onto captured rolling stock. However, these were not the only concerns.

Germany's manpower and mineral resources were also brought into question, General Friedrich Fromm's Ersatz Heer (Replacement Army) having limited replacements available to make good the expected battlefield losses. The supply of motor vehicles was inadequate and motor fuel was in relatively short supply, Germany having just three months' reserves of petrol and a one–month reserve of diesel. Tyres were a major problem as rubber was in short supply.

Yet in spite all of these potential problems, Hitler continued to forge ahead. The Generals, realising that resistance against Hitler was futile, pressed for the destruction of the Red Army as the primary aim of the campaign but Hitler objected. He believed that the capture of Soviet territory should be the key to the success of the campaign yet inexplicably announced that Moscow, the hub of the Soviet rail and communications network, was not important. He would only agree to an advance as far as Smolensk. Once this line had been reached it wasn't known what the German armies would then do.

On 17 December 1940 Directive 21 was submitted to Hitler for signing, but even at this late stage he interfered, lftering the plan to give priority to the drive on Leningrad rather than in the centre towards Moscow. This change was prompted by Hitler's interpretation of the rival Lossberg plan, undertaken by General von Lossberg under the jurisdiction of Jodl's OKW. The following day the directive was signed and issued to the army groups in outline as Operation Barbarossa.

Purges and Paranoia: A Brief Introduction to Stalin's Russia

In 1924 Lenin's death opened the door of power to Joseph Stalin. Under his iron rule the Soviet Union underwent colossal change. Industrialisation was widespread as Russia raced to become a modern industrial nation. By the mid 1930s Russia had one of the largest economies in the world, but it was built upon labour camps and forced collectivisation. However, as in Nazi Germany, the key to power in the Soviet Union lay with the army.

Stalin, ever suspicious of treason, turned his murderous paranoia towards the officer corps of the army, wiping it out in massive numbers. Beginning in June 1937, the Great Purge claimed the lives of almost 35,000 Red Army officers, many disappearing to labour camps in Siberia or facing summary execution. Among those killed were three out of five marshals of the Soviet Union, only Voroshilov and Budenny, Stalin's colleagues from the days of the First Cavalry Army in the Civil War, remaining. One of the marshals killed was Tukhachevski. He was the main proponent of mechanisation within the Red Army and in the years before his death had begun to reorganise the army along modern lines. However, with his death, the Red Army reverted to the arcane methods of World War One, with Voroshilov and Kulik opposed to the concept of the tank as a primary weapon. In addition to the loss of the marshals, all of the military district commanders and thirteen of fifteen army commanders were killed, plus in excess of half of all officers with the rank of general.

As in Germany, following the Ribbentrop–Molotov agreement in 1939, Stalin's attention turned to territorial expansion. In September 1939 the Soviet Union began its march west, occupying the eastern provinces of Poland. Shortly after the conclusion of the campaign, Molotov and Ribbentrop met again to renegotiate the demarcation line. The Soviets agreed to move their line east in exchange for Germany giving up her claims on territory in Lithuania. Germany's only interest in this region was reduced to the strip of land butting against East Prussia. In the winter of 1930 Stalin pressed his demands for territory against Finland but the Finnish David, a nation of just four million who had only gained independence from Russia at the end of the Great War, stood up to the Russian Goliath. The Soviets immediately deployed for war and invaded on 30 November. With overwhelming superiority in numbers, the Red Army attempted to smash its way through the Finnish positions but Finnish knowledge was far superior to Soviet brawn. Suffering a humiliating reverse, Stalin appointed General Timoshenko to renew the war in January 1940. Timoshenko opted to bulldoze his way through the Finnish lines by sheer brute force. Massing artillery, tanks and infantry, the Soviets launched their new attack in late January and slowly ate into the Finnish positions. Fighting such a war of attrition could only mean inevitable defeat for the Finns, yet the Russian advance was painfully slow, and it was not until the middle of March that the war was brought to a negotiated conclusion. Russian victory had not come cheap. For the loss of 25,000 killed and 45,000 wounded, the Finns inflicted upon the Red Army more than 50,000 killed and over 150,000 wounded. In all the Soviet Union mobilised 1,200,000 men to beat the 200,000-strong Finnish Army.

In the Soviet Union the unsatisfactory performance of the army compelled the High Command to begin a massive programme of reorganisation. Realising from the German victory in Poland, and later in the year in France, that ranks were the primary weapon of war, the Red Army began to rebuild its neglected armoured force. Hasty reorganisation brought together new mechanised corps and tank brigades, but they remained tied to infantry units and widely dispersed throughout the military districts.

Despite the setback in Finland, Stalin continued to bully his way into new territories in Eastern Europe. In June 1940, as Hitler began to think of invading Russia, the Red Army marched info the Baltic states and occupied each nation. At the end of the month an ultimatum was delivered to Rumania demanding Bessarabia and Northern Bukovina be handed over. Just days later the Rumanians acquiesced and the Red Amy moved in. Surprisingly the territorial gains left the Red Army at a distinct disadvantage. While it held its original positions, the Red Army had been well established in fixed and prepared defences, the Stalin line running along the 1939 border being a significant position if manned. However, by moving west, the frontier armies had to establish new bases, build new defences, airfields, roads to their bases and the entire infrastructure that was required to support an army of occupation. And all this had to be done on top of the reorganisation of the army. Already, barely a year after signing the pact with Germany, tensions began to develop between the two partners. During the occupation of Lithuania, the Red Army, in contravention of the agreement of September 1939, occupied the strip of land set aside for Germany, prompting Hitler to move twenty divisions to the East Prussian border during August as a show of force. Stalin continued his demands in Eastern Europe. Hitler though was not prepared to allow Stalin to gain access to his supplies of oil from Rumania or the iron ore in northern Norway. Therefore, in August 1940, the Germans successfully negotiated with the Finns to gain access through Finland to the Petsamo region, preventing Russia from making any claims. Furthermore, when at the end of the month Hungary and Bulgaria made territorial claims against Rumania, claims Russia supported, Hitler moved to aid Rumania. On 30 August the Germans announced the Vienna Award. This agreement gave Hungary control of Transylvania and Bulgaria Southern Dobrudja. However, the agreement also gave a German guarantee to Rumania that she would be protected against any outside aggression. As a result German military missions moved into Rumania to safeguard the oil at Ploesti. Surprised by the announcement, the Soviets protested that the agreement was a breach of the 1939 Non-Aggression Pact, under which Germany recognised Soviet ambitions in the Balkans. Hitler was quite ready deliberately to misinterpret this item of the agreement in order to further his own goals. When, less than a month later, Germany signed the Tripartite Pact with Japan and Italy, Stalin really began to see that Germany did not intend to honour the Non-Aggression Pact now that its usefulness was past. Almost immediately, Soviet foreign policy towards Germany hardened, yet the supply of raw materials continued to pour across the border. German supplies of finished goods continued to lag way behind.

The German pact with Japan came as a particular worry to Stalin. Similar to Hitler's fear of a war on two fronts, Stalin feared a two-front war against Germany in the west and Japan in the east. Having already fought a number of successful border skirmishes against the Japanese, the Soviet Union was keen to seek a settlement. When in June 1940 Stalin negotiated a peace agreement with Japan, he believed his eastern border to be secure. This new pact revived his anxieties. With the political situation between Germany and the Soviet Union deteriorating, the Germans invited Molotov to talks in Berlin in November 1940. Molotov arrived in the German capital on the 12th, meeting Ribbentrop and Hitler. Over the next few days a series of acrimonious talks were held. Ribbentrop tried to entice the Soviets with an offer of membership of the Tripartite Pact, but Molotov was unimpressed. The meeting broke up without agreement as the gulf between the two powers widened.

Barely had the discussions ended when Stalin continued plotting in the Balkans, offering Bulgaria a security pact on 25 November. The offer gave Bulgaria all of Dobrudja and access to the Aegean through Greece, but the Bulgarian government declined it. As the pressure built, with Germany moving more units into the Balkans, Russia complained on 17th January

1941 that German troop movements were a direct contravention of the alliance and could be seen to threaten the position of the Soviet Union. Naturally, Hitler ignored this protest.

In March 1941 the crisis leapt up another step as Bulgaria announced that she was joining the Tripartite Pact, following Hungary, Rumania and Slovakia who had already joined. German units marched into Bulgaria. With German hegemony over Europe growing, Turkey became nervous of her position, a feeling that was immediately picked up by Stalin. Offering the Turks an assurance that Soviet aid was available in the event of any outside aggression, the Soviets made it plain they were prepared to oppose any German move into the Dardanelles.

German pressure compelled Yugoslavia to join the Tripartite Pact on 25 March, but just two days later a coup toppled the pro-Hitler regime and replaced it with a pro-Allied one. Straight away the Soviets signed an agreement with the new government promising aid. Hitler was furious and ordered the invasion of Yugoslavia. By the 5 April 1941 German forces had concentrated on the border and on the 6th they invaded, just as Stalin withdrew his offer of aid to the Yugoslavs. The German army, at the height of its power, smashed the Yugoslav army in days and moved swiftly south, entering Greece off the march. Defeating the Allied forces in Greece, the Germans completed the occupation of the Balkans by the end of April. However, the invasion of Yugoslavia had a huge impact on the coming campaign against Russia. With German preparations for the attack well advanced, Hitler was forced on 7 April to postpone Barbarossa for five crucial weeks, from 15 May to 22 June.

From this point on, the attitude of the Soviet Union towards Germany crumbled. For the remaining few months of peace in the east, Stalin closed his eyes and ears to all signs and alarm bells of a German attack and tried to continue as though nothing was untoward. But the situation was tar from calm as Russia and Germany stood on the edge of tile abyss. German armies continued to mass as Hitler resolved finally that Russia must be defeated and destroyed during the summer of 1941.

NOTES

1   Abbreviation of the National Socialist German Workers party, more commonly known as the Nazi Party.

CHAPTER II

Preparations for War

With Hitler bent on war with the Soviet Union, the Axis armies undertook their mammoth preparations. The largest armada of military forces ever assembled massed against the western borders of the Soviet Union. How did Germany manage to surprise Stalin with an army of over three million men after months of preparation and could the disasters to come have been averted?

Throughout the winter of 1940–41 the Germans forged ahead with their plans for an invasion of the Soviet Union. Hitler, having signed and issued Directive 21 on 18 December, ordered the build up of forces against the Soviet frontier before the invasion in the middle of May. However, the German build up of arms did not go entirely unnoticed.

On 20 March 1941 General Golikov, head of the Military Intelligence Dept of the Red Army presented an appreciation of the current situation and possible developments to Stalin, which stated that there was evidence of an impending German attack against the western borders of the Union, expected to begin at the end of May or beginning of it. Despite indications of planned German aggression, Stalin would do nothing to endanger the Non-Aggression Pact with Germany. Having played nations off against one another for many years to strengthen the position of the Soviet Union, Stalin believed the German build up on the eastern borders of the Reich was just Hitler's attempt to play him at his own game. Even so, during the spring the Soviet armed forces began the induction of their reserves, the strength of the Red Army rising to 4,200,000.[1] Many of the reservists and reinforcements included officers only recently released from the brutality of the gulags in Siberia.

Not only did Stalin refuse to believe the information he was getting from his own intelligence services, he also refused to acknowledge that received from the British and Americans. Ever suspicious of the British, Stalin was of the opinion that Churchill wanted nothing more than to drag the Soviet Union into the war with Germany so that the German army would march east, away from the Channel coast. Despite the cynicism of this view, there was an element of truth to it. As Churchill would state after the start of hostilities, an enemy of Germany was a friend of Britain.

While Stalin cold-shouldered the West, in the Far East he forged a viable peace settlement with the Japanese. Following the entry of Japan into the Tripartite Pact, Stalin worried that the Soviet Union was vulnerable to attack by Germany in the west and Japan in the east. Already in economic and quasi-political alliance with Hitler, Stalin needed to settle the Japanese question. At her secret negotiations throughout the spring of 1941, in mid-April the Soviet Union and Japan signed a treaty of Neutrality, thereby securing the Soviet rear in case the Germans should attack. This adept political manœuvre would save the Soviet capital in the final days of 1941 as Stalin rushed highly trained Siberian troops from the east to the defence of Moscow.

With these political pieces in place, the Red Army continued a chaotic redeployment of its forces, Stalin forbidding any major movement of units to the western borders. Throughout April 1941 the 16th, 19th, 21st and 22nd Armies marched west, 16th and 19th Armies deploying into the Ukraine, 21st into the Gomel area and 22nd marching *en route* to Velikiye Luki. On 5 May Golikov again issued an appreciation of German intentions, estimating that the Wehrmacht had upwards of one hundred divisions near the border. When questioned by the Soviet foreign office, the Germans used the excuse that their units were training in Poland in preparation of an invasion of the British Isles and that bases this far east were out of range of the prying eyes of the RAF. Indeed, German training with tanks equipped with snorkel devices tended to prove this story. In reality these tanks were to be used in the opening phase of Operation Barbarossa, the Germans having to tackle the Bug river as one of their first obstacles.

Following Golikov's assessment, which was again disregarded by Stalin, on 19 May 1941 the Soviet agent operating in Japan, Richard Sorge, transmitted a report to his superiors in Moscow, also detailing information concerning the German intention to attack the Soviet Union in the summer of 1941. Sorge's report actually detailed the expected order of battle of the invasion force surprisingly accurately, as well as its proposed deployment.

In June 1941 the realisation that war with Germany was imminent was readily apparent to many in the Soviet Union. On 13 June, as tension mounted, Marshal Timoshenko, the Commissar for Defence, requested that he be allowed to bring the border districts onto a war footing in the light of Golikov's reports of the activities of the Germans across the Frontier. Stalin argued that he was not convinced the Germans were planning an attack at all and subsequently refused to allow the mobilisation of the border armies for war. As if he needed any further confirmation of the German intention to attack, on 15 June Richard Sorge again reported to Moscow that the Germans were about to launch an invasion, his report even going so far as to state that the Germans would make their move on 22 June. Stalin chose not to act upon this information.

While the Soviet Union began its slow mobilisation, in Germany preparations continued without interruption until the end of March. By the beginning of March 1941 the Wehrmacht had assembled thirty divisions against the Soviet border and had a further fifteen in the Balkans, plus many divisions *en route* to the east. However, the coup in Yugoslavia at the end of the month led Hitler to order the invasion and occupation of both Yugoslavia and Greece, an operation that would cost the German army dear in lost time later in the summer. Diverting forces away from the build up on the border, German units rapidly overran both nations; by 27 April Athens had fallen to German troops and the British had been expelled from continental Europe. However, the delay caused Hitler to postpone Barbarossa for five vital weeks, the start date for the offensive being moved back to 22 June, a good three to four weeks into the Soviet campaigning season. Indeed, by the end of April, German forces on the Soviet border numbered fifty–nine divisions while twenty-seven were operating in the Balkans; the former figure would have been higher had it not been for the campaign in the Balkans.

The Opposing Forces

By 21 June 1941 Germany had completed the assembly of its mammoth invasion force along the western frontiers of the Soviet Union. The campaign called for three army groups to lead separate advances into the Soviet interior, destroying the border forces close to the frontier in battles of encirclement followed by a pursuit of the remnants.

The Northern Sector

Facing the recently occupied Soviet Baltic provinces, Field Marshal Ritter von Leeb assembled the formations of Army Group North. His brief was to advance through Lithuania, Latvia and Estonia before punching through the pre-1940 Soviet border and reaching Leningrad. After reaching the city, von Leeb was to reduce the Soviet forces and link up with the Finns, who would have attacked from the north.

The Baltic region, across which von Leeb was to lead his forces, had only a few good roads upon which the German units could move, many of the off-road areas being swampy and thickly forested. The deeper one pressed into the region the thicker the forests became and the larger the areas of swamp. The culmination of the German northern attack would lead Army Group North to the region of the Valdai Hills between Moscow and Leningrad and on to Archangel. This whole area was extensively forested, marshy and entirely unsuitable for armoured warfare. In addition to these terrain features, the German units also had to deal with a number of river obstacles blocking their line of advance. The first major obstacle was the Dvina river, which runs east to west, barring progress through Latvia. Once this barrier was overcome, the next obstacle lay just south of the Baltic coast. Lakes Peipus and Pskov marked the border between the Soviet Union and Estonia and into the south of the lake flowed the Velikaya river, running south to north. This river line, incorporating the Stalin Line, had been heavily fortified in the pre-war period when it constituted the 1939 Soviet border and could readily be brought back up to strength if sufficient forces existed to man it. Finally, the last major river line on the road to Leningrad was the Luga, which also runs east to west before turning north just short of the Baltic coast. Again, this river, in an area of thick forest and extensive swamps, could readily be made defensible and had the potential to hold up the German advance.

To overcome the Soviet forces in the Baltic region von Leeb had at his disposal two infantry armies and one panzer group. Colonel-General von Kuchler 18th Army consisted of 145,000 men between Both's 1st Korp (1st, 11th and 21st infantry Divisions and 185th Assault Gun Brigade), Wodrig's 26th Korp (61st and 217th Infantry Divisions) and Chappius' 38th Korp (58th Infantry Division) with 291st Infantry Division in reserve, whose task was to clear the Baltic states of Soviet forces and support the left wing of the panzers as they marched along the more direct route to Leningrad. Once Leningrad was reached, von Leeb would invest the city while simultaneously pushing units east to prevent relief by any Soviet units that remained intact.

On the southern flank of the army group was Colonel-General Busch's 16th Army. His main task was to support the southern flank of the panzer group and maintain the junction of Army Group North with the northernmost army of Army Group Centre. This meant that as the armies advanced, 16th Army experienced a considerable lengthening of its front line. 16th Army comprised 165,000 men between Bockdorff-Ahlenfeldt's 2nd Korp (12th, 32nd and 121st Infantry Divisions and 600th Assault Gun Brigade), Hansen's 10th Korp (311th and 126th Infantry Divisions) and Wiktorin's 28th Korp (122nd and 123rd Infantry Divisions) and 253rd Infantry Division in reserve.

General Hoeppner's 4th Panzer Group formed the striking arm of the Northern Army Group. Numbering 680 panzers and 165,000 men, the group had two panzer korps under its command. Reinhardt's 41st Panzer korp (1st Panzer Division with 145 tanks, 6th Panzer Division with 245 tanks and 36th Motorised Division) and Manstein's 56th Panzer Korp (8th Panzer Division with 212 tanks and 3rd Motorised Division) led

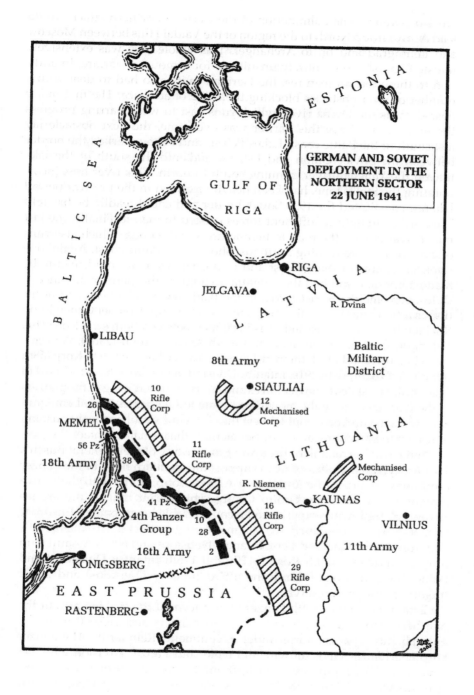

GERMAN AND SOVIET
DEPLOYMENT IN THE
NORTHERN SECTOR
22 JUNE 1941

ESTONIA

BALTIC SEA

GULF OF
RIGA

LATVIA

RIGA

JELGAVA

R. Dvina

LIBAU

Baltic
Military
District

8th Army

10
Rifle
Corp

SIAULIAI

26

MEMEL

12
Mechanised
Corp

56 Pz

18th Army

38

11
Rifle
Corp

LITHUANIA

3
Mechanised
Corp

1

R. Niemen

41 Pz

4th Panzer
Group

10

28

16
Rifle
Corp

KAUNAS

VILNIUS

16th Army

2

11th Army

KONIGSBERG

XXXXX

29
Rifle
Corp

EAST PRUSSIA

RASTENBERG

the German dash from the border into the interior. In reserve 4th Panzer Group had 3rd SS Motorised Infantry Division *Totenkopf.* General Keller's 1st Air Fleet was completely at the disposal of von Leeb's army group, having 430 aircraft on its complement.

The number of reserves available to Army Group North was slight considering the massive nature of its task. With Leningrad 500 miles away from their start lines, 16th and 18th Armies and 4th Panzer Group could rely upon the support of Schubert's 23rd Korp with 206th, 251st and 254th Infantry Divisions. In addition, the OKH set aside another two infantry divisions. Following Army Group North were the 207th, 251st and 285th Security Divisions. Army Group North deployed approximately 641,000 men.

Facing Army Group North were the forces of Colonel-General F I Kuznetsov's Baltic Military District. This formation had 370,000 men with 7,019 artillery pieces, 1,549 tanks and 1,344 aircraft.[2] However, many of the men of the front were recently inducted reserves and press-ganged units of the former Estonian, Latvian and Lithuanian armies. The district had under its control two armies, 8th and 11th. Eighth Army, commanded by Major-General Sobennikov deployed the nine divisions of 10th and 11th Rifle Corps echeloned from the frontier along the Baltic coast to the junction inland with 11th Army. Morozov's 11th Army completed the line to the junction with the Western Military District on its left flank, covering the approaches to Kaunas and Vilnius. This army also had, nine rifle divisions between 16th and 29th Rifle Corps. To support the frontier armies, the Baltic District had 3rd and 12th Mechanised Corps. Formed hastily following the success of the Panzerwaffe in the west, the reorganisation of the Red Army brought into being a number of these mechanised units. Each corps comprised two tank and one mechanised division with a theoretical strength of around 1,000 armoured vehicles. However, at the time of the German attack the corps were in varying stages of organisation. Third Mechanised Corp under General Kurkin had 740 tanks while 12th Mechanised Corp under Shestopalov by had 680 tanks. Each corp was designed to support a separate frontier army, 12th being allocated to 8th Army but held in reserve near Siauliai, while 3rd supported 11th Army from its base near Vilnius.

Behind the first line of frontier units the Soviets were in the process of forming another army, Berzarin's 27th. At the time of the German attack Berzarin had just one rifle division (67th) deployed at Libau and a rifle brigade on the island of Ruhnu in the Gulf of Riga. Farther into the interior the 27th was about to bring under its control the 22nd and 24th Rifle Corps and 5th Airborne Corp.

In all Kuznetsov had at his disposal nineteen rifle, four tank and two mechanised divisions. These units were deployed forward against the frontier and had only light fortifications facing the German border. No reserves were available to speak of close to the battle zone, 27th Army being in the process of forming up as the attack began. The only real reserve was the two armoured units held behind the front line, but the chronic lack of air support that was to dog the Soviet ground units until the middle of the war would greatly hamper their employment.

In high command reserve but available for action in the Baltic region was the 41st Rifle Corps along the Velikaya river, 21st Mechanised Corp near Opochka and 1st Mechanised Corp at Pskov.

The Central Sector

Field Marshal Fedor von Bock's Army Group Centre undertook its offensive between the southern wing of Army Group North and the northern edge of the Pripet Marshes. Von Bock was tasked with the destruction of the Soviet Western Military District.

The road to the east lay through Belorussia, but the terrain across which the German armies advanced was formidable. Metalled roads were rare and, of the decent roads available to the Wehrmacht, most were in the midst of massive belts of forests. The forests stretched upwards of fifty miles in depth and were dark and impenetrable. Therefore, the natural tendency of the Germans was to follow the good roads, but this effectively funnelled the advances stringing out the marching divisions over many miles. Across the line of the advance, as in the north, the central sector was cut by a number of major rivers.

On the border there were the Niemen and Bug river's across which 3rd and 4th Panzer Groups had to cross. Once these river lines were overcome the next obstacle was the Berezina, a short distance before the Dniepr river. The Dniepr running north to south across the line of the German advance, posed a very real threat to Army Group Centre. If Soviet units at the frontier managed to put up a protracted struggle, it was likely that reserve armies would have time to move from the east to man this easily defensible river line. If this happened, the Germans would be faced with a crossing against a prepared foe.

To carry out his assignment von Bock had been allocated two infantry armies and two panzer groups, some 1,180,000 men and 1,770 panzers. On the northern wing of the attack, deployed in the south-eastern tip of East Prussia and the north-eastern Poland against the northern face of the Soviet salient that jutted out into Poland around Bialystok, lay the forces of General Strauss' 9th Army and Colonel-General Hoth's 3rd Panzer Group.

Strauss' 9th Army comprised 248,000 men between Heitz's 8th Korp (8th, 28th and 161st Infantry Divisions and 184th Assault Gun Brigade), Materna's 20th Korp (162nd and 256th Infantry Divisions and 210th Assault Gun Brigade), Kuntze's 42nd Korp (87th and 129th Infantry Divisions), Ruoff's 5th Korp (5th and 35th Infantry Divisions) and Forster's 6th Korp

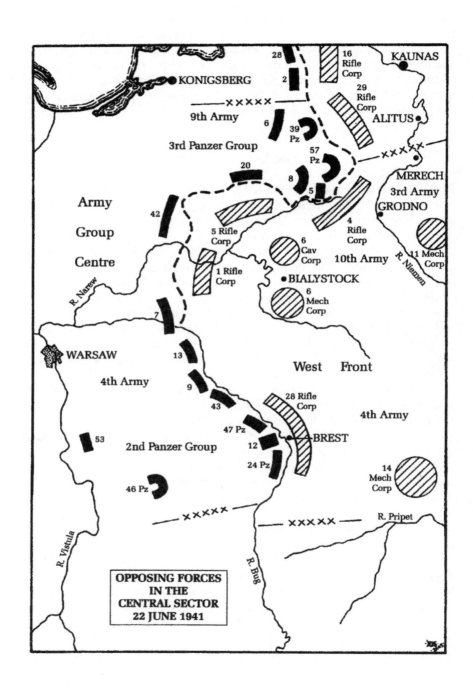

**OPPOSING FORCES
IN THE
CENTRAL SECTOR
22 JUNE 1941**

(6th and 26th Infantry Divisions). Their task was to secure the right wing of the army group and its junction with Army Group North, while also supporting the advance of 3rd Panzer Group and mopping up any pockets of resistance the panzers left behind.

Deployed immediately south of 9th Army was Hoth's 3rd Panzer Group. This force formed the deep northern pincer of Army Group Centre. With 39th and 57th Panzer Korps, Hoth had at his disposal over 840 tanks and 145,000 men. Schmidt's 39th Panzer Korp had 7th Panzer Division with 265 tanks and 20th Panzer Division with 229 tanks plus the 14th and 20th Motorised Divisions. Kuntzen's 57th Panzer Korp fielded 18th Motorised Division, 12th Panzer Division with 220 tanks and 19th Panzer Division with 228 tanks.

South of the Bialystok salient, around Brest-Litovsk, were Colonel-General Heinz Guderian's 2nd Panzer Group and General Kluge's 4th Army. Guderian's group, with 930 panzers and 248,000 troops, formed the southern pincer that would envelop the Soviets in the salient. This group comprised Schweppenburg's 24th Panzer Korp (10th Motorised Division, 3rd Panzer Division with 215 tanks and 4th Panzer Division with 176 tanks, 267th Infantry and 1st Cavalry Divisions), Vietinghoff's 46th Panzer Korp (10th Panzer Division with 1,82 tanks, 2nd SS Motorised Division *Das Reich* and Motorised Infantry Regiment *Grossdeutschland*) and Lemelsen's 47th Panzer Korp (29th Motorised and 167th Infantry Divisions, 17th Panzer Division with 202 tanks and 18th Panzer Division with 218 tanks). During the initial stage of the offensive, 46th Panzer Korp was held in reserve, together with 255th Infantry Division.

To support the panzers and mop up any pockets of infantry left in their wake there was Kluge's 4th Army. Like 9th Army to the north, 4th Army was to ensure the safety of the flank of the army group, the southern wing of von Bock's sector resting against the Pripet Marshes. To carry out this task the army had 310,000 men between Farmbacher's 7th Korp (7th, 23rd, 258th and 268th Infantry Divisions and 203rd Assault Gun Brigade), Geyer's 9th Korp (137th, 263rd and 292nd Infantry Divisions and 226th Assault Gun Brigade), Felber's 13th Korp (17th and 78th Infantry Divisions), Heinrici's 43rd Korp (131st, 134th and 252nd Infantry Divisions) and Schroth's 12th Korp (31st, 34th and 45th Infantry Divisions and 192nd and 201st Assault Gun Brigades).

German reserves were, as in the Northern Sector, limited. Army Group Centre had at its disposal Weizenberger's 53rd Korp (293rd Infantry Division) and an OKH reserve of six infantry divisions and one motorised brigade. For the security of the rear, Army Group Centre (Area 102) had 403rd, 221st and 286th Security Divisions.

Headquarters of 2nd Army, which had begun its move from the Balkans, had another two panzer (2nd and 5th, both battle weary after the Balkan campaign), one motorised (60th) and ten infantry divisions (including 46th, 93rd, 96th, 98th, 260th, 94th, 183rd, 73rd and 294th).

Air cover for the whole of the central region was provided by Field Marshal Albert Kesselring's 2nd Air Fleet with 910 planes split between Loerzers 2nd and Richthofen's 8th Air Korps. Axthelm's 1st Flak Korp provided ground protection.

Arrayed against these formidable forces was Lieutenant-General Pavlov's Western Military District. This formation had been severely impacted by the acquisition of land in Poland and as such had, during 1940 and 1941 been forced to move west, deploying well forward in the exposed Bialystok salient. With his armies arrayed neither offensively nor defensively, Pavlov had virtually lost the battle for the frontiers even before a shot was fired. The West Front total led some 647,000 men between 3rd, 10th and 4th Armies, which in all comprised twenty-four rifle divisions, twelve tank, six mechanised and two cavalry divisions.

Lieutenant-General V I Kuznetsov's 3rd Army deployment included 4th Rifle and 11th Mechanised (230 tanks around Grodno) Corps against the northern wing of the Bialystok salient and bore the brunt of the attack by Moth's 3rd Panzer Group. The 3rd had eight rifle, two tank and one mechanised divisions. In the centre of the salient lay 10th Army commanded by Major-General Golubev with eight rifle, three cavalry, two tank and one mechanised divisions. The army included 1st and 5th Rifle Corps, 6th Cavalry Corp and 6th Mechanised (1,000 tanks at Bialystok) Corp. In front reserve behind 10th Army was 13th Mechanised Corp (290 tanks near Minsk). On its right wing was 4th Army under Major-General Korobkov, which included 4th Rifle and 14th Mechanised (520 tanks) corps with eight rifle, two tank and one mechanised divisions. Deep inside Belorussia, Filatov's 13th Army was about to form around the reserve corps but would not be ready at the time of the German attack. Front command also held in deep reserve 2nd, 21st, 44th and 47th Rifle Corps, 4th Airborne Corp and 17th (thirty tanks at Baranovichi) and 20th Mechanised (ninety tanks near Minsk) Corps.

In deeper operational reserve the high command held the 20th Army, currently around Orel, with its 61st and 69th Rifle Corps and 7th Mechanised Corp, while the 21st Army was situated on the Volga with the 63rd and 66th Rifle Corps and 25th Mechanised Corp. Farther to the east, in the Ural region, the 22nd Army was moving west with its 51st and 62nd Rifle Corps and the 24th Army was even farther east in Siberia but moving west with its 52nd and 53rd Rifle Corps.

The Southern Sector

The third sector of the main war zone lay south of the Pripet Marshes. Here the Germans deployed their Southern Army Group under Field Marshal Gerd von Rundstedt. Due to the sheer length of the attack sector this German grouping was split into two elements. The northerly element, in southern Poland, comprised the 6th and 17th Armies and 1st Panzer Group. To the south, deployed along the Russo-Rumanian border were the German 11th and allied 3rd and 4th Romanian Armies.

The forces in southern Poland, facing the northern Ukraine and numbering 797,000 men,[3] were to attack a long the southern edge of the Pripet Marshes and, skirting the marshes all the way, push east to capture flanks and mopped up any Soviet units that were left behind. However, once again the German objectives for this sector lacked any real depth, the initial offensive calling for little more than the capture of Kiev, followed at a later date by an advance farther east into the industrial heartland around Kharkov and Rostov.

For this operation the 1st Panzer Group, commanded By Colonel-General von Kleist, had at its disposal 269,000 men between Weitersheim's 14th Panzer Korp (13th Panzer Division with 149 tanks), Mackensen's 3rd Panzer Korp (14th Panzer Division with 147 tanks, 4th and 298th Infantry Divisions and 191st Assault Gun Brigade) and Kempf's 48th Panzer Korp (11th Panzer Division with 143 tanks, 57th and 75th Infantry Divisions and 197th Assault Gun Brigade) and in reserve 9th Panzer Division (143 tanks) and 16th Panzer Division (146 tanks), 1st SS Motorised Division, Leibstandarte Adolf Hitler, 5th SS Motorised Division Wiking and 16th and 25th Infantry Divisions, a total of 750 panzers. During the opening phases of the attack the infantry divisions at the disposal of 1st Panzer Group were those of the neighbouring 6th Army. Kleist arrayed his units so that 3rd Panzer held the northern flank, 14th Panzer the centre and 48th Panzer the southern wing.

The German 6th Army, commanded by field Marshal von Reichenau, had Vierow's 55th Korp headquarters, Kienitz's 17th Korp (56th and 63rd Infantry Divisions), Koch's 44th Korp (9th and 297th Infantry Divisions) and Obstfelder's 29th Korp (10th and 299th Infantry Divisions) with 168th infantry Division in reserve. The 6th deployed behind the 1st Panzer Group but took up positions to its north and real as it advanced, protecting the armour from the many Soviet units that retreated into the marshes. Von Reichenau had at his disposal some 145,000 men during the initial stages of the operation but later would recover the infantry divisions temporarily seconded to 1st Panzer Army, placing his strength closer to a quarter of a million men.

Arrayed opposite Lvov was 17th Army under Colonel-General Stuplnagel with 228,000 men. These forces were deployed between Schwedler's 4th Korp (24th, 71st, 262nd, 295th, 296th Infantry Divisions and 243rd Assault Gun Brigade), Kubler's 49th Mountain Korp (68th and 257th Infantry and 1st Mountain Divisions) and Briezen's 52nd Korp (101st Light Division). In reserve the army had 97th and 100th Light Divisions.

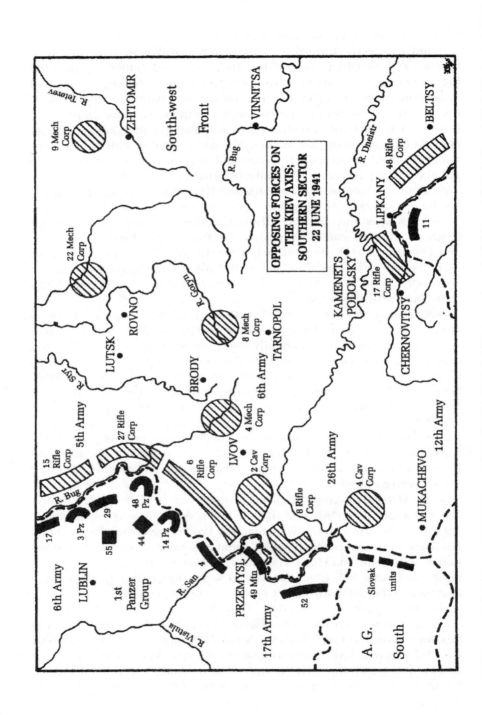

OPPOSING FORCES ON
THE KIEV AXIS;
SOUTHERN SECTOR
22 JUNE 1941

The Galician region through which the Germans struck was partially wooded and gently undulating, making it reasonable for armoured warfare but with excellent potential for effective defence. However, once the border area was clear and the Germans pressed into the interior, the land became increasingly suited to armoured warfare. With mile upon mile of treeless steepe stretching from Bessarabia in the west to the Donets and beyond to the east, the Germans found this ideal terrain to advance upon. However, for the marching infantry, the endless miles without any variation, in which the horizon lever seemed to come any closer, eventually became a wearisome and demoralising burden.

To the south lay the German 11th and Rumanian 3rd and 4th Armies. Deployed around the Rumanian border town of Jassy, General von Schobert's 11th Army had at its disposal Kortzfleisch 11th Korp (76th and 239th Infantry Divisions), Salmuth's 30th Korp (198th Infantry Division) and Hansen's 54th Korp (50th and 170th Infantry Divisions) with 22nd and 72nd Infantry Divisions and 90th Assault Gun Brigade in reserve, a total of 175,000 men. Also attached were four Rumanian infantry divisions, one cavalry brigade and two mountain brigades.

North of 11th Army was 3rd Rumanian Army under General Dimitrescu. This weak force had three cavalry brigades. South of 11th Army, 4th Rumania a was equally weak, being no more than a coastal defence force with four infantry divisions (organised into 5th Corp with two divisions and the 3rd Corp with another two divisions), a frontier brigade and a single armoured brigade. An independent corp (the 2nd) was deployed along the coast close to the mouth of the Danube. The 5th Rumanian Corp was deployed around Falcui and the 3rd to its south Inside Rumania, as reserve and deployed to tend off any threat from Hungary, the two German satellites being fervent enemies, the Rumanian army had ten infantry divisions, one reserve division and three cavalry brigades.

In OKH reserve, von Rundstedt army group held five infantry and one mountain divisions, one light division (99th) also being available directly to the army group. To defend the border regions of Slovakia and Hungary from any possible Soviet counter-thrust the Slovaks deployed two divisions and the Hungarians another two. Security of the rear area, designated Area 103, was entrusted to 444th, 454th and 213th Security Divisions. Lohr's 4th Air Fleet provided support across the entire sector with 1,800 aircraft.

To cover this extensive sector the Red Army had one established military formation, the Kiev Military District under the command of Colonel General Kirponos and one forming, the Odessa Military district. That latter unit was forming in the recently acquired lands bordering Rumania. Kirponos' Kiev Military District and Odessa Military District numbered 1,412,000 men, 26,500 artillery pieces, 8,000 tanks and 4,700 aircraft.

23

Kirponos had under his command 870,000 men in thirty-two rifle divisions, three cavalry, eight mechanised and sixteen tank divisions, split between the 5th, 6th, 26th and 12th Armies. Potapov's 5th Army, on the northern wing of the command, comprised eight rifle, two tank and one mechanised divisions between the 15th and 27th Rifle Corps and the 9th Mechanised Corp with the 22nd Mechanised Corp held in reserve. Muzychenko's 6th Army, deployed left of 5th Army, had eight rifle, two cavalry, two tank and one mechanised divisions split between 6th and 37th Rifle Corps, 5th Cavalry Corp and 4th Mechanised Corp with 15th Mechanised Corp held in reserve. Kostenko's 26th Army, sited farther south, had another eight rifle, one cavalry, two tank and one mechanised divisions deployed between the 8th rifle and 8th Mechanised Corps. Ponedelin's 12th Army, holding the extreme southern wing where it bordered the Odessa Military District, comprised eight rifle, two tank and one mechanised divisions between the 13th and 17th Rifle Corps. In reserve Kirponos could call upon the 31st, 36th, 49th and 55th Rifle Corps, 1st Airborne, 9th and 24th Mechanised Corps.

The substantial mechanised forces available to Kirponos were in varying stages of composition. Kondrusev's 22nd Mechanised Corp at Rovno had 650 tanks; Vlasov's 4th Mechanised had 890 tanks near Lvov, Ryabyshev's 8th Mechanised some 860 tanks around Uman and Karpezo's 15th Mechanised Corp at Zhitomir with 730 tanks. Rokossovsky's 9th Mechanised Corp at Zhitomir had 285 tanks, Sokolov's 16th Mechanised at Kamenets-Podolsky some 610 tanks, Feklenko's 19th Mechanised at Zhitomir with 280 tanks and Chistyakov's 24th Mechanised with 220 tanks at Proskurov.

On the extreme southern flank of the Soviet border were the newly-forming armies of the Odessa Military District under the command of Major-General Tyulenev. Following the Soviet occupation of Bessarabia, the Soviet high command deemed it necessary to raise another new army on the southern wing. The 9th Army became the core of the new Odessa Military District as additional units were sent south. At the time of the German attack the Odessa District had 9th and 18th Armies under Lieutenant-Generals Zakharov and Smirnov. 9th Army included 14th, 15th and 48th Rifle and 18th Mechanised (281) tanks) Corps while 18th Army had 9th Rifle Corp and 2nd Mechanised Corp (489 tanks). The district had thirteen rifle divisions, four tank, two mechanised and six cavalry divisions, in all some 320,000 men and 770 tanks.

In deep operational reserve and moving up to the Kiev region from the interior were the 6th and 19th Armies. The 16th Army deployed the 32nd Rifle and 5th Mechanised Corps while the 19th had the 25th Rifle Corp at Kharkov, 34th Rifle Corp in the northern Caucasus and 26th Mechanised Corp also in the Caucasus.

Finland and Norway

The Germans planned a secondary attack in alliance with the Finns. Unlike Rumania, where the German army was clearly the superior partner in Finland they were more equal with their allies. The main Finnish aim was the re-conquest of the lands lost in the Winter War of 1939–40. However, war in the frozen north was to be like no other the German army encountered. Ranging from heavily forested areas in the southern regions of Finland and Karelia, dotted with countless lakes and marshes, which froze in the winter and attracted hordes of mosquitoes in the summer, to the Arctic tundra in the north, this region meant that the Axis and Soviet soldiers who fought across it had to develop entirely new methods of survival.

The German plan was to sever the Soviet supply lines from Murmansk and bring about the isolation of Leningrad from the north. The Finnish plan was somewhat more limited, aiming at the recovery of the ground lost just a year and a half before. For the offensive the Finns deployed two armies, the South-Eastern Army north of Leningrad with 2nd Korp (2nd, 10th, 15th and 18th Finnish Infantry Divisions) and 4th Korp (4th, 8th and 7th Infantry Divisions), and the Army of Karelia under the command of General Heinrich with 8th Korp (1st, 5th and 11th Finnish and 163rd German Infantry Divisions), 36th German Korp (169th German and 6th Finnish Infantry Divisions and SS *Nord* Kampfgruppe). The German 36th Korp operated in isolation in the Salla region. The Finns also deployed their 3rd Korp with 3rd Finnish Infantry Division in the centre of their line, opposite the extreme southern flank of the Soviet 14th Army and before Belomorsk.

Even farther north, the Germans had additional forces with which they aimed to push from Norway and capture the Murmansk region. Dietl's Mountain Korp, part of the army of occupation in Norway, deployed in the Petsamo mining region. Dietl had at his disposal four divisions with 97,000 men and 100 tanks, mostly old and obsolete models. Total German and Finnish deployment stood at 407,000 men, of whom 150,000 were-Finns. The 5th Air Fleet provided air support but was relatively weak at just 400 aircraft.

Soviet forces in this region were thinly stretched along the border from the Arctic to the shores of the Gulf of Finland. All units were organised under Lieutenant General Popov's Leningrad Military District that totalled 426,000 men, 9,600 artillery pieces, 1,800 tanks and 2,100 aircraft. These forces were deployed between Frolov's 14th Army (104th, 122nd, 14th and 52nd Rifle and 1st Tank Divisions) from Murmansk to Belomorsk, Gorelenko's 7th Army with 54th, 71st, 168th and 237th Rifle Divisions between Lakes Onega and Ladoga and Pshennikov's 23rd Army with 42nd and 50th Rifle Corps and 10th Mechanised Corp north of Leningrad. Popov also had at his disposal the 1st Mechanised Corp north of Leningrad to support 23rd Army, plus the 77th, 191st and 8th Rifle Divisions held in reserve.

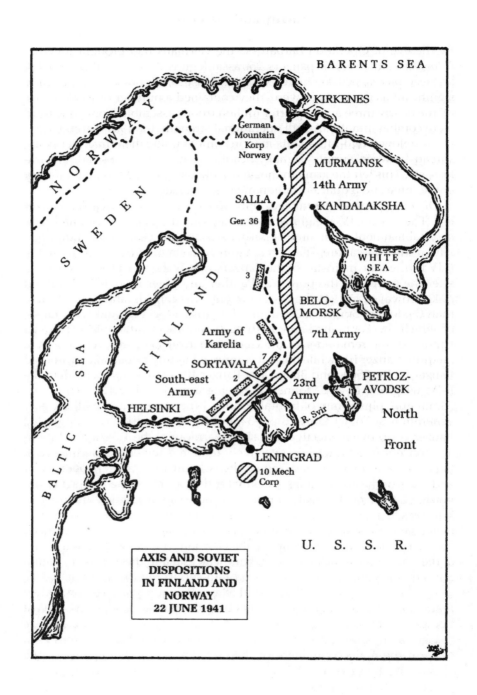

AXIS AND SOVIET
DISPOSITIONS
IN FINLAND AND
NORWAY
22 JUNE 1941

Germany and the Ostheer

By the eve of Operation Barbarossa the Germans had brought together 3,206,000 soldiers, 3,330 panzers, 250 assault guns, 2,840 aircraft, over 7,100 artillery pieces, 600,000 motor vehicles and 625,000 horses. Numerically significant as these forces were, they contained a number of weaknesses. Of the nearly three and a quarter million troops assembled, only one third were combat infantry. At full operational strength, the 1941 German division deployed two-fifths of its men in combat units, the remainder being spread between supply, signals, headquarters, workshops, administration, etc. This left the army in the field with just 1,300,000 combat infantry of the three and a quarter million men assembled.

Of 3,330 panzers assembled, only 439 were modern, heavier Panzer IVs. The Panzer IV, weighing 23 tonnes, was the heaviest German tank on establishment at the time of Barbarossa and the best armed. Equipped with a short 24-calibre, 75mm main gun and 60mm of frontal armour, the P-IV formed the mainstay of the Panzerwaffe as the war progressed, even after the arrival of the powerful Panther and Tiger models in 1942 and 1943. However, in 1941 the 24-calibre gun was considerably less effective than the longer Soviet 76.2mm gun that armed the T-34 and KV-1 tanks, of which the Germans knew nothing before their entry into the Soviet Union. Of the remainder of the German panzer fleet, 465 vehicles were medium Panzer IIIs while the rest comprised lightly armed and armoured Panzer Is, IIs, 35(t)s and 38(t)s. The Panzer III was less effective than the P-IV, weighing in at 22 tonnes and being armed with a 42 or 60-calibre 50mm gun, plus 50mm of frontal armour. When confronted with the new generation of Soviet tanks, the T-34 and Kv-1, even the latest upgraded Panzer IVs prove ineffective. The sloped armour of the T-34, a revolutionary concept in tank design, effectively tendered the entire German tank fleet obsolete, their 50 and 75mm shells bouncing off the sloped front and sides of the Soviet tanks. Luckily for the Germans, the Red Army did not have their new vehicles present in the western regions in sufficient numbers to greatly influence the course of the frontier battles and the few available were spread out in small groups among the many mechanised corps. The only effective weapons the Germans did have against the T-34 at the time of the attack were the 75mm Pak gun and the legendary 88mm anti-aircraft gun, which was pressed into service by the anti-tank units, whose main weapon, the 37mm and 50mm Pak guns, proved completely inadequate, the 37mm failing to penetrate the armour of the T-34 even at point blank range.

German mobile units were for the first two years of the war in the east, to form the main component of the German offensive. Organised into highly effective panzer and motorised infantry divisions, these mobile units were fast and packed a powerful punch. In early 1941 the strength of the German panzer division had been reduced from its 1940 level due to Hitler's call or an increase in the number of divisions. The end result was roughly the same number of tanks as operated in France, but twice the number of divisions, a waste of support resources.

At the time of Barbarossa the average army panzer division consisted of a panzer regiment of two panzer battalions, around 160 tanks in all. To support the panzers there was a motorised infantry brigade consisting of two infantry regiments. Each regiment had two infantry battalions mounted on lorries or half-tracks. Battalions had on average 600 men. Supporting the advance of the panzer divisions were the motorised infantry divisions, these units were mechanised infantry divisions with their own complement of tanks, the forerunners of the panzer–grenadier divisions. Each motorised infantry division had two infantry regiments, each of three battalions. In addition a panzer or assault gun battalion was attached, numbering somewhere between thirty and fifty AFVs. Fire support was usually provided by the Luftwaffe or self-propelled guns, each division having its own small allocation of tracked artillery.

Following in the wake of the panzers and having a less glamorous but equally important role were the massed ranks of the line infantry divisions. A German infantry division deployed three infantry regiments, each of three infantry battalions. In turn each battalion had three rifle companies and one machine-gun or heavy weapons company. Each regiment also hid an anti-tank company and infantry gun company with 75mm and 150mm artillery pieces. At divisional level there was an anti-tank battalion and an artillery regiment of nearly fifty guns. For fire support the infantry relied upon the assault gun rather than the panzer. Under the jurisdiction of the artillery arm, the assault gun units were organised into battalions, each unit having eighteen vehicles. However, unlike the panzer and motorised infantry divisions which relied upon motor vehicles to move their men and supplies, the infantry divisions were still extensively equipped with pack horses, carrying and moving everything from artillery pieces and ammunition to the trusty field kitchen.

The Luftwaffe deployed over half of its total operational strength for the offensive against the Soviet Union. Again though, the apparent strength of the German forces proves misleading. Of the 2,640 aircraft deployed only 2,130 were combat operational at the start of the offensive. When considering the scale of the undertaking, this force can only be considered inadequate.

To support the advance of the infantry and panzers the German armies required considerable logistical support and an efficient supply system. But in this vital area, once again the German forces operated with insufficient levels of equipment. Many of the trucks that supplied the vital resources needed to carry out the offensive were captured Czech and French vehicles. A core of German vehicles was in operation but these were insufficient numbers to provide for the requirements of the tanks, guns and men of the panzer and infantry divisions in the front line. The confusing array of vehicles in operation with the combat divisions and supply columns also presented the workshops with a logistical nightmare. For many models of vehicles, spare parts simply did not exist and when they broke down, they were either repaired as well as possible or simply abandoned by the road-sides. In order to supplement the lack of motor vehicles the line divisions were equipped with thousands of horses. Startling as it may seem now, the perception of the German army of World War Two as a mechanised and modern field army is wrong, the Germans making extensive use of horses to draw the artillery of the infantry divisions. Motorised tractors were gen-erally reserved for the panzer divisions, which needed the speed of these vehicles to keep up with the pace of the armoured advance.

Perhaps the greatest threat to the success of the German invasion though was the lack of a clearly defined strategy. Directive No 2 was very general in its aims for the campaign and did not clearly define one target or objec-tive as priority, in fact it diverted the main German thrust from a drive in the centre to the flanks. Therefore, the three-army groups all had their own widely separated objectives, which inevitably drew the advancing armies apart. Army Group North was tasked with the capture of Leningrad, while Army Group Centre was to advance to the Smolensk region and then await further orders. In the Ukraine, Army Group South was to take Kiev and the Donbas before moving into the Caucasus. This strategy inevitably led to large gaps on the flanks of each army group unless additional forces were committed, forces that were simply not available in sufficient number's to maintain the powerful attacks across the entire line. Even though 2nd Army continued to move up from the Balkans, and a force of twenty-eight divisions was available in the OKH reserve, this was wholly insufficient to cover even the natural expansion of the line as it moved east, let alone maintain the strength of the army group boundaries.

Another potential weakness, in fact the major weakness as the war progressed, hindering the German forces in the east was the fragmentary higher command structure. With Hitler head of state and the armed forces, he alone held the key to all the theatres in which the German army fought. In the west, the OKW (Oberkommando der Wehrmacht) had supreme authority while in the east, the OKH (Oherkommando des Heere) was in sole control of the operations in the Soviet Union only. With Hitler as supreme commander, the right German arm was unaware of the move-ment of the left, the two theatres being kept in isolation. This inevitably led to petty rivalries during the later years of the war, Jodl and Keitel of the OKW conspiring to deny the hard-pressed eastern front any form of aid or support. Even on the eastern front, the commanders of the German armies were kept in ignorance as to the situation of their neighbouring armies, each general being told only what he needed to know. This extended right up to army group level, Field-Marshals von Manstein, Model and others rarely knowing the situation on other sectors. Such intentional ignorance led to a lack of cooperation or mutual support between the neighbouring forces, weakening the already shaken German defences in the latter stages of the war.

The Soviet Union and the Red Army

Despite holding large numbers of men and equipment on the western marches of the Soviet Union, the Soviet armies were ill prepared to meet the onslaught that struck them. Having annexed large areas of territory between 1939 and 1941, the Red Army left its border fortifications far behind and had to redeploy its armies into the Baltic States, Poland and Rumania. Furthermore, the Red Army was undergoing a comprehensive restructuring at the time of the attack. Some Soviet divisions were fully re-equipped by the summer of 1941 and had a complete complement of men, others were only partially equipped, some not at all. Moreover, much of the equipment that the army and air force had at their disposal, despite being present in massive numbers, was obsolete and mechanically unsound. Many of the armoured units had moved to new barracks in the occupied regions, but their equipment remained to the east, awaiting transportation. Rifle units were in similar straits. Furthermore, the leadership of the Red Army had been decimated during the terrible years of the Purge and a great many divisional, army and front commanders were unsuited to their posts, lacking the necessary military knowledge to deal with the new, modern methods of warfare that the German army employed. Cavalry was still of paramount importance in the Red Army, with a number of cavalry corps on establishment with the frontier armies. In many cases, the mechanised forces look a secondary role to infantry, being regarded as the duty of the armour to support the attacks of massed infantry divisions, providing fire support where required, rather than *vice versa*. Most, of the frontier armies were equipped with their own mechanised corps, but only on the South-Western frontier, in the Kiev region, had the area commander any real understanding of their potential. Even so, the Soviet armoured force were hindered by the act that only command vehicles were equipped with radios, the remainder following a system of semaphore messages from the company command tank. This meant that Soviet armoured attacks were carried out rigidly on predetermined axes of advance and any sudden developments could not be reacted to. Most crews pressed home their attacks with reckless abandon until they either reached their target or were destroyed by the Germans. In the unlikely event of a successful breakthrough, the advantage gained was quickly lost as the freed armour hesitated, awaiting new instructions.

In all the Red Army deployed 4,700,000 men in 300 divisions, of whom 2,500,000 men, a force of one hundred and seventy divisions, were in the western border regions. These forces also deployed 24,000 tanks, 8,000 aircraft and 40,000 artillery pieces. However, like the German forces, the Red Army had a great deal of obsolete equipment on stock. Of the 24,000 tanks, barely a quarter were operational at the time of the German attack, the remainder being in workshops near their units or far to the rear. The few remaining operational tanks consisted in the main of old models, only 867 T-34s and 508 KVs being available for action against the panzer divisions. However, these few vehicles had a disproportionate influence upon the fighting, particularly the with the advent of the new generation of Soviet tanks, the German commanders found that their entire fleet of tanks was effectively rendered obsolete. With its revolutionary sloped armour design and outstanding cross-country performance, the T-34 set the trend for future tank design in both the Allied and Axis armies.

In the field, the Soviet divisions varied in strength but theoretically should have numbered between 7,000 and 14,500 men. The rifle divisions, like their German counterpart, the infantry division, formed the mainstay of the Soviet strength. Each division numbered around 14,500 men, being arranged into the triangular system similar to that adopted by the Germans, having three rifle regiments, each of three battalions having three rifle companies and a machine-gun company. Cavalry divisions were substantially weaker, numbering just 7,000 men.

The mechanised forces available to the Red Army were, at the beginning of the campaign, arrayed in a number of different formations. Many were grouped together into mechanised corps, each corp having two tank and one mechanised rifle divisions. Some tank units were organised into brigades but it was not until the middle of the war that soviet tank organisation really settled, the tank armies that were to lead massive advances across eastern Europe in the latter years coming into being in mid and late 1942.

Unlike the Germans, the Soviet could rely upon a well established and unified command structure, the whole being under the watchful eye of Joseph Stalin. In war, Stalin was supreme commander of Soviet armed forces, while Marshal Timoshenko was Commissar for Defence and General Zhukov Chief of the General Staff. The prosecution of the war against the Germans was based upon two separate command committees. The first was the State Committee for defence, GKO. Stalin was chairman of this committee, while members included Molotov (Foreign Minister), Malenkov (responsible for equipping the army and air force), Voroshilov (deputy chairman of the Defence Committee) and Rena (head of the NKVD and of intelligence). This bureau concerned itself with the general prosecution of the war. The second committee was referred to by its more common name, the Stavka. This group organised the planning and implementation of the military direction of the war on land, at sea and in the air. Again, Stalin was chairman, while Molotov, Timoshenko, Voroshilov, Budenny, Shaposhnikov, Zhukov and N G Kuznetsov were all members.

Throughout the war in the east, Soviet strength lay in its higher command, just as the German weakness lay in their lack of high command. War direction in the Soviet Union developed a level of expertise second to none by 1944, yet in the field the army remained relatively ignorant, lower levels of command consistently failing to show that *élan* which the Germans always had. However, in action the Soviet was invariably a cunning and stubborn soldier, having stamina generally not found among the easier living Western populations. After their high command, the main Soviet strength lay in the artillery, the god of war, as Stalin was fond of saying. Centrally controlled and organised, the Soviet artillery arm came to completely dominate its German counterpart as the war progressed, the Germans consistently failing to mass their artillery into effective groups, dispersing it between line divisions.

The Red Army Air Force, not a separate arm of service but rather a sub division of the Red Army, found itself in similar straits to the army. Having over 8,000 aircraft on establishment, the Soviet air force was the strongest in the world. But once again many of these aircraft were not operational, and the bulk of the remainder were obsolete. Furthermore, the majority were to be found lined up on airfields in the western USSR a target in waiting for the experienced pilots of the Luftwaffe.

NOTES

1   Halder estimated Soviet strength at 4,700,000 men while the OKH reckoned on 6,200,000, quite a considerable variation
2   Glantz, *Barbarossa 1941*, p 216
3   Glantz, *Barbarossa 1941*, p 217
4   Glantz, *Barbarossa 1941*, p 217

CHAPTER III

The Long Drive East

Following their lengthy preparation, the Nazis were ready to launch their crusade against Stalin's Bolshevik Empire. From the Barents Sea in the north to the Black Sea in the south, the largest offensive the world had ever seen was about to begin, an offensive which would ultimately end in the utter defeat of Western Europe's leading military power, but not before the Eastern colossus had itself been brought to the very edge of destruction.

Sunday 22 June 1941

NORTHERN SECTOR

Hoeppner's 4th Panzer Group attacked from the East Prussian frontier north of Memel and south of Tilsit. Supported by heavy artillery fire and air interdiction, Reinhardt's 41st and Manstein's 56th Panzer Korps struck Sobennikov's 8th Army, taking the Soviet command by surprise. Forward units were easily overrun.

The 56th Panzer Korp pierced the 8th Army's left flank and advanced rapidly through closely wooded territory, past Rasainiai to reach the Dubissa river and secure a crossing after a daring assault upon the Airogola viaduct. Rasainiai fell to supporting infantry after a brief battle. Reinhardt's 41st Panzer Korp launched its assault from Tilsit, striking a single rifle division in the centre of the 8th Army with two panzer, one motorised and one infantry divisions. The lone defending division, fighting desperately at the frontier, was unable to hold off the German attacks and crumbled, opening the road to Taurage. Pushing deep into the frontier zone, Reinhardt's progress was slower than Manstein's as Soviet forces threw in repeated counter-attacks.

Kuznetsov attempted to rally his forces throughout the day, but German air superiority prevented any effective measures at the border. The headquarters of the Baltic Military District (now renamed North-West front) at

Subach, together with many Soviet command and communications facilities, came under ferocious Luftwaffe attack.

As the panzers pressed forward the infantry began their long march. The 18th Army, moving out of its cramped assembly areas behind 56th Panzer Korp, fanned out into Lithuania, pushing north a long the coast towards Libau to prise the right flank of the 8th Army away from the coast. Farther inland, costly battles raged along forested tracks as small detachments of Soviet troops ambushed German units, holding up the advance before they were destroyed or retreated into the interior.

General Busch led his infantry forward on the right wing of Army Group North, pressing east from the East Prussian border towards the Niemen river. These units struck the right wing of 8th Army and the northern wing of 11th Army. Badly shaken, Kuznetsov's armies began to separate. Early in the day, as Manstein motored along the road to Airogola, Kuznetsov ordered the 3rd and 12th Mechanised Corps to concentrate for a counter-attack aimed at halting the Germans thrust towards Siauliai. Subordinating both corps to 8th Army command, Kuznetsov ordered an attack at midday on the 23rd. The 12th Mechanised ordered its forces to co-operate with the 3rd and attack the Germans at Taurage. However, due to the catastrophic collapse of communications, the front commander was largely unaware of the serious situation developing on the 11th Army sector. Essentially Kuznetsov was tackling the lesser of two evils, his movements merely delaying Reinhardt's advance momentarily while Manstein pushed almost unhindered towards the Dvina.

CENTRAL SECTOR

Bock's Army Group Centre began its offensive as the Luftwaffe arrived over Soviet air bases and military facilities behind the frontier. South-West of Vilnius, Hoth's 3rd Panzer Group ripped open the southern flank of Morozov 11th Army, pushing east for the Niemen river. With the 57th Panzer Korp on the left, 39th Panzer to its right and infantry following, Hoth severed the junction of the North-West and West Fronts. As a result, Kuznetsov was compelled to detach the 12th and 3rd Mechanised Corps from Sobennikov's 8th Army and bring them south to aid the crumbling 11th. However, the movement of the two mechanised corps was harried by the Luftwaffe, and would ultimately be halted by Reinhardt's armour in the first major tank battle of the campaign.

As the advance of the panzers got under way, Strauss's 9th Army hit forward elements of V I Kuznetsov's 3rd Army. The surprised Soviet forces, already out of touch with their high command and hard-pressed by German ground and air attacks, suffered fearful casualties. Supplies ran low towards the end of the day due to incessant Luftwaffe attacks upon forward dumps. The cohesion of the hard-pressed front line formations began to break after just the first few hours of combat,

Around Grodno German infantry were involved in fierce struggles with the Soviets. Kuznetsov vainly attempted to bring his armour into battle, but despite the fact that the 11th Mechanised Corp was deployed close to Grodno, it could not deploy, being impeded in its movements by Kesselring's 2nd Air Fleet. Soviet armoured losses on the approach roads were crippling.

In the centre of the army group, the 2nd Panzer Group launched a furious assault upon the garrison of Brest-Litovsk. Despite repeated attacks they were unable to capture the city, the NKVD border guards putting up ferocious resistance. After confused fighting in the outskirts, the Soviets withdrew into the citadel and prepared to withstand a prolonged German siege. North and south of the city, the remainder of Guderian's panzer group began their offensive. Lemelsen's 47th Panzer Korp moved across the Bug river north of the town and pushed towards Pruzhany, where it met resistance from elements of the 4th Mecanised Corp. Schweppenburg's 24th Panzer Korp succeeded in crossing the Bug south of Brest, As armour penetrated the Soviet defences, the marching infantry of Kluge's 4th Army got to grips with the Soviets left behind. As with the 3rd Panzer Group, infantry followed each armoured korp of Guderian's 2nd Panzer.

As in the north, in the centre the Germans had taken the Soviets entirely by surprise, the 3rd, 4th and 10th Armies together with front commander Pavlov having been caught entirely unawares. Many Soviet units were under sustained ground and air attack and disintegrated in the first few hours of fighting. However, isolated detachments fought ferociously, inflicting heavy casualties upon the attacking German divisions.

The Luftwaffe was extremely active throughout the day, bombing Soviet concentrations at Bialystok, Grodno, Lida, Volkovsky, Brest-Litovsk and Kobrin, the latter the head of Korobkov's 4th Army. Communications througout the now redesigned West Front collapsed, leaving Pavlov unaware of the disasters that were unfolding around him. In only two hours, unremitting Luftwaffe attacks succeeded in shattering the command structure of the 4th Army. Fuel and ammunition, dumps came under particularly fierce attack, while numerous airfields were disabled, Golubev's 10th Army, deep inside the Bialyslok cut, also came in for a considerable pounding, many of its supply facilities being lost.

Across the central sector the Soviet defences lay wide open. Golubev 's forces, despite ferocious fighting, were already losing their battle against the German 9th and 4th Armies. With much of his rear services destroyed, it was only a matter of time before the army bled to death. Golubev reported to Pavlov that his 6th Cavalry Corp had been virtually annihilated and the remnants of his frontier rifle divisions were falling back. In an effort to restore the situation, Pavlov ordered the 14th Mechanised Corp to move from Pruzhany and launch an immediate counter-attack to throw the Germans back to the border. Despite severe difficulties deploying, the 14th managed to engage 18th Panzer Division (47th Panzer Korp) and embroiled it in a protracted armoured duel for most of the day.

By dusk, the Germans had firmly invested elements of the 28th Rifle Corp in Brest-Litovsk and determined to capture the city as quickly as possible. Simultaneously, General Golubev decided to begin the withdrawal of his 10th Army behind the Narew river to prevent its encirclement, the collapse of his northern and southern flanks having endangered the whole army. The 6th Mechanised Corp was ordered to move up to the Narew to protect the rear of the retiring rifle divisions. In an effort to find out what was happening at 10th Army, Pavlov sent his deputy, General Boldin, to Golubev's unit. Late in the evening Boldin managed to locate Golubev, whose headquarters had been moved to some woods south-west of Bialystok. Here Boldin was informed that the 10th had suffered extremely severe casualties, and the 6th Mechanised Corp was severely short of tanks but was moving to the east bank of the Narew to cover the withdrawal of the frontier units. Reporting these developments to Pavlov, Boldin was ordered to put a shock group together to prevent any possible German penetration towards Volkovysk. During the night of 22–23 June Boldin tried to assemble his meagre force. He planned to attack towards Grodno from north-east of Bialystok where he presumed the 11th Mechanised Corp was already in action.

SOUTHERN SECTOR

Field Marshal von Rundstedt's Southern Army Group launched the first phase of its offensive against Soviet forces in the North-West Ukraine. Again the Luftwaffe was very active, attacking Soviet defences and airfields across the entire battle sector. Within hours the Luftwaffe destroyed nearly three hundred Soviet aircraft. While the Luftwaffe pounded Soviet ground and air forces, German panzers and infantry crossed the frontier. Kleist's 1st Panzer Group, with Reichenau's 6th Army in close support, crossed the border between Rava-Russki and Strumilov to exert pressure upon the junction of the Soviet 4th, 5th and 6th Armies. In the Rava-Russki region the 6th Rifle Corp was heavily engaged and, despite bitter fighting, failed to prevent German forces crossing the Bug. Assault groups successfully overpowered NKVD guards on bridges over the Bug, opening the road to the interior. The 3rd, 14th and 48th Panzer Korps of Kleist's 1st Panzer Group were able to begin their advance towards Kiev with only minor losses.

Stuplnagel's 17th Army also attacked, aiming to crush the Soviet 6th and 26th Armies deployed around Lvov. Fierce battles raged between Tomasov and Przemysl as German infantry struggled to break through the frontier units. Around Przemysl the 8th Rifle Corp of Kostenko's 26th

Army attempted to hold off these attacks but failed to prevent a crossing of the San river. Late in the day Przemysl fell to the Germans, but 8th Rifle Corp launched an immediate counter-attack, preventing the German exploitation of their gains.

As the day progressed, the Germans established secure bridgeheads over the Bug so that by noon, both the 6th and 17th Armies were across the rivers which barred their line of advance. Amid fierce fighting the Soviet border formations gave way to the attacks of the 3rd Panzer Korp, the 15th Rifle Corp on the right flank of Potapov's 5th Army crumbled, opening the junction of the 5th and 4th Armies. Shortly afterwards, the two armies lost contact. Further German pressure against the junction of the 5th and 6th Armies prompted Kirponos, the commander of the South West Front, as the Kiev Military District had been re-designated, to commit 22nd and 4th Mechanised Corps. However, by dusk he was aware of the danger presented by the deep advance of Kleist's panzers into the northern flank and began the difficult task of concentrating his armour to parry the German thrust. The main obstruction to the implementation of this decision was the complete superiority the Germans had already gained in the air.

NORWAY
Units of Dietl's mountain korp crossed the Russo-Norwegian border and moved into the Pechenga area. Soviet resistance was slight. The 52nd Rifle Division took up defensive positions to cover the approaches to Murmansk.

FINNISH SECTOR
Finland declared neutrality as Germany attacked but the Soviets responded by attacking Finnish shipping in the Gulf of Finland and firing from their base at Hanko.

Throughout the first day of fighting the Luftwaffe achieved spectacular successes, sixty Soviet airfields being bombed and nearly 1,500 aircraft destroyed, with a further 300 confirmed as downed in combat.

Despite their extensive preparations close to the border, the Germans had taken the Soviet forces by surprise. Many frontier units had been caught relaxing in their barracks as the offensive began, and a great number of the army and front commanders were absent from their units. This general lack of preparedness greatly increased the losses incurred during this first stage of the German attack.

Stalin, in a state of shock, refused even to believe that the Germans had attacked. As the frontier armies were torn apart, the Politburo ordered the Red Army to keep out of Germany. However, at 0530 the German ambassador in Moscow delivered a statement to Molotov, effectively declaring war upon the Soviet Union. incredibly, the radio link with the German foreign office was kept open and the Soviets asked the Japanese to mediate. However, as the morning progressed, it was clear that the German attack was not going to stop and the Soviet General Staff ordered the frontier armies to throw them back to the border. Only a couple of hours later Timoshenko issued Directive No 3 ordering all frontier armies to begin full-scale offensives towards the border. At noon Minister Molotov broadcast to the Soviet people that, in breach of the 1939 Non-Aggression Pact, Germany had attacked the Soviet Union and as a result both nations were at war. The pre-war military districts were re-designated combat fronts and Marshal Timoshenko, victor of the Winter War with Finland, appointed Commander-in-Chief of the Red Army.

23 June 1941

NORTHERN SECTOR

Kuchler's 18th Army continued to advance through the shattered Soviet border forces. Elements on the Baltic coast crossed the border into Latvia as they drove north.

Manstein's 56th Panzer Korp advanced a long the road to Kaunas, forward elements being only eighty in miles from the Dvina river, the first objective of the campaign. In an effort to halt the German drive, Kuznetsov launched a hasty counter-attack with elements of 3rd Mechanised Corp as the Germans cut across their line of manœuvre. However, poor coordination resulted in the loss of more than seventy tanks to the counter fire of 56th Panzer Korp and its Luftwaffe support. After this brief action, Manstein resumed his advance, reaching Kedainiai late in the day.

Kuznetsov's order of 22 June, calling or the 3rd and 12th Mechanised Corps to move to the aid of the 11th Army, brought Soviet armour into contact with Reinhardt's 41st Panzer Korp near Rasainiai. In an effort to avoid the attention of the ever-present Luftwaffe, Kuznetsov had ordered his armour to approach in small groups. Unfortunately this meant they entered the battle piecemeal, losing the advantage of greater numbers. The 12th Mechanised suffered particularly heavy losses to the attacks of the 1st Air Fleet as they moved down from Siauliai. In a short time, the narrow roads were littered with the wreckage of the Soviet corp, disabled tanks, armoured cars and lorries marking the route to the front. Only 28th Tank Division managed to engage the Germans, attacking the 1st Panzer Division but suffering heavy losses. The 3rd Mechanised corp threw its forces into the attack from the south-east. Supported by rifle units, the 3rd failed to make any headway, losing forty tanks and an equal number of artillery pieces in heavy fighting with the 6th Panzer Division. As the fighting developed, the 41st Panzer Korp was hard-pressed to prevent the Soviet forces from pushing it back through sheer weight of numbers.

As these dramatic events unfolded, the infantry of the 16th Army marched into the void left by the retreating Soviet 11th Army. Morozov exacerbated the problem on the southern wing of the North-West Front by ordering his army to fall back upon Kaunas and then Ionava. However, the Soviets left behind rear guard units who fought to slow the German advance. Despite this, Busch's men made steady progress towards the Niemen.

CENTRAL SECTOR

Pavlov's West Front struggled under the hammer blows of Bock's Army Group Centre. On the northern flank, Hoth's two panzer korps reached the Niemen at midday after a difficult march through thick forest and against stubborn defence from isolated units of NKVD border guards. Around Alitus, Kuntzen's 57th Panzer was involved in heavy fighting with Soviet tanks, while Schmidt's 39th Panzer Korp became embroiled in fierce combat around Merech, on the east bank of the Niemen. Soviet tanks from the Varena training grounds launched a ferocious counter attack that erupted into extremely bitter fighting. Once again the Soviets were pulverised by a combination of firepower from German ground and air forces. Having lost more than ninety tanks, the Soviet division was forced to pull back.

The slow advance of the panzers korps through the forests west of the Niemen had enabled the infantry to remain in close proximity to the armour. Later in the day, as Hoth's panzer korps broke free to the east, the infantry consolidated their gains and pushed farther along the Niemen.

On the right wing of the 3rd Panzer Group, 8th Korp wrestled Grodno from 4th Rifle Corp of 3rd Army. The 11th Mechanised Corp and elements of 4th Rifle Corp launched a counter-attack but failed to dislodge the Germans. With the disintegration of the Niemen position, Kuznetsov's 3rd Army was forced to retire to the south-east, away from Morozov's 11th Army. Due to their divergent withdrawals, a considerable gap developed between the North-West and West Fronts, through which Hoth poured his armour.

Guderian developed his attack on the southern flank of Army Group Centre, pushing east from Kobrin and Pruzhany and towards Slutsk. Bitter fighting erupted with elements of Golubev's 10th Army that were falling back around Bialystok. In their rear, the Germans invested Brest-Litovsk.

Pavlov decided to reinforce the hard-pressed frontier armies, committing his reserves. Filatov's 13th was ordered to move up to Molodechno. However, the 13th was woefully short of men and lacked even the most basic equipment, some combat units being armed with petrol bombs, nicknamed 'Molotov cocktails.' *En route* to Molodechno the army collected the remnants of two rifle divisions that had been thrown back from the centre. Pavlov, unaware of the real situation, was in the process of placing his meagre reserve directly inside the cauldron that the Germans were throwing around his front.

SOUTHERN SECTOR

The German attack from southern Poland progressed well as units of the Kleist's 1st Panzer Group advanced east despite meeting stiff resistance from pockets of Soviet armour that were scattered throughout the region, numerous engagements being fought by the German panzer and infantry units as they advanced. Kirponos, unlike Pavlov, recognised the importance of halting the German armoured thrust before it tore his entire front apart, and began to take effective steps to confront the panzers with his own formidable armoured forces. Sporadic tank battles flared up near Lutsk and Radekhov. The 11th Panzer Division took Berestechko during the afternoon, the fall of the town finally ripping apart the junction of the 5th and 6th Armies, enabling the Germans to close up to the Styr river.

Despite the failure of his efforts to halt the German assault, Kirponos continued preparations for an armoured counter-stroke. Armour north and east of Brody and around Radekhov was earmarked for the planned counter-attack. Kirponos knew that any unsupported armoured attack would fail and therefore allocated rifle corps from his reserve to support the assault. The 4th, 9th and 19th Mechanised Corps were ordered to attack immediately, while 15th and 8th Mechanised Corps moved into the battle area.

While the armour was embroiled in sporadic fighting with Soviet units, the infantry of the 6th and 17th Armies advanced on each flank. The 6th Army was advancing through the difficult terrain of the Pripet Marshes north of the 1st Panzer Group, fighting bitter and costly battles with the 5th Army while also supporting the advance of the tanks. Farther south, Stuplnagel's 17th Army advanced slowly but steadily upon Lvov, the 26th and 6th Armies fighting determined rearguard actions in an effort to prevent a major German breakthrough.

RED ARMY COMMAND

As the frontier armies collapsed, the Soviets began the organisation of the rear. The Central Committee met and created the High Command Headquarters, the Stavka. Stalin was the head of the Stavka, which also included marshals and heads of service, As part of the reorganisation of the Soviet command system, the Industrial Evacuation Group was formed. Tasked with evacuating any equipment of possible use to the Germans to the east, out of range of the enemy, this group was instrumental in the long-term survival and eventual victory of Soviet forces during the campaign in the east.

24 June 1941

NORTHERN SECTOR

The German 18th Army marched deeper into Lithuania. At Libau the 87th Rifle Division bloodily repulsed its 26th Korp after a direct assault upon the town. Quickly investing the garrison, the Germans continued their advance. Reinhardt's 41st Panzer Korp struggled against the 3rd and 12th Mechanised Corps around Rasainiai. The Soviets repeated their attacks with foolhardy bravery, but to no avail. Despite their setbacks, the Soviets threw additional forces into the attack, holding up the advance of Reinhardt's panzer divisions. To the east, Manstein pushed his units towards the Dvina against disorganised but stubborn Soviet resistance. Countless fire fights took place along forest tracks as struggling Soviet units stood and fought, only to be overcome by the weight of the German attacks. Ukmerge was taken during the course of the fighting, cutting the road to Daugavpils.

Busch's 16th Army also developed its attacks successfully, Kaunas, Lithuania's second city, falling to the 10th Korp as the Niemen was crossed. Morozov had given up Kaunas without a fight due to the 8th Army's inability to hold the line of the Niemen. He had planned to fall back to the east, but orders from Kuznetsov called for the recapture of Kaunas and an advance to the German frontier. Infantry of 23rd Rifle Division attempted to recapture the city, attacking along the Ionava to Kaunas road. Despite heavy fighting the attack failed, leading elements penetrating into the outskirts of the city only to be destroyed by the Germans. A furious counterattack by the 16th Rifle Corp east of Kaunas was flung aside. As the battle fizzled out, Morozov lost contact with North-West Front headquarters.

In support of the German ground forces, aircraft of the 1st Air Korp continued to be extremely active. Since the opening of operations, this korp alone attacked seventy-seven Soviet airfields, destroying 1,500 aircraft, 1,100 of these on the ground.

CENTRAL SECTOR

Fighting intensified as the Red Army fought stubbornly to hold up the German advance. Leading units of Kuntzen's 57th Panzer Korp entered Vilnius while the 39th Panzer Korp pushed east towards Minsk, into the very heart of the West Front. As the 3rd Panzer Group surged forward, the 9th Army suppressed the by-passed elements of the Soviet 3rd Army that were still operating to the rear of the advancing tanks. One such group, formed by the deputy of the West Front General Boldin, counter-attacked between Grodno and Bialystok. However, the support of the Luftwaffe was of vital impact again, pounding the Soviet units without mercy. The attacking units lost more than one hundred tanks during these raids. Within hours the Soviet assault had been brought to a halt.

On the southern flank of Army Group Centre, Guderian's 2nd Panzer Group made great gains. 17th Panzer Division was involved in fierce fighting at Slonim as Soviet 4th Army failed to hold the town. The 18th Panzer Division pushed towards Baranovichi, while 29th Motorised moved to support 17th Panzer at Slonim. On the right wing of 2nd Panzer Group, panzers forced back the extreme left wing of Korobkov's arrny, separating it from the main components that were being enveloped inside the pocket. Korahkov issued orders for his units to fight their way to the line Yaselda river–Slonim but already this position was imperilled. As a result the 4th Army faced a critical situation, compelling Korobkhov to begin the difficult task of extricating his forces from the Yaselda and, moving them back to the Shchara.

The withdrawal of Golubev's 10th Army from the Bialystok pocket placed increasing pressure upon the ever-lengthening left flank of the 2nd Panzer Group. Guderian was forced to commit his reserve 46th Panzer Korp to this flank to contain the Soviet forces. To the rear, the Germans launched yet another attack against the encircled Soviet garrison in Brest-Litovsk, while on the extreme right wing of the army group there was further heavy fighting at Maloryta.

Pavlov assigned 21st Rifle Corp with its three rifle divisions to 13th Army. The 13th also collected the remnants of a tank division at Molodechno.

SOUTHERN SECTOR
Developments in this sector were less dramatic compared with the battles to the north but no less successful. Both Reichenau's 6th Army and Kleist's 1st Panzer Group punched a hole through the junction of the 5th and 6th Armies and pushed east. As the panzers smashed the Soviet defences, infantry followed in their wake, mopping up pockets of Soviet resistance. However, the first indication of the Soviet counter-offensive was felt as two divisions of 22nd Mechanised Corp attacked 13th and 14th Panzer Divisions of 3rd Panzer Korp east of Vladimir Volynsky. With the panzers involved in close and heavy fighting, German infantry moved up to support their flanks and rear. As the fighting flared, troops of the 14th Panzer Korp reached Lutsk. The 15th Mechanised Corp also attacked but failed to halt the continued advance of 11th Panzer Division. Troops of 297th Infantry Division moved to protect the panzer's line of communication

On the southern wing of the attack, Stuplnagel's 17th Army also met with success. Having opened a twenty-mile gap between Muzychenko's 6th and Kostenko's 26th Armies, the Germans pressed on and captured Nemirov.

Despite these setbacks, Kirponos pressed ahead with the concentration of his armour against Kleist but experienced increasing disruption from Luftwaffe attacks. The Soviets were compelled to carry out much of their movement at night, as they were at the mercy of the Luftwaffe during the day.

In preparation of the counter-attack, the 4th and 22nd Mechanised Corps were ordered to remain with their parent units, while the 8th, 15th, 9th and 19th Mechanised Corps assembled at Lutsk, Rovno, Dubno and Brody, to strike the flanks of the German 6th Army and 1st Panzer Group.

On the extreme southern flank, opposite the Rumanian border, the Red Army high command activated the South front around the pre-war Odessa Military District. Commanded by General Tyulenev from his headquarters at Vinnitsa, the front comprised Cherevichenko's 9th and Smirnov's 18th Armies. The 18th had only recently been raised from elements of the 9th and 12th Armies.

FINLAND AND NORWAY
Finnish forces landed on Aaland and took control from the Soviet garrison. In the Arctic north, on the Russo-Norwegian border, Dietl's mountain korp began to advance from the Petsamo mining region, pushing east towards Murmansk.

DIPLOMACY
Slovakia joined the axis coalition and sent forces into Russia to fight alongside Army Group South.

25 June 1941

NORTHERN SECTOR
Leeb pushed relentlessly forward as the German advance forced back Kuznetsov's North-West front. The divergent withdrawal of Sobennikov's 8th and Morozov's 11th Armies placed the North-West Front under intense pressure, the gap between the two units increasing with every hour. The hard-pressed Kuznetsov called upon High Command to release Berzarin's 27th Army for defence of the Dvina line in an effort to plug the threatening hole in his defences.

Attached to the new army was Lelyushenko's 21st Mechanised Corp deployed around Daugavpils. Lelyushenko had available just ninety-eight tanks and one hundred and thirty artillery pieces, but in spite of this was ordered to halt Manstein's powerful 56th Panzer Korp. As the day progressed and 56th Panzer closed up to the Dvina, the Germans began to encounter elements of the 21st Mechanised, becoming embroiled in skirmishes with outlying Soviet units.

To the rear, the 41st Panzer Korp continued its fierce struggle at Rasainiai. Under heavy attack, the Germans were forced onto the defensive, attempting to hold the Soviet attacks frontally. However, the 12th Mechanised Corp brought the main part of its strength into the battle, attacking with its small complement of KV and T-34 tanks. These new weapons caused the Germans some considerable disquiet, especially the KVs that appeared impervious to all manner of German anti-tank weapons.

Along the Baltic coast the 291st Infantry Division was involved in further heavy fighting with 67th Rifle Division around Libau. The main part of the korp continued its advance inland towards Riga as the 291st threw siege lines around the port.

With enemy forces close to the Dvina, Kuznetsov undertook measures to prevent the German exploitation of their advance north of the Dvina. Sobennikov's 8th Army, bloodied but still intact, was ordered to bring its forces back to the river and establish a defensive line from Riga to Livani. Berzarin's 27th Army would dig in between Livani and Kraslava. Even farther to the rear, the Red Army took additional precautionary steps as General Popov, commander of the Northern Front, issued instructions for the fortification of a defensive line south of Leningrad, between Kingisepp and Lake Ilmen. Pyadyshev began the task of trying to create defences on this line from the scant resources in the area.

CENTRAL SECTOR

With disaster staring General Pavlov in the face, Marshal Timoshenko intervened, ordering the 3rd, 10th and 4th Armies to pull back to the line Lida-Slonim-Pinsk, a position that had in fact already been breached by German units. At this stage of the battle, Pavlov realised that his command had been less than spectacular. In an effort to restore the potential disastrous situation, he nervously issued orders to units that in some cases no longer existed, and to reserve units far from the combat area. Filatov's 13th Army was ordered to hold onto the Molodechno sector and protect Minsk, while the 3rd Army would stop the Germans at Lida. The 10th Army was to cover Slonim, which had already fallen to the Germans and the 4th Army covered Pinsk and the line of the Shchara river. However, it was too late to prevent German exploitation of the real areas, the bulk of the 10th and 3rd Armies being in virtual isolation around Bialystok and Volkovysk.

The 13th became embroiled in ferocious fighting with elements of Hoths's panzer group to the north of Minsk. The 39th Panzer Korp captured Molodechno and Lida, while to the south Guderian met with equal success, capturing Baranovichi after a brief battle. Leading German units were thus only a few miles apart, threatening to isolate those elements of the West Front that remained in the Bialystok salient.

As the battle for Minsk begun, 24th Panzer Korp struck cast, closing up to the Berezina. All that stood before the 24th Panzer Korp and the Dniepr were the ragged remnants of the 4th Army, fighting desperate running battles as the retreat together with miscellaneous divisions supposedly destined for the 13th Army.

Near Grodno, deep inside the developing pocket, Boldin's *ad hoc* combat group resumed its attack against Strauss's 9th Army.

By dusk the situation throughout the West Front theatre had deteriorated dramatically. Both the 3rd and 10th Armies were in operational isolation around Bialystok, the inner pincers of the 4th and 10th Armies drawing ever closer together. A narrow corridor remained open to the east, between Skidel and Volkovsky, through which thousands of desperate soldiers, ragged and short of the most rudimentary equipment, tried in vain to escape. Outside this fist pocket, the headquarters of Filatov's 13th Army, located close to Minsk, was brought under sustained attack, many of its personnel being killed or wounded. The survivors fled towards Minsk, leaving the tattered remnants of the 13th Army to fight their desperate final battle inside the cauldron. While its forces fell apart, Pavlov allocated 44th and 2nd Rifle Corps to 13th Army.

With the threat to the forces in the centre growing, Marshal Timoshenko ordered the 22nd Army to move from its position in the rear and deploy on the northern wing of the crumbling Western front. The 22nd, 19th, 20th, and 21st Armies of the Stavka reserve were ordered to form a Reserve Group under Budenny, establishing defensive positions along a line Nevel–Vitebsk–Mogilev–Zhlobin–Gomel–Chernigov.

SOUTHERN SECTOR

Kirponos continued to concentrate his armour in preparation for the planned assault upon 1st Panzer Group. Potapov had been assigned command of two mechanised corps and instructed to attack a long the line of the Lutsk–Brody railway north from Brody and Toropuv in the direction of Radekhov. To the north, another two corps were to advance from the Klevany area in a southerly direction. The attack was scheduled to begin at 0900 hours on the 26 June. As Kirponos prepared, the German 6th Army advanced slowly but steadily into his northern wing despite stubborn resistance from the 5th Army. The 1st Panzer Group penetrated deeper into the Soviet lines, 11th Panzer Division entering Dubno. On the dawn of Kirponos' attack, the 3rd Panzer was situated around Rovno, the 14th near Dubno and the 48th around Kremenets.

During that day's heavy fighting Lutsk fell to the Germans. To the south 17th Army fought a bloody campaign with the 26th Army around Lvov, the German and Soviet forces both suffering heavy casualties during all of these battles as they grappled for control of the city environs.

FINNISH SECTOR
Five hundred Soviet bombers struck Finnish cities and airfields. An emergency session of the Finnish parliament declared war on the Soviet Union. Finland's immediate aim was the recovery of the territory lost during the Winter War.

26 June 1941

NORTHERN SECTOR
With Manstein only a few miles short of the Dvina, Army Group North sent a special force of troops in advance of the main armoured forces. Their aim was the seizure of the bridge at Daugavpils. Audaciously attacking the startled Soviet guards, the 8th Panzer Division captured the road bridge, preventing its demolition. The Soviets tried vainly to prevent the Germans from securing a foothold, but to no avail. Lelyushenko's 21st Mechanised Corp, still north of the town, launched a limited counter attack with the forces on hand but was unable to prise the Germans away from the river. The Red Air Force even managed a number of air raids in an effort to blow the bridge, but the majority of its aircraft were shot out of the sky, leaving the crossing intact.

Reinhardt unleashed a fierce counter-attack with 1st and 6th Panzer Divisions slicing through 3rd and 12th Mechanised Corps. The 3rd was shattered in the fighting, being driven back into boggy ground where it was annihilated. Under intense fire, the Soviets retired, 12th Mechanised being the first to break off the battle. The attack between Siauliai and Rasainiai had cost Kuznetsov the bulk of his armoured reserve, 3rd and 12th Mechanised Corps no longer existing as coherent combat units after this battle.

While German tanks destroyed the Soviet armoured reserve, infantry of 18th and 16th Armies continued their forced marches. The 18th Army was involved in further bitter fighting at Libau and inland along the road to Riga. While Reinhardt had been bogged down with the Soviet armour at Rasainiai, the infantry had been undermining the Soviet positions. Elements of the 26th Korp had driven deep into the Soviet flank and were advancing along the road while the 38th Korp was striking into the rear of the 12th Mechanised around Siauliai. The 6th Army was struggling to catch up with Manstein's advanced force while simultaneously protecting the developing right flank of the army group.

CENTRAL SECTOR
Lead elements of 3rd Panzer Group were only eighteen miles north of Minsk while the 2nd Panzer Group was approaching rapidly from the south. Schmidt's 39th Panzer Korp smashed aside the 13th Army and fought its way into the city during the day. Farther north, 57th Panzer

Korp pushed deeper into the right wing of the Western front, advancing towards the Dvina. With Guderian's 2nd Panzer Group of the southern wing of the attack, 24th Panzer Korp advanced towards the Berezina, capturing Slutsk, while 47th Panzer Korp swung around and drove directly upon Minsk, 17th Panzer Division capturing Stolpce in the process.

Golubev's 10th had spent most of its forward munitions and, with no access to reserve stocks, began to fragment. In desperation, V I Kuznetsov's 3rd Army launched a counter-attack towards Lida in an effort to punch a hole to the east, but encountered strong resistance from Strauss's 9th Army. As these disasters unfolded, Korohkov's 4th Army struggled to free itself from the cauldron. A limited counter-attack at Slonim compelled Guderian to draw forces away from his eastward advance. As the German units swung around, the Soviets came under sustained and punishing air attack.

The collapse of the West Front prompted Marshal Timoshenko to establish a second defence line east of Minsk. Ershakov's 22nd Army was ordered to move up to the middle Dvina and Gerasimenko's 2lst to the lower Berezina. Koniev's 19th and Kurochkin's 20th Armies were to position themselves behind the northern flank of the West Front in order to reinforce the combat line as it fell back.

With the armoured forces pushing far ahead of the infantry, Army Group Centre subordinated command of the 2nd Panzer Group to the 4th Army.

SOUTHERN SECTOR

Kirponos launched his counter-attack at 0900 hours despite the fact not all his forces had been able to assemble in time or were already under heavy attack. Nevertheless, the counter-attack began as scheduled, Reichenau's 6th Army and Kleist's 1st Panzer Group being struck heavily on their flanks, forcing them to bring the bulk of 3rd and 48th Panzer Korps about to deflect the Soviet blows. Attacks by 15th Mechanised Corp, itself already under heavy attack, forced 57th Infantry Division back six miles. The attachment from Klevany by 9th Mechnised failed to prevent 13th and 14th Panzer Divisions pushing aside 22nd Mechanised Corp. The 11th Panzer Divison completed the capture of Dubno, while 299th, 11th and 75th Infantry Divisions struggled to fill the gap between the panzer divisions. The 19th Mechanised Corp struck at the flank of 11th Panzer Division but after heavy fighting was forced to fall back towards Rovno.

On his left wing Kirponos began to disengage his armies, ordering Muzychenko's 6th and Kostenko's 26th Armies to fall back from the crumbling Przemysl and Rava–Russki sectors and retire through Lvov. To the rear, Lukin's 16th Army was ordered north from its positions at Shepetovka in order to reinforce the hard-pressed West Front, denying

Kirponos the use of this reserve. However, 16th Army had forward elements already involved in bitter fighting with 14th Panzer Korp, which had closed up to the town over the last few of days. Shepetovka was a major supply base for the South-West Front and had to be held lest the units at the front die through lack of vital supplies.

FINLAND AND NORWAY
As the fighting along the border intensified, Finland officially declared war upon the USSR. The Soviet 14th Army launched an unexpected attack from the Murmansk area, but failed to break through the frontier.

27 June 1941

NORTHERN SECTOR
The 3rd Motorised Division crossed the Dvina south of 8th Panzer's bridgehead, consolidating the crossing at Daugavpils. Reinhardt also advanced rapidly following his victory at Rasainiai. In spite of the Soviet rearguard actions, 41st Panzer Korp pushed as quickly as it could across country for the Dvina at Jekabpils. The broken 12th Mechanised Corp attempted to erect defensive positions on the Musha river.

With 56th Panzer Korp already installed on the Dvina, Hitler began to meddle in affairs at the front, ordering 41st Panzer Korp to move up to the river behind 56th Panzer Korp. Krustpils was to be seized at the same time by the infantry of 18th Army. Leeb, realising the futility of this order, 'accidentally' failed to change Reinhardt's axis of advance and so he continued on to Jekabpils.

On the left wing of Army Group North, 18th Army penetrated deep into the Baltic States, but elements were still held up at Libau. Repeated attacks were repelled and artillery bombardment failed to dislodge the garrison. Further inland, the infantry of 16th Army mopped up in the rear of the 4th Panzer Group but remained far behind the panzers.

As the Soviet defences crumbled, Timoshenko ordered Kuznetsov to pull his armies back upon the 27th Army positions along the Dvina.

CENTRAL SECTOR
The final nail was hammered into the coffin around the West Front as 2nd and 3rd Panzer Groups linked up near Minsk. The meeting of the two German panzer groups sealed Pavlov's fate as the greater part of 3rd, 10th, 4th and 13th Armies were cut off between Bialystok and Minsk. There were three Soviet groups inside the pocket, two, each of six divisions, at Bialystok and Volkovysk consisting in the main of Kuznetsovs 3rd and Golubev's 10th Armies while the third larger group of fifteen divisions, was situated between Novgrudock and Minsk and comprised other elements of 3rd Army, most of Filatov's 13th Army

and part of Korobkov's 4th Army plus other miscellaneous units that Pavlov had thrown into the inferno. Pavlov ordered that the line of the Berezina be held at all costs. The loss of Slutsk continued the collapse of 4th Army.

Around the perimeter of the cauldron, the infantry of 9th and 4th Armies marched hard as they consolidated the gains made by the panzers. Fierce attacks were launched against the thin corridor connecting the Soviet pockets around Bialystok and Volkovysk, with heavy casualties being inflicted upon the Soviet units.

As the disaster unfolded, Timoshenko ordered Budenny to move his headquarters forward to Smolensk, taking Lukin's 16th Army under command. The 16th was at Smolensk. The 24th and 28th Armies were also ordered to form up to the rear, some 100 miles east of the reserve line.

SOUTHERN SECTOR
The Soviet attack towards Dubno from the north-east with 19th Mechanised and 36th Rifle Corps was completely disrupted when the Luftwaffe arrived over the battlefield to pound the attacking forces. The 9th Mechanised Corp attempted to coordinate its attack with 19th, but in heavy fighting lost contact with its neighbour. A mobile group of the 8th Mechanised struck from the south-west and succeeded in breaking through the German defences, advancing as fast as it could towards Dubno. However, the attack was held up by air attacks and intense fire from 16th Panzer Division. With the Soviets jabbing at the flanks of 1st panzer group, in the centre Weitersheims 14th Panzer Korp continued its bitter battle with 16th Army near Shepetovka.

On the northern wing of the army group, Reichenau's 6th Army bit deep into the positions of 5th Army. On the southern wing, Stuplnagel's 7th Army closed upon Lvov, and the withdrawal of Muzychenko's 6th and Kostenko's 26th Armies began. As the 49th Mountain and 52nd Korps provided diversionary attacks to the south, the 4th Korp attempted to storm the city with its five divisions, forcing the defenders of the city to decide between certain destruction and retreat. The 6th Army began the abandonment of its positions.

DIPLOMACY
Hungary declared war on the Soviet Union; the Hungarian government claimed that Soviet aircraft bombed the frontier.

28 June 1941

NORTHERN SECTOR
Lelyushenko launched his counter-attack towards Daugavpils elements breaking into the northern suburbs of the town. House-to-house fighting

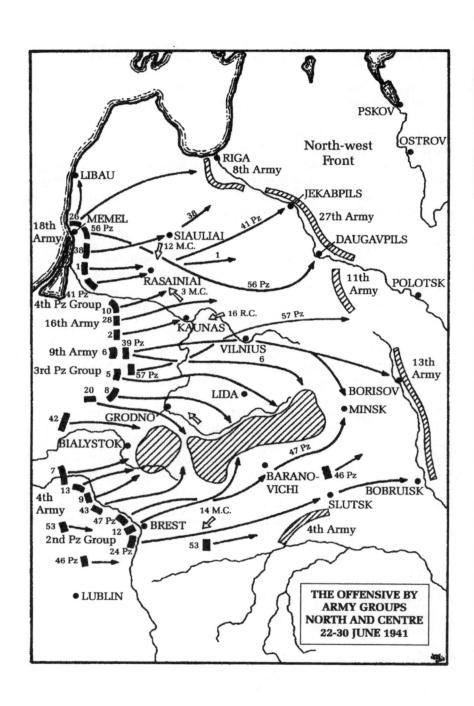

THE OFFENSIVE BY
ARMY GROUPS
NORTH AND CENTRE
22-30 JUNE 1941

erupted as the Soviets pressed their attacks home with vigour. Later on, 56th Panzer Korp managed to reinforce its units and began to inflict crippling losses upon Lelyushenko's corp.

Despite the failure of their attacks, the Red Air force launched a number of unsuccessful attacks in an effort to destroy the Dvina bridges. The battle, together with those over the previous week, had cost the North West front more than four hundred tanks and two hundred artillery pieces destroyed or captured plus six thousand soldiers captured and countless thousands more killed or missing in action.

CENTRAL SECTOR

Inside the Bialystok pocket, Kuznetsov's 3rd Army broke apart as it fought its last desperate battle in the forests of western Belorussia. Golubev's 10th Army, trapped at Volkovysk, also dissolved into the forests and surrendered to the Germans. General Boldin, leading a large group of stragglers from the 10th Army, began a difficult march east towards the Dniepr. At the other end of this vast series of pockets, the panzers were tied down in heavy fighting near Minsk as Soviet forces attempted to punch a path to freedom. The 13th Army suffered crippling casualties, four of its rifle divisions being destroyed in the heavy fighting.

Outside the pocket, elements of the 3rd and 2nd Panzer Groups pressed farther east. The 57th Panzer Korp continued its isolated advance along the road to Polotsk on the northern wing of the army group, while 24th Panzer Korp entered the outskirts of Bobruisk, throwing back the 4th Army.

To the rear, Pavlov was unaware of the encirclement of his armies but did nothing to attempt the extrication of his broken force. However, in Moscow the high command of the Red Army was increasingly worried by reports coming from Belorussia and moved to take measures to rectify the situation. Stalin decided upon the removal of Pavlov from command and put Eremenko in his place.

SOUTHERN SECTOR

Soviet armour attacking 1st Panzer Group suffered increasingly heavy losses as the battle entered its third day. Kirponos was aware that the attack had failed to halt the German panzer thrust, and therefore began the difficult task of extricating his shattered units. The mobile group of 8th Mechanised Corp continued its attack and was mercilessly pounded by the Luftwaffe, while 9th Mechanised Corp took up defensive positions. As 13th Panzer Division closed upon Rovno, the 9th Mechanised sprang an ambush inflicting heavy losses.

29 June 1941

NORTHERN SECTOR

Reinhardt reached and crossed the Dvina at Jekabpils, while Manstein began the battle to break out from the bridgehead at Daugavpils, despite having received no clear orders from group headquarters. The fighting on the river line succeeded in wearing down 21st Mechanised Corp to such an extent that it was left with just seven operational tanks, seventy-four artillery pieces and slightly more than four thousand men. Having failed to smash through the German lines on the 28th, the Soviet units went on the defensive. At 0500 hours Manstein attacked, giving the exhausted Soviet units no chance to regain their strength.

The renewed German attack endangered the junction of 8th and 27th Armies, threatening to overwhelm Kuznetsov's hastily erected defences along the Dvina line. Furthermore, elements of 38th Korp of the 18th Army captured Jelgava and, after a bitter battle, the 291st Infantry Division finally captured Libau. The bulk of the 26th Korp was closing on Riga, and in an audacious effort, Kampfgruppe Lasch broke into the city and seized control of the vital railway bridge across the Dvina. Two rifle divisions of 8th Army, falling back through Riga, launched a furious counter-attack against Lasch in conjunction with elements of the 12th Mechanised Corp. The German unit was compelled to fall back. Hitler would sentence Lasch four years later to death for surrendering Konigsberg to the advancing Soviet armies. The Soviet high command, sensing the imminent collapse of the Dvina position, began to build up additional reserves on the Velikaya river, south of Lake Peipus. The 24th and 41st Rifle Corps took up positions.

CENTRAL SECTOR

The encircled garrison of Brest-Litovsk was finally crushed by a combined attack from ground and air forces, supported by overwhelming artillery fire.

At this stage of the battle, Stalin and Timoshenko were aware of the encirclement of the West Front, mainly through listening to intercepted German wireless messages. In an effort to find out the true situation General Zhukov spoke to General Pavlov by over the radio to ask whether it was true that the Germans had isolated two of his armies to the east of Minsk. Pavlov replied that he thought this might well be true, clearly demonstrating that he was not in touch with developments at the front. Shortly after, Lieutenant-General A I Eremenko, accompanied by Marshals Voroshilov and Shapashnikov of the defence committee, arrived to take command of the West Front from the unfortunate Pavlov, who was informed he had been recalled to Moscow to report directly to Stalin.

SOUTHERN SECTOR

Kirponos called off his counter-attack after failing to halt Kleist's panzers and suffering heavy casualties. With his armour in tatters, he was compelled to order his armies to fall back but was hindered by a total lack of air support and scarcity of fuel for his vehicles. As the armies to his south fell back, Potapov's 5th Army was ordered to counter-attack in an effort to support 9th Mechanised Corp, which continued to inflict heavy casualties upon 13th Panzer Division.

Despite Kirponos's orders to cease attacks against 1st Panzer Group, 19th Mechanised and 36th Rifle Corps continued to attack in an effort to reach Dubno. On the southern wing of the attack, 8th Mechanised Corp was sliced in two and began the difficult task of extricating itself from a very perilous situation.

Stuplnagel's 17th Army fought its way into Lvov and was in the process of clearing out the Red Army. As the Soviets fell back through the city they committed horrendous atrocities against the Polish-Ukrainian population, the NKVD murdering more than three thousand political prisoners in a deadly blood bath.

With his armies suffering a terrible pounding, the Stavka authorised Kirponos to pull his forces back to a line Simovich–Novgorod Volynsky–Shepetovka–Proskurov–Kamenets Podolsky.

FINLAND AND NORWAY

The Finnish South-Western Army continued to attack the centre of the 23rd Army and severed the junction of the two central rifle divisions (the 43rd and 115th). The success of their attack prompted the Finns to push the 4th Corp rapidly forward in an effort to outflank the Vyborg defences.

In the far north, Dietl renewed his attack towards Murmansk with two mountain divisions. Fierce attacks struck the 4th and 52nd Rifle Divisions of the 14th Army. After initially strong resistance the forward elements of the 14th Rifle Division began to pull buck to the Titovka river. In an effort to prevent a close German pursuit, the 52nd Rifle Division threw in covering forces behind the 14th Rifle Division.

SOVIET COMMAND

With the armies in the field in total disarray, the Soviet defence committee issued harsh measures in an effort to slow the German advance. A scorched earth policy was to be introduced to deny the Germans any material gain in the occupied territories. Any livestock which could not be transported to the east was to be slaughtered and fields of crops burned, while entire factories were uprooted and loaded onto trains, to be taken east of the Urals out of the range of the Luftwaffe.

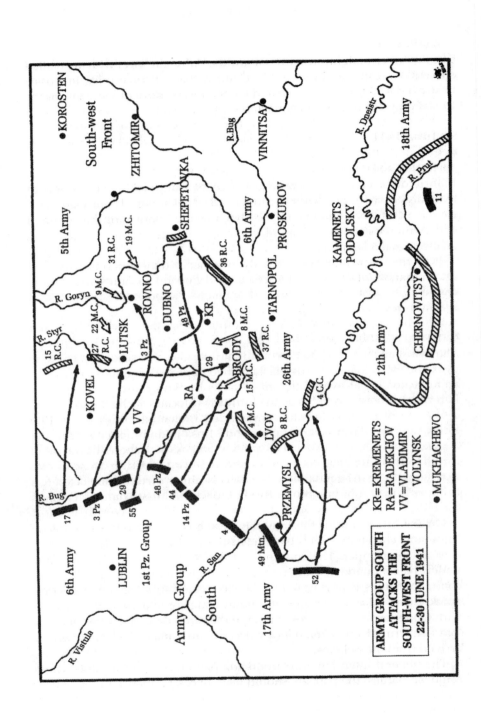

KOROSTEN

South-west
Front

ZHITOMIR

5th Army

SHEPETOVKA

31 R.C.   19 M.C.

9 M.C.

R. Goryn   22 M.C.   ROVNO

R. Styr   27 R.C.   LUTSK   DUBNO   48 Pz   KR   36 R.C.

15 R.C.   3 Pz   29   8 M.C.   37 R.C.

KOVEL   VV   RA   BRODY   15 M.C.

R. Bug   17   3 Pz   29   48 Pz   4 M.C.   LVOV   8 R.C.   4 C.C.

LUBLIN   55   44   14 Pz   PRZEMYSL

1st Pz. Group

R. San   4

Army Group   49 Mtn.

South   52

6th Army

17th Army

R.Bug

VINNITSA

6th Army

PROSKUROV

KAMENETS
PODOLSKY

TARNOPOL

26th Army

12th Army

CHERNOVITSY

MUKHACHEVO

R. Dniestr   18th Army

R. Prut   11

R. Vistula

KR=KREMENETS
RA=RADEKHOV
VV=VLADIMIR
    VOLYNSK

ARMY GROUP SOUTH
ATTACKS THE
SOUTH-WEST FRONT
22-30 JUNE 1941

THE AIR WAR
The first week of fighting in Russia saw the Luftwaffe meet with unrivalled success. An estimate by the OKL claimed that air force units in Russia destroyed 4,000 Soviet aircraft and gained firm control of the skies for the loss of only 150 of their own machines.

30 June 1941

NORTHERN SECTOR
Manstein forced 56th Panzer Korp free of Daugavpils and Reinhardt extended 41st Panzer Korp's bridgehead at Jekabpils. There were ferocious battles along the line of the Dvina as the infantry of the 16th and 18th Armies closed up, becoming embroiled in bitter fighting with hastily erected Soviet defences,

With the Dvina line well and truly breached, Kuznetsov was dismissed as commander of the North-West Front and General Sobennikov, formerly commander of 8th Army, appointed in his place, General F S Ivanov filled the vacant command of 8th Army.

CENTRAL SECTOR
The 24th Panzer Korp gained control of Bobruisk and secured a crossing over the Berezina. The Soviets launched repeated counter-attacks but were beaten off at every attempt. Attacks by Soviet aircraft against the Berezina bridges also failed as the Luftwaffe blocked each attack.

As one of his first acts as commander, Eremenko ordered the 13th Army to unify all units fighting around Minsk and immediately counter attack, However, this order was quickly amended to the withdrawal of forces to the Berezina. Eremenko's predecessor arrived in Moscow late in the day to be dragged before the fiercely angry dictator, subjected to a tirade of abuse and then promptly shot for his failure to halt the German forces.

On the other side of the line, the Germans carried out a number of command changes as they completed the destruction of the cauldrons close to the frontier. The 2nd and 3rd Panzer Groups, while remaining under the command of Guderian and Hoth, were brought under overall control of Klug's 4th Army, into what was termed 4th Panzer Army. Kluge quickly clashed with both of his subordinate commanders, particularly with Guderian, over the prosecution of the campaign. The infantry of the 'old' 4th Army were taken over by the headquarters of 2nd Army, which arrived from the Balkans.

The general intention was, upon completion of the Bialystok–Minsk cauldron battles, the panzers should lead a broad advance to the Dniepr and encircle the remnants of the West front and the new Reserve Front around Smolensk. The infantry of 9th and 2nd Armies were to mop up behind the panzers while also covering the flanks. However, this new command structure went against the fundamental concepts of armoured warfare. Instead of striking on a narrow sector with a great concentration of force, the blow was dissipated across a front of two hundred miles. OKH consulted with the command of Army Group Centre and stressed the importance of seizing the Dniepr crossings as rapidly as possible so that the Soviets were prevented from using the river line as a defensive position. The capture of Rogachev, Mogilev and Orsha were called for, in addition to the conquest of Vitebsk and Polotsk, which were to be secured on the Dvina in order to open up the northern pincer of a subsequent encirclement operation around Smolensk.

SOUTHERN SECTOR
The Soviet counter-attack against 1st Panzer Group finally ended as 9th Mechanised Corp began to fall back under intense German pressure. Rovno and Ostrog had both fallen.

After two days of intense fighting, the Soviets relinquished control of Lvov to 17th Army. Despite this loss, Kirponos managed to keep his force comparatively intact and, acting upon the orders of the Red Army high command, began to retire to a line from Korosten, through Novgorod Volynsky and Proskurov. Losses during the retreat from the frontier had been heavy, the South-West Front having lost more than 2,600 tanks since 22 June. Furthermore, despite his best efforts, Kleist was loose behind Kirponos' flank and drove on towards Kiev. In support, the infantry of Reichenau's 6th Army struggled to maintain the pace set by the panzers, skirting the southern edge of the Pripet Marshes, in which Potapov's 5th Army was taking refuge.

SOVIET COMMAND
In an effort to establish some semblance of authority and secure a bedrock of command, the State Committee for Defence, more commonly known as the GKO, was established. The new body was made up of senior commanders of the army, air force and navy and included party representatives such as Molotov, Voroshilov, Malenkov and Beria. The Supreme Command, also referred to as the Stavka (in place of the 'old' Stavka) was also established at the same time.

THE OSTHEER
By the end of June 1941 the Germans had pushed their forces hundreds of a miles east but the length of the line had also increased correspondingly, the Ostheer fanning out into the funnel of European Russia. Army reserves had begun to enter the line, so that at the end of the month the Ostheer increased its deployment to seventeen panzer, fourteen motorised infantry, eighty-three standard infantry, four light, two mountain and one

air landing divisions. In addition to these forces were those also in action in Finland and Norway.

The fighting during June had cost the Ostheer 25,000 killed.

> *The first week of war has seen the Ostheer annihilate the Soviet armies in Belorussia, harry those in the Baltic from the frontier to the Dvina and the formidable forces in the Ukraine repelled despite the commitment of their largest armoured units. Kirponos' spirited defence had been in stark contrast to Pavlov's rapid collapse, while the difficult terrain of the Baltic had saved Kuznetzov from a similarly bloody fate. Undoubtedly, the final days of June 1941 had shown the Wehrmacht at its finest, attacking with vigour and audacity to achieve its targets. However, the seeds of doubt had already been sewn as hard-pressed infantry struggled to maintain marches of thirty miles a day in blistering heat and against an opponent that, unlike their Western enemies, refused to surrender.*

1 July 1941

lvanov's 8th Army fell back to the Dvina and through Riga, escaping entrapment by Kuchler's advancing infantry. The 26th Korp stormed and captured the city after fierce street fighting with Soviet rearguards.

To meet the German blow along the Dvina, that was expected at any time, the North-West Front had only severely weakened forces at its disposal. Of its thirty-one divisions, twenty-two had below half their strength. Having been badly affected by the fighting at the border, Sobennikov had fewer than 1,450 artillery pieces and mortars remaining across his entire front command, while many hard-pressed front line divisions have been drastically reduced, some being down in only a few hundred men in the field.

CENTRAL SECTOR

Schweppenburg secured his bridgehead across the Berezina around Bobruisk. The infantry of Army Group Centre began the long process of disengaging from the Soviet forces remaining in the Minsk encirclement and marching east to support the armour.

SOUTHERN SECTOR

Reichenau's 6th Army and Kleist's 1st Panzer Group pushed through Kirponos' battered South-West Front, the 3rd, 14th and 48th Panzer Korps advancing around Rovno, Dubno and Kremenets. The northern flank of the 1st Panzer was being protected by the 17th, 44th and 29th Korps of the 6th Army against the dogged defence of Potapov's 5th, The difficult terrain of the Pripet Marshes made the going here very difficult.

To the south the final phase of the German offensive began as the armies on the Russo–Rumanian border attacked Tyulenev's newly created South Front. The 54th Korp attacked from Jassy, striking the junction of 9th and 8th Armies and hitting 48th Rifle Corp hard north of the town. From Stefanesti, north of Jassy on the banks of the Prut, the 30th Korp attacked while the 11th Korp, deployed on the northern flank, pushed north across the Prut around Lipkany to sever the junction of the 18th and 12th Armies. On the flanks of 11th Army the Rumanian 3rd and 4th Armies began their offensive operations.

FINLAND AND NORWAY

Fiege's 36th Korp joined the offensive from Finland, attacking 42nd Rifle Corp grouped in the Salla region. The Germans directed attacks towards Kandalaksha, aiming to sever communications between Murmansk and Russia proper. In conjunction with these attacks, 3rd Finnish Korp moved from Uhtua. The difficult terrain in this region severely hampered the attack of the 36th Korp.

2 July 1941

NORTHERN SECTOR

Hoeppner's 4th Panzer Group completed its regrouping operation on the Dvina and attacked from Jekabpils and Daugavpils, aiming to reach the Velikaya. Reinhardt's 41st Panzer Korp hit 12th Mechanised Corp hard, forcing the remnants of the corp and its thirty-five remaining tanks to withdraw. Lelyushenko's 21st Mechanised fought hard to hold off 56th Panzer.

Behind the combat line the Soviets moved the 1st Mechanised Corp down from the Northern Front to Pskov. Four rifle divisions of 41st Rifle Corp concentrated around Pskov, while 22nd Rifle Corp deployed at Porkhov with two divisions and 24th Rifle Corp at Ostrov with another two divisions.

CENTRAL SECTOR

Timoshenko began to take positive steps to deal with the next phase of the German offensive. Taking over direct control of the West Front, he appointed Eremenko his deputy and incorporated Marshal Budenny's Reserve Front into the West Front, bringing 19th, 20th, 21st and 22nd Armies into the combat line.

On the northern wing of Army Group Centre, the 19th Panzer Division of 57th Panzer Korp reached the Disna but was unable to cross in the face of fierce Soviet resistance. The 57th was meeting resistance from forward elements of the 22nd Army to the west and 11th Army to the north. The latter forces was compelled to abandon its exposed positions west of the

Dvina due to this latest German advance, hastily evacuating its remaining forces to the east bank.

To the south, elements of the battered 13th Army counter-attacked at Borisov where 18th Panzer Division of 39th Panzer Korp managed to establish another bridgehead over the Berezina river. Bitter fighting ensued, but despite repeated counter-attacks, the West Front was unable to dislodge the Germans. Just a little farther down stream, the 47th Panzer Korp was forcing its way east from Minsk towards the Berezina at Berezino, while the 46th Panzer Korp struggled to catch up and create a link between the 47th and 24th Panzer Korps.

SOUTHERN SECTOR

The 1st Panzer Group began to develop its attacks along the road to Kiev. Mackensen's 3rd Panzer Korp pushed forward on the left wing towards the Irpen river at Radomyshl, while the 14th Panzer headed for Zhitomir and the 48th for Berdichev. Once again the supporting infantry incorporated into the panzer group or with the 6th Army, provided support and flank cover.

On the road east from Lvov, fierce fighting raged as 17th Army pushed the 26th Army steadily back. Stuplnagel was pushing his korps forward along the general line of the Lvov railway, advancing towards Tarnopol and Proskurov.

Schobert's 11th Army made slow progress in Moldavia as the 9th and 18th Armies put up stiff resistance, Rumanian soldiers crossed the Prut at Stefanesti to support the 30th Korp, capturing Patrusheny after a brief struggle.

FINNISH SECTOR

A single tank division of the 10th Mechanised Corp attacked elements of the Finnish 4th Korp, pushing south towards Vyborg. Initial fighting saw the Soviets advance two miles, but a counter-attack by the Finns quickly threw the Soviet force back.

3 July 1941

NORTHERN SECTOR

The 4th Panzer Group stepped up the attack from the Dvina but encountered difficult terrain, slowing the advance. Rather than pushing directly along the main railway axes, the German panzers were trying to break across country. However, in heavily wooded and marshy terrain this tactic fell flat. Despite these difficulties though, the 8th, 27th and 11th Armies were again crumbling, front command at Pskov losing contact with its fighting units.

CENTRAL SECTOR

General resistance in the Bialystok pocket ended, only fanatical pockets continuing to hold out against the 9th and 2nd Armies. The greater part of Soviet 3rd and 10th Armies had been destroyed, while remnants of the 13th and 4th Armies fought on outside the pockets. The Luftwaffe launched crushing attacks against the few remaining active units inside the cauldron, inflicting heavy casualties upon the disorganised forces.

On the northern wing of the main combat line, the 19th Panzer Division forced a crossing of the Disna against determined opposition. The bulk of the 3rd and 2nd Panzer Groups were fighting along the Berezina, while the infantry of 9th and 2nd Armies, released from the fighting around Minsk, marched to their support.

SOUTHERN SECTOR

Smirnov's 18th Army fell back before Schobert's 11th, pulling its flank back upon Lipkany and Khotin as the 11th Korp extended its bridgehead across the Prut. North-east of Kishinev and near Beltsy, 9th Army was ordered to destroy the 30th and 54th Korp bridgeheads across the Prut at Jassy and Stefanesti. Strong counter-attacks by 48th Rifle and 2nd Mechanised Corps were beaten off after fierce fighting. The story here was the same as in the northern Ukraine and Belorussia. Disorganised armoured and infantry attacks were launched piecemeal, to be beaten off by superior German firepower and aerial attack. Consequently, Soviet casualties were severe

HOME FRONT: THE SOVIET UNION

Stalin made his first public broadcast to the nation since the German offensive began on the 22 June, calling upon the Soviet people to fight the Nazi aggressor and lead a Patriotic War against the Germans in defence of the 'Holy Soviet' motherland. By using such nationalist tones, Stalin skilfully swept the people of Russia into support for the war, gaining their loyally despite the general, if secretive, unpopularity of its regime. Many people, particularly those from ethnic areas such as the Ukraine and Baltic states, remained unmoved by his plea, seeing the German invasion as an opportunity to throw off the yoke of Soviet domination and oppression. During his speech, Stalin admitted that the provinces of Lithuania and western Belorussia had been lost to the Germans, whose attack was a treacherous betrayal of the 1939 Non-Aggression Pact. Furthermore, he assured the nation of support from the USA and Great Britain, while also calling for the formation of partisan hands in the occupied territories and the implementation of a scorched earth policy as the Germans continued to advance. Partisan forces began to gather in order to fight the Nazis at the front and rear.

In an additional new order, all males between the ages of 16 and 60 were called up for military service and women between 18 and 50 became eligible to serve the state. Behind the scenes, Stalin began to reorganise the Stavka and the GKO.

4 July 1941

NORTHERN SECTOR

The Germans advanced to the Velikaya river after breaking the back of Soviet resistance close to the Dvina. The 1st Panzer Division of 41st Panzer Korp reached Ostrov late in the day. The defending 24th Rifle Corp resisted bravely but was out–fought by the Germans and forced to fall back after suffering considerable casualties. The hastily established Soviet defences along the old Russo–Estonian border were easily pierced, 6th Panzer Division of 41st Panzer slicing through the Stalin Line behind the 1st Panzer.

Because of the rapid disintegration of this defence line, the Stavka ordered the immediate fortification of the Luga river line, preventing a German advance upon Leningrad. However, Popov's Northern Front, which was responsible for the defence of the southern approaches to Leningrad, was woefully short of soldiers and equipment to man the newly ordered position, its forces already being stretched thinly to the north where Finnish attacks pressed the Soviet armies back into Karelia and towards the northern suburbs of Leningrad. The Leningrad Soviet ordered the formation of three militia divisions to help in the manning of the Luga line. A single rifle division (177th) began to deploy before Luga, while another (191st) moved to cover Kingisepp and a third (10th) was ordered east of Luga. The 1st Mountain Brigade began to deploy around Schimsk.

While the German armour penetrated deep into the Soviet rear once more, the infantry protected their flanks. Divisions of the 26th Korp were marching rapidly north towards the Estonian border between the Baltic and Lake Peipus, while the 38th and 1st Korp were struggling in the wake of the panzers. On the southern wing, the 16th Army continued to push its units up behind the 56th Panzer but was constantly hampered by the fact it was tied down on its right by Hitler's insistence on protection of the junction with Army Group Centre. The 11th Army was being pushed steadily back before this tide of infantry, retreating generally north eastwards, away from the West Front and into operational isolation near Idritsa.

CENTRAL SECTOR

The 47th Panzer Korp reached the Berezina at Brodets ten miles south of Berezino, and stormed across. Remnants of 13th Army fought to prevent the consolidation of the bridgehead but were simply too weak. A single rifle division attempted to hold Germnan attacks at Studenka, while 1st Motorised Division hit the 39th Panzer Korp at Borisov.

Marshal Timoshenko, having taken command of the West Front on 2 July, arrived at his front headquarters to find the command in disarray. The West Front had been reduced to only two hundred operational tanks and fewer than four hundred aircraft. Due to the scale of losses suffered at the frontier, the Stavka began to man its new defence line, ordering Timoshenko to 'organise a reliable defence along the western Dvina and Dniepr rivers, and, after concentrating reserves … deliver a series of counter strokes along the Lepel, Borisov and Bobruisk axes.'[1]

With this in mind, Timoshenko began to plan a counter-attack. Attacking with 22nd Army at Polotsk to pin down the 57th Panzer Korp, the 20th Army moved forward along the line of the Dniepr to Shklov, while the 21st Army deployed to the south. Kurochkin's 20th Army, with seven rifle divisions, was ordered to drive the 39th Panzer Korp out of the Lepel area in conjunction with 5th and 7th Mechanised Corps, which would attack north of Orsha towards Senno. Each mechanised corp had just over 1,000 tanks.

As his new armies manœuvred into the line, Ershakov's 22nd Army took up positions trom Drissa to Vitebsk and Koniev's 19th Army assembled near Vitebsk. Kurochkin was digging his 20th Army in between the Dniepr and Dvina rivers, while the remnants of Remezov's 13th Army tried to hold the Berezina line forward of Orsha and Rogachev. Gerasimenko had by this time successfully deployed his 21st Army between Rogachev and Rechitsa, securing the southern flank of the West front against the Pripet Marshes. In addition, the last desperate survivors of the 4th Army, who escaped the Minsk pocket, were falling back to the east, hoping to rejoin the main combat line between the 13th and 21st Armies. To the rear, near Smolensk, the 6th Army had arrived from the Ukraine and was preparing to move up to the combat line, despite the attention of the Luftwaffe.

While the Soviets made these preparations for the continuation of the struggle, the Ostheer officially allocated the headquarters of the 2nd Army to take command of the infantry divisions of the old 4th Army. The new 2nd Army would operate in conjunction with Guderian's 2nd Panzer Group.

SOUTHERN SECTOR
Running battles were fought as Kleist pushed along the road to Kiev. Muzychenko's shattered 6th Army abandoned massive quantities of equipment as it withdrew, suffering heavy casualties to constant German air attacks.

To the left of Kirponos's battered armies, the South Front constructed a temporary bridge across the Dneistr at Khotin in order to facilitate the withdrawal of Smirnov's 18th Army across the river. The Luftwaffe targeted the bridge, launching heavy raids that succeeded in destroying the crossing and trapping elements of the 18th on the south bank. The bulk of the army was able to escape across a hastily erected reserve bridge. There was also heavy fighting around Mogilev-Podolski as the 30th Korp established a bridgehead over the Dneistr. German gains here increased the threat to the 26th and 12th Armies to the north, fighting in a salient position as they fell back. The German 17th Army was exerting pressure upon the rear of the 12th and 18th Armies as it pushed between the Bug and Dneistr rivers.

With his armies heavily committed, Rundstedt directed that, as soon is Zhitomir and Berdichev had fallen, the 1st Panzer Group was to turn its 14th and 48th Panzer Korps south towards Kirovograd, into the rear of the Soviet forces retreating before the 17th and 11th Armies. To support the advance on Kiev by the 3rd Panzer Korp, the 6th Army was divided into a northern and southern group. The northern group continued its advance upon Kiev with the 3rd Panzer, while the southern group accompanied 14th and 48th Panzer Korps south to link up with 11th Army. The 14th and 48th were to move from Berdichev in the direction of Pervomaisk, via Kazatin and Belaya Tserkov and bring about the encirclement of 6th, 12th, 26th and 18th Armies of South-West Front and South Front. Simultaneously Stuplnagel 's 17th Army was to advance through Vinnitsa and drive the Soviets into the arms of the panzers.

FINNISH SECTOR
The Finnish 14th Infantry Division launched new attacks along the Repola axis, meeting only limited resistance front the scattered Soviet forces in this region.

5 July 1941

NORTHERN SECTOR
The 41st Panzer Korp came under heavy attack at Ostrov as the 24th Rifle Corp counter-attacked. However, German fire crushed the assault, forcing the battered rifle divisions to fall back.

To the south, the 56th Panzer Korp advanced towards Opochka, but found the going extremely difficult in the trackless forest and marsh that cut across its line of advance.

CENTRAL SECTOR
Schweppenburg's 24th Panzer Korp succeeded in reaching the Dniepr during the afternoon, closing up to the river near the small settlement of Stary Bykhov. The Germans became embroiled in heavy fighting with retreating elements of Remezov's 13th Army. Simultaneously, 39th Panzer

Korp encountered strong resistance from Kurochkin 20th Army on the approaches to Vitebsk, the Soviets preventing the early capture of the city. The Soviet 5th and 7th Mechanised Corps also moved into the combat line and began to counter-attack in conjunction with the 20th Army, striking the exposed southern wing of the 39th Panzer.

SOUTHERN SECTOR

The 6th Army and 1st Panzer Croup unleashed a fierce attack upon Muzychenko's 6th Army. Furious fighting erupted around Zhitomir where the 14th Panzer fought a bitter battle. To the north the 3rd Panzer Korp pushed closer to the Irpen at Radomyshl.

In Moldavia, Tyulenev's Southern Front began to abandon its positions west of the Dneistr above Kishinev. The 9th Army continued to hold out around the Moldavian capital against the weaker forces of the 54th Korp.

FINLAND AND NORWAY

The German advance towards Salla ground to a halt amid ferocious Soviet defence and difficult conditions. SS *Nord* was attacking the town frontally, the 169th Infantry Division was attacking from the north and the 6th Finnish Infantry Division from the south. The Finns sent up their 14th Infantry Division to support the attack.

6 July 1941

NORTHERN SECTOR

Kuchler's 8th Army completed the occupation of Latvia and Lithuania and pushed into Estonia, the 26th Korp establishing strong positions from Lake Peipus, through Tartu and on to the Baltic coast at Parnu. Ivanov's 8th Army in turn anchored itself on a line between Lake Peipus and the Baltic Sea in an effort to prevent the Germans moving closer to Tallinn and Leningrad. Heavy fighting immediately erupted along the length of the line as the 26th attacked, breaking the Soviet position down.

The fighting on the Velikaya river also intensified as 11th and 27th Armies launched a number of counter-attacks against Reinhardt's 41st Panzer Korp. Fighting at Ostrov alone cost the Soviets more than 140 tanks destroyed, all just to gain time for the fortification of the Luga line.

To the rear of the main Soviet line, the Luga Operational Group was activated, but Pyadyshev had a command in name only.

CENTRAL SECTOR

Kuntzen's 57th Panzer Korp captured the bridges across the Dvina at Disna despite heavy and sustained Soviet air attack. Ershakov brought his 22nd Army up and launched a strong counter-attack. Furious fighting erupted as the Germans struggled to hold off each new Soviet assault. The

19th Panzer Division was preparing to attack towards Polotsk but was held up by these new Soviet attacks.

The Western Front launched its counter-attack during the morning, 39th Panzer Korp being embroiled in heavy fighting at Vitebsk as 20th Army prevented the Germans from storming the city. Counter-attacks by 5th and 7th Mechanised Corps unfolded. The 5th Mechanised opened the attack as it advanced upon Senno, followed shortly after by 7th Mechanised. Heavy fighting erupted with both the 39th and 47th Panzer Korps, the latter having closed up to the Dniepr to the immediate south of the 39th Panzer Korp.

Schweppenburg's 24th Panzer Korp came under sustained assault as the 21st Army attacked from Zhlobin, While these attacks were launched, the West Front brought up the 16th Army and began to insert it into the line at Orsha, covering the southern wing of the 20th Army.

SOUTHERN SECTOR

The 3rd Panzer Korp and 6th Army pushed through the broken Soviet positions on the road north-west of Kiev, while the 4th and 48th Panzer Korps approached from the west. Kirponos was no longer able to contain the German advance upon the city, his 5th and 6th Armies having been torn wide apart. Kiev itself had been uncovered and was open to German forces.

With his northern wing in danger of disintegration, 17th Army assailed Kirponos' centre. Stuplnagel launched a fierce attack across the Zbruch river east of Tarnapol, pushing the 26th Army back despite ferocious resistance.

In Moldavia, elements of the Rumanian 3rd Army took Chernovitsy, while the exposed 12th Army hastily retreated to prevent isolation as the 17th Army pushed into its rear. The fighting in the western Ukraine since the opening of hostilities had by early July cost the South-West Front 165,4000 killed or missing and 65,700 wounded, 4,400 tanks, 5,800 artillery pieces and 1,200 aircraft lost. During the same period the High Command fed twelve divisions and six brigades into the battle.

FINLAND AND NORWAY

The withdrawal of the 52nd and 14th Rifle Divisions to the Litsa river was completed, but Dietls' Mountain Korp was in close pursuit and attacked the Soviet river line. Fierce fighting raged all day, but the Germans were struggling in the difficult Arctic conditions.

7 July 1941

NORTHERN SECTOR
The 41st Panzer Korp overcame the 24th Rifle Corp barring its way at Ostrov and advanced north along the Velikaya towards Pskov, The 1st Korp advanced rapidly behind in support of panzers.

CENTRAL SECTOR
Elements of 20th Panzer Division crossed the Dvina at Ulla. After a furious battle, Soviet counter-attacks were repulsed. The 19th Panzer Division was struck by heavy Soviet attacks out of Polotsk and became embroiled in fierce fighting. The 7th and 12th Panzer Divisions of 39th Panzer Korp attacked the junction of 20th and 22nd Armies, a move that compelled Eremenko to order Koniev's 19th Army to close up to Vitebsk.

As these battles raged, Guderian moved his 47th Panzer Korp north to protect his left flank against the increasingly violent Soviet attacks at Senno. A little to the south, 24th Panzer Korp captured Bortniki as it extended its hold on the west bank of the Dniepr. Between these two korps the 46th Panzer was establishing strong positions.

SOUTHERN SECTOR
The 16th Panzer Division of 48th Panzer Korp was involved in pitched battles with Muzychenko's 6th Army near Starokonstantinovka. The 11th Panzer Division captured Berdichev after a brisk battle.

By this stage of the battle, the South-West Front had been reduced to 627,000 effectives, deployed between twenty rifle, one cavalry, four motorised and thirteen tank divisions and six tank brigades.

On the southern wing of the combat front, 18th Army was involved in heavy fighting with elements of the 30th Korp at Mogilev Podolski. The 48th Rifle and 2nd Mechanised Corps continued to counter-attack north east of Kishinev, joined also by 2nd Cavalry Corp. Amid heavy fighting, the 54th Korp beat back the exhausted Soviet units, indicting further heavy losses upon the already weakened divisions.

FINLAND AND NORWAY
The 52nd Rifle Division beat off the heavy attack of Dietls' Mountain Korp on the Litsa. German forces were just fifty kilometres away from Murmansk. The 36th Korp launched strong attacks upon Salla and, after a fierce battle, look the town. Repola fell to the 14th Finnish Division.

8 July 1941

NORTHERN SECTOR
Reinhardt's 41 Panzer Korp entered Pskov. Soviet losses were severe

as the 41st Rifle Corp fought a bitter defensive action around the town. Sobennikov ordered the armour of the 1st Mechanised Corp to support the hard-pressed rifle forces, but under Luftwaffe attack the tanks had a hard time moving into battle.

CENTRAL SECTOR

Army Group Centre destroyed the bulk of the Soviet forces trapped in the Minsk pocket. The 10th, 3rd, 4th and part of the 13th Armies had all been destroyed, but cadres of each unit have fought their way cast, so that newly formed armies could be created to fight another day. Already the 3rd and 4th Armies were in the process of being reformed and had elements in the line.

Soviet losses during the Frontier battle in Belorussia had been disastrous, 290,000 prisoners having been taken together with 2,500 tanks and 1,500 artillery pieces destroyed or captured. It was estimated that twenty-two rifle and seven tank divisions had been wiped from the Soviet order of battle, together with six mechanised brigades. Thousands of Soviet soldiers, possibly as many as 100,000, were killed during the fighting. Total Soviet losses were estimated to be in the region of half a million men. When considering that at the onset of the battle the West Front numbered 630,000 men, the defeat had been colossal.

To the east, the Germans continued their advance in spite of all that Timoshenko tried to throw in their way. The 39th Panzer Korp was involved in bitter fighting rear Vitebsk, but manœuvred successfully to strike at the flanks of the 22nd and 20th Armies. However, just as the attack hit the Soviet line, Koniev's 19th Army moved up, running head-long into the Germans. Leading German troops pushed into Vitebsk and became embroiled in furious street battles with Koniev's fresh army. The fighting left the greater part of the city in ruins, fires raging out of control in many of its historic buildings. Sebezh fell to flanking elements of 57th Panzer Korp, which broke free from the Dvina while Polotsk fell after a protracted battle with 22nd Army.

At Senno the 5th and 7th Mechanised Corps attacked repeatedly but failed to break through the junction of the 2nd and 3rd Panzer Groups.

SOUTHERN SECTOR

The 16th Panzer Division overcame rearguards of Muzychenko's 6th Army at Starokonstantinovka, while the 11th Panzer was involved in heavy fighting at Berdichev.

Kirponos, still aware of the importance of halting the German armour on the road to Kiev, began a new counter-attack in an effort to halt the German advance and close the grip between the 5th and 6th Armies. The 5th Army counter–attacked with 15th, 9th, 19th and 22nd Mechanised and 31st Rifle Corps to the north-west of Kiev but met strong resistance from the 3rd

Panzer Korp and infantry of the 6th Army. The bulk of these Soviet units had been severely worn down by the fighting during June, the 22nd Mechanised having just twenty tanks left and the 9th only sixty-four tanks.[2]

The Soviet forces in Moldavia called off their counter-attacks and the 48th and 35th Rifle Corps began to withdraw, covered by the 2nd Mechanised and 2nd Cavalry Corps.

FINLAND AND NORWAY
The Soviets reinforced their defences on the Litsa river. The Germans had abandoned their attacks for the time being.

9 July 1941

NORTHERN SECTOR
Pskov fell to the 41st Panzer Korp after a day of heavy fighting with 41st Rifle Corp. Manstein moved his 56th Panzer Korp up to Ostrov.

With Reinhardt firmly established along the Velikaya, Army Group North received orders from OKH regarding the objectives for the next phase of operations. The 41st Panzer Korp was to smash through the Soviet positions to the south of Lake Peipus and reach the Luga river around Luga city prior to its direct attack upon Leningrad. Simultaneously, Manstein was to lead his 56th Panzer Korp on a deep flanking attack towards Lake Ilmen.

Of its original complement of twenty-three divisions, the North-West Front had just seven near full strength and eleven with between 2,000 and 3,000 soldiers. Armoured strength was down to just 332 operational tanks. The heavy fighting in Latvia and Lithuania since 22 June had cost the North-West Front dear, some 73,900 soldiers being killed or reported missing and a further 13,300 wounded, Over 2,520 tanks, 3,500 artillery pieces and 990 aircraft had also been lost. As in the south, the Soviet Commend had fed new units into the battle as they withdrew, some fourteen divisions and one brigade joining the hard-pressed frontier armies.[3]

CENTRAL SECTOR
After a bloody last stand, the remnants of the Soviet forces trapped in the Minsk pocket were crushed, enabling the 9th and 2nd Armies to release infantry in support of the panzers in their drive east.

Having captured Polotsk, the 19th Panzer Division moved towards Nevel, but progress was slow in the face of difficult terrain and dogged Soviet defence. Vitebsk, burning and gutted, fell to 39th Panzer Korp, but furious battles continued as 19th Army launched repeated attacks aimed at throwing the Germans back. Farther south, the Soviets broke off their attacks at Senno.

The fighting in Belorussia since 22 June cost the West Front 418,000 casualties, 4,800 tanks, 9,427 artillery pieces and 1,777 aircraft lost. During the debacle, the Soviet Command reinforced the West Front with 45 divisions, giving the Front 579,000 men in early July.[4]

SOUTHERN SECTOR

Tanks of 14th Panzer Korp captured Zhitomir despite Soviet counterattacks. Elements of 5th Army cut the Zhitomir road but failed to prevent the German drive. Heavy fighting erupted along the line from Berdichev, Skvira and Fastov, where the 48th and 14th Panzer Korps were attacking the 6th Army. Units of the 4th Mechanised Corp and *ad hoc* forces of the Army hit the 11th Panzer Division hard at Berdichev.

With the Germans still advancing, Kirponos ordered his forces to fall back to the line Korosten–Novgorod-Volynsky–Shepetovka–Staro-Konstantinovka–Proskurov but the Germans had already penetrated far to the east of this line.

Thus far the fighting in the Ukraine had cost the Soviet forces dear. In ferocious battles the South-West and South Fronts had lost nearly 242,000 men, nearly 4,400 tanks, 5,800 artillery pieces and 1,200 aircraft.[5]

10 July 1941

NORTHERN SECTOR

Hoeppner's 4th Panzer Group launched new attacks towards the Luga, but encountered serious resistance from remnants of the Soviet forces scattered throughout the region. Reinhardt's 41st Panzer Korp broke out from Pskov, supported by the 38th Korp. In the heavy fighting around Pskov, the Germans threw the 118th Rifle Division back towards Gdov, leaving the road to Luga open. Soviet command hastily tried to plug the gap with 90th Rifle Division, but the Germans caught it on the march from Strugi-Krasnye. As the Germans approached Luga, 41st Panzer Korp was repulsed during a direct assault upon the town. The 1st and 6th Panzer Divisions swung north-west to try again at Sabsk, only to be repelled a second time. Manstein's 56th Panzer Korp, with 1st Korp in support, broke free from Ostrov, capturing Porkhov with 3rd Motorised Division after a fierce battle.

At this time the North Front forces on the southern approaches to Leningrad numbered 153,000, while the North-West Front had a further 272,000 against the Germans trying to push along the Leningrad axis.

CENTRAL SECTOR

Koniev's 19th Army renewed its attacks against 39th Panzer Korp at Vitebsk, launching a fierce attack with a single motorised division in an attempt to deter a renewed German advance. Hoth's 3rd Panzer Group found itself hard-pressed to hold off the Soviet thrust as it juggled forces between the outer pincer formed by 57th Panzer Korp and the inner one of 39th Panzer.

To the south, Guderian launched 24th Panzer Korp across the Dniepr, successfully gaining a bridgehead at Stary Bykhov. Reinforcements moved swiftly forward in their wake, and the hastily erected 13th Army defences collapsed as German panzers pushed east into the rear of the West Front. The four battered rifle divisions of 13th Army tried vainly to hold off the German attack, but simply could not halt Guderian's tanks.

SOUTHERN SECTOR

Near Korosten and Novrorod Volynsky, the northern group of German 6th Army was attacked by 31st Rifle (on the fight flank of the attack), 9th, 19th and 22nd Mechanised Corps (forming the centre and left of the attack). German attacks had isolated the 7th Rifle Corp on the Sluch river and the Soviet attacks strove to free this beleaguered force. The 31st Rifle Corp made little progress against the 17th Korp, while the mechanised forces advanced around ten miles. Farther south, Muzychenko's 6th Army also counter-attacked, hitting the right flank of 1st Panzer Group.

With German tanks close to Kiev, forces at Berdichev attacked to the south-east but were held up by the Soviet attacks. The fighting on the Berdichev, Zhitomir and Fastov position continued over the next five days as the Soviets threw in repeated attacks in a vain effort to halt the German armour. The 9th Panzer Division launched a strong attack south-east of Zhitomir and pushed closer to Skvir. As the Soviet withdrawal continued, the 26th Army was drawn into the battle.

FINLAND AND NORWAY

The Finnish Army of Karelia launched large-scale attacks, 4th Korp breaking through the positions of Gorolenko's 7th Army at Korpiselka. Finnish forces pushed towards the northern shores of Lake Ladoga aiming for Petrozavodsk and Olonets.

RED ARMY COMMAND

The Red Army reorganised its higher command structure. A number of Glavkom (theatre commands) were established in order to coordinate the front defences more effectively. The first was North-West under the command of Marshal Voroshilov, which comprised the North and North-West Fronts with Baltic and Northern Fleets, followed by Timoshenko's Glavkom West which had the West Front and Pinsk Flotilla under its command. Finally, to the south was Glavkom South-West under Marshal Budenny that comprised the South-West and South Fronts and the powerful Black Sea Fleet.

The importance of Army Group Centre's success in penetrating the Dniepr line cannot be overstated. Had the Red Army managed to establish an effective defence on the Dniepr, Army Group Centre would have been faced with the prospect of concentrating its forces for a set-piece river assault. The Soviet inability to react in time enabled Bock to push his forces forward without pause and begin the next great cauldron battle before his infantry had even joined with the armour after the Belorussian victory.

11 July 1941

NORTHERN SECTOR
Manstein's 56th Panzer Korp stalled in the difficult terrain between the Velikaya river and Lake Ilmen. After two gruelling days, the entire korp was forced to backtrack to Ostrov. Reinhardt's 41st Panzer Korp continued to manœuvred in the Luga area but was unable to cross the river.

CENTRAL SECTOR
Hoth's 3rd Panzer Group, together with Strauss's 9th Army, unleashed a new assault, pushing the 57th Panzer Korp north of Polotsk and Nevel in order to strike at those Soviet forces Hitler believed were building up at Velikiye Luki. However, as it transpired, this was nothing more than Ershakov's 22nd Army re-forming after its costly series of battles along the line of the Dvina river. The 39th Panzer Kurp simultaneously advanced from Vitebsk in the direction of Smolensk.

Guderian's 2nd Panzer Group successfully threw its full weight into the attack across the Dniepr and forced back Remezov's 13th Army. Elements of the 46th and 47th Panzer Korps forced the river at Shklov and Kopys, while the 24th Panzer exploited its already established bridgehead in the direction of Roslavl.

SOUTHERN SECTOR
Potapov's 5th Army continued to fight on in isolation around Korosten, being heavy embroiled with the infantry of the German 6th Army. Bitter fighting raged close to Novgorod Volynsky as the Soviet counter-attacks continued. The 13th Panzer Division of 3rd Panzer Korp, with 25th Motorised and 14th Panzer Divisions closely following, reached the Irpen river ten miles west of Kiev, but was inexplicably ordered to halt by Hitler.

Muzychenko's 6th Army continued holding the line from Berdichev to Ostropol in an effort to slow the German advance, while the 26th and 12th Armies fought determinedly on the line Ostropol to Bar. Between the 5th and 6th Armies the bulk of Kleist's 1st Panzer Group pushed east through a forty-mile void.

FINLAND AND NORWAY

Dietl renewed his attack on the Litsa line. Initial gains secure a minor bridgehead across the river, but then the 52nd Rifle Division managed to contain the German attack. Heavy fighting would continue along the river line for the next two weeks without any further German gains.

RED ARMY COMMAND

With the situation at the front increasingly desperate, the Stavka set about raising a new Front of Reserve Armies under the command of Lieutenant-General I A Bogdanov. This new formation comprised the yet to be raised 29th, 30th, 24th, 28th, 31st and 32nd Armies and would be arrayed on a long line running north to south before Moscow, the 29th, 30th, 24th and 28th Armies in the first echelon, the remainder in the second.

12 July 1941

NORTHERN SECTOR

The 10th Mechanised and 41st Rifle Corps were assigned to Luga Operational Group to reinforce the Soviet defence line along the river.

SOUTHERN SECTOR

Heavy fighting raged near Novgorod Volynsky as 31st, 9th, 19th and 22nd Mechanised Corps tried to free 7th Rifle Corp. Despite repeated attacks, the Soviets were repulsed with heavy losses. Mackensen's 3rd Panzer Korp established strong positions over the Irpen and stood poised to strike at Kiev but was forbidden to do so by Hitler's halt order. To the south, the 14th and 48th Panzer Korps began their surge towards the Bug, away from the Dniepr and into the rear of 6th, 12th and 26th Armies.

On the other side of the lines, the Soviets moved Vlassov's 37th Army up to cover the direct route into the city. Kirponos also pulled the headquarters of 26th Army into front reserve and then assigned it control of all forces east and north-east of Belaya Tserkov. It was ordered to link up with 5th Army to the north.

On the extreme southern wing, Rumanian forces advancing in Moldavia captured Balti.

13 July 1941

NORTHERN SECTOR

Army Group North hurriedly regrouped its 41st and 56th Panzer Korps, 41st being moved along the eastern shores of Lake Peipus to attack towards the lower Luga and 56th being moved from its original axis back to Ostrov to resume the advance to Lake Ilmen. After only a brief rest, the Germans resumed the offensive along and around the Luga. Heavy fighting saw 41st

Panzer Korp establish a number of small bridgeheads across the Luga south of Kingisepp. However, the sheer ferocity of the Soviet defence stalled 41st Panzer and 38th Korps. Manstein attacked with 56th Panzer Korp, 1st Korp continuing to support his operations. Elements of 8th Panzer Division reached Soltsy but were then attacked by 10th Mechanised Corp and rifle units of Group Vatutin. In heavy fighting the Soviets isolated 8th Panzer from 3rd Motorised on its left and SS *Totenkopf* to the rear.

The Soviets concentrated the new 34th Army around Staraya-Russa to forestall a German attempt to penetrate the Lovat line. On the southern approaches to Leningrad, the battered but still intact 8th Army was removed from North-West Front command and subordinated to the North Front, as was 41st Rifle Corp.

CENTRAL SECTOR

The 39th Panzer Korp continued to attack the 19th Army, having inflicted crippling casualties upon Koniev's green troops. To the south, 29th Motorised Division of 47th Panzer Korp advanced to within eleven miles of Smolensk, while 46th Panzer advanced north of Mogilev and 24th Panzer to the south. The 61st Rifle and 20th Mechanised Corps were isolated inside Mogilev and the 45th Rifle Corp close to it.

As West Front disintegrated, 21st Army launched the first of many counter-attacks. This fresh force attacked with the three rifle divisions of 63rd Rifle Corp from the Rogachev–Zhlobin area to the west, striking 43rd and 53rd Korps of the German 2nd Army. Simultaneously 67th Rifle and 25th Mechanised Corps attacked the southern flank of 2nd Panzer Group. Amid bitter fighting, the 63rd Corp threw the Germans out of both Rogachev and Zhlobin.

SOUTHERN SECTOR

The Soviets' attacks near Novgorod Volynsky begin to die down after four days of bitter fighting. Both 5th and 6th Armies began to abandon their attacks against the flanks of the German 6th Army and 1st Panzer Group following the heavy losses of the past weeks. The 9th Mechanised Corp has been reduced to thirty-two tanks, the 19th to thirty-three tanks and the 22nd to thirty tanks.[6]

CASUALTIES: THE OSTHEER

As an indication of the bitterness of the fighting, casualty returns by the Ostheer at the beginning of July showed, that since 22 June the armies in the line suffered 96,000 casualties.

14 July 1941

NORTHERN SECTOR

As Soviet defences before Leningrad crumbled, forward units of Reinhardt's 41st Panzer Korp closed up to the mouth of the Luga, expanding their small bridgeheads at Kingisepp.

South-west of Lake Ilmen the 8th Panzer Division captured Solsty. Morozov's 11th Army was counter-attacking along the Soltsy-Dno axis with two shock groups. The 'Northern Group' comprised a single tank division of 1st Mechanised Corp and two rifle divisions of 16th Rifle Corp, and struck 8th Panzer Division from the north. 'Southern Group' comprised three rifle divisions of 22nd Rifle Corp attacking Solsty from the east, while elements of the Luga Operational Group (LOG), comprising a militia division and 1st Mountain Brigade, attacked along the Novgorod axis.

At this stage of the battle Pyadyshev had arrayed his forces in three groups, the Kingisepp Group with two rifle and two militia divisions opposite 41st Panzer Korp, Luga Group in the Luga region with three rifle and one tank divisions and one militia division, and the Eastern Group at the far end of the line with a militia division and a mountain brigade.

CENTRAL SECTOR

The Germans progressed north and south of Smolensk as their plan to envelope the West Front proceeded. However, on the flanks of the broad advance, the 9th and 2nd Armies struggled to maintain, the pace set by the panzers, despite the fact that the weary soldiers of the two infantry armies marched an average of thirty miles each day, fighting battles with Soviet rearguards as they advanced. At Gorki and Mstislavl, the Germans were involved in fierce fighting with 13th Army.

As the German advance drew farther east the Stavka began to create another reserve line under General Artemev, commander of the Moscow District. This unit had the 32nd, 33rd and 34th Armies deployed, across the western approaches to Moscow, but the 34th Army had already become embroiled in heavy fighting near Lake Ilmen.

SOUTHERN SECTOR

As German forces closed upon Kiev, the South-West Front command was ready for the possibility of German parachute assaults across the Dniepr in order to counter this perceived threat the 3rd Airborne Corp was hastily deployed at Borispol.

FINLAND AND NORWAY

Unknown to Dietl, the Soviets landed a force of 1,500 men behind his line on the Litsa. They then marched inland to attack the Germans from the rear.

15 July 1941

NORTHERN SECTOR

The 41st Panzer Korp, carrying on its successful advance along the Luga, forced the river defences between Sabsk and Kingisepp and gained a small bridgehead. The Soviet divisions in this sector, only recently raised from Leningrad militia units, rapidly disintegrated in the face of concerted German attacks. As a result of the imminent collapse of their positions on the Luga, the Soviets began to construct yet another new defence line to the south of Leningrad, this time between the mouth of the Luga and Chudovo. Miles of pillboxes, trenches and anti-tank positions were hastily constructed, but seasoned, experienced soldiers to man the positions remained in short supply.

Near Lake Ilmen, Manstein struggled to beat off the attacks of 11th Army around Soltsy. The Germans were unable to prevent the encirclement of Manstein's force, prompting frantic calls for support from the infantry of 16th Army. However, 16th was still far behind 4th Panzer Group, being at least a week behind the most advanced panzer troops.

With only fragmented defences established along the Luga line, the road to Leningrad lay open to Leeb. However, Hitler's vacillation cost the Ostheer dear, a month of wasteful fighting on the Luga giving the Red Army the opportunity to rebuild its shattered armies and erect defences in depth. The opportunity taken so readily on the Dniepr was squandered on the Luga.

CENTRAL SECTOR

Nevel fell to 19th Panzer Division after a difficult march through marshy terrain. Soviet forces counter-attacked immediately but were held off. Slightly south, 39th Panzer Korp swung south to capture Yartsevo to the east of Smolensk, threatening the rear of the West Front. Lemelsen's 47th Panzer Korp fought its way into the suburbs of Orsha, while other elements of the korp were fighting around Grusino. Slowly but surely, a ring of steel closed around the West Front, for the second time.

SOUTHERN SECTOR

Kazatin fell to the 48th Panzer Korp after heavy fighting with the 4th Mechanised Corp. The 17th Army, advancing steadily against South-West Front, broke through the Stalin Line near Bar. The gradual encirclement of the southern flank of the South-West Front was well under way. Kirponos realised that the main German threat lay not on the road to Kiev but to the south, where they aimed to encircle his armies before they retreated to the Dniepr.

After heavy fighting, the Rumanian 5th Corp broke free from the Prut and marched towards Kishinev.

16 July 1941

CENTRAL SECTOR
On the left wing of Army Group Centre, 9th Panzer Division forced ahead from Nevel towards Velikiye Luki. In the centre, 47th Panzer Korp fought its way into the centre of Smolensk and captured much of the town. The very considerable Soviet forces fighting between Orsha, Smolensk and Yartsevo were in real danger of isolation, but a narrow corridor remained open to the east, through which the Soviet units began their efforts to withdraw. Try as they might, the Germans were unable to close this gap. Inside the pocket, 16th, 20th and 19th Armies milled around, suffering terrible casualties as German panzers, with Luftwaffe support, launched ferocious attacks upon any units that tried to break free.

FINLAND AND NORWAY
Finnish 7th Korp, advancing to the north of Lake Ladoga, captured Sortavala and reached the shores of the lake. The threatening Finnish advance in this region caused the separation of Soviet 7th Army between Lakes Onega and Ladoga from 23rd Army on its left, north of Leningrad.

17 July 1941

NORTHERN SECTOR
Soviet forces attacking 56th Panzer Korp along its long line from Lake Ilmen to Dno wore themselves out, having suffered crippling casualties. The 27th Army, attacking the lines of communication of the 56th Panzer Korp, was exhausted.

CENTRAL SECTOR
The 19th Panzer Division broke into and captured Velikiye Luki after hard fighting. Simultaneously, the 39th Panzer Korp struggled to push its way forward from Yartsevo as strong Soviet concentrations attacking from the east tried to hold off the German armour.

SOUTHERN SECTOR
In Moldavia, the Germans and Rumanians captured Kishinev. The Germans peeled north to cross the Dneistr at Dubossary and pushed into the rear of the South Front, while the 4th Rumanian Army pushed south-east, across the river at Tiraspol and on to Odessa.

18 July 1941

NORTHEN SECTOR
Fighting continued south of Soltsy as Berzarin's 27th Army launched

more attacks. Morozov's 11th Army renewed attacks against 56th Panzer Korp, but met with little success.

CENTRAL SECTOR

The Soviets launched strong counter-attacks in an effort to retake Velikiye Luki, The 2nd and 3rd Panzer Groups were involved in bloody fighting around the Smolensk cauldron as they struggled to contain the masses trapped in the pocket. Rokossovsky launched strong attacks against 7th Panzer Division, halting the German advance near Yartsevo. Bitter fighting raged for the next five days.

To the rear Stalin ordered the manning of the Mozhaisk line, with General Artemev in command.

SOUTHERN SECTOR

Reichenau dug his forces into strong positions facing the 37th Army at Kiev, while other elements of the army protected the long left flank against the incursions of the 5th Army. To the south, the 17th Army, having pushed on through the Stalin Line, crossed the Bug and established a firm bridgehead around Vinnitsa.

Additional elements of the 30th Korp of the 11th Army crossed the Dneistr at Mogilev Podolski and Soroki. The Stavka realised the danger posed to South-West and South Fronts, but only ordered a limited withdrawal of 6th, 12th and 18th Armies to a line Belaya Tserkov–Kitai Gorod–Gaysin. Tyulenev was also instructed to move 2nd Mechanised Corp up to Uman to block the German advance.

19 July 1941

CENTRAL SECTOR

The 10th Panzer Division of 46th Panzer Korp reached Elnya.

GERMAN COMMAND

With the battle for Smolensk barely underway, Hitler issued Directive No 33, instructing the infantry of Army Group Centre to continue their advance towards Moscow, while the panzer groups, so vital to the success of the German offensive, were to transfer to the northern and southern sectors of the line to aid the capture of Leningrad and of the eastern Ukraine. Hoth's 3rd Panzer Group was to be split apart, Kuntzen's 57th Panzer Korp moving up to the Leningrad area in order to aid the 18th Army and 4th Panzer Group in their assault upon the city, while 39th Panzer Korp was to attack to the east from the Volkhov river in the general direction of the Svir river, where a junction with the Finnish Army of Karelia was planned.

The 2nd Panzer Group was to drive south, into the rear of Kirponos' South-West Front, while 1st Panzer Group advanced north from the

Kremenchug bridgehead on the Dniepr, bringing about the encirclement of Budenny's Glavkom South-West in the Kiev region.

20 July 1941

CENTRAL SECTOR

While 10th Panzer Division consolidated its lines at Elnya SS *Das Reich* moved up on its left to support. The 24th Panzer Korp thrust to the Sozh river and gained a firm foothold between Krichev and Mstislavl.

With yet another defensive position broken, the Stavka ordered the Reserve Front to move its units forward and enter the main combat line. The 29th, 30th, 24th and 28th Armies all pushed west to aid the struggling 16th and 20th Armies at the mouth of the Smolensk pocket. The 29th Army was ordered to attack south from Toropets with the three rifle divisions of Group Maslennikov to bring pressure to bear upon the outer German perimeter, while 30th Army's Group Khomenko with another three rifle divisions attacked around Belyi and 24th Army's Group Kalinin attacked at Yartsevo with three more divisions. In addition, Kachalov's 28th Army was to hold down the threatening German advance at Roslavl with two rifle and one tank divisions.

SOUTHERN SECTOR

Elements of 48th Panzer Korp smashed through the Soviet lines and headed for Uman. At the end of the day, Monastyriche had fallen, severing the main escape route for 6th and 12th Armies. The 2nd Mechanised Corp held open a narrow corridor free to the east between 48th Panzer Korp and 17th Army.

FINLAND AND NORWAY

Dietl was forced off commanding heights to his rear by the surprise attack of the Soviet infiltration force. The already bitter fighting along the Litsa now intensified as the Germans fought to stabiliser their lines. Fighting would rage through to the end of the month without any significant gain for either side, but the Soviets achieved their goal of protecting Murmansk.

21 July 1941

CENTRAL SECTOR

Soviet forces trapped inside the Smolensk pocket began to pull back to the west of the Dniepr but suffered severe casualties due to constant German attacks. Fighting outside the pocket also intensified as 57th Panzer Korp came under furious attack near Velikiye Luki and 46th Panzer Korp struggled to repel Soviet attacks at Elnya.

SOUTHERN SECTOR
German tanks closed in upon Tarasche and Uman, all but enveloping the twenty-four divisions of 6th and 12th Armies. The two armies numbered 130,000 men, 1,000 artillery pieces and 384 tanks.[7] Kirponos ordered Kostenko to wheel his 26th Army south-west to protect the withdrawal of the two embattled armies. Heavy fighting erupted with German panzer units until 25 July. The 9th and 18th Armies, falling slowly back towards the Dniepr, numbered 280,000 men.[8]

FINLAND AND NORWAY
After heavy fighting, the Army of Karelia reached the eastern shore of Lake Ladoga at Salmy.

22 July 1941

NORTHERN SECTOR
After protracted fighting, 11th and 21st Infantry Divisions overcame elements of 27th and 11th Armies attacking near Soltsy, capturing the town after a bloody battle.

SOUTHERN SECTOR
The Stavka ordered 6th and 12th Armies to attack east to link up with 26th Army.

23 July 1941

NORTHERN SECTOR
Hoeppner's 4th Panzer Group became embroiled in bitter fighting with mixed Soviet forces on the hastily constructed Luga defence line. Pyadyshev, commander of the LOG, was dismissed and executed. General Popov, commanding the North Front, was placed in charge of this position in addition to his existing responsibilities to the north of Leningrad.

RED ARMY COMMAND
Attempting to rebuild the shattered Western Theatre, Stavka created a new Central Front between the West and South-West Fronts. Commanded by Colonel-General F I Kuznetsov, this formation comprised the newly reformed and redeployed 3rd Army (this unit recently having taken up defensive positions along the line of the Sozh river) and the 21st Army and was supported by 140 aircraft. The front later took under its control Kachalov's 28th and Remezov's 13th Armies as the German attacks in the centre developed.

GERMAN COMMAND
Keitel issued a supplement to Directive No 33, instructing the 3rd Panzer Group to move north to aid the capture of Leningrad and then move back to the centre in preparation for an advance as far east as the Volga. Hoeppner's 4th Panzer Group was to be taken out of the line altogether and withdrawn to Germany. Guderian was to join Kleist in the Ukraine and thrust east to occupy the Donbas and Caucasus. Halder emphasised the need for an autumn thrust upon Moscow, considering Leningrad and the Ukraine to be of secondary importance.

24 July 1941

CENTRAL SECTOR
After heavy fighting the Soviets recaptured Velikiye Luki.

SOUTHERN SECTOR
Heavy losses and a lack of supplies compelled the 6th and 12th Armies to abandon their break out efforts. Most rifle divisions inside the pocket were down to fewer than 4,000 men. Kirponos, in no position to support the faltering armies, requested permission to subordinate the armies to the South Front.

25 July 1941

NORHTERN SECTOR
Kuchler's 18th Army unleashed a major attack against lvanov 's 8th Army in Estonia that succeeded in ripping open the Soviet line. With the 26th Korp attacking between Lake Voru and Parnu and the 50th Korp around Sartu, the hard-pressed 10th and 11th Rifle Corps were stuck along the length of their weak defences. After bitter fighting, the 8th Army was compelled to abandoned its positions and fall back, the 10th Rifle heading for Tallinn and 11th for Narva.

CENTRAL SECTOR
Fighting around Smolensk raged as Army Group Centre ought to close the Yartsevo corridor. A large proportion of Soviet effort in the centre was being expended in keeping this corridor free for the withdrawal of the West Front. In addition, the sheer size of the pocket aided the Soviets, many units slipping through the fluid German lines, evading the panzers that rushed from one threatened sector to another. Despite this, there were considerable forces in danger of encirclement if the two panzer groups closed the neck of the pocket.

SOUTHERN SECTOR
As South-West Front fell back upon Uman, the Stavka transferred control of 6th and 12th Armies to South Front. Kirponos was no longer in touch with the two armies and could no longer get supplies through to them. The 26th Army struggled to hold on to the Rzhishev and Kanev sectors as Kleist's 1st Panzer Group launched strong attacks. The 3rd Panzer Korp decamped from its positions along the Irpen river, leaving 29th Korp to face 37th Army and 51st and 17th Korps to face 5th Army. Mackensen's panzers drove east along the Dniepr, while 14th and 48th Panzer Korps pushed south towards Pervomaisk in an effort to link up with 17th and 11th Armies and isolate the units that Stavka had just detached from Kirponos' command. In order to reinforce the Dniepr line, the Stavka raised Ryabyshev's new 38th Army, deploying it around Cherkassy.

General Tyulenev, commanding the South Front, ordered the trapped armies at Uman to pull back to the Zvenigorodka–Uman line and then punch through to the east, despite their already heavy losses and repeated failed attempts.

The 18th Army was ordered to launch a counter-attack with its 48th Rifle Corp in an effort to halt the progress of the German 30th Korp around Balta. Attacks by the 2nd Cavalry Corp of the 9th Army were to throw the Germans out of the town. The Germans were slowly but surely forcing a wedge between the junction of the 18th and 9th Armies near Balta.

26 July 1941

NORTHERN SECTOR
As the Germans delayed on the Luga, the Stavka activated the new 34th Army on the southern shores of Lake Ilmen. This new formation, having already encountered 16th Army around Soltsy, deployed on the southern shore of Lake llmen, between it and 11th Army to its south, and posed a very clear threat to the flank of 56th Panzer Korp and the 16th Army.

CENTRAL SECTOR
After an arduous battle, the Smolensk pocket was finally closed. The 20th Motorised and 17th Panzer Divisions effected a junction, but the neck of the pocket was still perilously thin and under constant attack. The 700,000 soldiers trapped inside the pocket tried to break through to the relief forces attacking from the outside. Desperate battles continued inside the pocket as the Soviets attempted to break free.

With the Reserve Front in the combat line, the West Front launched strong attacks against the German positions at Elnya, on the outer perimeter of the Smolensk pocket and upon the Yartsevo corridor. There were also further attacks by 21st, 13th and 28th Armies at Gomel, Rudnya and

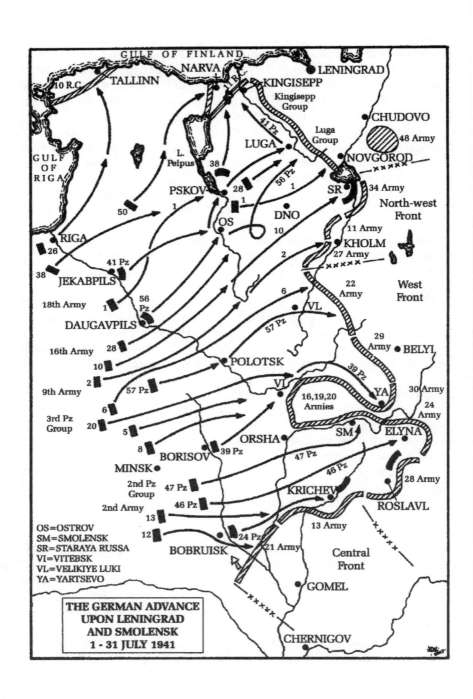

GULF OF FINLAND

10 R.C.
TALLINN
NARVA
T.R.C.
LENINGRAD
KINGISEPP
Kingisepp
Group
CHUDOVO
41 Pz
Luga
Group
48 Army
LUGA
NOVGOROD
GULF
OF
RIGA
L.
Peipus
38
56 Pz
1
SR
34 Army
North-west
Front
PSKOV
28
1
50
1
OS
DNO
RIGA
10
11 Army
26
2
KHOLM
38
41 Pz
27 Army
JEKABPILS
22
West
Army
Front
18th Army
56
Pz
1
6
DAUGAVPILS
VL
16th Army
28
57 Pz
29
Army
BELYI
10
POLOTSK
39 Pz
9th Army
2
VI
YA
57 Pz
30 Army
3rd Pz
6
16,19,20
24
Group
20
Armies
Army
5
SM
ELYNA
8
ORSHA
MINSK
BORISOV
39 Pz
47 Pz
28 Army
2nd Pz
46 Pz
Group
47 Pz
KRICHEV
2nd Army
46 Pz
ROSLAVL
13
13 Army
12
BOBRUISK
24 Pz
21 Army
Central
Front

OS=OSTROV
SM=SMOLENSK
SR=STARAYA RUSSA
VI=VITEBSK
VL=VELIKIYE LUKI
YA=YARTSEVO

GOMEL

THE GERMAN ADVANCE
UPON LENINGRAD
AND SMOLENSK
1 - 31 JULY 1941

CHERNIGOV

Roslavl that pinned down German 2nd Army as it attempted to secure the southern wing of 2nd Panzer Group.

The 61st and 45th Rifle Corps of 13th Army were under fierce attack at Mogilev. German forces, comprising four infantry divisions, penetrated into the town during the day and became embroiled in heavy fighting. At the end of the day, the Germans succeeded in overrunning most of the town.

FINLAND AND NORWAY
The left flank of the Army of Karelia reached Lake Onega at Petrozavodsk but was unable to release forces for the push to the Svir as the Soviets still had units fighting in their rear at Suoyarve. Other Soviet units were fighting hard on the right flank at Lake Yanisyarve.

27 July 1941

NORTHERN SECTOR
With the collapse of its positions south of Tallinn and the rapid advance of German 18th Army, 8th Army began to dig in around Tallinn. Kuchler quickly moved to invest the city, some 23,000 men having fallen back into Tallinn, while the remnants of 8th Army fled to Narva, hotly pursued by additional elements of 8th Army. With 41st Panzer Korp already across the Luga at Kingisepp, lvanov had a difficult time trying to fight his way through to Leningrad.

CENTRAL SECTOR
The 61st Rifle Corp attempted to break out of Mogilev, pushing towards Mstislavl and Roslavl. Elements of 45th Rifle Corp fought their way east across the Sozh and linked up with 13th Mechanised Corp.

With the panzer groups dispersing, Kluge's 4th Panzer Army was disbanded, the headquarters of the 4th Army becoming an active infantry formation once again. This allowed 2nd Army headquarters to take command of those infantry units in support of 2nd Panzer Group. Effectively, a new German infantry army entered the order of battle.

SOUTHERN SECTOR
Kostenko, having regrouped 26th Army, counter-attacked from the Dniepr and crashed into the exposed flank of 1st Panzer Group between Kiev and Cherkassy. In an effort to fend off this new Soviet thrust, Schwedler's 4th Korp marched to the relief of the armour and tackled Kostenko. Ferocious fighting ensued, but the Germans easily brought the Soviets to a halt. Bloody battles raged though as Kostenko launched repeated attacks with wave upon wave of infantry, unsupported by either aircraft or armour. On the southern wing of the South-West Front, 17th Army launched a

concerted attack against the Soviet forces that were becoming compressed in the Urnan sector. As these battles developed, the Stavka instructed Tyulenev to ensure the protection of Odessa and prevent its premature capture by the advancing Rumanian 4th Army. Rear Admiral Zhukov was placed in command of the landward defences of the port.

28 July 1941

NORTHERN SECTOR
After a protracted struggle, the Soviets abandoned the Kingisepp bridge-head across the Luga, units on the west bank withdrawing from the town, which fell to Reinhardt's 41st Panzer Korp.

SOUTHERN SECTOR
Tyulenev reported to Stavka: 'it is impossible to determine the situation in the 6th and 12th Armies ... because of the absence of communication.'[9] The Stavka believed the Germans were planning to seize the Dniepr crossings at Kiev and Cherkassy and therefore ordered the South-West and South Fronts to prevent the German advance. The Soviet command totally misread the German plan to isolate 6th and 12th Armies.

In Moldavia the 48th Rifle Corp of 18th Army pulled out of Kotovsk, while the anticipated counter-attack by 2nd Cavalry Corp towards Balta rattled the 30th Korp. Elements of the 35th Rifle Corp were fighting before Dubossary in an effort to prevent the Germans from expending a bridge-head across the Dneistr.

29 July 1941

NORTHERN SECTOR
Fighting continued in Estonia as Kuchler's 18th Army relentlessly battered Ivanov's 8th Army. On the line of the Luga, the LOG was deactivated, its forces continuing to operate in its three separate groupings.

SOUTHERN SECTOR
The 6th and 12th Armies continued to fight on inside their ever-decreasing pocket. In an effort to finally close the circle around the Soviet forces, Kleist ordered 48th Panzer Korp to push on to Pervomaisk. In turn 17th Army moved 49th Mountain Korp to the south-east, inadvertently opening an escape route up to the Soviet armies. Unfortunately they failed to take it.

In Moldavia, the 30th Korp continued to attack, pushing a wedge between the 18th and 9th Armies. Heavy fighting raged at Balta as the 2nd Cavalry Corp was outflanked.

RED ARMY COMMAND
As he delivered one of his regular reports, Zhukov clashed with Stalin over the need to hold on to Kiev. Accusing Zhukov of talking nonsense, Stalin dismissed his deputy, but at Zhukov's own request, kept him on active service, appointing him commander of the Reserve Front. Shaposhnikov was appointed Chief of the General Staff in place of Zhukov. Zhukov had advised Stalin to withdraw Kirponos' South-West Front behind the Dniepr and abandon Kiev. Stalin stated this was rubbish, prompting Zhukov to give up his post. Despite being demoted to commander of the Reserve Front, Zhukov retained his membership on the board of the Stavka.

30 July 1941

NORTHERN SECTOR
Elements of 1st Korp reached Schimsk forcing 11th and 27th Armies back upon a line Staraya Russa–Kholm. The 16th Army moved forces up to pursue the retreating Soviet forces.

CASUALTIES
German High Command claimed that between the 22 June and 30 July, the field armies captured 800,000 Soviet soldiers and destroyed or captured 12,000 armoured vehicles. The number of Red Army killed was thought to be in excess of three quarters of a million men.

31 July 1941

NORTHERN SECTOR
The 10th Korp of 16th Army advanced to the southern shores of Lake Ilmen. The 34th Army and its five rifle and two cavalry divisions fought to prevent the German advance.

CENTRAL SECTOR
Guderian's 2nd Panzer Army completed its redeployment on the southern flank of Army Group Centre, as did the 2nd Army. Even while the redeployment took place, 24th Panzer Korp struck Group Kachalov south of Smolensk, inflicting heavy casualties.

FINLAND AND NORWAY
The Finns began their attack towards Leningrad as South-Eastern Army struck Pshennikov's 23rd Army, the 2nd Korp driving towards Kexholm. The Finnish attacks upon Vyborg and Vousalmi continued.

THE COMBATANTS – END OF JULY 1941

At the end of July the German forces in the east had been substantially reinforced by a sizable part of their available reserves. In all the field armies deployed nineteen panzer, fifteen motorised and one hundred and two infantry divisions, an additional two panzer, one motorised and twelve infantry divisions having been committed. German losses had reached 213,000 men, of which only 47,000 had been replaced.[10] In July alone the Ostheer lost 63,000 men killed.

The Luftwaffe in the east had 1,050 aircraft available for action. The Soviet air force had been reduced to 2,500 planes.

The Red Army had suffered ghastly casualties, having only ninety-three operational divisions left in the line. During July the Soviet command raised a number of new armies. The 29th, 30th, 31st, 32nd, 33rd and 34th Armies were raised in the west, the 35th in the far east, the 36th in the Baikal area, the 43rd in Slavka reserve, 44th, 45th, 46th and 47th in the Trans Caucasus area.

1 August 1941

NORTHEN SECTOR

The 10th Korp attacked towards Staraya Russa but encountered strong resistance from 11th Army. Heavy fighting raged for over a week until the Germans were able to effect a break in the Soviet line.

CENTRAL SECTOR

Army Group Centre continued to attack the Smolensk pocket, but the German outer ring was under heavy attack as 30th, 29th and 24th Armies attempted to break through to the beleagured 16th, 20th and 19th Armies. Inside the pocket Orsha fell after a bitter struggle, and to the north there was heavy fighting near Vitebsk. On the southern flank, 21st Army counter-attacked around Gomel, hitting German 2nd Army. At the same time, Guderian unleashed his 2nd Panzer Group, ripping open the Soviet line to the north. Schweppenburg's 24th Panzer Korp, with Farmbacher's 7th in support, advanced towards Roslavl, taking it late in the day.

SOUTHERN SECTOR

Potapov 5th Army launched an unexpected counter-attack from the Pripet Marshes into the flank of 6th Army. Despite ferocious fighting around Ovruch, the Soviets were unable to break through the German line, but did succeed in drawing forces away from the fighting at Kiev. To the south, Ponedelin radioed the Stavka and South Front headquarters to inform them that the encirclement of 6th and 12th Armies was virtually complete, that no reserves were left and ammunition and fuel were running out.

In Moldavia the 2nd Cavalry Corp and 48th Rifle Corp of the 9th and 18th Armies respectively abandoned their feeble attacks around Balta and went onto the defensive. The remainder of the 9th Army also passed to the defensive.

2 August 1941

NORTHERN SECTOR
Busch's 16th Army fought its way along the southern shore of Lake Ilmen and cut a salient into the right flank of 34th Army. The Soviets battled to bar the road to Staraya Russa.

CENTRAL SECTOR
To support the attacks of 24th Panzer Korp around Roslavl, 9th Korp launched its attack from the Oster river.

SOUTHERN SECTOR
After an arduous march, 11th Panzer Division of 1st Panzer Group linked up with 101st Jaeger Division of 17th Army at Dobrianka, south-east of Uman. The 16th Panzer Division also linked up with Hungarian troops at Pervomaisk, encircling 6th and 12th Armies and part of 18th Army between Uman and Pervomaisk, a total force of over 200,000 Soviet troops. Budenny immediately ordered 26th Army to counter-attack towards Boguslav and Zvenigorodka to relieve the pocket. German forces also captured Kirovograd.

The isolation of the Soviet armies around Uman and Smolensk scratched close to a million Soviet soldiers and massive quantities of equipment from the Soviet order of battle. Despite desperate relief attempts, the Red Army effectively had to strike from its number nearly a third of its original operational strength. However, the sheer scale of the victory was in itself a problem for the Ostheer. Determined Soviet units were able to break out to the east as the Germans found it difficult to seal the pockets with their increasingly overstretched manpower resources. The lack of motorisation among German infantry divisions was clearly evident as the exhausted Landser struggled to cover the vast distances to catch up with the armoured units.

3 August 1941

NORTHERN SECTOR
Heavy fighting continued around Lake Ilmen as 16th Army increased its attacks.

CENTRAL SECTOR
Units of 9th Korp linked up with 24th Panzer Korp south of Roslavl, encircling 70,000 men of 28th Army.

SOUTHERN SECTOR
The Germans consolidated their positions around the Uman pocket as Budenny ordered 26th Army to counter-attack from the Dniepr and relieve the encircled armies. Kostenko's army had already suffered heavy losses in the fighting with 4th Korp along the Dniepr. On the Dniepr line 37th and 38th Armies became operational while a new 6th Army assembled around Dnepropetrovsk.

4 August 1941

NORTHERN SECTOR
Gerasimov took command of 23rd Army from Pshennikov.

CENTRAL SECTOR
The 9th Korp came under heavy attack and pulled back from the Moscow highway. This movement opened up an escape route for the units of the Central Front trapped around Roslavl.

SOUTHERN SECTOR
Potapov's 5th Army counter-attacked near Malin with two rifle divisions of 15th Rifle Corp from the west and north-west, the 9th Mechanised Corp from the north and 22nd Mechanised Corp from the south-east. Heavy fighting erupted with the 51st Korp of the German 6th Army. The 19th Mechanised and 31st Rifle Corps were engaged in fighting with the 17th Korp, which had attacked along the Korosten railway.

Tyulenev reported to the Stavka and Budenny, denouncing Ponedelin for his failure to evade German encirclement. The 9th and 18th Armies, fighting outside the pocket, were effectively isolated and were ordered to fall back to the Bug. The isolation of the 6th and 12th Armies around Uman had turned the flank of the 8th Army and presented the Germans with the opportunity to thrust into the rear of the 9th and 18th and reach the Black Sea coast around Nikolayev. Tyulenev was faced with the difficult task of extricating his battered armies and saving what he could to fight on from farther east.

GERMAN COMMAND
Hitler visited the headquarters of Army Groups Centre and South over the next two days to hear the views of his field commanders. All pressed for the continuation of the advance towards Moscow rather than the diversion of resources onto the flanks. Hitler rejected these opinions on the grounds of economic necessity.

5 August 1941

CENTRAL SECTOR
Soviet resistance in the Smolensk pocket ended. Army Group Centre claimed to have taken 309,000 prisoners and destroyed or captured 3,200 tanks, 3,100 artillery pieces and 1,000 aircraft.

Around the Roslavl pocket, 7th Korp counter-attacked, closing the corridor opened by the withdrawal of 9th Korp. The Central Front was once again firmly sealed.

SOUTHERN SECTOR
Heavy fighting continued around Malin as the 5th Army pressed home its attacks. The 1st Airborne Corp joined the assault.

The Rumanian 4th Army closed in around Odessa, encircling the Soviet garrison inside the port. The Red Army had been ordered to fight to the last man to prevent the fall of Odessa to the Rumanian forces.

6 August 1941

NORTHERN SECTOR
Kholm and Staraya Russa fell to units of 16th Army. The Germans had established a continuous line from Lake Ilmen to Velikiye Luki. Pronin's 34th Army, already in action south of Lake Ilmen, was ordered to recover Staraya Russa.

CENTRAL SECTOR
Guderian's 2nd Panzer Group launched new attacks with 3rd and 4th Panzer Divisions of 24th Panzer Korp aimed at capturing Gomel. The Stavka allocated 43rd Army to the Reserve Front.

SOUTHERN SECTOR
Potapov's assault around Malin struggled to make any headway in the face of serious German resistance. The 9th and 22nd Mechanised and 1st Airborne Corps had managed a five-mile advance in three days of heavy fighting. The 29th Korp fought its way into the suburbs of Kiev but was halted by 37th Army.

Fighting in the Uman pocket continued with increasing numbers of Soviet soldiers surrendering to 11th and 17th Armies. Elements of 6th Army tried to break out to the east while 12th Army pushed south, each without success. Farther east, the Soviet retreat to the Dniepr accelerated, 9th Army falling back upon Nikolayev. Elements of the 14th Panzer Korp, pushing south, reached and captured Voznesensk. The 2nd Cavalry Corp, having been transferred to this exposed flank, failed to prevent the fall of the town. While these forces advanced, the 11th Army unleashed a major new attack from Dubossary and split apart the front of the 9th Army, effectively isolating those units protecting the approaches to Odessa from the remainder of the army.

FINLAND AND NORWAY
Finnish forces smashed through 23rd Army and pushed on to Lake Ladoga near Khitola. Elements of 23rd were isolated north of Sortavala but continued to fight on here and at Khitola. Fighting also raged south and west of Kexholm.

7 August 1941

NORTHERN SECTOR
Under Stavka instructions, the Red Army introduced Aklimov's 48th Army around Novgorod. It fielded one militia, three rifle and one tank divisions and one mountain brigade.

On the Baltic coast the Germans reached Kunda, slicing lvanov's 8th Army in two. The 10th Rifle Corp fell back into Tallinn while the 11th retreated towards Narva.

CENTRAL SECTOR
The Stavka allocated 49th Army to the Reserve Front.

SOUTHERN SECTOR
The 6th and 12th Armies launched a final effort to try to break free but failed. Barely 11,000 men escaped the pocket during the battle.

With the threat to its rear now acute, the 18th Army began to fall back towards the east, fighting their way against roving German armour and infantry forces.

8 August 1941

NORTHERN SECTOR
In heavy rain, Army Group North resumed its offensive towards Leningrad but the once fluid line had, after a month of inactivity, been solidified. The 41st Panzer Korp launched its attack from the lower Luga at 0800 hours with 38th Korp in support.

The Germans planned to advance from the Luga in three groups. The northern group, comprising 41st Panzer and 38th Korps, attacked from the Kingisepp bridgehead towards Leningrad, while the Luga group, comprising 56th Panzer Korp, was to attack on the direct road through Luga towards Leningrad. The southern group (1st and 28th Korps) was to attack 48th Army along the Schimsk–Novgorod–Chudovo axis. On the extreme left, 18th Army was to complete the conquest ol Estonia, while

16th Army defeated 11th, 34th, 27th and 22nd Armies along the Staraya Russa–Velikiye Luki line with its 10th, 2nd, 50th and 23rd Korps and then pushed into the Valdai hills. The Stavka, expecting a German attack south of Lake Ilmen, ordered 48th, 34th, 11th and 27th Army to strike at 16th Army.

At Tallinn the Germans began to lay down artillery fire upon the city. Soviet warships situated in the harbour mounted a counter-battery.

CENTRAL SECTOR
Guderian concluded the fighting near Roslavl as the encircled elements of 28th Army surrendered, 38,000 prisoners falling into German hands. A further 200 tanks and 200 artillery pieces had been destroyed or captured. The remnants of 28th limped east to fight another day.

The 2nd Army began an offensive around Gomel, aiming to destroy 21st Army and open the junction of the South-West Front.

SOUTHERN SECTOR
Fighting on the northern wing of Army Group South died down as 5th Army abandoned its attacks at Malin. German 17th Korp counter-attacked and captured Korosten, thereafter going onto the defensive itself.

The Germans completed the destruction of the Uman pocket. Yet another Soviet force had been destroyed. Over 103,000 men marched into German captivity, leaving behind 300 tanks and 800 artillery pieces. Among the prisoners were Generals Ponedelin and Muzychenko.

With the final destruction of the Uman grouping, the 18th and 9th Armies began a wholesale flight to the Southern Bug.

FINLAND AND NORWAY
The Finns formed the 1st Korp (7th, 19th and 2nd Infantry Divisions) to destroy the Soviet units fighting on the shores of Lake Ladoga.

9 August 1941

NORTHERN SECTOR
Heavy fighting raged at Kingisepp as 41st Panzer Korp struggled to break free of its Luga bridgeheads. At Novgorod, 48th Army was involved in bitter fighting with 1st and 28th Korps as the German southern group opened its attack.

SOUTHERN SECTOR
Fierce fighting raged around the environs of Kiev as the Soviets launched counter-attacks in an effort to keep the 6th Army out of the city. The German 17th and 11th Armies turned their attacks from the Bug, pushing towards the Dniepr and shattered the South Front as it withdrew.

Stuplnagel pushed his forces east to the river line, while Schubert marched south-east towards the Black Sea coast and Nikolayev.

10 August 1941

NORTHERN SECTOR
Fighting along the Luga line intensified as 3rd Motorised Division of 56th Panzer Korp launched a frontal assault upon Luga city. Fierce battles ensued as the 269th Infantry and 85 *Polizei* Divisions of 50th Korp attacked in support of 56th Panzer.

Busch's 16th Army renewed its attack along the southern shore of Lake Ilmen. The Soviets defended their positions with determination, embroiling the Germans in bitter battles.

SOUTHERN SECTOR
Strong German attacks towards Kiev reduced the hastily committed 3rd Airborne Corp and shattered 147th Rifle Division to mere shells. The Soviet 9th Army had retired to Nikolayev and began the difficult task of evacuating its forces to the eastern bank of the Bug.

FINLAND AND NORWAY
Finnish forces close to Vousalmi were involved in protracted battles with the defending 7th Army. Two Soviet divisions had been trapped at Kexholm and another was pinned down a Sortavala.

11 August 1941

NORTHERN SECTOR
The 41st Panzer and 38th Korps penetrated Soviet defences on the Luga and secured bridgeheads at lvanovskoye and Bolshoi Sabsk. The 8th Panzer Division moved up to support 41st Panzer Korp's attack.

SOUTHERN SECTOR
In an effort to strengthen the shaky Kiev defences the Soviets moved a rifle division up to reinforce the line. German attacks closed upon the southern outskirts of the city, hitting the 295th Rifle Division.

FINLAND AND NORWAY
The Finnish South-Eastern Army captured Vousalmi. To the north Dietl was strengthened by the addition of' two infantry divisions moved up from Norway.

12 August 1941

NORTHERN SECTOR
South of Lake Ilmen 10th Korp had pushed nine miles towards Staraya Russa. The Soviets counter-attacked with 34th Army, having concentrated eight rifle divisions, a tank and a cavalry corp. They aimed to press from the south and trap 10th Korp against the southern shores of Lake Ladoga. To support 34th Army's attack towards Morino, 48th Army was to attack north of Schimsk towards Utorgozh and 11th Army from the south of Staraya Russa. However, 48th and 11th Armies had been heavily attacked and forced onto the defensive, 48th Army losing Schimsk as 1st and 28th Korps advanced.

CENTRAL SECTORS
The 24th Panzer Korp succeeded in encircling another portion of Kuznetsov's ill-fated Central Front near Krichev, elements of 28th and 13th Armies being isolated.

The 2nd Army continued its attack on the Gomel axis, throwing three divisions across the Dniepr south of Zhlobin.

SOUTHERN SECTOR
Vlassov's 37th Army counter-attacked before Kiev and restored the city defences following the earlier limited penetration by 6th Army.

The OKH ordered Army Group South to destroy all enemy forces between Zaporozhe and the mouth of the Dniepr, trapping 9th, 18th and Coastal Armies against the Black Sea.

GERMAN COMMAND
Keitel issued another supplement to Directive No 34, detailing the objectives for the next phase of the offensive. With the infantry forces of Army Group Centre remaining on the defensive, 3rd Panzer Group would move north to assist Army Group North's assault upon Leningrad, while 2nd Panzer Group joined the southern wing of Army Group Centre to operate in conjunction with Army Group South in its operations to conquer the Kiev region, leading to the capture of the Donbas and Kharkov.

13 August 1941

NORTHERN SECTOR
As the Kingisepp bridgehead collapsed, Voroshilov threw one of his scarce reserve divisions into the battle.

South of Lake Ilmen, 34th Army hammered 10th Korp. The Germans held an exposed salient on the southern shore of the lake and were in danger of encirclement. To prevent this, Leeb ordered 56th Panzer Korp over to this sector. However, 56th was heavily embroiled in fighting on the Luga and unable to disengage.

14 August 1941

NORTHERN SECTOR
Soviet defences on the Luga began to crumble as 41st Panzer Korp shattered 41st Rifle Corp. Most of the Soviet unit was encircled close to the river but then broke out towards Krasnogvardievsk (now Gatchina). The Germans pushed forces into the breach, destabilising the entire Luga position.

In Estonia, 18th Army struck Tallinn and Narva. Soviet positions at Narva became untenable, compelling lvanov to pull back to evade isolation as the Germans thrust towards Leningrad.

South of Lake Ilmen, 34th Army continued to attack around Staraya Russa. The 34th had advanced twenty miles in two days.

CENTRAL SECTOR
The 24th Panzer Korp completed the destruction of the Krichev group, capturing 16,000 Soviet soldiers.

SOUTHERN SECTOR
As 11th Army approached the Black Sea coast, the retreating 9th Army destroyed naval installations at Nikolayev.

RED ARMY COMMAND
With the front line in tatters, the Stavka raised another new command in the central sector. Bryansk Front, commanded by General A I Eremenko, the former deputy commander of the West Front under Timoshenko, comprised General Petrov's 50th Army (seven rifle and one cavalry divisions) and General Golubev's 13th Army (eight rifle, one tank and two cavalry divisions). There were three rifle and one cavalry divisions in reserve. Eremenko was given the task of halting the eastward advance of 2nd Panzer Group and 2nd Army. Stalin and the Stavka still believed Guderian was about to strike east from Roslavl in order to encircle Moscow. However, Guderian had begun to turn his forces south, smashing the junction of the Bryansk and Central Fronts even as the Bryansk Front took to the field.

15 August 1941

NORTHERN SECTOR
Manstein's 56th Panzer Korp gave up its hard won positions on the Luga line to Lindemann's 50th Korp and marched north in order to support 41st Panzer Korp's attack from its bridgehead at Kingisepp. As soon as he was on the move, Manstein was ordered to backtrack and march his

entire force south to aid the 10th Korp near Lake Ilmen. Manstein moved his korp back to Dno to strike at 34th Army.

The bloody struggle on the Luga had yielded Army Group North 21,000 prisoners and the destruction or capture of 300 tanks and 600 artillery pieces.

SOUTHERN SECTOR

With the situation in the south becoming increasingly acute, the South Front rushed the 2nd Cavalry Corp up to Krivoi-Rog to prevent the early German capture of the town. However, the corp became embroiled in bitter fighting as it attempted to aid the difficult withdrawal of the 18th and 9th Armies to the Ingulets river. Most of the 18th Army was already on the east bank and was pulling back upon Snegirevka. The 9th Army was fighting fierce defensive battles around Nikolayev.

FINLAND AND NORWAY

Sortavala fell to the Finnish 7th Infantry Division of the 1st Korp after heavy fighting. The defending 198th and 168th Rifle Divisions retreated after heavy losses. East of Viipurii the Finns penetrated across Lake Vuoksa, endangering the rear of 23rd Army.

16 August 1941

NORTHERN SECTOR

Soviet rearguards gave up Kingisepp, retreating along the road to Gatchina. The 1st and 28th Korps entered Novgorod amid heavy fighting with 48th Army.

CENTRAL SECTOR

The Bryansk Front was involved in heavy fighting with the 2nd Panzer Group and 2nd Army, fierce fighting raging around Konotop and Chernigov.

SOUTHERN SECTOR

Budenny signalled the Stavka that he required the readjustment of the line in order to prevent the destruction of his armies. He recommended the withdrawal of the right wing and formation of a front reserve. Stalin in turn ordered the withdrawal of all South-West Front units behind the line of the Dniepr, with the exception of Vlassov's 37th Army, which was to cover the approaches to Kiev between Loyev and Perevochna. Potapov's 5th Army, isolated in the Pripet Marshes, was also to fall back across the Dniepr and Desna rivers to rejoin the main combat line.

17 August 1941

NORTHERN SECTOR
Attacks headed by 41st Panzer Korp captured Narva. The 8th Army had already evacuated most of its forces from Estonia. The 48th Army launched a desperate counter-attack in an effort to prevent the Germans turning north from Novgorod and isolating Leningrad from the east. Busch's 16th Army held off the attacks of 34th Army, while 56th Panzer Korp deployed along the right wing of 10th Korp.

CENTRAL SECTOR
Rakutin's 24th Army began to attack the Elyna salient, pinning down five German divisions. The battle would rage until 21 August. After a brief struggle, Unecha fell to 24th Panzer Korp. Schweppenhurg was ordered to block the withdrawal of 21st Army from Gomel, where 2nd Army was attacking.

SOUTHERN SECTOR
Elements of 14th Panzer Korp entered Dnepropetrovsk and were dragged into bitter street battles with the defending 6th Army. To the South-West, the broken 9th and 18th Armies fell back across the Ingulets, Nikolayev having been abandoned. German forces were heavily attacking at Krivoi-Rog with the intention of pressing on to the Dniepr at Dnepropetrovsk and Zaporozhe.

GERMAN COMMAND
Brauchitsch and Halder tried one last appeal to Hitler to resume the advance in the centre. Their arguments were set forth in a memorandum but failed to change Hitler's decision. The advantage that the Wehrmacht had gained on the road to Moscow seemed about to be squandered in return for territorial gains to the south. However, even if Brauchitsch and Halder had been successful at this stage, there would still have been a delay launching the next phase of the offensive in the centre. Hoth's 3rd Panzer Group had already left the Moscow axis and was marching north to join Leeb's attack on Leningrad while Guderian had orientated his forces to the south to strike into the Ukraine.

18 August 1941

CENTRAL SECTOR
The 2nd Army and 2nd Panzer Group captured Pochep. German forces pushed on to Gomel and Starodub, threatening to separate the junction of 21st and 13th Armies.

SOUTHERN SECTOR
Soviet engineers blew the Dnepropetrovsk dams ahead of schedule. The rise in river level downstream destroyed the crossing points of 9th and 18th Armies. At the far end of the line, the 1st SS Motorised Division *Leibstandarte Adolf Hitler* fought its way into Kherson. The battle for the town would continue for the next three days.

19 August 1941

NORTHERN SECTOR
The 26th Korp opened the final assault upon Tallinn, artillery fire opening the battle. Heavy fighting erupted at Harku. North of Lake Ilmen, 1st Korp made progress at Novgorod, forcing 48th Army out of the city with serious losses.

Following his redeployment onto the flank of 10th Korp, Manstein unleashed a ferocious attack against 34th Army. Slicing through the thinly held Soviet flank, 3rd Motorised and SS *Totenkopf* Divisions inflicted heavy casualties as they pushed across the rear of those units fighting 10th Korp. Simultaneously, 10th Korp counter-attacked and pinned 34th Army frontally, the entire attack taking the Soviets completely by surprise.

CENTRAL SECTOR
Elements of 2nd Army fought their way into Gomel, while 24th Panzer Korp pushed south towards Starodub, into the rear of 21st Army. The movement south compelled Guderian to commit 47th Panzer Korp to protect the increasingly exposed eastern flank. However, 47th was immediately brought under sustained attack at Pochep. The attacks of 2nd Army and 2nd Panzer Group had successfully forced apart the Central and South-West Fronts, severing 21st Army from Central Front. Bitter fighting raged at Unecha where 13th Army was fighting in isolation.

SOUTHERN SECTOR
Potapov pulled out of positions in the Korosten sector. Reichenau's 6th Army spotted the Soviet withdrawal and launched an immediate attack, inflicting heavy casualties upon the rear of 5th Army.

The 14th Panzer Korp was involved in heavy fighting at Dnepropetrovsk, while other units of the Korp reached Zaporozhe. Despite efforts to rush the Soviet defences, the Germans were unable to capture the hydroelectric dams spanning the river. Fierce battles ensued as the Germans fought to gain a bridgehead on the eastern bank.

The Stavka altered its defensive plans in the Kiev region. Kirponos was ordered to pull 5th Army back across the Dniepr, while Vlassov held its strong bridgehead on the west bank at Kiev. To protect the weak right wing, Podlas' 40th Army was formed to fortify and hold the Desna near Novgorod Seversky, forming a link between 21st and 13th Armies. Tyulenev was ordered back across the Dniepr.

20 August 1941

NORTHERN SECTOR

The Germans launched strong attacks upon Tallinn, making slow progress into the Soviet defensive lines.

Reinhardt's 41st Panzer Korp pushed towards Krasnogvardievsk, drawing the German ring around Leningrad fighter. The 8th Panzer and SS *Polizei* Divisions, together with 269th and 96th Infantry Divisions isolated the remnants of the Luga Group. In ferocious fighting six rifle, two militia and one tank divisions were destroyed, costing the Soviets 30,000 men, 120 tanks and 400 artillery pieces.[11]

Aklimov's shattered 48th Army pulled back from Chudovo after being heavily attacked by 21st Infantry Division of 1st Korp. The loss of the town severed the Moscow–Leningrad railway line. German forces reached the Volkhov and prepared to push north to isolate Leningrad from the south east. Despite the weakness of Aklimov's 48th Army, reduced as it was to just 6,200 men, Northern Front ordered it to hold the line from Lyuban to Gruzino and halt the German advance along the Volkhov.

CENTRAL SECTOR

The 13th Army fell back to the line of the Sudost river.

SOUTHERN SECTOR

The 18th Army had retired to the west bank of the Dniepr near Lopatikha and began its evacuation to the east bank, while the 9th Army was in the process of pulling back across the river at Kherson.

FINLAND AND NORWAY

High Command ordered 23rd Army to pull back to a shorter line between Lake Pukya and Lake Vuoksa.

21 August 1941

NORTHERN SECTOR

The 4th Panzer Group attacked the Krasnogvardievsk position but was repulsed. Bitter fighting began along the line of Soviet fortifications.

On the southern shore of Lake Ilmen, 34th Army suffered under the attacks of 10th and 56th Panzer Korps. The Soviets attempted to fall back, but Manstein's panzers threw the Soviet units into disarray.

CENTRAL SECTOR

On the northern wing of Army Group Centre, the Germans prepared to counter-attack with 19th and 20th Panzer Divisions and 110th and 121st Infantry Divisions at Velikiye Luki to retake the town.

Rakutin halted his attack at Elnya after heavy losses. Guderian's 2nd Panzer Group became increasingly committed to the fighting in the Ukraine, 24th Panzer Korp taking Kostobobr and 47th Panzer striking at Pochep. Inside the salient, east of Kiev, 21st Army was under intense pressure from 2nd Army and began to pull out of Gomel.

SOUTHERN SECTOR

The Soviet 5th Army began to fall back to the Dniepr, but 51st Korp attacked its 27th Rifle Corp as it withdrew. The Germans surged forward and gained a crossing of the river at Okuminovo.

On the extreme southern flank, Kherson fell to the 1st SS Motorised Division *Leibstandarte Adolf Hitler* of 11th Army, German units reaching the mouth of the Dniepr.

FINLAND AND NORWAY

Kexholm fell to the 2nd Finnish Korp, which then pushed into the rear of 23rd Army as it attempted to pull back.

GERMAN COMMAND

Hitler revised Directive No 34. Army Group South was, upon completion of the Kiev operation, directed to conquer the Kharkov and Donbas industrial centres and then move into the Caucasus to overrun the Soviet oilfields at Maikop and Grozny. This was pushing the capabilities of the already over-extended German armies too far, demonstrating Hitler's total lack of comprehension of the concept of logistics and movement. He also entirely disregarded the opinion of his military staff, the protestations of Halder and Brauchitsch once again being ignored. Halder's proposal of 18 August had been turned down, without comment.

22 August 1941

NORTHERN SECTOR

The 26th and 38th Korps launched strong attacks against the retreating 8th Army, harrying it along the coast road to Leningrad.

On the southern wing, 56th Panzer and 10th Korps reached the Lovat river in strength near Staraya Russa, having defeated 34th Army. The counter-attack led by 56th Panzer had cost 34th Army 12,000 captured and 140 tanks and 240 artillery pieces destroyed or captured Army Group North's casualties since the opening of hostilities had reached 80,000 men.[12]

CENTRAL SECTOR
The Germans unleashed their attack upon Velikiye Luki, slicing through the Soviet line and outflanking the town. Heavy fighting ensued as infantry closed the battle with the defending Soviet units.

SOUTHERN SECTOR
The German 6th Army unleashed a major attack aimed at pulling down the Soviet defences before Kiev and undermining the entire Dniepr position.

Tyulenev successfully evacuated 9th and 18th Armies to the eastern bank of the Dniepr despite the raised river level.

SOVIET COMMAND
With its armies shattered, the Stavka disbanded Voroshilov's Glavkom North-West. Sobennikov was relieved as commander of North-West Front, Kurochkin being appointed in his place. The Stavka also disbanded Popov's North Front and created two new formations, Karelia Front under Lieutenant General Frolov and Leningrad Front under Stalin's civil war companion, Marshal Voroshilov, with Popov as chief of staff. Voroshilov's force was instructed to protect the northern approaches to Leningrad with 23rd Army and the southern perimeter with the existing militia units and 8th Army. The 55th and 42nd Armies would be formed in the final days of August, but until then the Soviets struggled on with what they had. Frolov was ordered to halt the Finnish advance north of Lake Ladoga with his 7th and 14th Armies. The 32nd Army would enter the fighting with this front some time later, near Lake Onega.

Since the renewed German attack towards Leningrad had begun on 10 July, the North Front had lost 40,500 killed and missing and a further 15,000 wounded.[13]

23 August 1941

CENTRAL SECTOR
German progress was made along the roads to Velikiye Luki against stiff Soviet resistance.

SOUTHERN SECTOR
The German 6th Army struck at 5th Army as it fell back through the Pripet Marshes to the Dniepr, the Soviets suffering heavy casualties as they tried to cross at Okuninek. After a brief but hard fought action, the Soviets fled towards Oster. Elements of Reichenau's army had already crossed the Dniepr, reaching the Desna at Oster and cutting off Potapov's line retreat. The thrust also threatened the northern flank of 37th Army.

FINLAND AND NORWAY

The fighting on the Finnish front and the northern approaches to Leningrad had cost the North Front 36,800 killed and missing and a further 35,700 wounded since the opening of hostilities.[14]

24 August 1941

NORTHERN SECTOR

At Tallinn, the Soviets pulled back into the city. German infantry penetrated Pirita and closed up to Minna Harbour, forcing the Soviets to commit their last reserves. During the night, the Germans overran Paldiski after fierce hand-to-hand fighting, bringing them to within six miles of Tallinn.

Reinhardt's 41st Panzer Korp reached Krasnogvardievsk, only twenty miles from Leningrad and was involved in fierce action with 41st Rifle Corp. On the middle Luga, Luga city fell to 50th Korp. Since the beginning of the German offensive towards the Luga, the North Front had lost 55,000 of the 153,000 men engaged.[15]

Schmidt's 39th Panzer Korp (12th Panzer and 18th and 20th Motorised Divisions) completed its deployment alongside 1st and 28th Korps, its target being the envelopment of Leningrad from the south-east. The 4th Panzer Group and 18th Armies were to push on to the city from the south, and west, while the bulk of 16th Army held south of Lake Ilmen and along the line of the Volkhov. Popov attempted to hold the western approaches to the city with 8th Army, the south-eastern approaches with 48th Army and the Volkhov positions with the Novgorod Group (two rifle divisions and one mountain brigade).

CENTRAL SECTOR

The 57th Panzer Korp made progress towards Velikiye Luki throughout the day, lead units of the assault force penetrating to within a mile of the city.

On the southern wing, 24th Panzer Korp captured Novo Sybkov, while 21st Army launched a counter-attack near Gomel, striking 2nd Army. The recent fighting between Central Front and 2nd Panzer Group had cost the Soviets 80,000 captured.

FINLAND AND NORWAY

The Karelia Front took up blocking positions near Kastenga with its 14th and 7th Armies, aiming to halt the Finnish Army of Karelia. The advancing Finnish South-Eastern Army successfully crossed the Gulf of Vyborg with its 8th Infantry Division and isolated Vyborg and three rifle divisions. The Finns moved the 18th and 12th Divisions of the 4th Korp up from the east and inflicted heavy losses upon the Soviets.

25 August 1941

NORTHERN SECTOR
The 39th Panzer Korp attacked 48th Army, forcing it back and taking Lyuban. The 18th Motorised Division pushed ahead towards Kolpino and the 20th Motorised towards Volkhov.

CENTRAL SECTOR
Velikiye Luki was surrounded by 57th Panzer Korp, which stormed the city and began the destruction of the isolated elements of 22nd Army.

Trubchevsk fell to Lemelsen's 47th Panzer Korp after a brisk battle. The Germans were deep into the northern wing of the South-West Front, threatening the rear of 21st and 40th Armies. Konotop fell to the Germans.

With the large-scale destruction of its forces facing the southern wing of Army Group Centre, the Stavka disbanded Kuznetsov 's badly mauled Central Front, transferring 3rd and 21st Armies to the Bryansk Front, which already deployed 50th and 13th Armies. Since 26 July the Front had lost 79,000 killed and missing and 28,000 wounded.

The new 20th and 43rd Armies were sent up to the West Front, deploying to the north of the Elnya salient. Stavka also ordered the West, Reserve and Bryansk Fronts to mount counter-attacks along the line Smolensk–Elnya–Novozybkov in order to deter the 2nd Panzer Group's southerly thrust. The Western Front was to attack with 16th, 19th, 20th and 30th Armies towards Dukhovschina, the 22nd and 29th Armies were to support by moving upon Belyi and Velizh, The West Front was given the target of Smolensk. The 24th and 43rd Armies were to flatten the Elnya salient.

SOUTHERN SECTOR
Budenny suggested to the Stavka that either 5th Army be transferred to the Central Front or 21st and 3rd Armies be moved over to South-West Front, The Stavka turned down the requests and instead ordered the newly forming 40th Army, with 135th and 239th Rifle Divisions, 10th Tank Division and 2nd Para Corp, to deploy onto the northern wing of the South-West Front.

South Front was allocated the reformed 6th Army (General Malinovksy) and 12th Army (General Galanin), which had been hastily formed around Dnepropetrovsk.

26 August 1941

NORTHERN SECTOR
The 26th Korp penetrated the shrinking Tallinn perimeter from the east and south, capturing the last airfield inside the pocket. Heavy fighting

continued at Pirita, while the Minna Harbour was under intense artillery fire and Paldiski was isolated. Soviet ships in the harbour stepped up their counter-barrage, inflicting heavy losses upon the attacking Germans. As the remnants of the garrison struggled to hold out, Front command ordered the evacuation of the city. Rearguards fought for every yard of the city, defending the Kadriorg Park against German attack.

The 18th Army and 4th Panzer Group commenced their attack upon Leningrad, drawing Voroshilov's Leningrad Front into bitter fighting on the city's southern perimeter.

CENTRAL SECTOR
Kuntzen's 57th Panzer Korp was involved in heavy fighting with 22nd Army in Velikiye Luki. Farther south, the 24th Panzer Korp rushed the Desna at Novgorod-Seversky and secured a bridgehead. By dusk the 2nd Army had also reached the river and was embroiled in heavy fighting with Potapov's retreating 5th Army, which was trapped to the west. The left flank of 2nd Panzer Group was increasingly over-extended as the spearhead pushed south, 47th Panzer Korp struggling to hold off the persistent Soviet attacks. Guderian was forced to call upon the supporting infantry to take over some sections of his front in order to relieve his ever extended armoured korps.

The rapid advance of the German armoured forces to the south threatened to undermine the newly deployed 40th Army, imperilling the northern wing of the South-West Front. As Guderian pushed south, the Stavka informed Eremenko that: 'it seemed possible to envelop the Starodub position, destroy the enemy in Starodub and close up the 21st and 13th Armies.'[16]

SOUTHERN SECTOR
Heavy fighting raged at Dnepropetrovsk as 13th Panzer Division came under strong attack from the Soviet 6th Army.

Tyulenev was relieved of command of the South Front and Ryabyshev of 38th Army appointed in his place.

FINLAND AND NORWAY
The Finns reached the Vuoksi river, seven miles from Viipurii.

27 August 1941

NORTHERN SECTOR
As the Soviets began the evacuation of Tallinn, the Germans pushed their rearguards back to the final defence line. During the night the destruction of the last supplies was begun.

With the crisis at Leningrad deepening, the GKO assumed direct control of the Karelia, Leningrad and North-West Fronts. The Stavka also began the deployment of 54th, 52nd and 4th Armies along and east of the Volkhov.

CENTRAL SECTOR
Attacks by 3rd Panzer Group forced the 22nd and 29th Armies back over the Western Dvina. Soviet counter-attacks brought the German advance to a halt, but not before elements of 22nd Army had been isolated near Velikiye Luki.

28 August 1941

NORTHERN SECTOR
Bitter battles raged inside Tallinn as the Germans pressed closer to the port, destroying isolated Soviet units as they advanced. During the day the Soviets moved their ships out of the harbour, beginning the hazardous journey east to Leningrad. By dusk the last elements that would escape had boarded their ships.

Reinhardt's 41st Panzer Korp took Ishora, only a few miles short of the suburbs of Leningrad.

CENTRAL SECTOR
The 16th, 19th and 20th Armies launched attacks along the line from Dukhovschina to Yartsevo.

The right wing of the South-West Front launched a strong counter attack against 24th Panzer Korp on the Desna.

SOUTHERN SECTOR
After protracted fighting, 12th Army fell back from Zaporozhe. As the Soviets withdrew, engineers destroyed the hydroelectric dam and disabled the generators, denying them to the Germans and flooding large areas to the south of the town.

With the battle for the Dniepr line under way, Rundstedt ordered the 1st Panzer Group to gain as many crossings over the river as possible, 6th and 17th Armies being ordered to do the same.

FINLAND AND NORWAY
Gerasimov was ordered to pull 23rd Army units close to Viipurii back to the Mannerheim Line.

29 August 1941

NORTHERN SECTOR
Tallinn fell to 26th Korp after a ferocious struggle. Of 23,000 Soviet soldiers

taken out of the city, only 5,000 reached the safety of Kronstadt. Twenty-four of twenty-nine transport vessels were sunk by Keller's 1st Air fleet and mines in the Gulf of Finland.

On the approaches to Leningrad there was heavy fighting at Kolpino and at Tosno and Mga where 12th Panzer and 20th Motorised Divisions, supported by three infantry divisions, closed up to the Neva.

Leeb ordered the encirclement of Leningrad and the capture of the Neva crossings, and the towns of Uritsk, Pulkovo, Pushkin, Kolpino and Ishora. To achieve their targets the German forces were organised into two groups, the Krasnogvardievsk Group and Slutsk–Kolpino Group. The former had 38th Korp (1st, 58th, 291st and 254th Infantry Divisions) on the left and 41st Panzer (1st and 6th Panzer and 36th Motorised Divisions) in the centre, with 50th Korp (SS *Polizei* and 269th Infantry Divisions) on the right. The Krasnogvardievsk Group aimed to take Krasnogvardievsk, reach the Gulf of Finland and isolate the Soviet forces west of Leningrad.

The Slutsk–Kolpino Group had 28th Korp with 121st, 96th and 122nd Infantry Divisions and part of 12th Panzer Division. Its task was to push along the Ishora river and capture Slutsk and Kolpino. To the east, 39th Panzer Korp (20th Motorised and balance of 12th Panzer Divisions) was to widen the corridor south of Lake Ladoga and then drive east from Sinyavino. The 8th Panzer Division was held in reserve behind 41st Panzer Korp.

CENTRAL SECTOR
The 30th Army launched a ferocious counter-attack east of Velizh aimed at relieving 22nd Army near Velikiye Luki. Initial attacks penetrated the German lines, enabling General Dovator to lead his Cavalry Group on a week-long raid inside German lines.

The 16th, 19th and 20th Armies continued their attacks along the Dukhovschina–Yartsevo line.

FINLAND AND NORWAY
Finnish armour moved towards Viipurii, encountering resistance from the hastily erected Soviet defences, after a brief battle, the Finnish South Eastern Army captured the town. Later in the day Kivennapa also fell.

After protracted fighting, 36th Korp reached the old Russo–Finnish border in the Salla region. German and Finnish forces penetrated twenty five miles along the road to Kandalaksha but were halted on the Verma river.

30 August 1941

NORTHERN SECTOR
Mga fell to 39th Panzer Korp after heavy fighting, severing the last rail

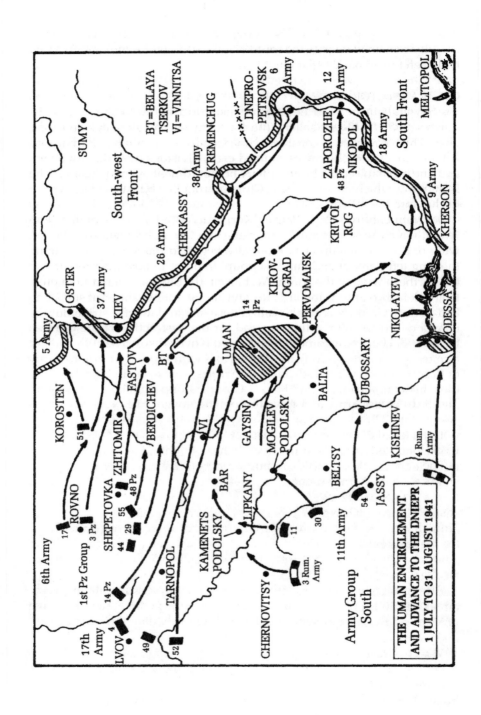

THE UMAN ENCIRCLEMENT
AND ADVANCE TO THE DNIEPR
1 JULY TO 31 AUGUST 1941

link out of Leningrad to the rest of the Soviet Union. Only a narrow land corridor remained open to the south of Lake Ladoga. Akimov's 48th Army had been forced back to the line Mga–Kirishi.

CENTRAL SECTOR
The Soviets launched a determined offensive to drive the Germans from the Elnya salient. Inside the salient, the 4th Army had five infantry divisions, all of which had been in constant action since the beginning of Barbarossa. Against this force Zhukov assembled eight divisions (five rifle, two tank and one mechanised). A brief artillery bombardment opened the attack by 24th Army, which penetrated the German front line but struggled to push farther into the salient.

Schweppenburg's 24th Panzer Korp succeeded in overcoming 40th Army, which was vigorously attacking the Desna bridgehead. The left wing of Eremenko's Bryansk Front also began to counter-attack, striking the long left flank of 2nd Panzer Group. In order to take the pressure off the northern wing of the South-West Front, the Stavka ordered Eremenko to attack in two groups towards Roslavl and Starodub, aimed at smashing 2nd Panzer Group. Eremenko called for a single powerful strike but the Stavka overruled him, calling instead for the destruction of the German forces at Pochep, Novgorod-Seversky and Novozybkov. The 50th and 3rd Armies were to attack along the Roslavl axis with support from 43rd Army of Reserve Front, while 13th and 21st Armies were to encircle and destroy the main components of 2nd Panzer Group. Group Ermakov was to operate ahead of 3rd Army and drive through to Novgorod-Seversky.

SOUTHERN SECTOR
Reichenau's 6th Army was involved in heavy fighting as it forced its way into Kiev. Vlassov defended the city street by Street.

FINLAND AND NORWAY
As the Finns advanced north of Leningrad, Raivola fell.

31 August 1941

NORTHERN SECTOR
The 48th Army launched a fierce counter-attack with two rifle divisions, all NKVD division and a mountain brigade, forcing 39th Panzer Korp out of Mga and reopening the railway line to Moscow. General Antonyuk took over command of 48th Army from Akimov.

With his forces at the gates of the city, the weather began to turn against Leeb, the onset of the autumn rains bringing movement to a standstill. Progress became difficult as the untracked components of the armies bogged down.

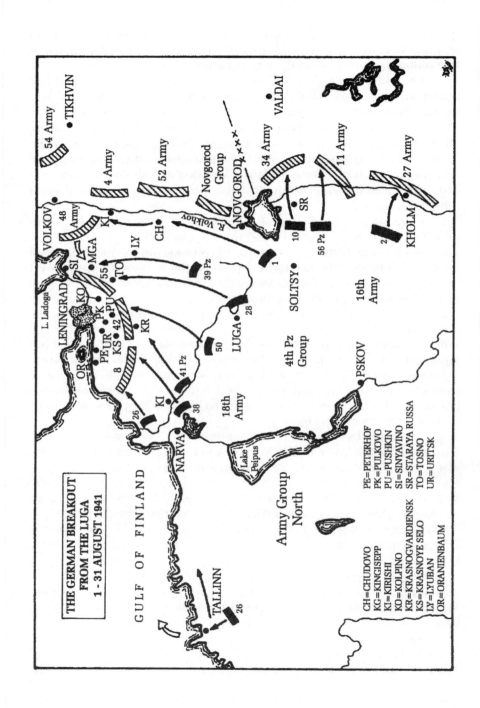

THE GERMAN BREAKOUT
FROM THE LUGA
1 - 31 AUGUST 1941

GULF OF FINLAND

TALLINN
26

NARVA

Lake
Peipus

PSKOV

Army Group
North

18th Army

16th Army

4th Pz
Group

LUGA
28

SOLTSY

50

41 Pz

KR

39 Pz
55
TO

1

10
56 Pz
2
KHOLM

SR

NOVGOROD

R. Volkhov

CH

LY

MGA
SI
KO
KS
PEUR
PK
PU
42
8
26
38
KI
OR
LENINGRAD

L. Ladoga

VOLKOV
48
Army
KI

4 Army

52 Army

Novgorod
Group

34 Army

11 Army

27 Army

VALDAI

54 Army

TIKHVIN

CH=CHUDOVO
KG=KINGISEPP
KI=KIRISHI
KO=KOLPINO
KR=KRASNOGVARDIENSK
KS=KRASNOYE SELO
LY=LYUBAN
OR=ORANIENBAUM

PE=PETERHOF
PK=PULKOVO
PU=PUSHKIN
SI=SINYAVINO
SR=STARAYA RUSSA
TO=TOSNO
UR=URITSK

With Leningrad directly threatened, the Stavka authorised Popov to raise a new army, 55th, in the Slutsk and Kolpino areas in order to defend the southern approaches of the city. A new 42nd Army was also formed. The 55th, under Major-General Lazarev, had four rifle divisions and one militia division while 42nd, under Lieutenant General Ivanov, had one rifle and two militia divisions.

On the far right wing of Army Group North, 16th Army pushed deeper into the Valdai Hills with its 56th Panzer, 2nd and 10th Korps. Demyansk fell to 19th Panzer Division of 57th Panzer Korp as Army Group Centre's left wing drove north. The 20th Panzer Division of 57th Panzer Korp and 2nd Korp isolated a large Soviet force near Lake Selinger and closed upon Ostashkov.

CENTRAL SECTOR
The 24th Panzer Korp launched strong attacks out of the Novgorod Seversky bridgehead in an effort to penetrate the heart of the South-West Front. On the left flank, 47th Panzer Korp came under increasing pressure by persistent Soviet attacks at Trubchevsk.

SOUTHERN SECTOR
With 2nd Panzer Group deep in the northern flank of the South-West Front, 1st Panzer Group renewed its attack, aiming to roll up Kirponos' left wing. Frelenko's 38th Army was unable to prevent 3rd Panzer Korp from crossing the Dniepr south-east of Kremenchug and establishing a bridgehead on the eastern bank. Elements of 52nd Korp began to cross into the Kremenchug bridgehead.

At the end of August the South Front held the Dniepr line from the mouth of the river to the Vorskla river. The 9th and 18th Armies stood from the Black Sea to the Dniepr bend south of Dnepropetrovsk. The newly formed 12th and 6th Armies held the Zaporozhe and Dnepropetrovsk sectors. Sofronov's Coastal Army continued to hold on to Odessa. Army Group South deployed 6th Army around Kiev, 17th Army from Cherkassy to the south of Kremenchug, 1st Panzer Group at Dnepropetrovsk and 11th Army and 3rd Rumanian Army on the lower Dniepr, opposite Nikopol.

FINLAND AND NORWAY
Terioki fell to the Finns as they closed up to the pre-war Russo–Finnish border.

THE OSTHEER
The first major casualty returns compiled by the German High Command showed that by the end of August the Ostheer had more than 410,000 casualties, 46,000 men losing their lives during August alone. In the same

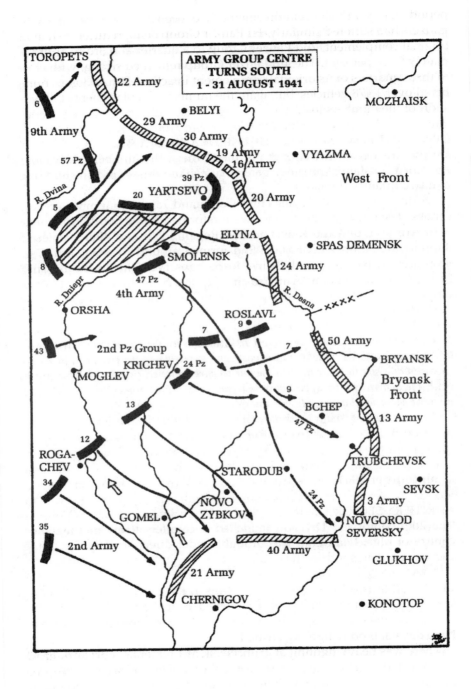

ARMY GROUP CENTRE
TURNS SOUTH
1 - 31 AUGUST 1941

period barely 217,000 reinforcements had been fed into the line. The panzers had suffered similarly, 1st Panzer Group being reduced to half its original complement, 2nd Panzer Group to a quarter and 3rd to approximately forty per cent. The 4th Panzer Group remained strong, with close to three quarters of its original complement in action. Panzer losses numbered over 1,478 vehicles, but again the number of replacements fell way short of the numbers lost.

OPPOSING DEPLOYMENT AT THE END OF AUGUST 1941
Despite the decreasing strength of the Ostheer, the number of divisions remained constant at nineteen panzer, fifteen motorised and one hundred and two infantry divisions.

During August the Soviet High Command raised a number of new armies. The 6th and 12th Armies were reformed in the South Front area, 37th Army around the Kiev Fortified Region, 38th and 40th Armies to support the South-West Front, 42nd formed around Krasnogvardievsk, 48th around Novgorod., 49th in Moscow reserve, 50th in the Bryansk Front, 51st Independent Army in the Crimea, 52nd Independent Army along the line of the Volkhov, 53rd in central Asia and 55th Army at Slutsk-Kolpino.[17]

> The hard fought battles of August 1941 had pushed the Soviet armies back to the gates of Leningrad in the north and to the line of the Dniepr in the south. Only in the centre had the line remained relatively stable, providing the Stavka with the opportunity to replenish its broken armies on the road to Moscow. However, Hitler's unexpected decision to deal with the Soviet armies in the Ukraine would take Stalin by surprise once again, and lead to the greatest battle of encirclement of the war so far.

1 September 1941

NORTHERN SECTOR
The 20th Motorised Division launched a counter-attack and regained control of Mga. Leningrad was brought under direct artillery fire as the Germans dug in south of the city.

CENTRAL SECTOR
The 16th, 19th and 20th Armies launched concerted attacks along the Dukhovschina–Yartsevo line in an effort to penetrate through to Smolensk. Nine days of bloody fighting ensued.

There was heavy fighting at Trubchevsk as Eremenko's Bryansk Front attacked 47th, Panzer Korp. The threat to the left flank of 2nd Panzer Group compelled Guderian to commit his reserves. After a relatively short period of rest, 46th Panzer Korp was thrown into the battle. Schweppenburg's 24th Panzer Korp extended its bridgehead around Novgorod-Seversky.

FINLAND AND NORWAY
The 23rd Army pulled back to the 1939 Russo-Finnish border after a running battle with the Finnish South-Eastern Army. The Soviets attempted to hold the Finns on the line of the Sestra, bitter fighting raging along this position throughout September.

2 September 1941

NORTHERN SECTOR
Army Group North tightened its grip around Leningrad as 18th Army dug in to prevent a breakout by the 8th Army from Oranienbaum. On the southern outskirts, 18th Army prepared to complete the isolation of the city from the east. The 50th Korp held the right flank together with 38th Korp, while the left flank comprised 39th Panzer Korp, which would move upon Schlusselberg. The 28th Korp of 16th Army also deployed alongside the right wing of 8th Army.

The 54th Army had begun to form in the Leningrad sector, bringing together four rifle divisions and two tank brigades.

CENTRAL SECTOR
The Bryansk Front began to counter-attack after a two-hour artillery preparation. The Germans seemed hardly affected by the attacks, but 3rd Army suffered heavy losses to German counter-fire.

SOUTHERN SECTOR
Heavy fighting raged along the Dniepr as the Germans exerted pressure upon the thinly spread armies of the South-West Front. Reichenau's 6th Army at Kiev hit the 37th Army, while 26th and 38th Armies struggled to hold off German attacks between Cherkassy and Kremenchug.

Stavka ordered Budenny to secure the defence of Chernigov but he had nothing left to plug the line. Guderian's southerly drive with 3rd and 4th Panzer Divisions had forced apart 21st and 3rd Armies, isolating 21st Army from the main component of the Bryansk Front.

3 September 1941

NORTHERN SECTOR
Pitched battles were fought south off while fighting along the Volkhov intensified as 1st and 39th Panzer Korps pressed 48th Army back.

CENTRAL SECTOR
The 24th Panzer Korp pushed south from the Desna, leading units capturing Krolovetz after a brief struggle.

4 September 1941

NORTHERN SECTOR
The Germans completed the occupation of Estonia. Rearguards of 8th Army, cut off to the west of the Narva, were forced to surrender. At Leningrad, Kuchler began to deploy his heavy artillery around Tosno to bombard the city into submission.

CENTRAL SECTOR
The 24th Army penetrated into the Elnya salient from the north and south, pushing shock groups into action and threatening the German positions.

SOUTHERN SECTOR
Budenny requested permission to create a reserve by taking two rifle divisions from the Kiev garrison and two from 26th Army. Shaposhnikov replied for the high command, refusing any regrouping of the South-West Front armies. Kirponos planned to use his meagre reserve to launch a counter-attack at Kremenchug.

Rundstedt ordered 1st Panzer Group into the Kremenchug bridgehead. Kirponos ordered 38th Army to eliminate the bridgehead.

FINLAND AND NORWAY
Finnish forces captured Beloostrov, north of Leningrad, but 23rd Army offered ferocious resistance.

The Finnish Army of Karelia unleashed a new attack against 7th Army. Having massed nine divisions, the Finns outnumbered the Soviets considerably.

5 September 1941

NORTHERN SECTOR
With the collapse of the defences south of Leningrad, Popov was dismissed as commander of Leningrad Front, Marshal Voroshilov, Stavka member and close associate of Stalin's, being appointed in his place. Voroshilov's forces consisted of the battered but still intact 8th Army in the Oranienbaum pocket, Ivanov's 42nd Army defending a line from the Gulf of Finland to Pustoshka and Lazarev's 55th Army from Pustoshka to the Neva river.

CENTRAL SECTOR
Fighting around the Elnya salient continued as 19th Rifle Division penetrated into the town. The 100th, 103rd, 309th and 120th Rifle Divisions supported the attacks, placing the Germans under intense pressure. The fighting compelled Kluge to commit four divisions from his reserve. To the south, 46th Panzer Korp captured Sosnitza.

FINLAND AND NORWAY
Olonets fell to the Finns as 7th Army was pushed back towards the Svir.

6 September 1941

NORTHERN SECTOR
The Germans struck Soviet forces on the approaches to Lake Ladoga, three hundred aircraft bombing the 1st NKVD Division before Schlusselberg. Ground attacks followed, 28th and 39th Panzer Korps hitting the Soviet unit on a narrow front.

Hitler ordered Leeb to encircle and starve Leningrad into submission rather than storm the city.

CENTRAL SECTOR
Elnya fell to 24th Army. Other units of the army pressed forward to the Desna. This relatively minor action was hailed in Moscow as a great victory, proving to the world that the Germans could be beaten, even if only through the use of sheer attrition to wear down their armies. From this victory the first Guards units were created. The 24th Army, which conducted the direct assault on Elnya, suffered 10,000 killed and missing and 21,000 wounded. With the Elnya offensive brought to a close, the Red Army counted the cost of their victory. Of 103,000 men committed, 31,000 became casualties. Since 10 July the Western Front armies suffered 310,000 killed and missing and 159,600 wounded. In addition the Reserve Front lost 45,700 killed and missing and 57,000 wounded since 30 July. Bryansk Front suffered 51,000 men killed and missing and a further 28,600 wounded since 16 August. The Soviets also lost 1,350 tanks, 9,300 artillery pieces and 900 aircraft.[18]

Group Ermakov was isolated on the southern wing. Stalin allowed Eremenko to pull his force back but criticised him bitterly as he did so. 21st Army, having become separated from the main part of the Bryansk Front, was transferred to South-West Front command, thereby forming the northern wing alongside the recently raised 40th Army.

7 September 1941

NORTHERN SECTOR
After a week of heavy fighting, 20th Motorised and 12th Panzer Divisions broke through 48th Army and advanced north upon Schlusselberg. Sinyavino fell during the fighting.

CENTRAL SECTOR
Heavy fighting raged in the Chernigov, Konotop and Oster sectors as the southern wing of Army Group Centre folded back the northern flank of the South-West Front.

SOUTHERN SECTOR
Potapov's 5th Army was in imminent danger of being split apart by German attacks. The 2nd Army pushed from the north-east and 6th Army from the east. The Stavka refused 5th Army permission to fall back. The 5th SS Motorised Division *Wiking* launched strong attacks north from the Dnepropetrovsk bridgehead. After heavy fighting the Kamenka Heights fell to the Germans.

8 September 1941

NORTHERN SECTOR
The Germans began their assault against the Moonzun islands. To defend the islands the Soviets had 23,600 men and 140 artillery pieces of the 8th Army. These forces were split between 18,600 men on the islands of Saaremaa and Muhu and a further 5,000 on Hiiumaa and Vormsi. The Germans began their attack upon Vormsi after an artillery barrage softened the defences. Three divisions were committed, two to land on the islands and one to defend the coasts. The small Soviet force defended stoutly, holding up the German attack.

On the southern shore of Lake Ladoga, Antonyuk's 48th Army broke apart, enabling 20th Motorised and 12th Panzer Divisions to take Schusselberg, severing the last land route out of Leningrad. Some 2,500,000 civilians, together with the greater part of the Leningrad Front, were encircled between the Germans to the south and Finns to the north. The fighting effectively cut apart 48th Army, forcing half away to the east and confining the remainder inside the city. With Leningrad isolated, German bombers launched heavy raids upon the city, inflicting severe damage upon the warehouses and factories.

CENTRAL SECTOR
Chernigov fell to 13th Korp of 2nd Army. Shaposhnikov ordered the West Front over onto the defensive, calling off the costly Dukhovschina–

Yartsevo attacks. The offensive had weakened the West Front considerably.

FINLAND AND NORWAY
Finnish forces took Lodenoye Pole, severing the Leningrad to Murmansk railway and securing a crossing over the Svir river. Heavy fighting raged as the Finns attempted to enlarge their bridgehead.

On the extreme northern wing the Germans unleashed a new attack towards Murmansk. Bitter fighting raged as artillery and aerial attacks supported the infantry assault.

9 September 1941

NORTHERN SECTOR
Army Group North commenced its main assault upon Leningrad as 41st Panzer Korp, with 38th Korp in support, attacked towards Krasnoye Selo. The 41st penetrated the Soviet positions, its 36th Motorised and 6th Panzer Divisions advancing six miles and cutting the Krasnoye Selo to Krasnogvardievsk road. The 6th Panzer was involved in heavy fighting at Krasnoye Selo. Attacks by 28th Korp failed to make progress in the face of fierce resistance by 55th Army. Furious artillery fire fell upon the Soviets, but the Baltic Fleet, anchored around Kronstadt, lay down a counter-barrage in support of the hard-pressed units.

CENTRAL SECTOR
The 24th Panzer Korp extended its bridgeheads across the Seim as it advanced towards Konotop. Backmach fell to the Germans.

SOUTHERN SECTOR
Elements of 17th Army crossed the Dniepr, consolidating the positions of 1st Panzer Group at Kremenchug. Belatedly, the Stavka ordered 5th and 37th Armies to fall back behind the Desna, but 2nd Army had already broken into the rear of this position, trapping the Soviet armies between itself and 6th Army that was advancing north of Kiev.

The Stavka ordered the withdrawal of 5th Army and right wing of 37th Army to the Desna.

FINLAND AND NORWAY
The fighting on the Litsa line intensified as the Germans pushed slowly forward to heights 173.7 and 314.9. Intense Soviet resistance brought the speed of the advance down to a crawl.

10 September 1941

NORTHERN SECTOR
After a fierce three-day battle the Soviet survivors on Vormsi pulled back to Hiiumaa.

Near Leningrad 1st Panzer Division reached the Duderhof Heights, which were defended by Lazarev's 55th Army. To the east, the 54th Army counter-attacked towards Sinyavino in an effort to smash the tenuous German hold around Leningrad. The Sinyavino battle would rage for another sixteen days and result in a meagre six-mile advance.

With the battle for Leningrad fully engaged, OKH ordered Leeb to hand over 41st Panzer Korp to Army Group Centre. Schmidt reported that 39th, Panzer was having difficulty overcoming the 54th Army. In an effort to strengthen this thrust, Leeb transferred 8th Panzer Division to 39th, while 254th Infantry Division filled the gap left in the line by the departure of 41st Panzer Korp. The 28th Korp was to move west towards Pushkin.

CENTRAL SECTOR
Konotop and Romny fell to Schweppenburg's 24th Panzer Korp, forcing back the 40th Army. Shaposhnikov ordered Reserve Front onto the defensive, joining the West Front in digging in along their current positions. Koniev also took over as commander of the West Front.

SOUTHERN SECTOR
Near Kiev, 5th Army fell back to the Desna, only to find 2nd Army firmly dug in. For the men of 5th Army the end was in sight, their line of retreat being firmly blocked. The 38th Army counter-attacked at Kremenchug and penetrated a short way into the German bridgehead. Over the previous few days the Germans had piled forces into the bridgehead, having the 52nd, 55th and 11th Korps deployed there.

Realising the scale of the disaster developing around his armies, Marshal Budenny urgently requested permission to withdraw from the Kiev salient. Stalin, having learned nothing from the disasters at Minsk and Smolensk, was furious that Budenny should even suggest withdrawal and absolutely forbade any retreat, condemning the greater part of the South-West Front to annihilation.

11 September 1941

NORTHERN SECTOR
German forces on the Baltic coast began to bombard Muhu Island, softening the defences in preparation for their landing.

Slutsk and Pushkin, on the southern approaches to Leningrad, fell to the Germans, while a furious battle raged for control of Krasnoye Selo. On the Duderhof Heights, the 1st Panzer Division gained territory but at considerable cost. Height 167 fell after heavy fighting.

Voroshilov's failure to halt the German attack prompted the Stavka appointment of General Zhukov to command the defence of the city. Zhukov would turn around Soviet fortunes at Leningrad, dismissing weak commanders and using draconian measures to instil discipline into the faltering combat units. At the beginning of his tenure, the Leningrad Front deployed 425,000 men, two thirds of them facing the Germans to the south of the city. To the east 54th Army had a further 85,000 around Volkhov, behind Antonyuk's badly bruised 48th Army.[19]

CENTRAL SECTOR
In heavy rain 46th Panzer Korp reached Putivl and 47th Panzer Korp took Glukhov.

SOUTHERN SECTOR
Budenny and Kirponos again requested permission to pull out of the exposed Kiev salient but Stalin insisted that Kiev be held and that the Soviet defence should be anchored on the line of the Dniepr.

The Germans began to deploy the 48th Panzer Korp into the Kremenchug bridgehead, 16th Panzer Division leading the way. Novo-Alexandrovka fell to the 1st SS Motorised Division *Leibstandarte Adolf Hitler* as the Germans conquered the Dniepr Elbow.

FINLAND AND NORWAY
Following the fall of Lodenoye Pole, 7th Army retired behind the line of the Svir, taking up strong positions on the southern bank.

12 September 1941

NORTHERN SECTOR
After a fierce battle, Krasnoye Selo fell to 1st Panzer Division. The Germans tried to push on but were halted at Pulkovo as the Soviets piled forces up in front of them, A naval brigade was committed to reinforce the militia division at Krasnoye Selo, while other militia held fast at Pulkovo. However, the German advance had outflanked the 42nd Army positions at Krasnogvardievsk. The 41st Panzer Korp advance threatened to outflank the 42nd Army's defences at Krasnogvardievsk, opening up the rear of 55th Army.

The 6th Panzer Division of 41st Panzer, supported by SS *Polizei* and 169th infantry Divisions of 50th Korp, attacked from the Ishora river in an attempt to take Krasnogvardievsk and push ahead to Pushkin and Slutsk. East of Slutsk a single rifle division stood fast. The 28th Korp unleashed its attack with 96th and 121st Infantry Divisions towards Slutsk and Pushkin, aiming to link up with 41st and 50th Korps.

On the Volkhov, the Stavka disbanded 48th Army, absorbing its elements into 54th Army. Stalin ordered Kulik, commanding 54th, to restore the broken front line south of Lake Ladoga, while 4th Army (General Yakovlev) and 52nd Army (Genral Klykov) were ordered up to the Volkhov line. Yakovlev's 4th was forming on the Volkhov, pulling together three rifle and one cavalry divisions.

CENTRAL SECTOR

Schweppenburg's 24th Panzer Korp continued to push south, becoming embroiled in heavy fighting at Nezhin.

As the situation on the central axis plunged towards disaster, the Stavka revised its standing orders to the Bryansk Front. Eremenko was ordered to halt his already failed offensive and regroup his battered armies in order to strike at the left flank of 2nd Panzer Group. The Stavka ordered 13th Army to be reinforced at the expense of 50th Army.

SOUTHERN SECTOR

First Panzer Group launched its attack from the Kremenchug bridgehead. Despite counter-attacks by 38th Army, 16th Panzer Division pushed through the Soviet defences, closing up to Khorol. The 14th Panzer Division moved to follow 16th. After heavy defensive fighting, 38th Army began to withdraw.

Potapov's 5th and Vlassov's 37th Armies fought desperate actions against the advancing 2nd and 6th Armies between the Desna and the Dniepr.

FINLAND AND NORWAY

The Finns launched strong attacks across the Svir, capturing Podporogye but being unable to press any farther south.

RED ARMY COMMAND

The Stavka disbanded Timoshenko's Glavkom West, Budenny simultaneously being dismissed as commander of the Glavkom South-West, his sacking being greatly influenced by his requests for the evacuation of the Kiev salient. Marshal Timoshenko took over command of the southern theatre.

GERMAN COMMAND

Hitler decided to suspend the costly attacks upon Leningrad and starve the city into submission. The armoured units of Army Group North, would shortly re-deploy to the central region, leaving Army Group North with only 39th Panzer Korp as armoured support.

13 September 1941

NORTHERN SECTOR
German units landed on Muhu Island after heavy artillery and aerial attacks. The main landings fell at the Gulf of Lyu, but severe Soviet coun- ter-attacks repulsed the German force. Another German force landed on the island of Saaremaa.

Army Group North renewed its assault upon Leningrad, 41st Panzer Korp (1st Panzer and 36th Motorised Divisions) and 38th Korp (1st and 58th Infantry Divisions) penetrating 42nd Army lines north of Krasnoye Selo and closing up to Uritsk. The 42nd Army, with one militia division and the naval brigade in place, counter-attacked. As the fighting spread, Krasnogvardievsk fell to elements of 41st Panzer and 50th Korps. For his failure to hold, General lvanov was dismissed as commander of 42nd Army and General Fedyuninsky appointed in his place.

SOUTHERN SECTOR
Elements of 3rd Panzer Division reached Lubny from the north, while 16th Panzer Division continued its attack, reaching the southern outskirts of the town. The Soviets threw in a scratch force, halting German progress temporarily. Mirgorod fell to 9th Panzer Division, while 14th Panzer moved to cover the 16th left flank. The South-West Front was to all intents and purposes isolated. During the night the South-West Front radioed Shaposhnikov to advise him of the seriousness of the situation. Even now, Stalin continued to insist upon no withdrawal. Manstein was appointed to command 11th Army.

14 September 1941

NORTHERN SECTOR
The Germans land on Muhu again, this time gaining a firm foothold.

At Leningrad, Zhukov was forced to commit a rifle division from his reserve to reinforce the hard-pressed 42nd Army at Uritsk. Zhukov's plan was to build up 42nd Army positions, forming a block upon which the German attack would falter. Simultaneously, the revitalised 8th Army would strike from Oranienbaum with two rifle divisions into the flank of the German armies. The 8th Army was ordered to counter-attack immedi- ately but failed to move, General Shcherbakov claiming his force was too weak. Zhukov dismissed Shcherbakov and ordered 8th to attack the next day under its new commander, General Shevaldin.

South of Leningrad, Zhukov ordered 55th Army to defend the Pushkin, Krasnogvardievsk and Kolpino sectors. The 54th Army was commanded to recapture Mga and Schlusselberg.

CENTRAL AND SOUTHERN SECTORS
The 3rd Panzer Division pushed slowly south, lead elements linking up with 16th Panzer Division near Lokhvitsa. This junction, albeit a tenuous one, brought about the encirclement of the South-West Front in a gigantic pocket east of Kiev. Kirponos and his command, together with 5th, 37th, 38th, 21st and 26th Armies, were cut off.

15 September 1941

NORTHERN SECTOR
On the southern perimeter of Leningrad, the Germans renewed their attacks, 50th and 41st Panzer Korps battering 42nd Army, hitting the Pulkovo Heights. Heavy fighting raged in Uritsk. The Soviets counter attacked at Sinyavino and Mga in an effort to break the siege. As the fighting raged, the Germans lost 6th Panzer Division, this unit leaving Leningrad for the centre.

FINLAND AND NORWAY
Dietl again tried to smash the Soviet defences on the road to Murmansk, but was frustrated by strong Soviet resistance. Once again the 14th Army drew away the focus of the German attack by launching an unexpected coastal raid.

16 September 1941

NORTHERN SECTOR
Before 8th Army could launch its delayed attack, 41st Panzer and 38th Korps struck. Advancing quickly against disorganised resistance, the Germans reached the coast and finally isolated 8th in the Oranienbaum pocket.
  The 1st Panzer and SS *Polizei* Divisions entered Pushkin and Aleksandrovka. Fighting at Slutsk and Kolpino enabled 28th Korp to penetrate the Soviet defences. However, despite these furious battles, 42nd Army continued to receive a trickle of reinforcements. Ferocious fighting raged at Uritsk.

CENTRAL SECTOR
The Germans began to pull 2nd Army out of its positions in order to redeploy onto the Moscow axis. Guderian's 2nd Panzer Group was unable to disengage as it was involved in heavy fighting around the Kiev pocket, Priluki falling to 47th Panzer Korp.

SOUTHERN SECTOR
Soviet forces in the Kiev pocket attempted to break out. However, the armies were fighting in isolation, 26th Army around Orzhitsa, 37th Army

in two groups to the south-east of Kiev and 5th and 21st Armies around Piryatin.

17 September 1941

NORTHERN SECTOR
After heavy fighting the Soviets fell back from Muhu to Saaremaa. The 18th Army launched a final, furious attack upon the Leningrad defences in a bid to take the city by storm. Guns of 42nd and 55th Armies were hard-pressed to hold the Germans at Kolpino and Pulkovo but after bitter fighting, halted their attacks.

During the final days of September, 41st, 56th and 57th Panzer Korps, together with the headquarters of the 4th Panzer Group left Army Group North in order to redeploy for Operation Typhoon.

SOUTHERN SECTOR
Army Group South launched concentric attacks against Kirponos's South West Front. As the front began to break up, Stalin belatedly agreed to let Kirponos evacuate his forces. It was far too late to save the trapped armies, many having already been reduced to remnants.

Manstein's 11th Army forced its way across the Dniepr at Berislav, 22nd Infantry Division undertaking a hazardous assault crossing. The army then advanced over the Nogaisk Steppe towards the Azov coast. The 11th deployed 30th Korp (72nd, 22nd and SS *Leibstandarte Adolf Hitler* Divisions), 49th Mountain Korp (170th Infantry and 1st and 4th Mountain Divisions) and 54th Korp. Manstein planned to push across the river in force and isolate the Crimea from the rest of the Ukraine by seizing the narrow Perekop Isthmus. The 30th Korp moved towards Melitopol, 54th to Perekop and 49th Mountain along the eastern bank of the Dniepr. To the rear, 3rd Rumanian Army advanced behind the main German force with its mountain and cavalry corps.

18 September 1941

NORTHERN SECTOR
Pushkin fell to 1st Panzer and SS *Polizei* Divisions after fierce fighting, while 28th Korp captured Slutsk, forcing 55th Army back. The Germans tried to develop the advance, 1st Panzer taking Pulkovo but was halted by 42nd Army at Aleksandrovka.

SOUTHERN SECTOR
The Soviets launched strong counter-attacks at Romny in an effort to punch a corridor through 24th Panzer Korp. Inside Kiev, 37th Army took a beating as 6th Army fought its way into tile heart of the city.

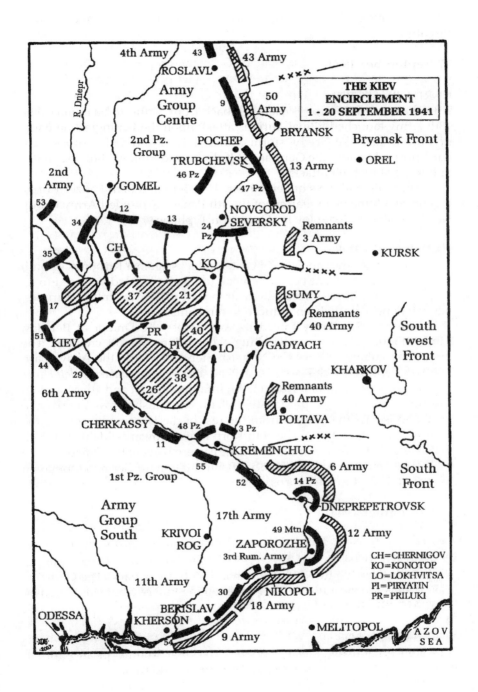

THE KIEV
ENCIRCLEMENT
1 - 20 SEPTEMBER 1941

4th Army   43   43 Army
ROSLAVL
Army   9   50
Group   Army
Centre   BRYANSK   Bryansk Front

R. Dniepr

2nd Pz.   POCHEP   OREL
Group
            TRUBCHEVSK   13 Army
2nd   46 Pz
Army   GOMEL   47 Pz
53   12   NOVGOROD
    34   13   SEVERSKY   Remnants
                    24   3 Army
35   Pz
        CH   KURSK
                KO
51   17   37   21
    KIEV   SUMY   South
                        Remnants   west
44   PR   40   40 Army   Front
    29   PI   LO   GADYACH
6th Army   38   KHARKOV
            26
        4   Remnants
CHERKASSY   48 Pz   3 Pz   40 Army
        11   POLTAVA
        55   KREMENCHUG   South
1st Pz. Group   52   Front
                    14 Pz   6 Army
Army   DNEPREPETROVSK
Group   17th Army
South   KRIVOI   49 Mtn   12 Army
        ROG   ZAPOROZHE
            3rd Rum. Army   CH=CHERNIGOV
11th Army   KO=KONOTOP
        30   NIKOPOL   LO=LOKHVITSA
    BERISLAV   18 Army   PI=PIRYATIN
ODESSA KHERSON   PR=PRILUKI
        54   9 Army   MELITOPOL   AZOV
                            SEA

19 September 1941

NORTHERN SECTOR

Fighting at Uritsk raged unabated. Germans fought in the suburbs of Uritsk but could not break through the Soviet positions. The 55th Army successfully stabilised its front at Pulkovo, Kuzmino and Portolovo, containing each German assault. Following 6th Panzer, the 1st Panzer and 36th Motorised Divisions together with headquarters of 41st Panzer Korp left the Leningrad sector.

> With the movement of German armour away from Leningrad, the first battle for the city drew to a close. Zhukov had displayed for the first time against Army Group North his ability to mount a ferocious defence when all seemed lost. Had the ineffective leadership of Voroshilov continued, Leningrad would undoubtedly have fallen to the Ostheer. Such a victory would have released additional German forces for the thrust east and had a serious impact upon the ability of the Soviet command to mount an effective defence of the capital.

SOUTHERN SECTOR

Heavy fighting raged at Romny as the Soviets hit 24th Panzer Korp. There was heavy fighting in Kiev as 6th Army pounded the remnants of 37th Army. German attacks isolated the Soviet forces inside the city. To the south, 11th Army advanced steadily from Berislav.

20 September 1941

NORTHERN SECTOR

To distract German attention from the southern perimeter of Leningrad, 8th Army attacked with four divisions from the Oranienbaum bridgehead.

SOUTHERN SECTOR

Kiev fell to 6th Army, 37th Army retreating east in an effort to break out of the cauldron and rejoin the main combat line.

Kirponos and his headquarters staff, a column of over one thousand men, tried to break out of the pocket, but the Germans ambushed the straggling line near Lokhvitsa, inflicting terrible casualties. After fierce fighting, the few survivors surrendered but Kirponos was not among them, having fallen in the battle. Potapov was captured. Bagramyan managed to break out with a force of around fifty men. Generals Kostenko, V I Kuznetsov, Lopatin and Moskalenko also escaped the pocket.

21 September 1941

NORTHERN SECTOR
The Leningrad sector became relatively quiet, with only small-scale actions taking place. West of the city 38th Korp counter-attacked, halting 8th Army's attacks at Oranienbaum.

SOUTHERN SECTOR
Heavy fighting raged around Glukhov and Romny as the Germans launched strong counter-attacks. There was also bitter fighting inside the Kiev pocket as the leaderless South-West Front fought its last bloody, unco-ordinated battles. An increasing number of Soviet soldiers surrendered, 2nd Panzer Group alone claiming 30,000 prisoners, 1st Panzer Group 43,000 and 6th Army a further 63,000. To the south-east of Kiev 37th Army began to surrender.

22 September 1941

SOUTHERN SECTOR
The Germans claimed to have taken 290,000 men prisoner in the Kiev pocket as Soviet resistance collapsed. Farther south, 11th Army reached the entrance to the Crimea, 54th Korp attacking the Perekop Isthmus. The six defending Soviet divisions held, up the German advance. Elements of 49th Mountain Korp and 30th Korp took up positions south of the Dniepr bend and at Melitopol.
    Around Odessa the Soviets launched a sharp counter-attack against their Rumanian besiegers and actually expanded their perimeter, advancing around Grigoryevka.

FINLAND AND NORWAY
Hitler ordered the attack on Murmansk to be discontinued.

23 September 1941

NORTHERN SECTOR
The Soviets on Saaremaa fell back to the Salme position and attempted a final stand. Heavy fighting raged along this position for a week.
    After a brief lull, 18th Army launched a new attack upon the Soviet forces south of Leningrad. Heavy fighting erupted at Pulkovo, but lack of armour prevented a German breakthrough with only twenty panzers available to aid its attack, 18th Army was quickly embroiled in close quarters fighting with 42nd and 55th Armies. Only 39th Panzer Korp remained with Army Group North, this unit being destined to pursue operations east of the Volkhov.

SOUTHERN SECTOR

Inside the Kiev pocket the remnants of 37th Army gave up the struggle and surrendered.

24 September 1941

NORTHERN SECTOR

Despite determined attacks, 18th Army was unable to break through to Leningrad. The 54th Army continued its counter-attack at Sinyavino but met with a singular lack of success.

The Soviets began to place pressure upon the Germans in the Valdai Hills area. Sporadic attacks failed to force the Germans back and a counter-attack by the 3rd SS Motorised Division *Totenkopf* forced the Soviets back.

SOUTHERN SECTOR

Inside the Kiev pocket, 5th and 21st Armies surrendered. Elements of 5th Army fought on, joining with the remnants of the South-West Front headquarters group in its attempt to break free.

Hansen's 54th Korp launched another ferocious attack at Perekop with its 45th and 73rd Infantry Divisions. The narrow confines of the Isthmus prevented the Germans from encircling the defending divisions, giving them no option other than costly frontal attacks.

The main part of Army Group South redeployed for the continuation of the advance east. Reichenau's 6th Army assembled for a thrust towards Kharkov, while Stuplnagel's 17th Army was to advance into the Donbas. The strike component of the army group, 1st Panzer Group, moved up to the Dniepr bridgeheads at Zaporozhe and Dnepropetrovsk in preparation for the drive to the Azov Sea and the expected encirclement of the South Front.

FINLAND AND NORWAY

General Meretskov took command of 7th Army defending the line of the Svir.

26 September 1941

NORTHERN SECTOR

Kulik abandoned his attack at Sinyavino. For his failure and mismanagement, Kulik was recalled to Moscow and demoted, Khozin taking over control of 54th Army.

The fighting in the Valdai Hills continued as the Soviets attempted to maintain the pressure on 16th Army.

SOUTHERN SECTOR
The Kiev pocket was destroyed, the last units of 26th Army surrendering around Orzhitsa. Soviet losses were thought to exceed 665,000 captured and many thousands, possibly in excess of 100,000, killed, together with 400 tanks, 28,400 artillery pieces and 340 aircraft destroyed or captured. The South-West Front alone reported 531,400 killed and missing and 54,000 wounded while 6th and, 12th Armies of the South Front recorded another 53,000 killed and missing plus 26,000 wounded.[20]

The disaster at Kiev effectively destroyed the South-West Front, 5th, 21st, 37th and 26th Armies being annihilated and 40th and 38th severely mauled. The South-West Front had been reduced to just 150,000 men. To the south, 54th Korp managed to punch a hole through the Perekop Isthmus defences, capturing the town of Perekop. The fighting had been so severe that 49th Mountain Korp was pulled back from the main front between the Dniepr and the Azov Sea to provide support to the exhausted 54th. This left 30th Korp to hold the line from the Dniepr elbow to the Azov Sea, with only the Rumanian 3rd Army in support, a tenuous situation at best. To warn the Germans of the dubious fighting ability of the Rumanian divisions, an attack by 9th and 18th Armies easily penetrated the front line, forcing Manstein to send part of 49th Mountain back to its original positions.

27 September 1941

NORTHERN SECTOR
The fighting in the Valdai Hills continued without success for the Soviets.

SOUTHERN SECTOR
The Soviets deployed Belov's 2nd Cavalry Corp to protect the junction of the depleted 40th and 21st Armies before Sumy. German forces in the Ukraine reached Novomosskovsk and Spaskoye.

28 September 1941

SOUTHERN SECTOR
Heavy fighting raged before Sumy as the 48th Panzer Korp pushed forward against 2nd Cavalry Corp. The 9th Panzer and 25th Motorised Divisions struck the Soviet corp hard and inflicted heavy losses.

29 September 1941

CENTRAL SECTOR

The 2nd Panzer Group was ready to attack towards Moscow. Guderian retained 24th and 47th Panzer Korps but gave up 46th to 4th Panzer Group. In compensation, 48th Panzer Korp, 34th and 35th Korps were allocated to 2nd Panzer. The 47th Panzer Korp deployed on the left flank near Shostka, 24th in the centre at Glukhov and 48th on the right around Putivl. The infantry of 34th and 35th Korps held the outer flanks. Unfortunately, the bulk of 48th Panzer Korp had been unable to assemble as it was bogged down in fighting near Sumy. It's attack against the 2nd Cavalry Corp ran into trouble as the fresh 1st Tank Brigade launched a counter-attack.

SOUTHERN SECTOR

Heavy fighting continued on the Perekop Isthmus as 54th Korp attacked. After a fierce battle, Armyansk fell, but the German advance stalled yet again at the Ishun defences, a historic Tartar ditch system dug across the narrowest stretch of the Isthmus. The recent fighting had already cost the Soviets 10,000 captured, 110 tanks and 135 artillery pieces destroyed.[21]

After an appeal to the Stavka, Stalin authorised Admiral Oktybrski to begin the evacuation of Odessa, the Soviet force inside the port having resisted the half-hearted attacks of the Rumanian forces for two months. Those divisions still inside the city were to be taken off to the Crimea by ships of the Black Sea Fleet.

Army Group South redeployed in preparation for the next phase of operations. Field Marshal von Rundstedt was to conquer the Donbas industrial region and gain the Don at Rostov. 1st Panzer Group was attacking towards Rostov while 17th Army made for Voroshilovgrad. 6th Army was to force its way forward on the northern flank and capture Kharkov in addition to maintaining the junction with 2nd Army of Army Group Centre. The main problem posed to Army Group South was the fact that 1st Panzer Group had been reduced to only two panzer korps, 14th and 3rd, following the transfer of 48th to Guderian. The army group had two panzer, two motorised and thirty-six infantry divisions supported by three Italian, six Rumanian, three Hungarian and two Slovak divisions.

THE OPPOSING FORCES ON THE EVE OF OPERATION TYPHOON

The German Moscow offensive aimed to isolate the Soviet capital in a double pincer movement, Strauss's 9th Army and Hoth's 3rd Panzer Group pushing to the north and Guderian's 2nd Panzer Group and the 2nd Army advancing to the south, the infantry forming the inner wings of the encirclement and the panzers the outer. The centre was to be pinned by Kluge's 4th Army and Hoeppner's 4th Panzer Group in order to prevent the transfer of Soviet units to the flanks. This would bring about the destruction of what the Germans believed were the last Soviet field armies in European Russia. It had originally been intended that Guderian's armoured fist would launch its attacks from just south of Smolensk, but there had not been enough time to assemble the 2nd Panzer Group in this sector following the conclusion of the fighting at Kiev. Therefore, the attack would be launched from Glukhov, from where the 2nd, Panzer would march north-east in the direction Orel–Moscow.

Army Group Centre had been comprehensively restructured in preparation for the new offensive, deploying a formidable array of armies across the Moscow axis. The northern wing, comprising 3rd Panzer Group with 41st and 56th Panzer Korps and 9th Army, had three panzer, two motorised and eighteen infantry divisions, while 4th Panzer Group with 46th, 57th and 40th Panzer Korps and the 4th Army numbered five panzer, two motorised and fifteen infantry divisions. To the south, 2nd Panzer Group had two panzer, two motorised and five infantry divisions among 24th, 47th and 48th Panzer, 34th and 35th Korps, and 2nd Army had eight infantry divisions. To support the ground forces there was 2nd Air Fleet and 8th Air Korp of 4th Air Fleet. In full the German forces in the centre numbered 1,929,000 men in 78 divisions, 14,000 artillery pieces, 1,000 panzers and 1,390 aircraft.[22]

Many German units had been reinforced for Operation Typhoon but still lacked the strength they had in June. The 1st Panzer Group had approximately five hundred and fifty tanks, the 2nd four hundred and sixty and the 3rd six hundred and twenty tanks. The 4th Panzer had been significantly reinforced, fielding nearly seven hundred tanks.

Since the first day of fighting in June to the end of September, the Ostheer suffered 550,000 casualties. However, just 350,000 had been replaced. In spite of the fall in strength among German combat units, the number of divisions in the field had in fact risen. At the end of September, the field armies comprised nineteen panzer, fifteen motorised and one hundred and three infantry divisions. During September one infantry division left the front but two entered the line. Germany's allies also increased their commitment. The Rumanians had eleven divisions and nine brigades in action, the Hungarians three brigades, the Italians three divisions, the Slovaks two divisions and the Spanish a single division, the 250th *Azul* Infantry Division, in the line. In the far north the Finns fielded sixteen divisions.

The Red Army planned to block the expected German attack upon Moscow with Koniev's Western Front deployed between Lake Selinger and Elnya, Marshal Budenny's Reserve Front between Elnya and Roslavl and the Bryansk Front between Roslavl and Kirov, commanded by Eremenko.

Koniev's Western Front fielded 22nd, 29th, 30th, 19th, 16th and 20th Armies, 558,000 men. The Reserve Front had 24th and 3th Armies in the line and 31st, 49th, 32nd and 33rd Armies behind the front, in the rear of the Western Front. This formation had 448,000 troops. Eremenko's Bryansk Front deployed 244,000 men between 50th, 3rd and 13th Armies to hold the southern wing of the Moscow axis. In total the Soviet armies on the Moscow axis comprised eighty-three divisions, nine cavalry and thirteen tank brigades, 7,600 artillery pieces, 990 tanks, 671 aircraft and 1,250,000 men.

On the southern wing of the Moscow axis, the Red Army had the remnants of the South-West Front and South Front. Following the debacle at Kiev, the Stavka disbanded Glavkom South-West, appointing Timoshenko to command the shattered, and demoralised South-West Front. This front comprised 40th Army, 21st, 38th and 6th Armies, nearly 200,000 men. The South Front had 12th, 18th and 9th Armies. Most of these armies had suffered heavy casualties in the fighting along the Dniepr and were in dire need of reinforcement. To the rear, the Stavka began to raise a new 37th Army around Voroshilovgrad.

> The destruction of the Soviet armies in the Kiev pocket had been an outstanding achievement. Not only had the armies in the Ukraine been massively defeated, their extremely capable commander and his staff had been killed or captured. Across the southern line, the Red Army was now thinly spread, enabling the Germans to conquer the rich industrial Donbas region and draw up to the Don.
>
> Had the victory in the Ukraine robbed the Germans of success at Moscow though? The presence of some three quarters of a million men on their right flank would have proved a serious threat to the advance of the central armies upon Moscow and therefore had to be addressed. However, the battle had drawn the very forces needed for the push to the capital away from the central axis. The battle of Kiev was a necessity and a valuable victory. Hitler had correctly concentrated on defeating the enemy army at the expense of the early capture of the enemy capital. The first great dilemma and moment of decision had passed, apparently with overwhelming success. In fact the dilemma should never have arisen. Had the German Army possessed adequate reserves for the enormous risk it had undertaken, the advance in the centre and south could have been conducted simultaneously. Hitler's greatest failure lay not in the decision to turn south but in spreading his limited forces so thinly that one objective could only be achieved at the expense of others. Germany quite simply lacked the resources to achieve the targets she set herself.

NOTES

1   Glantz, *Barbarossa* 1947, p 78
2   Erickson, *The Road to Stalingrad,* p 169
3   Kirosheev, *Soviet Casualties and Combat Losses in the Twentieth Century,* Table 75. This recently published book offers valuable information on Soviet commitments and casualties throughout the Russo-German War. After a half century of denial, the massive scale of Soviet losses has finally been documented.
4   Kirosheev, *Soviet Casualties and Combat Losses in the Twentieth Century,* Table 75
5   Glantz, *Barbarossa* 1947, p 169. Exact numbers were 241,954 troops lost, including 172,323 killed and wounded, 4,381 tanks, 5,806 artillery pieces and 1,218 aircraft.
6   Glantz, *Barbarossa* 1941, p 224
7   Glantz, *Barbarossa* 1947, p 224
8   Glantz, *Barbarossa* 1941, p 224
9   Glantz, *Barbarossa* 1941, p 120
10 Glantz, *Barbarossa* 1941, p 84
11 Glantz, *Barbarossa* 1941, p 223
12 Glantz, *Barbarossa* 1941, p 222
13 Kirosheev, *Soviet Casualties and Combat Losses in the Twentieth Century,* Table 75
14 Kirosheev, *Soviet Casualties and Combat Losses in the Twentieth Century,* Table 75
15 Glantz, *Barbarossa* 1941, p 112
16 Glantz, *Barbarossa* 1947, p 91
17 Glantz, *Barbarossa* 1941, p 69
18 Kirosheev, *Soviet Cesualties and Combat Losses in the Twentieth Century,* Table 75
19 Glantz, *Barbarossa* 1947, p 108
20 Kirosheev, *Soviet Casualties and Combat Losses in the Twentieth Century,* Table 75
21 Manstein, *Lost Victories,* p 214
22 Glantz, *Barbarossa* 1941, p 141

CHAPTER IV
Target: Moscow

With victory at Kiev now behind them, the Ostheer turned its attention to the last battle before final victory, the destruction of the Red Army around Moscow. However, the battle would unleash two of Russia's greatest weapons, the clinging autumn mud and numbing cold of winter. Combined with General Zhukov's and the Stavka's developing skills, the German Army would face war of a ferocity it had never encountered before, and stare into the abyss of defeat at the very moment victory was within reach.

30 September 1941

NORTHERN SECTOR

German units broke through the Russian defences at Salme on the island of Saaremaa. After heavy fighting, the remnants of the garrison fell back to the Syerve peninsula. Further bitter fighting continued there.

On the main combat line, the Russian forces were being bled white. Since 10 July the North-West Front had lost 97,000 killed and missing plus 47,800 wounded, 1,500 tanks, 9,900 artillery pieces and 1,700 aircraft while the relatively new Leningrad Front lost 65,500 killed, and missing and 50,800 wounded since 23 August.[1]

CENTRAL SECTOR

Guderian opened the offensive towards Moscow, 24th and 47th Panzer Korps attacking Eremenko's left wing South-West of Orel. Near Glukhov, the German armour launched a furious attack, inflicting heavy casualties upon Group Ermakov and 13th Army. After heavy fighting, 24th Panzer Korp gained the Chinel Heights and 47th Panzer Korp encountered strong resistance at Shuravka. Ermakov's five divisions retreated in disorder, exposing the left flank of 13th Army. Despite the severity of the attack and a thirteen-mile German advance, Eremenko believed this to be a German diversion in advance of the main attack.

The 48th Panzer Korp bucked the trend of the main offensive as it came under heavy attack from both the 1st Tank Brigade and 2nd Cavalry Corp. Fighting would continue until 5 October.

SOUTHERN SECTOR

Kleist's 1st Panzer Group attacked from the Dniepr elbow. Fierce fighting erupted as 3rd and 14th Panzer Korps crossed the Samara near Novomosskovsk, striking the right wing of Cherevichenko's South Front. To the south, Manstein's 11th Army pinned Cherevichenko frontally, preventing the withdrawal of forces to cover the hard-pressed right wing.

The Soviets created a new 6th Army around Krasnograd. It had three rifle and two cavalry divisions.

FINLAND AND NORWAY

After an arduous advance, the Finnish Army of Karelia smashed Soviet positions at Petrozavodsk, reaching Lake Onega and the line of the Svir. The fighting on the Finnish front since the summer had been very costly for the Axis forces, the Finnish army suffering 5,000 casualties and the Germans 21,000.

SOVIET CASUALTIES

The Red Army and Navy suffered 2,129,677 killed and missing in action during the first quarter of the war, and a further 687,626 wounded.[2]

THE OSTHEER

At the end of September the Germans fielded nineteen panzer, fifteen motorised and one hundred and three infantry divisions in the east. Germany lost 51,000 killed in the East during September. Germany's allies also deployed increasingly significant forces. Rumania deployed eleven divisions and nine brigades, Hungary three brigades, Italy three divisions, Slovakia two divisions, Spain one division and Finland sixteen divisions.

1 October 1941

CENTRAL SECTOR

Guderian forced units deeper into Eremenko's left flank. Group Ermakov launched a brief counter-attack in an effort to close the hole between itself and 13th Army but was quickly forced back onto the defensive. The 24th pushed towards Orel while 47th Panzer Korp attacked towards Bryansk, aiming to link up with 2nd Army, which had entered the battle against 50th and 43rd Armies. Late in the day, 24th Panzer successfully encircled two divisions of 13th Army and had fully isolated Group Ermakov. Sevsk fell to 47th Panzer Korp, which then wheeled north-east towards Karachev

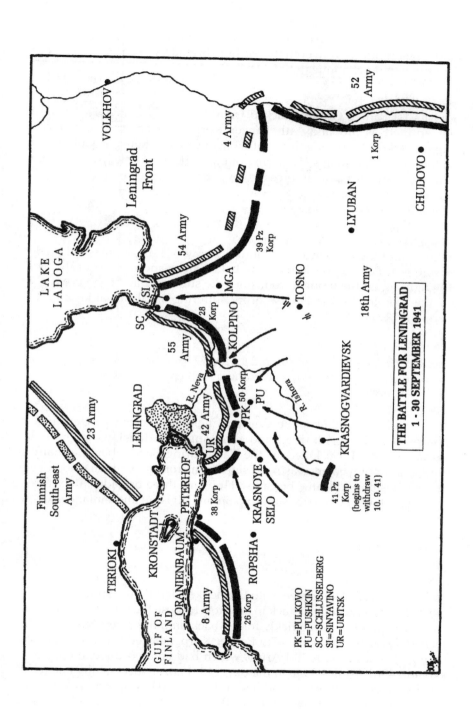

THE BATTLE FOR LENINGRAD
1 - 30 SEPTEMBER 1941

VOLKHOV

Leningrad Front

52 Army

4 Army

1 Korp

CHUDOVO

LAKE LADOGA

54 Army

39 Pz Korp

LYUBAN

SI

SC

28 Korp

MGA

KOLPINO

TOSNO

18th Army

55 Army

R. Neva

50 Korp

PU

KRASNOGVARDIEVSK

LENINGRAD

42 Army

UR

PK

R. Ishora

23 Army

Finnish South-east Army

PETERHOF

KRASNOYE SELO

41 Pz Korp (begins to withdraw 10. 9. 41)

TERIOKI

KRONSTADT

ORANIENBAUM

38 Korp

ROPSHA

8 Army

26 Korp

GULF OF FINLAND

PK=PULKOVO
PU=PUSHKIN
SC=SCHLUSSELBERG
SI=SINYAVINO
UR=URITSK

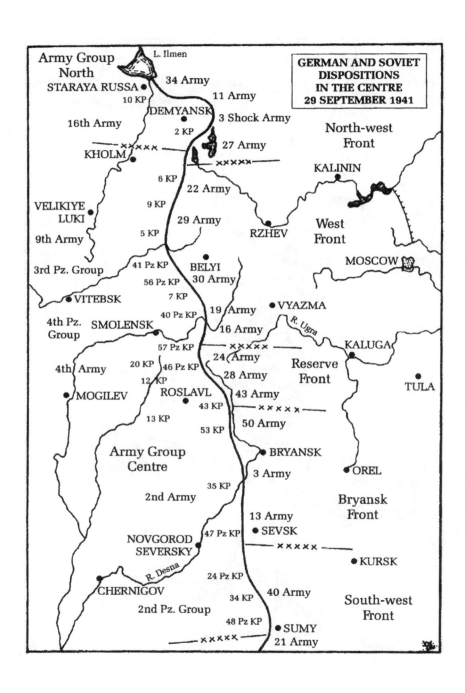

GERMAN AND SOVIET
DISPOSITIONS
IN THE CENTRE
29 SEPTEMBER 1941

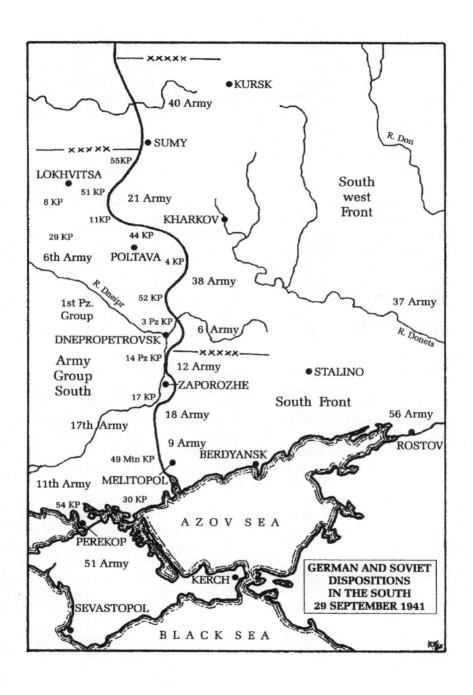

KURSK

40 Army

SUMY

55KP

LOKHVITSA

51 KP

8 KP

21 Army

KHARKOV

11KP

29 KP

44 KP

6th Army   POLTAVA   4 KP

R. Dneipr

1st Pz.
Group

52 KP

38 Army

3 Pz KP

DNEPROPETROVSK

6 Army

South
west
Front

R. Don

37 Army

R. Donets

Army
Group
South

14 Pz KP

12 Army

STALINO

17 KP

ZAPOROZHE

17th Army

18 Army

South Front

56 Army

9 Army

BERDYANSK

ROSTOV

49 Mtn KP

11th Army

MELITOPOL

30 KP

54 KP

PEREKOP

AZOV SEA

51 Army

KERCH

SEVASTOPOL

BLACK SEA

GERMAN AND SOVIET
DISPOSITIONS
IN THE SOUTH
29 SEPTEMBER 1941

and Bryansk. Eremenko still had not realised that this attack was part of the main German thrust towards Moscow and only ordered Ermakov to recover Sevsk.

Just two-days fighting had left the southern flank of the Soviet defences before Moscow in tatters. The Stavka moved Lelyushenko's 1st Guards Rifle Corp (two rifle divisions, 4th and 11th Tank Brigades) to take up blocking positions on the road to Orel and ordered 49th Army to redeploy to protect the Orel–Kursk axis.

SOUTHERN SECTOR
As 1st Panzer Group pushed units towards the Azov Sea, the infantry armies joined the offensive. Both 6th and 17th Armies launched ferocious attacks around Gadyach in an effort to break open the South-West Front before Kharkov, while on the southern flank 30th Korp of 11th Army pressed along the Azov coast, forcing the left wing of the South Front to the north, into the arms of Kleist's panzers.

FINLAND AND NORWAY
After a month of heavy fighting, Petrozavodsk fell to the Finns.

2 October 1941

CENTRAL SECTOR
At 0530 hours Army Group Centre began its offensive towards Moscow. Intense artillery fire and aerial attacks smashed into the Soviet lines as 4th and 9th Armies, with 3rd and 4th Panzer Groups and 8th Air Korp in support, attacked the northern wing and centre of the West Front. Furious battles erupted as 30th and 19th Armies were shattered, their flanks caved in and forced apart by 9th Army and 3rd Panzer Group. The 56th Panzer Korp pushed elements towards Vyazma and Kholm, while 41st Panzer Korp advanced upon Rzhev. After only a few hours, a twenty-mile hole had been torn open between the 30th and 19th Armies The Germans had massed a force of twelve divisions and more than four hundred tanks against the four Soviet divisions at the junction of the two armies. The twelve divisions of 4th Army attacked around Roslavl, hitting 43rd Army while 4th Panzer Group smashed the junction of 43rd and 24th Armies. By the end of the day, 4th Army had advanced twenty-four miles and struck the second echelon of 33rd Army. Koniev vainly attempted to counter attack, mounting artillery strikes and ground attacks.

To the south, 2nd Panzer Group and 2nd Army continued to attack the flanks of the Bryansk Front. Guderian forced 13th Army away to the north-east, breaking the junction of Bryansk and South-West Fronts. The deterioration of their positions prompted Stalin to order Fremenko to restore his lines, 49th Army being allocated as reinforcement around Bryansk. Eremenko suggested to Shaposhnikov that he adopt a flexible defence but he flatly refused. Lelyushenko's 1st Guards Rifle Corp continued its march, being ordered to destroy the German forces on the road from Glukhov and Sevsk. 5th Parachute Corp was also sent to support it.

SOUTHERN SECTOR
The 17th and 6th Armies attacked the northern wing of the South-West Front, while Kleist's plunged deep into the rear of the South Front. The 11th pushed 30th Korp along the Azov coast, herding the South Front into the developing trap.

SOVIET COMMAND
With the German offensive before Moscow clearly identified, the Stavka suspended all offensive action, only limited local attacks being continued. In the centre, what reserves were available were scraped together into a mobile group under the command of General Boldin.

3 October 1941

CENTRAL SECTOR
Hoth's 3rd Panzer Group pushed towards Rzhev and Vyazma, crashing into 32nd Army in West Front's second echelon and reaching the Dniepr. Strauss's 9th Army followed. General Boldin, with an *ad hoc* shock group of two rifle and one motorised divisions and two tank brigades, counter attacked to restore the junction of 30th and 19th Armies. The 30th Army launched its own attack with a motorised and rifle division from Belyi against 3rd Panzer but failed to make any headway. 4th Panzer Group and 4th Army were involved, in heavy fighting with 19th, 16th, 20th and 24th Armies.

After a rapid advance, 24th Panzer Korp surprised the defenders of Orel, German tanks entering the town as trams continued to roll along the main roads and dismantled factory equipment lined the railway sidings. The 17th and 18th Panzer Divisions of 47th Panzer Korp pushed north from the Orel area, advancing across the rear of 13th Army and on into the rear of 3rd in the direction of Karachev. In an effort to halt 47th Panzer Korp, Eremenko threw two rifle divisions into a counter-attack towards Seredina Buda but was brushed aside. Towards the end of the day, Eremenko requested permission to withdraw but was turned down. Group Ermakov, severely depleted and fighting in operational isolation, was ordered to push east and protect the approaches to Dmitrev Lgovsky.

4 October 1941

CENTRAL SECTOR

Boldin continued to counter-attack with his group but was unable to halt 3rd Panzer Group. Heavy fighting raged as the Russian force launched repeated attacks. The 3rd Panzer continued to hit 19th and 32nd Armies. Belyi fell to 3rd Panzer Group, while 10th and 2nd Panzer Divisions of 40th Panzer Korp fought close to Vyazma and Yukhnow. The 4th Panzer Group all but destroyed 43rd Army and broke apart 33rd Army. The wings of 20th and 24th Armies had been turned and a seventy-mile gap torn between Reserve and Bryansk Fronts. Spas Demensk and Kirov also fell to the Germans during the bitter fighting.

To the south, 24th Panzer Korp heading for Tula, having taken Mglin, while 47th Panzer thrust into the rear of Bryansk Front, vanguards nearing Karachev. The 2nd Army launched ferocious attacks across the Bolva river, pinning the 3rd and 50th Armies between it and 47th Panzer Korp. Following the unexpected fall of Orel, 1st Guards Rifle Corp detrained at Mtsensk, aiming to halting the German drive upon Tula. Katukov's 4th Tank Brigade had only recently been formed and was fully equipped with T-34 tanks.

West Front command reported to the Stavka that its situation was difficult and that Boldin's counter-attack had failed. Budenny's Reserve Front reported its own situation to be out of control. Despite these dire warnings, the Stavka reacted slowly to developments.

FINLAND AND NORWAY

The Finns launched a heavy attack across the Svir but were repulsed by 7th Army after bitter fighting. Fierce battles continued along the river line for the remainder of the month.

After a warning from the USA that any Finnish offensive towards the Murmansk railway would be seen as an act of war on America, Mannerheim decided that the Finns would not attack in this sector.

THE PARTISAN WAR

While the Russian armies suffered, behind the German line the actions of hostile partisan groups began to hinder the movement of support forces and supply columns. In the Central Sector particularly, where the extensive Belorussian forests provide excellent cover, attacks upon supply columns and outposts increased alarmingly. Brutal reprisals followed in an effort to deter further attacks, but this in itself led to more fighting, each side acting in reprisal against the atrocities committed by the other.

5 October 1941

NORTHERN SECTOR
After continued heavy fighting, the 1,500 surviving Soviet soldiers on Saaremaa fell back to Hiiumaa Island.

CENTRAL SECTOR
Fierce fighting raged across the Moscow axis as the Germans deepened their pincer attacks around the West and Bryansk Fronts. The 4th Panzer Group captured Yukhnow and Mosaisk and 4th Army took Sukhinichi as 43rd Army retreated. Koniev ordered Boldin to block the German advance upon Vyazma from the north, while 16th Army did so from the south. The 16th Army was to hand over its existing sector to 20th Army and redeploy into the Vyazma sector by 6 October.

The 24th Panzer Korp moved upon Tula. However, the advance was hindered by an alarming lack of fuel, movement being stalled as the lead tanks ran out of gasoline. The 48th Panzer Korp was in action on the southern wing, taking Rylsk while 47th captured Karachev.

With the front collapsing, Stavka ordered the West, Reserve and Bryansk Front to begin withdrawing during the night. At 2300 hours 31st and 32nd Armies were transferred to West Front command. Stalin hastily summoned an emergency session of the Stavka when news was received of strong German armoured columns pushing from Yukhnow and decided upon the Mozhaisk line as the rallying point for the broken West Front. Koniev was ordered to fall back upon the Rzhev–Vyazma line and Budenny back to a line Vedreniki–Mosalsk.

SOUTHERN SECTOR
With his armies falling apart before the German attacks, Tyulenev was dismissed from command of South Front, Cherevichenko being appointed in his place. Under his command were 12th, 18th and 9th Armies. Cherevichenko ordered his armies to block the German advance along the Azov coast by standing on a line Bolshoi Tokmak–Melitopol–Lake Molochnoe but this condemned them to encirclement as Kleist continued to advance largely unopposed towards the Azov coast.

Stuplnagel, who was commanding German 17th Army, reported sick. On 8 October General Hoth would take over command of the 17th Army, and Reinhardt, commanding 41st Panzer Korp took over 3rd Panzer Group.

6 October 1941

CENTRAL SECTOR
During the night of 5–6 October the Russian forces attempted to disengage

and withdraw to the Mozhaisk line. Vyazma fell as 16th and 19th Armies retreated.

Farther south, Bryansk Front was in imminent danger of encirclement. The 17th Panzer Division of 47th Panzer Korp captured Bryansk and crossed the Desna. German tanks attacked Eremenko's front head quarters, six miles south of the city, Eremenko only narrowly escaping capture as his staff was scattered. Zhizdra fell to the Germans after a brief struggle.

Katukov's 4th Tank Brigade continued to counter-attack, having stopped 24th Panzer Korp dead. Brigade Eberbach, the leading unit of 24th Panzer Korp, were unable to prevent a breakthrough at Kamenevo.

The 48th Panzer Korp launched a flanking attack against 2nd Cavalry Corp and undermined its hard won positions.

As the disintegration of the main line accelerated, the Stavka took precautionary steps by ordering the Mozhaisk line to full readiness. It also ordered the West and Reserve Fronts to fall back from the Vyazma line. The 31st and 32nd Armies, grouped under the overall command of General Boldin, were ordered to cover the withdrawal of the shattered West and Reserve Front armies. A number of divisions were already being rushed to the Mozhaisk sector to prepare for the next German onslaught. Six rifle divisions, six tank brigades and ten artillery regiments would have been deployed, plus the 2nd Cavalry Corp under Belov, which assembled nearer Moscow. With the situation at the front already in consideration and confusing command change, the 30th Army relieving the 31st Army while the divisions of the 16th Army were transferred to the 20th Army. Rokossovsky's 16th Army headquarters was to take command of those troops fighting in the Vyazma area.

SOUTHERN SECTOR

The 1st SS Motorised Division *Leibstandarte Adolf Hitler* reached Berdyansk on the Azov coast, isolating a large part of South Front against the sea. The majority of the 18th and 9th Armies were cut off, a force of nearly 150,000 men. The 12th Army retreated north-east towards Stalino, minor elements of 18th Army also falling back upon Stalino while 9th Army retreated to Taganrog. Units of 11th Army launched powerful attacks along the coast from the west, inflicting heavy casualties.

With the Russian forces on the southern wing thus off, 6th and 17th Armies attacked from Mirgorod and Poltava. The junction of 6th and 38th Armies was crushed during the initial German assault.

GERMAN COMMAND

In a minor re-designation, the Germans renamed 1st and 2nd Panzer Groups the 1st and 2nd Panzer Armies.

SOVIET COMMAND

With the situation on the Moscow axis becoming more desperate, Stalin recalled Zhukov from Leningrad. Zhukov left Fedyuninsky to command the Leningrad Front before setting off for the central sector.

7 October 1941

CENTRAL SECTOR

As the temperature in the central region dropped and incessant rain fell, tanks of 56th Panzer Korp moving from the north linked up near Vyazma with elements of 46th and 40th Panzer Korps pushing up from Spas Demensk. The Germans put up blocking positions to prevent the break out of Soviet forces. Inside the tenuous pocket, 19th and 20th Armies pulled back in relatively good order, but 24th Army was partially encircled, and destroyed in heavy fighting north-east of Elnya. The Germans had effectively trapped 16th, 19th, 20th and 24th Armies and part of 32nd Army west of Vyazma.

There was heavy fighting near Kamenevo as 1st Guards Rifle Corp attacked 24th Panzer Korp. The 18th Panzer Division linked up with elements of 2nd Army near Zhizdra, isolating 3rd and 13th Armies south of Bryansk and 50th Army to the north.

Having returned from Leningrad, Zhukov was appointed to command the defence of the Soviet capital. As he took command, he found the West and Reserve Fronts out of touch with Moscow and therefore set out to discover the true picture.

SOUTHERN SECTOR

South Front tried to break out of its encirclement to the east. Repeated attacks failed to punch a hole through the German line, 1st Panzer and 11th Armies exacting a terrible price on the Red Army divisions. Manstein's 11th pushed 49th Mountain Korp along the coast, linking up with Kleist at Osipenko and denying the Soviet forces access to the sea. At this point 11th Army handed operational control of 49th Mountain Korp to 1st Panzer Army and brought 30th Korp back to the Ishun defences, in preparation for the offensive into the Crimea. The 30th would support the attack by the weakened 54th Korp. 30th Korp had at its disposal the 22nd, 72nd and, 170th Infantry Divisions while 54th Korp had 46th, 73rd and 50th Infantry Divisions.

> Yet again the Red Army had been out-manœuvred by the Ostheer and was reduced to fighting desperate battles in encirclement. In the centre and south, the Wehrmacht had sliced away huge portions of the Soviet field armies with impunity. However, while the Soviets had stood hundreds of miles west of Moscow, they had had the opportunity to throw new armies into the field,

before the Germans could resume their push east. Now, with Moscow scant miles to the rear, the Stavka was faced with the prospect of defending the capital with a decimated force. Only skill and tenacity, and a little help from the weather, would keep total defeat at bay.

8 October 1941

NORTHERN SECTOR

The Germans began new attacks in the Valdai Hills pushing east from Demyansk.

CENTRAL SECTOR

Around Bryansk, infantry and armour of 2nd Panzer and 2nd Armies pounded 50th and 3rd Armies, which were ordered to break out to the east. Eremenko ordered all his units to pull back by night to escape from the pockets. The 3rd and 50th Armies pushed thirty miles to the east. Fighting would continue for another two weeks, at the end of which the Bryansk Front would have been almost annihilated.

Zhukov went out to West Front to establish just what was happening to the Soviet armies. He found Koniev easily enough and was given details of the encirclement of the Russian armies at Vyazma and the envelopment of Eremenko to the south. Of Budenny's front, nothing was known. He tried to find the Reserve front headquarters but when he did, Budenny was nowhere to be found.

SOUTHERN SECTOR

The South Front was crushed on the Azov coast as 1st Panzer Army launched concentric attacks upon 18th and 9th Armies. Mariupol fell after bitter fighting, but despite the overwhelming German fire, small units of Soviet soldiers managed to slip through the pocket and escape to the east to fight another day. The weather, which had broken in the Ukraine on 8 October, became worse and began to affect the state of Rundstedt's advance.

9 October 1941

CENTRAL SECTOR

Heavy fighting raged in and around both the Vyazma and Bryansk pockets as the Soviet forces launched repeated attacks in an effort to break out. The Stavka ordered 19th and 32nd Armies to make their way to the east towards Sychevka or Gzhatsk. The 20th Army was ordered to push southeast. However, during heavy fighting, Gzhatsk fell to 10th Panzer Division and 2nd SS Motorised, Division *Das Reich*.

Inside the Bryansk pockets 3rd and 50th Armies, fighting close to Dyatkovo, attempted to fight eastward but ran into strong German forces. The 13th Army, in action at Trubchevsk and Suzemka, fought its way south-east and managed to break through the German ring.

Kempf's 48th Panzer Korp began to push towards Kursk and Livny on the extreme southern flank of Army Group Centre, while 24th Panzer Korp was involved in further costly fighting with Lelyushenko's 1st Guards Rifle Corp as it pushed nearer to Mtsensk.

With the front line in tatters, the Mozhaisk Line was upgraded to the Moscow Reserve Front, commanded by General Artemev. Moscow began the placement of its limited reserves, placing a rifle division each at Volokolamsk (316th), Maloyaroslavets (312th) and Mozhaisk. The Stavka also began the formation of a new 5th Army under Lelyushenko and a 26th Army under Sokolov at Tula. The latter force was based upon the 1st Guards Rifle Corp.

10 October 1941

CENTRAL SECTOR

Inside the Vyazma pocket, the Stavka gave control of the mixed forces to Lukin and ordered him to break east towards Sychevka and Gzhatsk. On the road to Moscow, heavy fighting erupted at Maloyaroslavets.

To the south, 24th Panzer Korp finally reached Mtsensk. Many tanks had been lost in the fighting with 1st Guards Rifle Corp blunting Guderian's army. Meanwhile, 13th Korp of 2nd Army forged a crossing of the Ugra river west of Kaluga despite stubborn Soviet resistance. Around Bryansk, 50th Army fell back to the north-east under heavy attack while 3rd Army fought its way south near Dmitrov Lgovsky.

Following the collapse of their defences around Vyazma, the Soviets disbanded the Reserve Front, its units being incorporated into the battered West Front. Zhukov took personal control of the front with Koniev as deputy. With Bryansk Front also in tatters, Zhukov deployed the reformed 26th Army along the line of the Zusha river to provide cover to the southern wing of his line. The 16th Army was deploying around Volokolamsk, 5th at Mozhaisk, 43rd at Maloyaroslavets, 49th at Kaluga and 33rd at Naro-Fominsk, the latter being in front reserve.

SOUTHERN SECTOR

Sixth Army captured Sumy as Army Group South struggled to maintain its link with 2nd Army. Hitler repeatedly called for 6th Army to move south together with 17th Army, to lend support to 1st Panzer Army. Halder insisted this would open a vulnerable gap between the two German army groups.

Kleist's 1st Panzer Army had almost completed the destruction of

18th and 9th Armies. Outside the pocket, the 1st SS Motorised Division *Leibstandarte Adolf Hitler* of 3rd Panzer Korp forced its way into Taganrog, becoming involved in fierce fighting with remnants of 18th Army.

FINLAND AND NORWAY
The heavy fighting in Karelia since 23 August had cost the Karelia Front nearly 30,000 killed, and missing and 32,000 wounded.[3]

GERMAN COMMAND
OKH altered its plan to expand the offensive in the centre and destroy North-West Front. Third Panzer Group was to push on to Kalinin, Torzok and Vishny Volochek, linking up with Army Group North after its advance through the Valdai Hills. 9th Army would support 3rd Panzer's drive. Fourth Army and 4th Panzer Group were to push directly east towards Moscow as 2nd Panzer Group and 2nd Army enveloped the city from the south.

11 October 1941

CENTRAL SECTOR
The attacks by 3rd Panzer Group towards Kalinin met fierce resistance from 22nd and 29th Armies and progress was slow. The 4th and 9th Armies both attempted to push forces east while simultaneously trying to destroy Lukin's isolated armies. Lukin attempted his first break out from the Vyazrma pocket but was held back by the Germans. Heavy fighting raged through the day as repeated attacks failed to punch out to the east.

Soviet forces encircled to the south of Bryansk, launched a desperate attack in an effort to break out but were halted with heavy casualties. As the isolated armies surrendered, the Germans started to move 2nd Army onto the southern flank of 2nd Panzer Army.

Schweppenburg's 24th Panzer Korp was involved in furious fighting at Mtsensk as 1st Guards Corp continued to slow the advance, despite their own heavy losses. Fierce battles raged at Kaluga as 13th Korp pushed 49th Army back.

SOUTHERN SECTOR
The 18th and 9th Armies surrendered to 1st Panzer Army. In all, 106,000 Soviet soldiers were captured and 210 tanks and 670 artillery pieces either captured or destroyed. Kleist began to redeploy his units for the advance towards Rostov, while Hoth moved north to attack Voroshilovgrad. Unfortunately, the deterioration of the weather had brought movement to a standstill, only the tired and sodden infantry being able to slog forward through the clinging mud. On the Azov coast the weather was not quite

so bad and Kleist managed to cross the Mius north of Taganrog, the SS *Leibstandarte Adolf Hitler* Division reaching the city during the day. Russian resistance though was fierce.

12 October 1941

NORTHERN SECTOR
The Germans began the bombardment of Hiiumaa Island.

CENTRAL SECTOR
Staritza, on the road to Kalinin, fell as 1st Panzer Division forced 30th Army back. With Moscow threatened from the north-west, the Stavka formed the Kalinin Group to the right of West Front. Koniev was placed in command but his force consisted of three weakened rifle divisions and one tank brigade.

On the approaches to the Mozhaisk line, the 2nd SS Motorised Division *Das Reich* captured Gzhatsk. Pogoreloye fell to 36th Motorised Division and Zubtsov to Lehr Motorised Brigade.

Inside the Bryansk pocket, 50th Army began to fight its way north-east towards Belev. The 13th Korp captured Kaluga, forcing back 49th Army.

Closer to Moscow, the GKO ordered the construction of extensive defences before the city. Nearly half a million civilians will be drafted to complete the work.

SOUTHERN SECTOR
Bogoduchov fell to 6th Army after a brief battle.

13 October 1941

NORTHERN SECTOR
The Soviet High Command ordered the evacuation of Hiiumaa. Forces were to be evacuated to Hanko.

CENTRAL SECTOR
The 3rd Panzer Group fought its way into Kalinin, caving in the Kalinin Group's front. The 29th Army attempted to block the Kalinin sector with its eight rifle divisions. On the left wing, Rzhev fell to 1st Panzer Division.

Inside the Vyazma pocket, Rokossovsky fought his way east with a command column of 16th Army. Lukin was captured. On the Bryansk Front sector Eremenko was wounded during a German air strike and had to be evacuated. Zakharov took command of the front.

Farther south, the West Front had dug in along the Mozhaisk position. Using limited forces from High Command reserve, the Soviets placed four rifle divisions and four tank brigades on the line. Fighting immediately erupted at Mozhaisk as the Germans struck the 32nd Rifle Division. Intense fighting also raged west of Borovsk as the 43rd Army fought to hold off the Germans.

SOUTHERN SECTOR
Due to bad weather, Army Group South had come to a standstill. Many divisions were stuck in mud, awaiting the onset of the cold weather to solidify the sodden ground and return a modicum of mobility. However, the cold would bring with it a whole set of new problems for the badly equipped Ostheer. With fifty percent of its transport arm already out of action, Army Group South was hamstrung. Supplies of all essential items were running worryingly low.

14 October 1941

NORTHERN SECTOR
The first snows fell on Leningrad, presaging the onset of winter.

CENTRAL SECTOR
With the temperature plummeting below freezing, 3rd Panzer Group continued the costly battle for Kalinin. The German penetration threatened the rear of 22nd, 29th and 31st Armies.

In the centre of the Moscow axis, the Germans hit the defending Siberian rifle division before Borodino. The Siberians, with two tank brigades in support, launched strong counter-attacks that pinned down 4th Army. The Soviets had assembled fourteen divisions, sixteen tank brigades and forty rifle regiments, a force of some 90,000 men along the Mozhaisk line. Deployed before Volokolamsk was 16th Army, 5th Army being to its south at Mozhaisk, 43rd Army at Maloyaroslavets and 49th Army near Kaluga. In addition, 33rd Army was in the process of assembling at Naro-Fominsk.

Farther south, 24th Panzer Korp struggled to penetrate the Soviet positions at Mtsensk while 47th Panzer Korp attempted to move towards Fatezh.

SOUTHERN SECTOR
On the northern wing of Army Group South 6th Army took Akhtyrka.

15 October 1941

CENTRAL SECTOR
Heavy fighting raged around Kalinin as 29th Army launched repeated counter-attacks. The fighting raged until 29 October. Borovsk fell as the 43rd Army was pushed out of the town.

Resistance in the Vyazma pocket ended, 650,000 prisoners, 1,200 tanks and 5,400 artillery pieces falling to the Germans. The West Front had been virtually annihilated during the battle, fifty-five divisions being badly mauled or destroyed.

SOUTHERN SECTOR
The Soviets began to evacuate their rearguard from Odessa. Since the beginning of the siege, the Red Army had evacuated 86,000 men to the Crimea and during the night of 15–16 October took out another 35,000.

On the main battlefront, German 6th Army captured Krasnoploye. While the Germans continued to make limited progress, the South-West Front attempted to straighten its line and create a front reserve. Lopatin's 37th Army was raised around Voroshilovgrad from these units. The Stavka ordered the 56th Army to protect the approaches to Rostov. South-West Front ordered, its forces to fall back to a line Kastornoye–Stary Oskol–Novy Oskol–Vayluki–Kupyansk–Liman by the end of October.

16 October 1941

NORTHERN SECTOR
Heavy snow fell during the night as the German and Soviet forces along the Volkhov began new offensives. The Soviets deployed 54th Army near Lake Ladoga and 4th and 52nd Armies and Novgorod Operational Group on the line of the Volkhov, in all a force of 135,700 men. For their attack the Germans concentrated 39th Panzer. Korp with two panzer and two motorised divisions, 1st Korp with three divisions, both to attack along the Volkhov towards Volkhovsroy while 38th Korp attacked towards Malaya Vyshera to protect the southern wing of the salient.

The German attack struck first, crashing into the junction of the 4th and 52nd Armies as elements drove forward upon Kirishi, Bodogosh, Tikhvin and Malaya Vyshera.

CENTRAL SECTOR
Fighting erupted at Volokolamsk. Panfilov's 316th Rifle Division attempted to stem a German attack by two infantry and 29th Motorised and 2nd Panzer Divisions. The 110th Rifle Division was also heavily attacked.

SOUTHERN SECTOR
The siege of Odessa ended after the successful evacuation of remaining Soviet units from the port. At 0200 hours rearguards fell back to their final positions around the harbour and commenced the destruction of the port facilities. Within a few hours these men had also been taken out of the city, leaving the blazing ruins to the Rumanians. The Coastal Army and Black

Sea Fleet lost 16,578 killed and missing during the defence of Odessa, and a further 24,690 wounded.[4]

17 October 1941

CENTRAL SECTOR

The Germans captured Kalinin. To the south the remnants of 50th Army fighting north of Bryansk surrendered, while 3rd Army continued to fight on in isolation at Dmitrev-Lgovsky.The Stavka created the Kalinin Front. This new formation, based upon Koniev's Kalinin Group comprised 22nd, 29th and 30th Armies. The Vatutin Operational Group, with two rifle and two cavalry divisions and one tank brigade was also attached. The new front's objective was to prevent 3rd Panzer Group from penetrating into the rear of West and North-West Fronts.

The fighting around Volokolamsk intensified as Dovator's Cavalry Corp was struck by the German divisions north of the town.

SOUTHERN SECTOR

Taganrog fell to the 1st SS *Leibstandarte Adolf Hitler* Motorised Division as the Army Group South fought its way closer to Rostov.

18 October 1941

CENTRAL SECTOR

Fortieth Panzer Korp broke into Mozhaisk but had to fight for every yard of ground. By the end of the day, 2nd SS Motorised Division *Das Reich* and 10th Panzer Division had cleared the town. These units then moved forward towards Dorohov, which was defended by the 50th Rifle Division. The 57th Panzer Korp penetrated the Soviet line at Maloyaroslavets and Borovsk, while fierce fighting continued at Kaluga. Tarusa also fell as 49th Army was pounded. With steady progress being made by the German forces south-west of Moscow, communications between the capital and Tula became tenuous, particularly in the hard-pressed Naro-Forminsk and Podolsk sectors. To bolster the line, 33rd Army was committed and 43rd Army reinforced.

SOUTHERN SECTOR

Reichenau's 6th Army captured Grayvoron. Fifty-fourth Korp began an attack aimed at breaking through the Perekop Isthmus and opening the road to the Crimea. Kuznetsov's 51st Independent Army, with twelve rifle and four cavalry divisions, had constructed formidable defences on the narrow neck of land, but Kuznetsov had then spread his forced thinly to cover the extensive Crimean coast. The Russians had more than 200,000 troops in the Crimea, having been reinforced by the recently evacuated

A Stug III carrying infantry into action.

A Soviet combat team advances. The Soviet troops proved to be masters of close combat in the streets of Stalingrad.

German infantry with the versatile MG-34, late 1941. These troops are ill-prepared for the harshness of the Russian winter.

Precursor to the Russian winter, oozing mud which brought movement to a halt.

A Stug III in the ruins of Stalingrad. Infantrymen are hitching a ride to the front. (Source: Bundesarchiv)

Knocked-out T-34's and a Pak 37 anti-tank gun. The Pak 37 proved virtually useless against the sloped armour of the T-34. (Source: IWM)

The forgotten face of the German Army: horse drawn transport columns supplying the front. (Source: R Tomasi)

German infantry advancing into a burning Soviet village. (Source: US National Archives)

T-34's on the move in closely wooded terrain in the late summer of 1941.

German artillery in action in Stalingrad. The grain elevator can be seen dominating the background. (Source: The Robert Hunt Library)

A German column on the move, winter 1941. (Source: Ukrainian Central State Archive of Cine-photo Documents.

A Panzer III advances toward surrendering Soviet troops. (Source: Ukrainian Central State Archive of Cine-photo Documents)

A column of Panzer IV's advance across the steppe. (Source: Christopher Ailsby Historical Archives)

German infantry marching into Stalingrad. Air raids had set the city alight in August 1942.

Panzer III's pause before continuing to push across the steppe.

Soviet riflemen advance past a knocked out Panzer IV.

19 October 1941

NORTHERN SECTOR
The fighting in the Valdai Hills bogged down as the 3rd SS Motorised Division *Totenkopf* and 30th Infantry Division stalled in the face of determined Soviet resistance.

CENTRAL SECTOR
Vereya fell to the 7th Korp as the Soviets abandoned the town. The 43rd Korp captured Lichvin after a costly battle. Group Vatutin was disbanded and amalgamated with 31st Army.

SOUTHERN SECTOR
The 54th Korp continued to attack on the Perekop Isthmus while 1st Panzer Group entered the suburbs of Stalino and fought its way into the town, forcing 18th Army back.

20 October 1941

NORTHERN SECTOR
The Soviets prepared to launch the second Sinyavino Operation to break the German stranglehold on Leningrad. Leningrad Front had concentrated eight rifle divisions among the 55th Army and Neva Group, a force of 63,000 soldiers, 475 artillery pieces and 97 tanks. These men were to push east to link up with Kulik's 54th Army near Sinyavino. The Germans had 54,000 men facing the attack in strongly established positions.[5]

CENTRAL SECTOR
Elements of 5th Korp, holding the southern flank of 9th Army, crossed the Ruza river. Continuing their attacks on the Mozhaisk axis, German forces captured Borovsk, the Russians falling back upon Naro-Fominsk where 43rd Army was in defensive positions. Dorohov became a focal point of Russian resistance on the road to the capital. Units of the 50th Rifle Division and the 20th and 22nd Tank Brigades defended the settlement. Some 13,000 men of the battered 3rd Army broke out of their encirclement at Dmitrov Lgovsky and rejoined. the combat line near Ponyri.

SOUTHERN SECTOR
Heavy fighting raged in Stalino as the 1st SS *Leibstandarte Adolf Hitler* Division fought its way through the city.

21 October 1941

SOUTHERN SECTOR
Sixth Army fought its way into the western outskirts of Kharkov but became embroiled in bitter fighting with 21st and 38th Armies.

22 October 1941

CENTRAL SECTOR
24th Panzer Korp launched a furious attack against the elements of 3rd Army that barred its way to Moscow but failed to push much farther from Mtsensk. Farther south, 48th Panzer Korp captured Fatezh after a long struggle with 13th Army.

SOUTHERN SECTOR
With the battle for the Crimea underway, Stavka appointed Vice-Admiral Levchenko to command all forces in the peninsula. His forces comprised Coastal and 51st Armies. Batov took over 51st Army from Kuznetsov.

23 October 1941

NORTHERN SECTOR
Malaya Vyshera fell to 38th Korp.

CENTRAL SECTOR
German forces broke into Naro-Fominsk and fought for control of the southern half of the town.

SOUTHERN SECTOR
The 6th and 17th Armies, having failed to penetrate into Kharkov, began to develop attacks around the city in on effort to envelope 21st and 38th Armies. The battle for the Perekop continued as 54th Korp launched repeated frontal attacks against 51st Army.

SOVIET COMMAND
Following the disasters of the previous few weeks, the Stavka established two new operational commands. The two areas, Northern under Zhukov's command, covered the line from the Leningrad to the Moscow axis and Southern under Marshal Timoshenko, covered the Ukraine.

Zhukov had already repelled the Germans before Leningrad and was back in favour with Stalin, having been transferred to the Moscow sector to prevent the German capture of the city.

24 October 1941

NORTHERN SECTOR
Heavy fighting erupted around Leningrad as the Leningrad Front launched its Sinyavino operation. Despite repeated attacks, Soviet units were repelled by the well dug in German divisions. General Fedyuninsky was placed in command of 54th Army as the incompetent Marshal Kulik was sacked.

CENTRAL SECTOR
Heavy fighting raged on the approaches to Torzok as Kalinin Front battled to prevent 3rd Panzer Group from reaching the city. Bitter battles raged for the next week.

As 2nd Panzer Army penetrated Soviet positions south of Moscow, 24th Panzer Korp taking Chern and 53rd Korp Belev, the Stavka ordered Eremenko to pull back to a line between Tula and Yelets to cover the southern approaches. However, Bryansk Front had suffered crippling casualties in the fighting around Bryansk and Orel and was close to disintegration. The 24th Panzer had also suffered heavy losses and was so short of fuel that its remaining supplies were given up to Brigade Eberbach, which henceforth formed the spearhead of 2nd Panzer Army's assault upon Moscow. Heavy fighting continued in Naro-Fominsk.

Having completed the destruction of the Vyazma pocket, 9th Army had redeployed and moved to join the 3rd Panzer Group fighting around Kalinin.

SOUTHERN SECTOR
Reichenau's 6th and Hoth's 17th Armies entered Kharkov while Belgorod, a little to the north, was taken by 6th Army, forcing the Soviets to either abandon Kharkov or lose 21st and 38th Armies entirely.

Kleist fanned out into the Donbas as the Soviet defences at Stalino collapsed. Hitler had had his eyes on the industry of this region since the beginning of the campaign, but the Soviets had evacuated or destroyed many of the mining and manufacturing facilities and pressed more than 100,000 mine workers into the ranks of the South Front, reinforcing its shattered armies.

25 October 1941

CENTRAL SECTOR
Resistance in the pocket south of Bryansk was quelled, the greater part of 3rd, 13th and elements of 50th Armies having been destroyed in the fighting. Fifty thousand prisoners had fallen into German hands and an equal

number had been killed. The Germans continued to make minor gains throughout the Moscow axis as assault units pushed forward through the mud. Ruza fell to the 10th Panzer Division. Volokolamsk railway station fell to German units.

SOUTHERN SECTOR
Kharkov fell to 6th Army after costly street fighting with 21st and 38th Army rearguards.

26 October 1941

CENTRAL SECTOR
The German 4th Army was under fierce Soviet attack and forced onto the defensive, while 53rd Korp reached the Oka river and 43rd Korp moved up to Belev.

SOUTHERN SECTOR
Near Stalino, the Soviets were falling back, abandoning the Donbas to the Germans. Fierce fighting continued at Ishun as 11th Army began to prise open the Soviet defences.

27 October 1941

CENTRAL SECTOR
Elements of 5th Korp captured Volokolamsk after a long battle with three rifle divisions of 16th Army. In the centre, 4th Army repulsed renewed Soviet attacks. Heavy fighting erupted at Serpukhov. Lead elements of Brigade Eberbach reached Plavskoye, while 53rd and 43rd Korps consolidated their positions on the Oka river.

28 October 1941

SOUTHERN SECTOR
Kramatorsk fell to the Germans. First Panzer Army pushed across the Mius river as it advanced towards Rostov, and the 17th Army fought to secure a crossing over the Donets river. Reichenau's 6th Army was established along the northern Donets. The Ishun defences began to collapse under the weight of 11th Army attacks.

29 October 1941

NORTHERN SECTOR
The Sinyavino Operation had failed to achieve a breakthrough to Leningrad, despite days of bitter fighting.

CENTRAL SECTOR
Brigade Eberbach was just two miles from Tula and launched a direct assault upon the town. However, 50th Army defences proved too strong, Eberbach losing many tanks to Soviet anti-tank batteries. To the south, 53rd Korp advanced towards Yepifan to protect the open southern flank of 2nd Panzer Army.

30 October 1941

CENTRAL SECTOR
Following his failure to rush Tula, Guderian skirted east of the town, moving upon Dedilovo. He planned to let the supporting infantry clear Tula.

SOUTHERN SECTOR
Manstein pushed deep into the Crimea as the Ishun defences collapsed. Soviet forces were in total disarray, many soldiers surrendering to the approaching German units and more fleeing to the rear, creating a rout on the roads leading south to Sevastopol.

SOVIET COMMAND
As the situation at the front deteriorated, the Stavka activated 56th independent Army of the North Caucasus Front. The intention was to protect the approaches to Rostov and the road into the Caucasus.

31 October 1941

CENTRAL SECTOR
Army Group Centre was exhausted as it struggled to push closer to Moscow. Ninth Army was bogged down around Kalinin, while 3rd Panzer Group was involved in heavy fighting with 19th and 30th Armies. In the centre, 49th, 43rd and 33rd Armies held up 4th Army and 4th Panzer Group on the Nara and at Serpukhov, while on the southern wing Guderian had by-passed Tula.

SOUTHERN SECTOR
The 51st Army retreated in confusion, Alma falling. Even at this early stage of the battle, the fighting in the Crimea had netted the Germans 65,000 prisoners.

To give an indication of the catastrophic supply situation the Germans faced, of 724 trains that were due to deliver supplies to Army Group South during October, only 195 had arrived. Furthermore, of these, 112 were held over from September.[6]

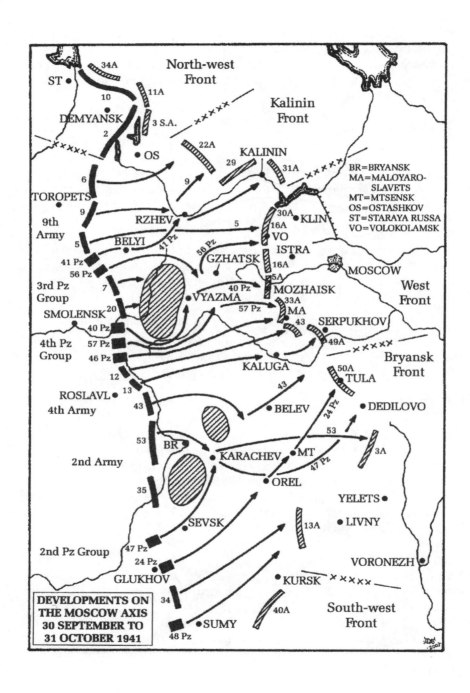

North-west Front

Kalinin Front

ST

34A

10

11A

DEMYANSK

2

3 S.A.

×××××

OS

22A

KALININ

29

31A

×××××

6

9

TOROPETS

9

RZHEV

5

30A

KLIN

16A

VO

9th Army

5

BELYI

41 Pz

56 Pz

GZHATSK

ISTRA

16A

MOSCOW

41 Pz

56 Pz

7

VYAZMA

40 Pz

MOZHAISK

5A

West Front

3rd Pz Group

SMOLENSK

20

57 Pz

33A

MA

SERPUKHOV

4th Pz Group

40 Pz

57 Pz

46 Pz

43

49A

×××××

12

KALUGA

Bryansk Front

ROSLAVL

4th Army

13

43

43

BELEV

50A

TULA

24 Pz

DEDILOVO

53

BR

KARACHEV

MT

53

47 Pz

3A

2nd Army

35

OREL

YELETS

LIVNY

SEVSK

13A

2nd Pz Group

47 Pz

24 Pz

VORONEZH

GLUKHOV

34

KURSK

×××××

SUMY

40A

South-west Front

48 Pz

BR=BRYANSK
MA=MALOYARO-
SLAVETS
MT=MTSENSK
OS=OSTASHKOV
ST=STARAYA RUSSA
VO=VOLOKOLAMSK

**DEVELOPMENTS ON
THE MOSCOW AXIS
30 SEPTEMBER TO
31 OCTOBER 1941**

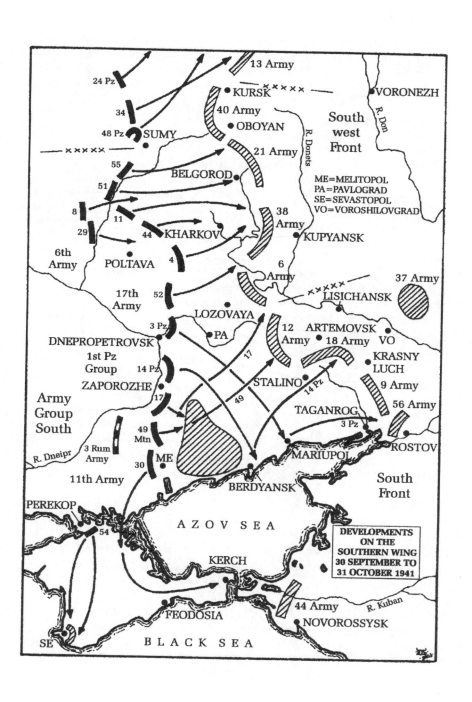

DEVELOPMENTS
ON THE
SOUTHERN WING
30 SEPTEMBER TO
31 OCTOBER 1941

ME=MELITOPOL
PA=PAVLOGRAD
SE=SEVASTOPOL
VO=VOROSHILOVGRAD

THE OPPOSING FORCES: END OF OCTOBER 1941
During October the Germans had received a single mountain division, bringing their strength in Russia to nineteen panzer, fifteen motorised and one hundred and four infantry, mountain and light divisions. Furthermore, it was estimated by the German high command that since 22 June the Red Army had lost 3,200,000 men captured, 19,000 tanks, 28,000 artillery pieces and 14,600 aircraft destroyed or captured. These losses alone outnumbered the entire force the Germans had assembled for the campaign, but still the Red Army fought on with stubborn determination. In the same period, the Ostheer had suffered 686,000 casualties, including 145,000 killed and 29,000 missing. During October alone 88,000 men had been lost, 41,000 of them killed. Ostheer strength stood at 2,700,000 men while just one third of the original motor pool was still operational.[7]

The Stavka had raised three new armies (the 10th, 26th and 57th) during the recent fighting and began to move them closer to Moscow. A reformed 28th Army deployed near Lake Onega, 39th around Yaroslavl, 58th near Gorki, 59th at Saratov and 60th before Stalingrad. To the extreme south, the 61st Army assembled around Astrakhan. In addition, the Stavka appointed Marshal Shaposhnikov Chief of Staff of Soviet Armed Forces. Facing the Germans the Russians had 269 divisions, 65 brigades and 2,200,000 men.[8]

1 November 1941

CENTRAL SECTOR
The 24th Panzer Korp closed in upon Dedilovo but encountered fierce resistance from the reformed 50th Army. A little farther south, 53rd Korp ran into strong Soviet forces before Teploye that were attempting to attack the open southern flank of 24th Panzer Korp.

2 November 1941

SOUTHERN SECTOR
Manstein's 11th Army captured Simferopol as it closed in upon Sevastopol. The 49th Mountain Korp was reallocated to 1st Panzer Army command.

3 November 1941

CENTRAL SECTOR
Heavy fighting continued around Teploye as 53rd Korp struggled to withstand Soviet attacks. Kempf's 48th Panzer Korp fought its way into and captured Kursk.

4 November 1941

SOUTHERN SECTOR
Eleventh Army captured Feodosia after a brief battle with 51st Army.

5 November 1941

NORTHERN SECTOR
There was fierce fighting on the road to Tikhvin as 39th Panzer Korp pushed east.

SOUTHERN SECTOR
First Panzer Army renewed its attack in the Donbas, forcing 9th Army back. 14th Panzer Korp thrust forward towards Schakhty. Realising the potential danger to Rostov, Timoshenko requested additional forces. Stalin responded that all equipment was needed in the centre.

7 November 1941

NORTHERN SECTOR
As the Germans closed upon Tikhvin, the Luftwaffe launched a number of heavy air raids on Leningrad. The Soviet situation was becoming untenable as their efforts to halt the German salient pressing towards the Svir failed. Reinforcements were urgently airlifted to the crumbling Tikhvin sector to bolster 4th Army.

CENTRAL SECTOR
Army Group Centre began to redeploy for the next phase of Operation Typhoon. Third Panzer Group took up new positions between 9th Army and 4th Panzer Group, aiming to strike directly towards Moscow and envelop the city from the north. The continuing drop in the temperature saw winter take an early hold, causing the first cases of frostbite among the ill-equipped German units. Most men were still wearing summer tunics and no supplies of winter uniforms existed to the rear. Only the Luftwaffe had made provisions for operating in the winter, and the infantry had to endure the worst winter in living memory virtually without protection.

SOUTHERN SECTOR
First Panzer Army forced 9th Army back twenty miles along the road in Rostov. The weight of the German attack was then switched south, bringing pressure to bear upon 56th Independent Army. Rundstedt aimed to penetrate directly into Rostov rather than enveloping the city from the north-west.

8 November 1941

NORTHERN SECTOR
39th Panzer Korp, with 1st Korp in support, entered Tikhvin and ought its way through the town. The 4th Army was close to collapse, having lost contact with the headquarters of Leningrad Front and threatening the rear of 7th Independent Army on the Svir. Elements of 44th Rifle Division pulled back along the Tikhvin–Lodenoye Pole road, while 191st Rifle Division fell back east.

CENTRAL SECTOR
The 53rd Korp continued to fight off 3rd Army attacks around Teploye. Schweppenburg's 24th Panzer Korp, which had been earmarked to support 53rd Korp, was forced to deal with new attacks from Tula by 50th Army. Heavy fighting raged at Uzlovaya as a rifle division and tank brigade struck the German lines.

West Front expected the next phase of German attacks from Volokolamsk and Tula. Zhukov proposed a number of preemptive attacks to hinder German redeployment. The 16th Army was to lead the first attack at Volokolamsk.

9 November 1941

NORTH SECTOR
Tikhvin fell to 39th Panzer Korp, but fighting continued on the eastern outskirts as the Germans tried to press towards the Svir amid temperatures of minus forty degrees centigrade. The 4th Army was fighting to prevent the Germans from effecting a junction with the Finns. With the disintegration of his army, Yakovlev was relieved and Meretskov appointed in his place. Meretskov was also given coordination of 4th, 7th and 52nd Armies. The fact that the Soviets were holding back the Germans at all was astounding. With just 300 men, the 44th Rifle Division prevented the Germans from exploiting their gains towards Vologda. Soviet forces in the area were very weak, the 54th Army numbering 55,600 men, 4th Army 62,700 and 52nd Army just 42,000. The Novgorod Group fielded 32,000 men.

The collapse of their defences along the Volkhov compelled Soviet High Command to rush 65th Rifle Division to this sector, its arrival being expected by 11 November.

SOUTHERN SECTOR
German pressure upon the outer defences of Rostov mounted as Kleist pushed forward. Timoshenko planned to launch his own counter-offensive and called for additional weapons from the High Command. Again

he was refused, so he had to build up a reserve by scraping together spare units from his existing forces. From these forces he reinforced 37th Army. Timoshenko's plan was to halt the German attack by breaking into the exposed northern flank of 1st Panzer Army with 37th, 12th, 18th and 9th Armies, while 56th Independent Army pinned 1st Panzer frontally. Lopatin's 37th Army deployed around Krasnodar and Kolpakchy's 18th at Voroshilovgrad, both beginning the movement to their new sectors. The counter-attack would draw in twenty-two rifle and nine cavalry divisions and five tank brigades. The 18th and 12th Armies were to block the German advance at Voroshilovgrad.

> *From the Karelian forests in the north to the vast expanse of steppe in the south, the early onset of winter and tenacious Soviet defence had brought the German advance to a standstill. Inadequate replacements and over-extended lines of communication hampered an already exhausted army. Hitler's generals sought to finish off an enemy who refused to accept defeat with forces close to breaking point. Nearly five months of continuous combat, heavy casualties and a lack of replacement soldiers and equipment was sapping the strength of the combat divisions. However, the seemingly endless resources of the Red Army also appeared to be nearing their end. With the fighting closer to Moscow than ever, the field armies were shadows of their former selves. Battered, exhausted and having retreated some six hundred miles, the Red Army refused to die. Yet in this hour of need the Soviets were finding a new generation of generals, men who would make the Germans reap what they had sown.*

10 November 1941

CENTRAL SECTOR
Group Belov counter-attacked at Serpukhov, the intention being the encirclement of 13th Korp. Belov committed 2nd Cavalry Corp, two tank divisions and two tank brigades.

SOVIET COMMAND
The Stavka disbanded Bryansk Front, incorporating the 50th Army into Western Front and 3rd and 13th Armies into South-West Front.

GERMAN COMMAND
Hitler issued objectives for the continuation of Operation Typhoon. Army Group North was to build upon its gains at Tikhvin, effecting a junction with the Finns on the Svir before pounding Leningrad into submission. The Germans did not anticipate the surrender of the city, having decided there were insufficient resources available to feed the civilian population. Army Group Centre was to continue the attacks on the Moscow axis and

destroy Soviet forces in and around the city. It was then to push cast to the Urals. Army Group South, tasked with capturing Rostov, was to reduce the Soviet forces encircled at Sevastopol using 11th Army and then cross the Kerch Strait into the Kuban. This would begin the advance to and capture of the Maikop oilfields, a gigantic task given the early onset of the Russian winter and the weakened state of Army Group South.

These objectives proved just how out of touch Hitler and his staff really were with the situation at the front. To expect the Ostheer, with its exhausted and under-strength divisions, to maintain an advance in the middle of winter, without winter equipment, and bring about the destruction of the Red Army in the field was utter delusion.

11 November 1941

NORTHERN SECTOR
The Soviets laid plans for a counter-attack at Tikhvin. Fourth Army was to hit 39th Panzer Korp in three groups, Northern, Eastern and Southern, its aim being to split up and isolate the German force. Once Tikhvin was retaken, 4th was to press on to Budogosh and Gruzino. Other units of 4th Army were also to press north to help 54th Army seal off 1st Korp at Volkhov. The 54th would then unfold its main attack upon Kirishi. On the southern flank, 52nd Army and Novgorod Group were to attack the 38th Korp at Malaya Vyshera. Those units of 4th Army operating in 54th Army area, comprising five rifle divisions and a tank brigade, were amalgamated into the latter force.

CENTRAL SECTOR
Elements of 50th Army (one rifle and one cavalry division) and 49th Army (a single rifle division) launched a concentric attack aimed at pinning down 31st and 131st Infantry Divisions of 43rd Korp north of Tula. Heavy fighting erupted that continued for the next five days.

The 53rd Korp began to gain the upper hand against Soviet forces attacking around Teploye. However, 53rd had to call up armoured support to repel the Soviet attack, 24th Panzer Korp arriving in dribs and drabs from the fighting around Tula, where 50th Army resisted stubbornly.

SOUTHERN SECTOR
First Panzer Army halted its attack upon Rostov to briefly rest and refit.

12 November 1941

NORTHERN SECTOR
Meretskov created a small reserve and counter-attacked at Tikhvin. The three Soviet groups around the town closed in, struggling for each house.

The Soviets were attacking with two rifle divisions, a single tank division and two rifle regiments.

Klykov's 52nd Army began its counter-attack at Malaya Vyshera but the attacks were weak and uncoordinated.

CENTRAL SECTOR

The temperature dropped to minus twelve degrees centigrade. German army and group commanders, meeting in conference at Orsha, decided upon the next phase of operations towards Moscow. Halder proposed that the advance be resumed as quickly as possible, the majority of army and korp commanders agreeing with this proposal. The reports of the field commanders convinced Halder that Army Groups North and Centre were even weaker than he had suspected.

The conference decided that Army Group North should go over to the defensive, while Groups Centre and South continued the drive east. Army Group Centre was to complete the envelopment of Moscow; the northern wing attacking with 9th Army and 3rd Panzer Group, while 4th Army and 4th Panzer Group secured the centre and 2nd Panzer and 2nd Armies pushed from the south. The northern pincer was to attack on 15 November through Klin and across the Moscow–Volga Canal, and the southern pincer on 17 November, pushing north-east through Tula and Kashira. Army Group South was to continue its attacks towards Rostov and following the capture of the city extend its offensive into the Caucasus.

3rd Panzer Group had three panzer, two motorised and three infantry divisions, 9th Army ten infantry divisions, 4th Panzer Group four panzer, one motorised and seven infantry divisions, 4th Army two panzer, one motorised and twelve infantry divisions and 2nd Panzer Army four panzer, three motorised and six infantry divisions. Of 460 tanks available to 2nd Panzer at the end of September, only fifty remained in action. The other panzer groups had suffered similar losses, as had the infantry armies. With only fifty operational tanks, 2nd Panzer Army was expected to encircle Moscow from the south and contain the forces inside the pocket while also protecting the eastern perimeter from counter-attack.

Predicting that the renewed German offensive was imminent, Zhukov alerted the West Front, ordering it to prepare to meet the next wave of German attacks. The West Front, having lost nearly three quarters of a million men in October, numbered barely a quarter of a million now. However, the Soviet high command had put in motion a series of moves that would create a significant strategic reserve around Moscow.

On the eve of the German attack, the West Front deployed 30th Army with two rifle divisions and a single tank brigade, 16th Army with four rifle and six cavalry divisions and four tank brigades, 5th Army with five rifle divisions and five tank brigades, 33rd Army with four rifle divisions and one tank brigade, 49th Army with seven rifle divisions and 50th Army with seven rifle divisions, two cavalry divisions and two tank brigades. Protecting the northern flank of the West Front was Koniev's Kalinin Front, which deployed 22nd Army with six rifle divisions and one cavalry division, 29th Army with five rifle divisions and one cavalry division and 31st Army with five rifle divisions. In reserve, the Kalinin Front had a rifle division and tank brigade.

Left of 50th Army were 3rd and 13th Armies of the South-West Front, which became embroiled with 2nd Army as the Germans struck towards the Don. The 3rd Army had five rifle divisions and two cavalry divisions, while 13th had nine rifle and two cavalry divisions.

13 November 1941

NORTHERN SECTOR
There was heavy fighting around Tikhvin while 52nd Army continued to attack 38th Korp near Malaya Vyshera. The temperature was minus twenty-two degrees centigrade.

14 November 1941

CENTRAL SECTOR
Fighting erupted as 16th and 49th Armies launched spoiling attacks north of Volokolamsk and east of Serpukhov. The 49th Army hit 98th, 13th, 17th and 137th Infantry Divisions of 12th and 13th Korps with five rifle divisions (415th, 5th Guards, 60th, 94th and 17th) north-east of Serpukhov, making minor gains. The 2nd Cavalry Corp also entered the battle, 112th Tank Division trying to exploit any gains by 49th Army but was halted in its tracks. German counter-attacks by 263rd and 268th Infantry Divisions threw the tank division back.

Knowing the resumption of the German attack was imminent, the Stavka sent out an alert to the armies at the front.

15 November 1941

NORTHERN SECTOR
The Soviets withdrew from Volkhov. Following the fall of Tikhvin, 39th Panzer Korp began to move away from the Volkhov sector, going south to support 16th Army.

CENTRAL SECTOR
In frosty but clear weather, the Germans resumed the attack against the West Front, heralding the final phase of Operation Typhoon. Soviet estimates put the German attack force at 233,000 men while the defending West Front had 240,000 men, 1,254 artillery pieces and 502 tanks.[9]

Fighting erupted as 3rd and 4th Panzer Groups attacked 3rd Panzer, with elements of 9th Army in support, crashed into 30th Army around Kalinin and pushed towards Klin. Despite fierce resistance, 30th Army was forced to yield ground. German infantry and armour headed for the Volga as they sought to smash open the entire northern wing of the Soviet front. Fourth Panzer Group pounded the Russians as it crashed into 16th Army before Istra.

The 49th and 50th Armies halted attacks by 2nd Panzer Army north of Tula.

SOUTHERN SECTOR
in the Crimea 11th Army conquered the greater part of the peninsula, only the defenders of Sevastopol and the remnants of 51st Army in flight to Kerch remaining in the field.

16 November 1941

CENTRAL SECTOR
The 16th Army launched a spoiling attack with four divisions (126th Rifle, 17th and 24th Cavalry and 58th Tank) on its right wing in an effort to prise apart the 9th Army and 56th Panzer Korp of the 3rd Panzer Group. Heavy fighting with 14th Motorised and 7th Panzer Divisions saw the virtual destruction of the attacking divisions, despite the commitment of 20th and 44th Cavalry Division to back up the attack. The Germans then counter attacked, pushing towards the Lama, which was crossed during the afternoon.

Fourth Panzer Group then struck 16th Army at Volokolamsk, inflicting crippling casualties upon the heavily outnumbered units. As 16th fought its ferocious battles, on its northern flank 30th Army crumbled. Battered by 9th Army and 3rd Panzer Group, the Soviets suffered a terrible pounding. Only two days after the resumption of the offensive, it looked as though the Moscow defences were on the verge of collapse.

The Soviets continued to attack 13th Korp, inflicting heavy losses on the hard-pressed German infantry.

SOUTHERN SECTOR
With temperatures in the Ukraine as low as minus twenty degrees centigrade, 1st Panzer Army began its offensive towards Rostov. Even as the attack rolled on, Rundstedt believed that the assault served no purpose, as the German forces would be unable to maintain their hold upon the city due to the weakness of the combat divisions. Predicting the German attack, the Stavka had laid plans for a counter-stroke against Army Group South. Striking into the exposed northern flank of 1st Panzer Army as it

advanced, the Soviets planned to encircle and destroy the army against the sea. With 18th, 9th and 37th Armies pushing from north and east towards the Azov coast and 56th Army fighting in Rostov, the Germans would find themselves pinned frontally in street fighting while their flank and rear were overrun. The defensive operation before Rostov had already cost the South-West Front's 6th Army 11,200 killed and missing and 2,000 wounded, while the South Front had lost 132,000 killed and missing and 15,000 wounded.[10]

In the Crimea, the battle for Kerch ended. The remnants of the 51st Army fled across the Kerch strait. Twelve rifle and four cavalry divisions had been mauled during the fighting and 100,000 men captured. During the entire Crimean battle the Coastal and 51st Armies, together with elements of the Black Sea Fleet, suffered 48,000 killed and missing and 15,000 wounded. The Germans also captured or destroyed more than 700 artillery pieces and 160 tanks in and around the burning port.[11]

17 November 1941

CENTRAL SECTOR
The Stavka transferred 30th Army from the Kalinin to the West Front to cover the crumbling Klin sector and provide support to 16th Army. Rokossovsky's flanks had collapsed under the force of the German attacks and his divisions were being bled to death, three having lost touch with army headquarters.

SOUTHERN SECTOR
Kleist pinned down 18th Army as it attempted to counter-attack. The 3rd Panzer Korp led the assault that aimed to bypass and isolate Rostov. The 37th Army also counter-attacked, attacking without artillery preparation. It pushed ten miles into the German flank. In spite of this, 3rd Panzer Korp continued to concentrate its firepower upon 56th Independent Army. Fifty-sixth had at its disposal 86,500 soldiers, while the South Front, minus 12th Army, had a further 262,000 men.[12]

To support the attack upon Rostov, Manstein's 11th Army handed the 73rd Infantry Division over to 1st Panzer Army control. This move weakened Manstein's plan of attack on Sevastopol.[13]

18 November 1941

NORTHERN SECTOR
Klykov's 52nd Army infiltrated the German lines and succeeded in encircling elements of 38th Korp at Malaya Vyshera. Despite fierce counter-attacks, the Germans were unable to break out, bitter street fighting raging as the Soviets pressed into the town.

Lake Ladoga froze, enabling the Soviets to move supplies across its surface into Leningrad.

CENTRAL SECTOR

Third and Fourth Panzer Groups and Ninth Army continued to crush the Soviet defences to the north of Moscow. Kluge's 4th Army attempted to cross the Oka river but encountered fierce Soviet resistance. On the southern wing, 3rd Panzer Division of 24th Panzer Korp crossed the Upa south-east of Tula and launched attacks against the three left flank divisions of 50th Army, while 4th Panzer Division pushed towards Dedilovo. Simultaneously the Soviets counter-attacked from Venev, breaking the German lines. Panic ensued as the German position collapsed, and it seemed likely that a rout would develop. Guderian hastily rallied his force, counter-attacking with 47th Panzer Korp. Pushing from the south into the deep right flank of West Front, 47th Panzer captured Yepifan, while 53rd Korp moved towards the Don.

SOUTHERN SECTOR

As fighting raged in Rostov, 37th Army continued to counter-attack. Progress was slow, prompting Halder to urge 17th and 6th Armies to move units forward to relieve the pressure upon 1st Panzer Army.

19 November 1941

NORTHERN SECTOR

Fighting around Tikhvin intensified as 4th Army's northern group fought to cut the Tikhvin–Volkhov road and prevent the German withdrawal while the southern group aimed to cut the Tikhvin–Budogosh road. The Germans moved 61st infantry Division up to reinforce the Tikhvin sector. Fifty-second Army continued to batter 38th Korp at Malaya Vyshera.

CENTRAL SECTOR

Attacks by 3rd Panzer Group had forced apart 16th and 30th Armies, prompting West Front to form Group Zakharov with three divisions and two brigades to cover the gap in the line before Klin. To reinforce 30th Army, Zhukov moved 58th Tank Division, with just 350 men and 15 tanks, from 16th Army.[14]

A new thrust by 4th Panzer Group hit the right wing of 5th Army, pushing it back towards Zvenigorod and threatening its junction with 16th Army. In an effort to prevent an immediate collapse, the Stavka diverted a rifle division and tank brigade from the already under-strength 33rd Army to the 5th. To cover the increasingly exposed Volokolamsk–Istra axis that was being pressed hard by 4th Panzer Group, the Soviets had three rifle and two cavalry divisions plus 1st Guards Tank Brigade. The slow pace of the advance compelled Hoeppner to commit 40th Panzer, 9th and 5th Korps to the attack.

SOUTHERN SECTOR
Third Panzer Korp fought its way through the heavily defended streets of Rostov. Fighting was extremely bitter as 56th Army defended every street, exacting a high price on the 14th Panzer Division as it pushed deeper into the city. The 60th Motorised Division was embroiled in heavy fighting as it tried to protect the exposed flank and rear of 14th Panzer. To the north 37th Army launched a fierce attack and routed 14th Panzer Korp, throwing it back and threatening the rear of 3rd Panzer Korp in Rostov.

20 November 1941

NORTHERN SECTOR
The Germans reinforced their force in Tikhvin with a newly arrived infantry division from France. The Germans had five divisions in Tikhvin.

CENTRAL SECTOR
The 16th and 5th Armies, together with 30th and 50th were under intense attack. Rokossovsky's 16th Army was hard-pressed before Klin, suffering heavy casualties as 3rd Panzer Group launched repeated attacks. Fourth Panzer Group continued its costly attacks, pushing fourteen miles into the Soviet positions on the Volokolarnsk–lstra axis.

Fiftieth Army had been badly mauled in the fighting around Tula, its left flank divisions having crumbled under the German attacks. The Stavka transferred a rifle division from 3rd Army to reinforce 50th. The 48th Panzer Korp took Tim, propping up the increasingly exposed right flank of 2nd Panzer Army.

SOUTHERN SECTOR
The struggle continued in and around Rostov, where Kleist was embroiled with 56th Independent Army. Most of the city had fallen to the Germans, along with the still intact Don bridge and 10,000 prisoners. The 56th continued to launch furious counter-attacks, preventing the removal of forces to protect the growing threat to the north where 37th Army was attacking. The southerly movement of 1st Panzer Army had opened a threatening gap between it and 17th Army. Third Panzer Korp was forced to move 13th and 14th Panzer Divisions to Tuslov to hold off the threat presented by 37th Army.

SOVIET COMMAND
The Stavka issued formation orders for 1st Shock Army, based around the old 19th Army and 20th and 10th Armies.

21 November 1941

CENTRAL SECTOR
Fourth Panzer Group, having penetrated the junction of 5th and 33rd Armies, turned to hit the flank of 33rd Army in an effort to cut the Naro Fominsk–Kubinka road and open up the rear of 5th Army. The threat to the northern wing grew as 3rd Panzer Group pounded 16th and 30th Armies. Zhukov ordered Rokossovsky to ensure that Klin and Solnechnogorsk were held, despite the fact that German attacks had already encircled Solnechnogorsk and penetrated into the outskirts of Klin. To the south, 2nd Panzer Army advanced steadily, capturing Uzlovaya with 53rd Korp after a bitter battle.

SOUTHERN SECTOR
First Panzer Army's control of Rostov was increasingly threatened by the attacks of 9th and 37th Armies from the north. The 56th Independent Army kept up the pressure on 3rd Panzer Korp, launching constant attacks from across the frozen Don. Fighting continued into and through the night. Just as Rundstedt stated before the offensive, while 1st Panzer could conquer Rostov it could not hold the city, its own weakness and the growing strength of the Soviet forces arrayed against it proving too much.

22 November 1941

CENTRAL SECTOR
Reinhardt's 3rd Panzer Group fought in Klin and Solnechnogorsk. The 16th Army was unable to hold the German attacks. Late in the day, 4th Panzer Group penetrated between 5th and 16th Armies, entering Istra and threatening to unhinge the Soviet defences west of Moscow. Lead units of 3rd Panzer Group were only thirty miles north of Moscow while 2nd Panzer Army was fighting near Venev and Tula as it launched strong attacks in an effort to dislodge 50th Army. Heavy fighting around Tula compelled Zhukov to move Boldin's 2nd Cavalry Corp from Serpukhov to Kashira, blocking the line of the German advance to Moscow. Boldin was instructed to prevent the fall of Kashira to 2nd Panzer Army at all costs. On the southern wing of 2nd Panzer Army, 48th Panzer Korp came under heavy attack near Tim. Timoshenko was trying to bring pressure to bear upon the flank of the German forces to the south of Moscow in an effort to divert attention away from the city, but his own

lack of resources prevented any significant penetration of the German positions.

23 November 1941

CENTRAL SECTOR
Heavy fighting raged at Venev as the Germans struggled to take the town from the Venev Group, a force of one rifle regiment and two tank brigades.

SOUTHERN SECTOR
Elements of 37th and 9th Armies reached the Tuzla river to the rear of the German forces in Rostov.

GERMAN COMMAND
Guderian met Bock and stressed the tiredness of his troops. Bock relayed this information to Brauchitsch, but it was obvious that Brauchitsch was not allowed to make any decisions, being completely under Hitler's control.

24 November 1941

CENTRAL SECTOR
After a bitter battle, Klin fell to 7th Panzer Division of 56th Panzer Korp, 30th Army being sent reeling to the east. The battle on the road to and for Klin left 30th with only twenty operational tanks and two hundred artillery pieces. Solnechnogorsk also fell to 2nd Panzer Division of 40th Panzer Korp, while 5th Korp drew level with 4th Panzer Group, opening the road to the Moscow–Volga Canal. Istra, already under attack, formed the lynchpin of the Soviet defences. A single Siberian rifle division (78th) was deployed the hold the town and the nearby reservoir, taking up positions along the Istra river. The Stavka had ordered the battered 16th Army to fall back to a new line south of Solnechnogorsk. The 5th Army was falling back to a line Istra–Zvenigorod.

The 24th Panzer Korp took Venev after a fierce battle, while 43rd Korp pushed forward to the Upa. The 5th Motorised Division captured Michailov.

SOUTHERN SECTOR
First Panzer Army began to withdraw from Rostov, Rundstedt ordering his forces to retire quickly to the line of the Mius river due to the growing Soviet threat on the northern flank. Rundstedt felt his forces were at risk of encirclement if they remained in Rostov, the only viable option being the withdrawal of his forces westward. OKH agreed with Army Group South's decision to withdraw.

25 November 1941

NORTHERN SECTOR
After the heavy fighting at Tikhvin and Malaya Vyshera, Kuchler decided he had no option other than to go onto the defensive all along the Volkhov. For the first time in the campaign, the Germans had lost the initiative, albeit on a limited front.

CENTRAL SECTOR
The 4th Panzer Group secured its hold on Solnechnogorsk and continued to pound both the 16th and 30th Armies. The 7th Panzer Division took Peshki and reached the banks of the Moscow–Volga canal near Yakhroma, capturing the bridge across the canal intact.

Farther south, elements of Boldin's 2nd Cavalry Corp, fighting 17th Panzer Division of 47th Panzer Korp on the road to Kashira, suffered a terrible battering and were unable to halt the German advance.

Despite these setbacks, the Soviets continued to build up new formations to the rear. Zhukov refused to feed reserve units into the line until the Germans were completely exhausted. The recently formed 1st Shock Army assembled its seven rifle brigades at Zagorsk, while 20th Army formed near Moscow. Golikov was *en route* to Ryazan with his hastily raised 10th Army. The 1st Shock Army was a new creation among the Soviet order of battle, being specifically tasked with breaking through the German front to the north of Moscow once the counter-offensive began. The shock armies were essentially the same as the normal rifle army but with increased artillery forces at their disposal.

26 November 1941

CENTRAL SECTOR
Fierce battles raged at Istra as 2nd SS Motorised Division *Das Reich* and 10th Panzer Division attacked the 78th Rifle Division in the town. The 10th Panzer was operating with just seven tanks.[15] The 17th Panzer Division pushed towards Kashira amid running battles with 2nd Cavalry Corp. Fifty-third Korp reached the Don and encircled a Siberian division against the river near Donskoye. The isolated force continued to fight on, 53rd Korp's weakness preventing the destruction of the pocket.

Boldin's 2nd Cavalry Corp was elevated to Guards status, being renamed 1st Guards Cavalry Corp.

27 November 1941

CENTRAL SECTOR
The Kalinin Front began a series of counter-attacks against the left flank of Army Group Centre. Ninth Army repelled repeated Soviet attacks but had to divert forces from the support of 3rd Panzer Group to deal with this threat. Heavy fighting raged at Istra as hand-to-hand battles surged through this small town.

The fighting at Kashira intensified as the Guard's cavalry counter attacked, halting the northward march of 17th Panzer Division. The 53rd Korp was unable to prevent the escape of the encircled unit at Donskoye, which rejoined the main combat line despite the loss of much of its heavy equipment.

28 November 1941

NORTHERN SECTOR
A newly reinforced and revitalised 4th Army launched furious attacks at Tikhvin, pinning down 1st Korp. 52nd and 54th Armies continued their attacks against the northern and southern flanks of the salient. Slowly but surely 18th Army was squeezed back to the west.

CENTRAL SECTOR
With 7th Panzer and 14th Motorised Divisions just twenty miles north of Moscow at Yakhroma, the Soviets deployed 1st Shock Army from reserve. The advance had cost the Germans their last ounce of strength, many units being severely depleted in the costly fighting and atrocious weather. After a bitter battle, 2nd SS Division *Das Reich* and 10th Panzer Division captured Istra. Farther south, 43rd Korp came under heavy attack as West Front attempted to pin down 4th Army.

Behind the combat line, 10th Army completed its march to Ryavan. Golikov's army stood poised to enter the fighting south of Moscow where it threatened the exposed right wing of 2nd Panzer Army. To reinforce the hard-pressed 16th Army, the 5th, 33rd, 43rd and 49th Armies each gave up a rifle division. Operational Group Lizyukov was formed around these divisions, later going on to become 20th Army. The 5th Army was instructed to form a mobile reserve to secure its junction with 16th Army. Its group numbered just 800 men and 21 tanks.[16]

SOUTHERN SECTOR
The 56th and 9th Armies recaptured most of Rostov, 3rd Panzer Korp retreating from the cement factory. The bulk of 1st Panzer Army fell back to the Mius, hotly pursued by the South Front. With Rostov virtually lost and 1st Panzer Army in retreat, Hitler countermanded Rundstedt's order and insisted that the 1st Panzer hold its positions.

29 November 1941

CENTRAL SECTOR

Lead units of 4th Panzer Group took Dmitrov on the eastern bank of the Moscow–Volga canal. The 16th and 30th Armies received substantial reinforcement, much needed following their bloody battles with 3rd and 4th Panzer Groups. First Shock Army and 10th Army were allocated to West Front as reinforcement, but held in reserve behind the wings of the front until the German attack ground to a halt. As yet both 1st Shock and 10th Armies needed fleshing out, being short of men and equipment.

On the southern wing, 47th Panzer Korp came under fierce attack and was forced to pull back from Skopin. The 24th Panzer also came under heavy fire around Tula. To the rear of the combat line, the Red Army brought up yet more reserve armies. The 60th deployed around Tarasovka, while 24th was situated on the Moskva near Davidkovo. In addition, 26th Army was at Noginsk and 61st at Ryazan.

SOUTHERN SECTOR

Fierce fighting continued as 1st Panzer Army withdrew to the Mius, giving up Rostov to 56th and 9th Armies. These two units pressed the Germans relentlessly but were unable to rout the retreating force.

30 November 1941

CENTRAL SECTOR

North of Moscow, 2nd Panzer Division of 40th Panzer Korp captured Krasnaya Polyana. Heavy fighting also raged at Kryukovo and Dedovsk as 46th and 40th Panzer Korps of 4th Panzer Group and 5th Korp of 3rd Panzer Group closed around 16th and 5th Armies. The Stavka reluctantly released 1st Shock and 20th Armies from reserve to shore up the crumbling 16th and 30th Armies, 1st Shock being ordered to counter-attack at Yakhroma and 20th Army at Krasnaya Polyana.

With the German offensive weakening noticeably, Zhukov proposed to the Stavka that the forces on the Moscow axis launch their counter offensive within the next few days. As the Germans pressed closer to Moscow, the force of their attacks lessened appreciably. Using his reserve, Zhukov intended to strike at the flanks of Army Group Centre, bringing about its encirclement and destruction in a cauldron battle before Moscow. The northern wing, comprising 30th, 1st Shock, 20th and 16th Armies, was tasked with isolating and destroying 3rd and 4th Panzer Groups. These armies would then push west to Smolensk, where the southern pincer would also have penetrated the German front. This southern attack consisted of 10th and 50th Armies, whose task was to destroy 2nd Panzer Army. In the centre, 4th Army would be pinned down on the Nara and prevented from transferring forces to the flanks by the attacks of 5th 33rd, 43rd and 49th Armies. The Soviets brought together 718,000 men on the Moscow axis, with 7,985 artillery pieces and 720 tanks against the cold and exhausted forces of Army Group Centre. At this stage of the battle, Army Group Centre had been reduced to 801,000 soldiers, 14,000 artillery pieces and 1,000 tanks, many being inoperable due to the intense cold. There were also 615 aircraft but again most of these were grounded due to the weather and lack of adequate supplies.[17]

Von Bock in conversation with von Brauchitsch: 'My one hope of reaching Moscow is to continue the attack frontally ... I emphasise that Army Group Centre is at the end of its strength.'[18]

SOUTHERN SECTOR

Hitler ordered Rundstedt to halt his retreat to the Mius and hold firm on positions between the Mius and the Don. Rundstedt maintained that he would be unable to prevent a Soviet breakthrough on this line and pulled back quickly to the Mius, to break off contact with the Russians and because there were defensive positions already established on this river line. Hitler accused Rundstedt of defeatism and relieved him of his post, appointing Reichenau in his place. This was the first of many dismissals over the coming few weeks, Hitler sacking his generals as each new defeat was reported from the front.

THE OSTHEER

The number of divisions in the East fell by one at the end of the month with the departure of a single infantry division, standing at nineteen panzer, fifteen motorised and one hundred and three infantry divisions. Ostheer equipment strength stood at 36,000 artillery pieces, 1,453 tanks and 3,688 aircraft.[19] German losses on the Eastern Front during November amounted to 57,000 men (36,000 killed), bringing losses since June to 770,000. Some 400,000 men, had been replaced. Of the 600,000 motor vehicles committed to the Eastern Front in June, the Ostheer had lost 150,000 destroyed and a further 250,000 were under repair.

THE RED ARMY

At the end of November 1941, the Red Army had in reserve nine armies (10th, 26th, 28th, 39th, 57th, 58th, 59th, 60th and 61st) with fifty-nine rifle and seventeen cavalry divisions. At the front the army had two hundred and nineteen divisions with 4,196,000 men, 32,194 artillery pieces, 1,984 tanks and 3,688 aircraft.[20]

1 December 1941

NORTHERN SECTOR

Fighting at Tikhvin continued as the Leningrad Front launched fierce attacks against 1st Korp. The 18th Army had the bulk of its strength against the southern perimeter of Leningrad, 26th Korp being deployed around the Oranienbaum pocket, and 28th and 50th Korps facing the city. Only 1st and 38th Korps were east of the Volkhov, covering the exposed line from the southern shores of Lake Ladoga to Novgorod on Lake Ilmen. South of Lake Ilmen, holding the line from Staraya Russa to the junction with 9th Army near Ostashkov, was 16th Army. Army Group North had a total strength of thirty German and one Spanish divisions.

CENTRAL SECTOR

Kluge's 4th Army launched a new attack with 20th Korp, striking 33rd Army in an effort to break open the road to Moscow. The attack was made in three groups, 267th Infantry Division attacking south-west of Zvenigorodka, 258th and 292nd Infantry and 3rd Motorised Divisions north of Naro-Fominsk while 183rd Infantry, 20th Panzer and part of 15th Infantry Divisions attacked south of Naro-Fominsk. After heavy fighting, the 267th Infantry Division was thrown back to its start lines, while 1st Guards Motorised Division put up a ferocious defence at Naro-Fominsk. However, by noon the 258th Infantry and 3rd Motorised had pushed ahead five miles north and south of Naro-Fominsk[21] and were close to Akulovo, having sliced apart 33rd and 5th Armies. Realising the danger, Zhukov rushed reserves up to the hard-pressed armies. Heavy fighting raged at Naro-Fominsk as 4th Army launched additional attacks.

The 2nd Panzer Army was trying to smash its way through to Moscow, but the intensification of the fighting prompted the Stavka to commit 10th Army from the reserve. This unit threatened the southern wing of 2nd Panzer, forcing Guderian to draw forces away from his advance to the north to protect the exposed flank.

As the offensive stalled, Field Marshal von Bock, ill with stomach cramps, reported to Hitler that he no longer considered it possible to achieve the objectives set for his forces and strongly urged that his armies be allowed to suspend offensive activity. Hitler disagreed and ordered the offensive to be continued until the Red Army had been broken and Moscow captured.

On the northern wing of the Moscow axis, the Stavka ordered the Kalinin Front to assemble a shock group to attack Kalinin, its aim being to break into the rear of the German forces at Klin.

SOUTHEN SECTOR

Kleist's 1st Panzer Army, together with elements of 17th Army, continued their fighting withdrawal to the Mius as the South Front launched constant attacks. Reichenau continued the withdrawal, Hitler having agreed to allow it now that it was in motion, but wanted the 1st Panzer to stop a short distance before the river, a stupid and pointless decision. Kleist disagreed with this decision, and let Halder know it during a telephone conversation. The weakness of the German forces meant they would be unlikely to hold this line, especially since there was an excellent position just a few miles behind them. Reichenau though refused to pull back, being convinced that Hitler's decision was the right one. Brauchitsch went to see Hitler and at the same time Reichenau called from the front to inform Hitler that the Soviets had broken through and were pressing towards the Mius. Hitler then gave permission to fall back to the river line.

2 December 1941

CENTRAL SECTOR

North of Moscow, 4th Panzer Group pushed forward as far as Khimki, only twelve miles from the city, but the Russians launched strong counter-attacks which pushed the Germans back from the town. Fourth Army continued to attack 33rd and 43rd Armies at Golizno and Akulovo, being embroiled in furious fighting in both sectors. After a bitter struggle, Akulovo fell. From here 4th Army could see the spires of the Kremlin on the eastern horizon, but this was as close as they would get to their objective. Efremov took command of a composite group of one rifle and two tank brigades to force the Germans back. The group counter-attacked, striking the flank of 20th Korp and almost isolating elements at Aprelevka.

To the south, 2nd Panzer Army launched an attack upon Tula, taking 50th Army by surprise. The Germans aimed to encircle the town with two shock groups formed around 3rd and 4th Panzer Divisions. These would attack to the west from the area north of Tula, while a third group, comprising 31st and 296th Infantry Divisions of 43rd Korp, attacked east from the north-west of the city. Despite a day of bitter fighting, which cut the Tula–Moscow road, the Germans were unable to break through and went onto the defensive. The 47th Panzer Korp, situated farther east, was brought under intense pressure as the Soviets began to counter-attack.

SOUTHERN SECTOR

The fighting around Rostov has been costly for the Soviets. The South Front had suffered 11,000 killed and 13,000 wounded since 17 November, while 56th Army lost 4,000 killed and 5,000 wounded.[22]

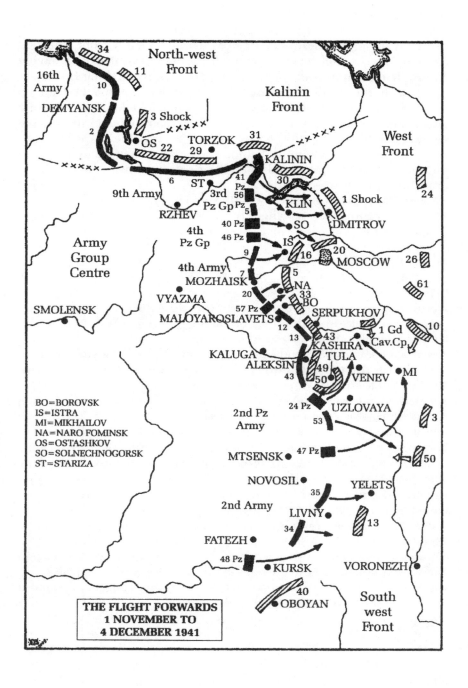

THE FLIGHT FORWARDS
1 NOVEMBER TO
4 DECEMBER 1941

North-west
Front

Kalinin
Front

West
Front

16th
Army

DEMYANSK

3 Shock

TORZOK

KALININ

9th Army

3rd
Pz Gp

RZHEV

KLIN

1 Shock

DMITROV

Army
Group
Centre

4th
Pz Gp

SO

4th Army

MOZHAISK

MOSCOW

SMOLENSK

VYAZMA

NA

MALOYAROSLAVETS

BO

SERPUKHOV

1 Gd
Cav.Cp.

KALUGA

KASHIRA

ALEKSIN

TULA

VENEV

MI

24 Pz

2nd Pz
Army

UZLOVAYA

BO=BOROVSK
IS=ISTRA
MI=MIKHAILOV
NA=NARO FOMINSK
OS=OSTASHKOV
SO=SOLNECHNOGORSK
ST=STARIZA

MTSENSK

47 Pz

2nd Army

NOVOSIL

YELETS

LIVNY

FATEZH

KURSK

VORONEZH

OBOYAN

South
west
Front

3 December 1941

CENTRAL SECTOR
Bitter fighting raged at Dimitrov as 1st Shock Army struck 3rd Panzer Group. To the south, 4th Army had the tables turned on it, being brought under heavy attack at Akulovo and Golizno. Kluge extricated his battered 258th Infantry and 3rd Motorised Divisions and abandoned the recently won territory. Akulovo was retaken as the Germans were forced back to the Nara.

4 December 1941

NORTHERN SECTOR
Meretskov's 4th Army forced the Germans to give ground around Tikhvin, while 52nd Army subjected 38th Korp to further pressure.

CENTRAL SECTOR
The temperature fell to minus thirty-five degrees centigrade. Vehicles no longer started; engines froze while they ran and the breaches of artillery pieces froze shut. In spite of the severe cold, the fighting carried on.

North of Moscow, the German advance ground to a halt, 3rd and 4th Panzer Groups lacking the strength to push forward. In the centre, 4th Army fell back to the Nara, having failed to dislodge the West Front in the Akulovo and Gruzino sectors. As the Germans withdrew, 33rd, 43rd and 5th Armies launched fierce counter-attacks. Around Tula, 24th Panzer Korp failed to break through the Soviet defences and was struck by 50th Army, which also attacked 43rd Korp.

With the Germans exhausted, over-extended and at the end of supply lines stretching over a thousand miles, Zhukov prepared to begin the counter-offensive that would throw the Ostheer away from Moscow and destroy Army Group Centre in a massive double envelopment. Koniev's Kalinin Front, despite reinforcement, fielded 100,000 men between 22nd, 29th and 31st Armies with 980 artillery pieces, sixty-seven tanks and eighty-three aircraft while West Front, commanded by Zhukov, deployed 558,000 men among ten armies. The ten armies, 30th, 1st Shock, 20th, 16th, 5th, 33rd, 43rd, 49th, 50th and 10th, plus Group Belov, had 4,348 artillery pieces, 624 tanks and 199 aircraft. On the southern wing of the attack sector, the Soviets deployed the elements of Timoshenko's South-West Front, comprising 3rd and 13th Armies and Group Kostenko, 60,000 men with 388 artillery pieces, thirty tanks and seventy-nine aircraft.

GERMAN CASUALTIES
Since 22 June the Ostheer had suffered 830,000 casualties.

SOVIET CASUALTIES

Since the beginning of Operation Typhoon the West Front had suffered 254,000 casualties, while the Reserve Front lost 127,000 and the Bryansk Front 103,000. In its brief period of operations to date, the Kalinin Front lost 2,000 killed and missing and 21,000 wounded. The Soviets also lost 2,785 tanks, 3,800 artillery pieces and 290 aircraft.

> *The brutality of the fighting since the resumption of Typhoon, and the unexpectedly early onset of winter had left the Ostheer in a state of near collapse. Barely twenty miles from Moscow, with the spires of the Kremlin visible on the horizon, the German Army had shot its bolt. Hitler had pushed his forces forward on a seven hundred-mile journey, a journey strewn with thousands of fallen comrades on both sides of the combat line. However, the very weakness of the Ostheer was exactly what Zhukov was waiting for. With skill and masterly cunning, he had assembled a powerful strike force on the flanks of the exposed German positions in the centre. It was now the Germans' turn to defend as the Red Army took to the offensive.*

NOTES

1   Kirosheev, *Soviet Casualties and Combat Losses in the Twentieth Century*, Table 75
2   Kirosheev, *Soviet Casualties and Combat Losses in the Twentieth Century*, Table 75
3   Kirosheev, *Soviet Casualties and Combat Losses in the Twentieth Century*, Table 75
4   Kirosheev, *Soviet Casualties and Combat Losses in the Twentieth Century*, Table 75
5   Erickson, *The Road to Stalingrad*, p 254
6   Ellis, *Brute Force*, p 69
7   Glantz, *Barbarossa 1941*, p 161
8   Details from Glantz, *Barbarossa 1941*, p 151
9   Glantz, *Barbarossa 1941*, p 169
10 Kirosheev, *Soviet Casualties and Combat Losses in the Twentieth Century*, Table 75
11 Kirosheev, *Soviet Casualties and Combat Losses in the Twentieth Century*, Table 75
12 Kirosheev, *Soviet Casualties and Combat Losses in the Twentieth Century*, Table 75
13 Manstein, *Lost Victories*, p 223
14 Erickson, *The Road to Stalingrad*, p 258
15 Ailsby, *SS Hell on the Eastern Front*, p 42
16 Erickson, *The Road to Stalingrad*, p 261
17 Erickson, *The Road to Stalingrad*, p 272
18 Ellis, *Brute Force*, p 72
19 Ellis, *The World War Two Databook*, p 175
20 Erickson, *The Road to Stalingrad*, p 161
21 Detail of divisional action taken from Glantz, *Barbarossa 1941*, pp 175–6
22 Kirosheev, *Soviet Casualties and Combat Losses in the Twentieth Century*, Table 75
23 Erickson, *The Road to Stalingrad*, pp 272–3
24 Kirosheev, *Soviet Casualties and Combat Losses in the Twentieth Century*, Table 75

CHAPTER V
Zhukov's First Strike

With its back against the wall, the Red Army prepared to break once and for all the seeming invincibility of the Wehrmacht. Forces moved east from Siberia and men hastily called up into reserve armies stood ready to attack through the snow to drive the Germans west.

5 December 1941

CENTRAL SECTOR
At 0300 hours the 31st Army began attacking 9th Army forces south of Kalinin, penetrating their defences. Lead units were involved in bitter fighting at Turginovo. During the morning, at 1100 hours, 29th Army attacked north of Kalinin. By early afternoon both armies had established limited bridgeheads across the Volga. At 1600 hours 5th Army of West Front launched probing attacks against the German forces to the south.

With the temperature on the Moscow axis down at minus thirty degrees centigrade, a metre of snow lying on the ground and the Red Army launching ferocious attacks north of Moscow, Hitler reluctantly agreed to the suspension of Operation Typhoon. He blamed the failure to reach Moscow on the unusually early onset of winter. He instructed the Ostheer to go onto the defensive but called for the field armies to hold their positions and halt the Soviet attacks.

6 December 1941

NORTHERN SECTOR
There was bitter fighting as 4th Army closed upon Tikhvin. Heavy fighting raged at Malaya Vyshera as 52nd Army attacked 38th Korp in an effort to penetrate the southern flank of the salient.

CENTRAL SECTOR

The 30th, 1st Shock and 20th Armies began to counter-attack north of Moscow along the Moscow–Volga Canal and near Krasnaya Polyana. Elements of 30th Army penetrated the forward positions of 3rd Panzer Group and pushed eight miles along the road to Klin from the north-east. Further attacks by 1st Shock and 20th Armies at Dmitrov and Solnechnogorsk hit 3rd Panzer Group hard. Elements of 1st Shock Army fought their way into Yakhroma. Under intense pressure, the 1st, 2nd, 6th and 7th Panzer and 14th Motorised Divisions of 3rd Panzer Group began a fighting withdrawal to Klin, threatening to expose the left wing of 4th Panzer Group. Heavy fighting raged at Krasnaya Polyana where 20th Army also attacked 3rd Panzer Group.

The 10th Army marched directly into battle, striking 2nd Panzer Army on its southern wing and pushing towards Michailov and Novomosskovsk. The 17th Panzer Division struggled to hold off Soviet attacks south of Kashira, but by the end of the day was threatened as 2nd Guards Cavalry Corp cut the Mordves–Venev road. With the collapse of his right wing imminent, Guderian ordered his army to fall back to defensive positions on the Don, Shat and Upa rivers. South of 2nd Panzer Army, Soviet 13th Army hit 2nd Army near Yelets.

7 December 1941

CENTRAL SECTOR

Elements of 30th Army broke through 3rd Panzer Army lines north-east of Klin and attacked the headquarters of 56th Panzer Korp. Leading units of 30th Army were just five miles from Klin. The 1st Shock and 20th Armies pressed west from Yakhroma and north from Krasnaya Polyana. making slow but steady progress amid ferocious German resistance. The 6th Army joined the offensive, three divisions attacking 35th Infantry Division on the right wing of 3rd Panzer. Both 20th and 16th Armies aimed to destroy the Germans at Krasnaya Polyana from where they would thrust forward to Solnechnogorsk.

To the south, 2nd Panzer Army was forced back by 50th and 10th Armies, and Michailov fell to 10th Army as 10th Motorised Division fought a bloody delaying action. Group Kostenko also joined the attacks on the southern wing, striking 2nd Army on the Kastornoye–Livny axis. The 50th Army began attacks around Tula aimed at cutting 2nd Panzer Army's escape route.

GERMAN COMMAND

Field Marshal Brauchitsch, Chief of the Army General Staff, tendered his resignation to Hitler, who did not formally accept. Hitler and Brauchitsch had had a shaky relationship since the early days of Barbarossa,

Brauchitsch taking a back seat as the Führer dictated the direction of the campaign.

THE PACIFIC THEATRE
In the Far East, the Japanese attacked the American Pacific Fleet at Pearl Harbour, inflicting grievous damage and considerable casualties. The ramifications of the event were not lost upon Stalin, who realised that the Japanese had firmly committed their resources to a war with the USA and Britain. For the Germans this meant that they would have to face the full might of the Red Army, no longer able to hope for the withdrawal of Soviet forces to the east to defend against Japanese aggression. Stalin had effectively secured his rear and was fighting with his armies on only one front, while the Germans had tied themselves down to fighting in North Africa, albeit with a very minor force, protecting the western provinces of their territory from the still active British and fighting in the East against the USSR. With the Red Army on the offensive before Moscow and German forces falling back westwards, it was clear that the campaign in Russia would be long and bitter.

8 December 1941

NORTHERN SECTOR
There was heavy fighting inside Tikhvin as two rifle divisions broke through the German defences. With Tikhvin on the brink of capture, Hitler agreed to allow 18th Army to pull back to the Volkhov but it was too late, 1st Korp being forced back under pressure.

CENTRAL SECTOR
The danger to 3rd Panzer Group of encirclement increased as 30th Army pushed past Klin from the north, cutting the Moscow–Kalinin road. First Shock Army progress was slower than expected, but its attacks towards Klin made steady progress. The 16th and 20th Armies continued to strike near Krasnaya Polyana, forcing the Germans back. Elements of 16th Army pushed west towards Istra, hitting 4th Panzer Group. Bitter fighting raged at Snegiri, where 2nd SS Division *Das Reich* was fiercely attacked by 9th Guards Rifle Division.

On the southern wing, 50th Army launched strong attacks around Tula but was held back by 296th infantry and 3rd Panzer Divisions. New attacks by 3rd Army towards Yefremov struck 34th Korp hard. The 150th Tank Brigade separated the 45th and 95th infantry Divisions north of Yelets and exploited the gap, 55th Cavalry Division storming into the rear of 2nd Army. Timoshenko prepared to commit the new 61st Army between 10th and 3rd Armies. Group Belov also joined the attack, striking the Germans north-east of Tula.

9 December 1941

NORTHERN SECTOR

During the night of 8–9 December, the Soviets launched a furious attack into Tikhvin. Two rifle divisions attacked simultaneously from the north and south, supported by heavy artillery fire. After a bitter battle Tikhvin was cleared.

The Red Army had succeeded in wresting the initiative from Army Group North, forcing the 18th Army back to the Volkhov. However,1st Korp retired intact, despite the loss of 7,000 men in the Tikhvin battle. On the southern flank, 38th Korp also retreated to the Volkhov as 52nd Army pressed forward from Malaya Vyshera.

South of Lake Ilmen, 16th Army was relatively unaffected by the recent Soviet attacks, holding a line from Staraya Russa to Ostashkov with its 10th and 2nd Korps and 39th Panzer Korp.

CENTRAL SECTOR

First Shock Army captured Fedorovka, west of Klin. After the very heavy losses of the first few days of the counter-offensive, Zhukov ordered his armies to avoid frontal attacks, and instead to seek out open flanks to penetrate into the German rear. The 20th Army continued to advance amid heavy fighting while 16th Army supported the attack. Rokossovsky split his 16th Army into two offensive groups. Group Remezov was to strike out from the right wing, while Group Beloborodov attacked on the left towards Istra. Hoeppner attempted to reinforce the crumbling Klin sector by moving up 10th Panzer Division to help 3rd Panzer Group. *Das Reich* abandoned Snegiri to the Soviets after bitter fighting.

On the southern wing, Venev fell to Group Belov, which then pushed towards Stalinogorsk. Under heavy pressure from these attacks, 47th Panzer Korp began to withdraw from its exposed positions east of Tula as 24th Panzer Korp came under renewed attack by 50th Army. The 10th Army attack stalled due to fierce resistance by 112th Infantry Division along the Shat and Don rivers. Yelets tell to Group Moskalenko of 5th Army as 2nd Army retired. Group Kostenko of 13th Army was supporting the attacks of 3rd Army, hitting 53rd Korp near Livny and isolating part of the German force. A dangerous gap, twenty miles wide, had opened between 2nd Army and 2nd Panzer Army, through which 5th Cavalry Corp and 121st Rifle Division surged ahead.

10 December 1941

NORTHERN SECTOR

Following the fall of Tikhvin, the Stavka created the Volkhov Front under General Meretskov. The new front became operational on 17 December and incorporated 26th Army and 59th Army in addition to its existing forces. The 26th Army would later become 2nd Shock.

CENTRAL SECTOR

There was heavy fighting around Klin and Solnechnogorsk as the German panzer groups fought to escape the developing Soviet pincers. Third Panzer Group was fighting in operational isolation around Klin, while on the southern flank, 47th Panzer Korp fell back upon Yepifan.

With his lines falling apart, Guderian managed to extricate 53rd Korp from its near disastrous battle around Livny, having brought this korp and 24th Panzer back to the line of the Don, Shat and Upa rivers. During the heavy fighting, 95th Infantry Division had suffered fifty per cent casualties, while 45th Infantry Division had been all but destroyed. Heavy fighting along the river lines brought the 10th Army's attack to a complete halt. However, the gap between 2nd Panzer Army and 2nd Army had widened to eighty-five miles, elements of 2nd Army being cut off from the body of their force with 2nd Panzer.

11 December 1941

CENTRAL SECTOR

Solnechnogorsk fell to 20th Army and lstra to 16th Army. The retreating Germans blew the Istra dam, flooding large areas and stopping 16th Army dead. Fifth Army launched new attacks towards Ruza and Kolyubakovo, aimed at supporting the advance of 16th Army.

The 50th Army renewed its attacks south of Shchekino near Tula but with little success. Group Belov, operating in advance of 10th Army, sliced through 2nd Panzer Army and advanced south of Venev, entering Novomosskovsk. Stalinogorsk was also brought under heavy fire and fell later in the day. Zhukov ordered Belov to swing south-west to pin down 2nd Panzer Army in conjunction with 50th Army. Belov was to push south from Tula, while 50th advanced towards Plavsk. Tenth Army was also to regroup to effect a wider encirclement at Plavsk.

Guderian was worried by the widening gap between 2nd Panzer and 2nd Armies, realising that if it was not closed there was the real danger that the Soviets would push forces through and effect a junction with those attacking north of Moscow, isolating Army Group Centre.

SOUTHERN SECTOR

German 6th, 17th and 1st Panzer Armies fought bitter defensive battles to prevent the penetration of South-West Front into the Donbas and eastern Ukraine. The main weight of the Soviet attacks fell upon 1st Panzer Army on the line of the Mius but pressure was building up to the north as Timoshenko prepared to cross the Donets in force.

GERMAN POLITICS

Hitler declared war upon America. For a nation already deeply committed to the war in Russia, this decision defied logic. Hitler voluntarily placed Germany in a position of total disadvantage. With American resources openly at the disposal of the British, the future for Germany in the long term looked bleak. Had Hitler not declared war, it was likely that the United States would still not have entered the conflict in Europe, American opinion against any involvement in the war in Europe being divided.

12 December 1941

NORTHERN SECTOR

The 18th Army abandoned its hard won territory east of the Volkhov, giving up all gains made during Typhoon.

CENTRAL SECTOR

The 1st, 6th and 7th Panzer and 14th Motorised Divisions of 3rd Panzer Group fought on the outskirts of Klin, while 2nd Panzer Division held open the road to the west. The 30th and 1st Shock Armies were closing in from the north and east. Army Group Centre subordinated command of 3rd Panzer to the equally hard-pressed 4th Panzer Group. The 16th Army struggled to make any headway in the flooded Istra area. The 18th and 354th Rifle Divisions attempted a crossing of the swollen Istra river but were held up by fierce German artillery fire. Rokossovsky redeployed his army into two groups, Groups Remizov and Katukov, to envelop the Istra reservoir from north and south. Fifth Army was to support the attack with its own three-division mobile group.

The situation on the right flank continued to deteriorate as 2nd Army was separated from 2nd Panzer Army. Yefremov was evacuated as 2nd Army fell back. To the left of 2nd Army, 2nd Panzer Army was prised away from 4th Army to the north, leaving both flanks of 2nd Panzer exposed.

Hitler blamed the entire debacle in the centre upon Field Marshal von Bock, dismissing him, from command of Army Group Centre. Field Marshal Kluge succeeded the ill von Bock.

13 December 1941

CENTRAL SECTOR

Elements of 29th and 31st Armies, advancing around Kalinin, cut the German line of retreat from the town. The mobile groups of 6th and 5th Armies pushed forward near lstra, 5th Army group moving towards Ruza. Exploiting the cracks in the German line, 2nd Guards Cavalry Corp pushed forward, closely followed by a tank brigade.

To the south, 2nd Panzer Army fell back to the Plava but was threatened on both flanks as the Soviets pressed their attacks home. On the northern wing, 43rd Korp became separated from 24th Panzer Korp by more than twenty-five miles. Guderian's flanks were uncovered.

14 December 1941

CENTRAL SECTOR

Group Chanchibadze, with two cavalry and one motorised divisions (assigned to 30th Army) cut the road west from Klin, isolating 1st, 2nd, 6th and 7th Panzer and 14th Motorised Divisions. As the group pushed west, it entered Dyatkovo but was halted by heavy fire from elements of 6th Panzer and 14th Motorised Divisions.

15 December 1941

NORTHERN SECTOR

The 1st Korp completed its withdrawal to the Volkhov and, together with 38th Korp, fought to prevent the Red Army from crossing the river. Despite their efforts, the Soviets gained a bridgehead south of Lake Ladoga, threatening to break the ring around Leningrad.

CENTRAL SECTOR

After a bitter battle, the Germans were forced back into Kalinin, fierce street battles erupting as 29th and 31st Armies pushed into the town. Klin fell to 365th and 371st Rifle Divisions of 30th Army and 348th Rifle Division, 50th and 84th Rifle Brigades of 1st Shock Armies after running battles during the night. The 3rd Panzer Army was retreating in disarray. Farther south 2nd Guards Cavalry Corp, operating ahead of 5th Army, cut the German line of retreat west of Zvenigorod, forcing 4th Panzer Group to accelerate the pace of its withdrawal.

> *The battle around Klin had virtually destroyed the cohesion of the panzer forces north of Moscow. Amid terrible winter conditions, with engines frozen solid and weapons inoperable, the Germans could not counter the Soviet attacks. Never had a modern Western army encountered such difficult conditions and yet the Wehrmacht fought on, the struggle having taken on a brutality that forbade any quarter.*

16 December 1941

CENTRAL SECTOR

Ninth Army was unable to hold its positions on the Volga and gave up Kalinin. The 31st and 29th Armies forced the Germans to the Volga between Lake Selinger and Kalinin, threatening to expose the northern flank of Army Group Centre. Soviet forces claimed to have inflicted 10,000 casualties on the Germans at Kalinin.

The West Front transferred 30th Army to Kalinin Front, to bring greater pressure to bear upon the rear of 9th Army. The 39th Army was allocated to Kalinin Front from the High Command reserve.

Group Chanchibadze was ten miles north-east of Volokolamsk, while Group Remizov, now under 20th Army direction, was nine miles west of the Istra reservoir. Katukov was nearly fifteen miles west of Istra. These units were forcing 46th Panzer Korp back to the west. To the south, Dedilovo fell to Group Belov and Bogoroditsk to 10th Army.

17 December 1941

NORTHERN SECTOR
Meretskov's Volkhov Front was officially activated. The new front comprised 4th, 52nd, 59th and 2nd Shock Armies, the latter having only recently been raised around the core of 26th Army. To the left of Volkhov Front was Kurochkin's North-West Front, deployed between Lake Ilmen and Ostashkov with 11th Army, 34th Army, 3rd Shock Army and 4th Shock Army, the latter having been formed around the old 27th Army.

SOUTHERN SECTOR
Manstein began a new attack in the Crimea, aiming to destroy the Soviet forces isolated in Sevastopol. At 0800 hours an overwhelming artillery barrage, supported by air strikes, struck the Soviet positions. German infantry moved closely behind the rolling artillery barrage, hitting the Soviet defences hard. On the northern perimeter, 30th Korp was pinned down in the Belbek Valley and suffered heavy casualties, while to the south 54th Korp made minor gains before also being halted by sustained machine-gun and artillery fire.

18 December 1941

CENTRAL SECTOR
The West Front launched a series of frontal attacks aimed at pinning 4th Army and preventing the transfer of reinforcements from the centre to the flanks. The 5th, 33rd, 43rd and 49th Armies attacked, but 33rd and 43rd Armies were soon bogged down along the Nara river and at Naro-Fominsk.

Zhukov ordered 50th Army to thrust towards Kaluga. The army formed Group Popov (one rifle, one tank and one cavalry divisions) to punch through the gap between 43rd Korp and 2nd Panzer Army. The

Stavka reactivated the Bryansk Front commanded by Cherevichenko. The front incorporated 61st, 3rd and 13th Armies and Group Kostenko, with a strength of eighteen rifle and seven cavalry divisions, two tank, one rifle and one motorised rifle brigades. The Stavka planned to use the Bryansk Front to penetrate the southern wing of the Moscow axis while also maintaining the line between the West and South West Fronts. General Malinovsky took over command of the South Front following Cherevichenko's move to the centre.

19 December 1941

CENTRAL SECTOR
Groups Katukov and Remizov outflanked Volokolamsk from the north and south-east. The right flank of 4th Army was on the brink of collapse as Soviet attacks pounded the German lines. Forty-seventh Panzer and 53rd Korps of 2nd Panzer Army were forced back across the Plava.

Belov's 2nd Guards Cavalry Corp was ordered to break into the German rear and advance upon Yukhnow to destabilise 4th Army. The 10th Army was to support the attack, securing the group's flanks at Sukhinichi and Mosalsk.

SOUTHERN SECTOR
Heavy fighting raged around Sevastopol as 11th Army launched repeated attacks against the seemingly impregnable Soviet positions. Kozlov's Trans-Caucasus Front was responsible for the defence of Sevastopol but could do little to aid the port.

GERMAN COMMAND
Field Marshal Brauchitsch, having tendered his resignation, was formally relieved of his post. Hitler decided to appoint himself Commander in Chief of the Army.

20 December 1941

CENTRAL SECTOR
Volokolamsk fell to Groups Remizov and Katukov, while 2nd Guards Cavalry Corp of 5th Army pushed to Zvenigorod. The Soviets had drawn up to the Lama, Ruza and Moskva rivers, but were being held by 78th Infantry Division, 46th Panzer Korp, 11th Panzer Division and 7th Korp.

Group Popov was in sight of Kaluga, 43rd Korp having fallen back to the North-West and 2nd Panzer Army to the south-west. Elements of 10th Army pushed west towards Odoyevo and Livny, having crossed the Plava.

The 39th Army joined the Kalinin Front.

GERMAN COMMAND
Under the mantle of Commander in Chief of the German Army, Hitler instructed the Ostheer to fight on its present positions, no further retreat west being permitted. The success of this order probably saved Army Group Centre from defeat before Moscow.

On the home front, Goebbels issued an appeal to the civilian population to donate winter clothing to the Ostheer. The response from the German people was tremendous but only a fraction ever reached the soldiers at the front, the bulk being claimed by the men of the rear.

21 December 1941

NORTHERN SECTOR
Budogosh fell as the Germans retreated to the Volkhov.

CENTRAL SECTOR
Popov Group stormed Kaluga, 31st Cavalry Division penetrating into the town only to be thrown back by 137th Infantry Division. This division had been given strict orders to hold Kaluga, and following the Soviet attack, counter-attacked and encircled Group Popov. Fiftieth Army attempted to push through to Kaluga but was held back by the Germans.

Group Belov attacked towards Odoyevo and Yukhnow, while elements of 10th Army pushed towards Kozelsk and Sukhinichi.

SOUTHERN SECTOR
The battle for Sevastopol reached its peak as the Germans broke through the positions of 40th Cavalry Division north-east of Severnaya Bay. Only the hasty commitment of reserves prevented the collapse of the position.

22 December 1941

CENTRAL SECTOR
Kalinin Front prepared to launch a new offensive with 22nd, 39th, 29th, 31st and 30th Armies, the aim being to destroy the German forces around Rzhev. The front deployed thirty rifle and five cavalry divisions and two tank brigades.[1]

23 December 1941

SOUTHERN SECTOR
Heavy fighting raged at Sevastopol as the Germans pounded the city with artillery and sustained attacks.

24 December 1941

CENTRAL SECTOR

Second Army withdrew from Livny and Chern as 10th Army piled pressure on the exposed German southern flank.

The Bryansk Front became officially operational but was well below its regulation strength, many of its divisions having as few as four thousand men.

25 December 1941

NORTHERN SECTOR

With temperatures well below zero, the citizens of Leningrad struggled to endure the privations of the siege. On this single day, 3,700 people died of starvation, hypothermia or exhaustion.

CENTRAL SECTOR

Against the northern wing of Army Group Centre 39th Army completed its concentration, having brought together five rifle divisions. Other Soviet attacks began to falter, 20th and 16th Armies stalling as they tried to cross the Lama and Ruza rivers.

Guderian became the latest victim of Hitler's purge, being dismissed from 2nd Panzer Army. Hitler condemned Guderian for his failure to halt the Soviet attacks, an unreasonable charge given the exhausted state of his army. General Schmidt was appointed to command 2nd Panzer.

SOUTHERN SECTOR

With German attention fixed firmly upon Sevastopol, the Soviets prepared to launch an offensive into the Kerch peninsula. Units of the Trans-Caucasian Front aided by the Azov Flotilla set sail from the Kuban in two groups which were to land north and south of Kerch. Group A comprised 44th Army with 23,000 men, thirty tanks and 130 artillery pieces, while Group B had 3,000 men of 44th Army together with 13,000 of 51st Army. The landing was due to begin on 26 December.

26 December 1941

CENTRAL SECTOR

On the northern flank, the Soviets launched a new attack with 39th Army. The attack fell around Rzhev and aimed to break the centre of 9th Army. Farther south, despite repulsing and encircling the Popov Group, the hard-pressed forces of 2nd Panzer Army relinquished control of Kaluga to 50th Army.

SOUTHERN SECTOR
Manstein launched more attacks upon Sevastopol but failed to break the Soviet positions. Later in the day, the Soviets began the Kerch–Feodosia operation. Elements of 51st Army landed north of Kerch, while a smaller component of 44th Army went ashore at Cape Opuk, near Feodosia. Both units were able to gain a firm foothold despite the horrendous conditions, and proceeded to attack 42nd Korp's single infantry division. Sponek requested permission to withdraw to the Ak-Monai narrows but was instead ordered to launch an immediate counter-attack and drive the Soviet forces into the sea.

27 December 1941

NORTHERN SECTOR
Soviet troops reached the Volkhov at Kirishi, clearing the Germans of all their gains on the east bank of the river.

SOUTHERN SECTOR
The 42nd Korp counter-attacked north of Kerch and succeeded in inflicting heavy casualties upon the Soviet forces. The Germans were unable to clear up the Soviet bridgeheads because of a lack of strength, enabling the Soviets to land reinforcements and strengthen those units that were already ashore.

28 December 1941

SOUTHERN SECTOR
Manstein continued to attack Sevastopol, gaining territory around Fort Stalin. Fighting on the Kerch peninsula resulted in the destruction of Soviet forces south of Kerch, but those to the north could not be dislodged. Sponek again requested permission to fall back to the Ak-Monai narrows but was overruled by Manstein, who knew the only chance of defeating this new threat was to push the Soviets back into the sea before they became well established on the peninsula.

29 December 1941

SOUTHERN SECTOR
Another force of 23,000 men of 44th Army landed in the Crimea. The new landing came ashore at Feodosia, where German defences were virtually non-existent, consisting mainly of Rumanian forces and rear area personnel. The Soviets threw the Rumanians back and established a firm bridgehead, threatening the rear of 42nd Korp. With his rear open and his force in danger of being isolated, Sponek took immediate action and

withdrew from the peninsula to the Ak-Monai narrows, the withdrawal beginning during the night of 29–30 December. With this new danger to his rear, Manstein suspended attacks upon Sevastopol and began to move 30th Korp east to the aid of 42nd Korp.

30 December 1941

SOUTHERN SECTOR
The Soviets poured forces into the Crimea as 42nd Korp retreated to the Ak-Monai narrows, fighting rear guard battles as it fell back.

31 December 1941

NORTHERN SECTOR
More than 52,000 civilians had perished in Leningrad during December, testimony to the severity of the weather and the terrible conditions of the siege. The fighting along the Volkhov since 10 November cost the Soviets dear, 54th Army losing 6,000 killed and 11,000 wounded, 4th Army nearly 9,000 killed and 16,000 wounded, and 52nd Army 1,000 killed and 2,000 missing. The Novgorod Group lost a further 2,000 killed and 1,700 wounded.[2]

CENTRAL SECTOR
Kozelsk fell to 10th Army. The Soviet forces were becoming increasingly weak. Rokossovsky reported that 16th Army had suffered heavy casualties, many battalions being down to a few hundred soldiers. The Bryansk Front reported that its units were burnt out, 3rd Army numbering 16,000 men and 138 artillery pieces while 13th Army had 11,800 men and eighty-two artillery pieces.[3]

SOUTHERN SECTOR
Fighting intensified as 42nd Korp was attacked at Feodosia. Having already begun the transfer of 30th Korp, Manstein had no option but to suspend offensive action around Sevastopol. At Feodosia the Soviets had already landed 40,500 men, 236 artillery pieces and forty-three tanks.[4]

THE OSTHEER, DECEMBER 1941
During December the Germans committed three infantry divisions to the front, bringing their strength up to nineteen panzer, fifteen motorised and one hundred and six infantry divisions.[5] The Luftwaffe had 2,500 aircraft in the east against the same number of Soviet planes. Luftwaffe losses since June 1941 totalled nearly 2,100 aircraft destroyed and 1,300 badly damaged.

Across the eastern front, Germany's allies deployed twenty-nine divisions, four Rumanian divisions and six brigades, three Hungarian divisions, three Italian, two Slovak and one Spanish divisions and sixteen Finnish divisions.

Germany lost another 40,000 killed in the east during December, bringing the total number of troops killed during 1941 in the east to 302,000.

SOVIET CASUALTIES
The Red Army and Navy lost 1,007,996 killed and missing and 648,521 wounded during the final quarter of 1941.[6]

PRODUCTION
During 1941 the Germans produced 3,790 tanks and self-propelled guns, 11,200 artillery pieces, 51,085 trucks and 11,776 aircraft. The Soviets produced 6,590 tanks, 42,300 artillery pieces and 15,735 aircraft.[7] German oil production totalled 5,700,000 tons of natural oil and 3,900,000 tons of synthetic oil while 5,800,000 tons were consumed.

1 January 1942

SOUTHERN SECTOR
Timoshenko unleashed his assault in the Ukraine. Planning to attack all along his sector, Bryansk Front was to attack towards Kursk and Orel with 3rd, 13th and 61st Armies in conjunction with 21st and 40th Armies on the northern wing of the South-West Front. South-West Front was to attack with 38th and 6th Armies in the Chuguyev–Balakleya–Izyum area to capture Kharkov and Krasnograd. The South Front, with 57th, 37th and 9th Armies was to attack towards Pavlograd and seize Dnepropotrovsk and Zaporozhe. The 57th was to push through Barvenkovo to Pavlograd, while 37th Army attacked towards Bolshoi Tokmak. Fifty-first and 44th Armies were to continue their offensive in the Crimea.

The offensive began at dawn, heavy fighting erupting along the Siem river as 40th and 21st Armies launched vigorous attacks towards Oboyan and Kursk. The left wing of 40th pushed twenty miles into the German positions, while 21st Army cut the Belgorod–Kursk road.

In the Crimea, 42nd Korp counter-attacked but was unable to crush the Soviet bridgehead at Feodosia. The 42nd was too weak to destroy the Soviet force.

2 January 1942

CENTRAL SECTOR
North-West Front received new orders for operations against Army Groups North and Centre. The 3rd and 4th Shock Armies were to seize Ostashkov

and Toropets and smash the junction of two army groups. The attack was planned for 9 January and aimed to destroy the northern wing of Army Group Centre, completing the envelopment of the German armies before Moscow. Already hard-pressed by the Kalinin Front, 9th Army requested permission to withdraw from its positions on the Volga to a shorter line to the rear. Hitler categorically forbade a withdrawal, ordering 9th to hold its line. To the south, West Front recaptured Maloyaroslavets as 4th Army fell back.

SOUTHERN SECTOR
The fighting on the Kerch peninsula had cost the Soviets 30,000 killed and missing and 7,700 wounded of 62,000 originally committed. The Soviets also lost thirty-five tanks, 133 artillery pieces and thirty-nine aircraft.[8]

3 January 1942

CENTRAL SECTOR
Elements of 10th Army encircled 4,000 men of 216th Infantry Division in Sukhinichi. The beleaguered force, only recently arrived from the West, was attacked by tank and infantry forces and brought under sustained artillery fire. Despite its inexperience the division held, compelling the Soviets to divert forces from their westward drive.

SOUTHERN SECTOR
South-West Front attacked 6th Army around Kharkov but with little success. Timoshenko ordered the 21st and 38th Armies to take Belgorod by the 5th. In the Crimea, 44th and 51st Armies attacked at Feodosia and Kerch.

Zhukov's concentrated and directed assault against Army Group Centre had successfully, over the course of a month, forced the Germans to relinquish territory at great cost. However, with the road to victory partially traversed, Stalin undertook to reconquer all. Despite the protests of Zhukov, the Stalin offensives were about to begin and the gains of the past month would be squandered in localised attacks from the frozen north to the Don in the south.

5 January 1942

NORTHERN SECTOR
The Volkhov Front began a series of probing attacks along the line of the Volkhov, testing German defences. Within the next few days the front would unleash a new offensive to smash the right flank of 18th.

CENTRAL SECTOR
Belev fell to 10th Army.

SOUTHERN SECTOR
As the Soviet attacks began to bog down, Timoshenko launched a new thrust towards Belgorod with 38th Army. The attack was aimed at dislodging the Germans north of Kharkov and bringing about the collapse of Army Group South. However, the Germans were aware of Soviet intentions around Belgorod and launched strong counter-attacks against 21st Army.

In the Crimea, Soviet forces launched new landings at Sudak and Evpatoriya but the now alert German units repelled them.

SOVIET COMMAND
Buoyed by the successes of the offensive in the centre, Stalin called a meeting of the Stavka to plan the next phase of operations. He aimed to expand attacks along the entire front, but Zhukov wanted to push the offensive against Army Group Centre. Stalin overruled him and proceeded with a larger offensive.

6 January 1941

NORTHERN SECTOR
In line with Stalin's plan, the Volkhov Front continued making probing attacks, searching for weaknesses in the German defences before the main offensive was launched.

CENTRAL SECTOR
The month-long Soviet offensive in the centre had cost the Red Army heavily. The Western Front had lost 102,000 killed and missing and 160,000 wounded, the Kalinin Front 27,000 and 55,000 respectively, the South-West Front's 3rd and 13th Armies 10,000 killed and 12,000 wounded and the Bryansk Front 1,300 killed and 4,200 wounded. Equipment losses had also been heavy, the Fronts losing 429 tanks, 13,000 artillery pieces and 140 aircraft.[9]

SOUTHERN SECTOR
The 38th Army fought its way slowly towards Belgorod, while 21st and 40th Armies pressed their attacks against the German defences before Kharkov.

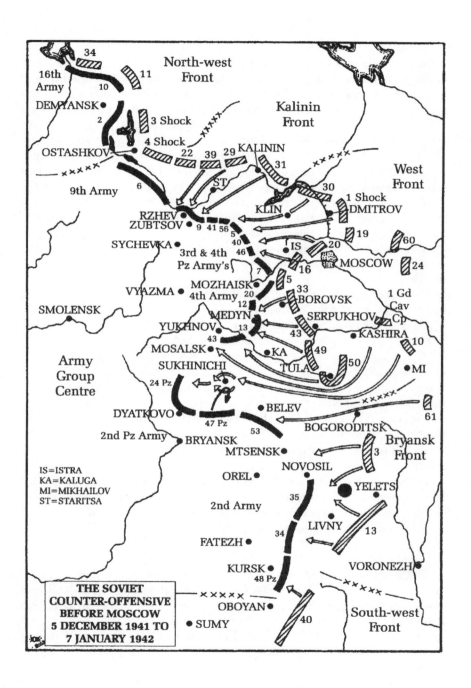

THE SOVIET
COUNTER-OFFENSIVE
BEFORE MOSCOW
5 DECEMBER 1941 TO
7 JANUARY 1942

7 January 1942

NORTHERN SECTOR
To the accompaniment of massed artillery fire, the Volkhov Front launched its offensive along the Volkhov. Fierce fighting developed as the partially deployed 2nd Shock and 59th Armies attacked 1st and 38th Korps. The hastily prepared Soviet attacks failed to penetrate the German positions.

South of Lake Ilmen, the North-West Front began probing attacks against 10th and 2nd Korps of 16th Army, concentrating its efforts in the 11th Army sector near Staraya Russa. The Germans had recently brought 18th Motorised Division down to this sector and in heavy fighting it inflicted severe casualties upon the Soviet units. For the operation the Soviets assembled 106,000 men between 1st Shock, 11th, 34th and 53rd Armies. The 3rd SS *Totenkopf*, 30th and 290th Infantry Divisions absorbed the main force of the Soviet attacks. All three divisions lost considerable numbers during the fighting.

CENTRAL SECTOR
Kalinin Front reached the Volga near Rzhev, having mauled six German divisions during the fight around the town.

The Bryansk Front renewed its attacks in the Bolkhov–Orel–Kromy area with 61st Army. The 3rd and 13th Armies would join the attack shortly.

8 January 1942

NORTHERN SECTOR
The Volkhov Front continued to attack with 2nd Shock, 59th and 52nd Armies but was unable to break the German defences. Both 1st and 38th Korps put up bitter resistance, preventing even minor penetrations of the front line.

North-West Front launched further probing attacks against 16th Army, which resulted in unexpected successes. The 2nd Korp, deployed near Lake Selinger was severely mauled and began to crack, two divisions having been destroyed in the heavy fighting.

CENTRAL SECTOR
The 39th Army attacked west of Rzhev, while 29th Army pinned down 9th Army around the town. However, the 9th repulsed most of the Soviet attacks, preventing the capture of Rzhev. West of Moscow, 5th and 33rd Armies struck around Mozhaisk but were repelled by 4th Army. There was heavy fighting at Sukhinichi as 10th Army launched repeated attacks against 216th Infantry Division.

The Stavka issued new instructions to the Kalinin Front. While 39th Army crushed the Germans at Rzhev, 30th Army was to pin down and destroy 9th

Army at Sychevka. To fully develop the attacks by 39th Army, the Stavka allocated 11th Guards Cavalry Corp as reinforcement. The 22nd Army was to cut the Rzhev–Velikiye Luki railway line at Nelidovo and exploit these gains in the direction of Belyi. The Kalinin Front had available 346,000 men.

New directives were also issued to the West Front, calling for 1st Shock, 20th and 16th Armies to break open 4th Panzer Army at Volokolamsk and push on to Gzhatsk. As these attacks developed, 5th Army (seven rifle, one motorised divisions, three rifle brigades and one tank brigade) and 33rd Army (seven rifle and one guards motorised divisions) would attack 4th Army before Mozhaisk. To the south 43rd, 49th (six rifle divisions, four rifle brigades and two tank brigades) and 50th Armies and Group Belov were to push to the north-west and reach Vyazma, penetrating the southern wing and rear of 4th Army. Tenth Army continued its westward advance on the southern flank, separating 4th Army from 2nd Panzer Army. To carry out its attack West Front had 713,000 men

On the southern wing the Bryansk Front began its offensive around Bolkhov, committing 317,000 men to the operation.

SOUTHERN SECTOR
Heavy fighting raged before Kharkov as 38th, 40th and 21st Armies pressed home their attacks with little success.

9 January 1942

NORTHERN SECTOR
The 3rd and 4th Shock Armies began to attack across the frozen surface of Lake Selinger but encountered fierce resistance from 16th Army. Third Shock planned to punch through the German defences and advance upon Kholm and Velikiye Luki, crushing the southern flank of 16th Army, while 4th Shock Army exploited the hole in the German line and rushed forward to storm Vitebsk. The 22nd Army provided support on the left flank. As the North-West Front increased the pressure upon the right wing of 16th Army, the German defences at Peno, near Andreapol, began to crumble. Elements of 11th Army penetrated into the German rear and closed up to Staraya Russa.

CENTRAL SECTOR
Bitter fighting continued at Rzhev as 29th and 39th Armies pounded 9th Army. The Germans threw back each Soviet attack, albeit with heavy casualties. Farther south, 49th Army was involved in heavy fighting as it advanced towards Vyazma, while 10th Army stormed Lyudinovo, taking the town after a fierce battle with 2nd Panzer Army. The 10th Army was ordered to take Kirov and then cut the Vyazma–Bryansk railway. The 3rd and 13th Armies joined the 61st Army attacks upon Bolkhov.

10 January 1942

NORTHERN SECTOR
The attacks of 2nd Shock and 59th Armies failed to open the German defences along the Volkhov and died down. Sokolov was sacked from command of 2nd Shock and replaced with Klykov. The Soviets prepared to renew the attack in the next few days, this time in conjunction with an attack by the Leningrad Front from the Neva river. It was hoped that this attack would draw the Germans away from the Volkhov, enabling Meretskov to effect a breakthrough. On the southern flank, the offensive by North-West Front progressed slowly as 3rd and 4th Shock Armies smashed their way through the strong German defences north of Lake Selinger.

CENTRAL SCTOR
The 39th Army pushed south past Rzhev, having torn a hole in the German line. Twenty-ninth Army continued to attack Rzhev itself.

SOUTHERN SECTOR
The German 6th Army launched a ferocious counter-attack against the flanks of 21st and 40th Armies, disrupting the Soviet attacks and compelling them to move forces to meet this new threat. Germans broke into the rear of 21st Army and smashed the junction of the two armies during the day.

11 January 1942

NORTHERN SECTOR
A lull settled over the Volkhov as the Soviets regrouped. To the south, 3rd and 4th Shock Armies continued to attack 16th Army, but only made slow progress.

CENTRAL SECTOR
The 11th Cavalry Corp (three cavalry and one guards motorised divisions and 6,000 men) passed through the gap created by 39th Army, pushing south towards Vyazma. Simultaneously, 29th Army launched new attacks upon Rzhev but failed to enter the town. To the south, 10th Army took Kirov and pushed on to Zhizdra and Chiplyavea. The 216th Infantry Division continued to hold at Sukhinichi.

SOUTHERN SECTOR
The counter-attack by 6th Army around Kharkov inflicted heavy casualties upon 21st and 40th Armies, while in the Crimea 44th and 51st Armies tried to break the German line near Feodosia, albeit unsuccessfully.

12 January 1942

NORTHERN SECTOR
The Leningrad and Volkhov Fronts began probing attacks east of Leningrad in preparation for Operation Iskra, the effort to break the siege of the city. Farther south, 16th Army struggled against the attacks of North-West Front, finding it increasingly difficult to prevent the penetration of its front line by 3rd and 4th Shock Armies. Leeb requested permission to pull his forces back as the 2nd and 10th Korps were in imminent danger of collapse. Hitler ordered Leeb to stand fast, withdrawal being strictly prohibited. Angered by the decision, Leeb requested that he be relieved of his command.

13 January 1942

NORTHERN SECTOR
Leningrad and Volkhov Fronts renewed their offensive. Near Lake Ladoga, 54th Army attacked towards Pogoste and Tosno. However, alongside 54th Army the 4th Army was hit by German attacks and forced onto the defensive. Elements of 2nd Shock and 52nd Armies struck 38th Korp near Gruzino establishing minor bridgeheads across the Volkhov. Heavy fighting raged at Mostki, Spasskaya-Polist and Zemtitsky as the Soviets encountered strong German defensive positions. On either flank, 59th and the remainder of 52nd Armies met with little success, failing to push forward from their start lines.

South of Lake Ilmen, 11th Army continued to fight around Staraya Russa, while 3rd and 4th Shock Armies slashed at 16th Army, striking 10th and 2nd Korps hard. Despite a spirited defence, the German line began to crack.

CENTRAL SECTOR
Heavy fighting raged around Rzhev as 29th and 39th Armies pressed deeper into the positions of 9th Army, while 20th and 1st Shock Armies, with 2nd Guards Cavalry Corp in support, overcame the German defences around Volokolamsk. Furious fighting ensued as the Soviet units pressed into and through the town, pushing 4th Panzer Army back. The 4th Panzer lost contact with 4th Army to its south, 33rd Army cutting its lateral communications as it advanced upon Vyazma.

14 January 1942

NORTHERN SECTOR
Near Leningrad 54th and 4th Armies both attacked but only made minor gains. Along the Volkhov, 2nd Shock, 59th and 52nd Armies only managed

to advance yards against 1st and 38th Korps. Farther south, 4th Shock Army finally began to make progress into the positions of 16th Army before Andreapol.

CENTRAL SECTOR
Bitter fighting raged at Rzhev as 22nd, 29th and 39th Armies threw repeated attacks against 9th Army. Medyn fell to 43rd Army as the West Front maintained the pressure against the centre and south of 4th Army.

SOUTHERN SECTOR
In the Crimea, 30th Korp had redeployed to the Kerch peninsula and prepared to strike the Soviet forces around Feodosia. Manstein planned to smash the newly landed Soviet forces and push them back to Kerch.

15 January 1942

NORTHERN SECTOR
After bitter fighting, 4th Shock Army penetrated the German line at Andreapol and pushed into tile rear of Army Groups North and Centre.
   The Germans fell back in order to evade encirclement, fighting running battles with the advancing Soviets as they went.

SOUTHERN SECTOR
The 11th Army unleashed its attack upon the Soviets around Feodosia. Elements of 30th Korp struck 44th Army, fighting intensifying during the day as the Germans pushed into the Soviet positions. Luftwaffe attacks hit the headquarters of 44th Army, wounding its commander. The 44th and 51st Armies began to fall back to the Ak-Monai narrows.

16 January 1942

NORTHERN SECTOR
The remnants of the Andreapol garrison succumbed to the attacks of 4th Shock Army after a bitter struggle, while the main elements of 10th Korp retreated to Toropets.

CENTRAL SECTOR
The Soviets drop a force of 400 paratroops at Myatlevo, capturing the airfield near the town. Fierce German resistance disrupted further Soviets attacks.

SOUTHERN SECTOR
Ferocious battles raged around Feodosia as 30th Korp smashed 44th Army, inflicting heavy casualties. The Germans closed up to the port while pushing the attack east towards Kerch.

17 January 1942

NORTHERN SECTOR
Leeb was dismissed as commander of Army Group North, mainly due to his disagreement with Hitler over the withdrawal of 16th Army. Kuchler was appointed to command the army group and Lindemann took over 18th Army.

Amid heavy fighting, 16th Army fell back from its positions north of Lake Selinger. The collapse of the front endangered the entire German position as the rear of Army Group Centre was exposed to envelopment.

Kurochkin suggested that 11th Army be reinforced and moved from Staraya Russa to Kholm to seal off the German forces at Demyansk. The Stavka accepted this in principle, but maintained that the main task of 11th Army was to push to Soltsy with its 1st and 2nd Guards Rifle Corps and into the German rear at Pskov.

CENTRAL SECTOR
Model assumed command of 9th Army, Strauss having reported sick a few days earlier. Army Group Centre attempted to rebuild its left flank following the collapse of 16th Army, withdrawing 3rd Panzer Army from the Rzhev salient to new positions between 16th and 9th Armies. The success of Soviet attacks in this area increased the need for a speedy re-deployment, the Germans having nothing with which to plug the gap torn in their line. In due course 59th Korp would go into action after it completed its long journey from France.

SOUTHERN SECTOR
Feodosia fell to 11th Army, 10,000 Soviet prisoners being taken. With additional casualties of 7,000 killed, the 44th Army was in tatters. The fall of Feodosia partially restored the German position on the Kerch peninsula, prompting Hitler to order the immediate dismissal and arrest of General von Sponek. His withdrawal from Kerch in late December resulted in a charge of cowardice in the face of the enemy, from which he was lucky to escape with his life. Army Group South also lost its commander as Field Marshal von Reichenau died unexpectedly of a heart attack.

18 January 1942

NORTHERN SECTOR
On the shores of Lake Ladoga, 18th Army struggled to hold off fierce Soviet attacks, being pushed out of Schlusselberg. With this minor victory the Red Army created a narrow corridor through to Leningrad. However, the corridor was barely half a mile wide and under continuous German artillery fire and aerial attack.

To the south, 16th Army fell back upon Toropets following its defeat at Andreapol, both 3rd and 4th Shock Armies extending their attacks into the German flank, threatening to unhinge the junction of Army Groups North and Centre. The remnants of the Andreapol garrison reached Toropets after a harrowing march. Barely forty men from the original force had survived the bitter cold and incessant Soviet attacks during the retreat.

CENTRAL SECTOR
The Soviets made another attempt to disrupt the rear of Army Group Centre by landing 450 paratroops between Yukhnow and Vyazma, near Znamenka-Zhelanie. Two battalions of 201st Airborne Brigade, totalling 1,600 men, landed twenty-five miles south of the town over the next four days. The majority of the men were lost during the drop, fewer than four hundred surviving to fight on.

SOUTHERN SECTOR
South-West and South Fronts launched new attacks as 38th Army attacked towards Kharkov and 6th, 57th, 9th and 37th Armies pushed upon Krasnograd and Pavlograd. The two fronts attacked with 204,000 troops.[10]
    In the Crimea, the 11th Army flushed out those elements of 44th Army that remained in Feodosia.

GERMAN COMMAND
Following the death of Field Marshal von Reichenau, von Bock was appointed to command the forces of Army Group South. Bock, only recently relieved from command of Army Group Centre after being blamed by Hitler for the failure to reach Moscow, was tasked with halting the Soviet attacks around Kharkov and the stabilisation of the German line on the Donets and Mius.

19 January 1942

CENTRAL SECTOR
The Germans brought the 59th Korp forward to Vitebsk in an effort to rebuild the shattered left flank of Army Group Centre. Thirty-third Army recaptured Veriya. Zhukov directed 5th Army towards Gzhatsk and 33rd to Vyazma. The German 4th Army had pinned its defences upon these two locations. To the rear, Soviet paras effected a junction with elements of 49th Army near Myatlevo, other units of this army capturing Kandorovo. More Soviet paratroops landed in the rear of 9th and 4th Armies near Vyazma.
    The 2nd Panzer began a counter-attack against the left wing of 10th Army with 208th infantry and 4th and 18th Panzer Divisions, the eventual

aim being the relief of Sukhinichi. Heavy fighting raged around Lyudinovo, where the Germans forced the 322nd Rifle Division out of the town.

Koniev issued new orders to his armies, ordering 22nd to secure the right wing and rear of 39th and 29th Armies, 29th to take Rzhev, 39th to destroy the Germans at Sychevka, 31st to push towards Zubtsov, 3rd Shock to advance on Velikiye Luki and 4th Shock on Velizh.

SOVIET COMMAND

Stalin began to interfere in the conduct of offensive operations. North-West Front was instructed to hand over 3rd and 4th Shock Armies to Kalinin Front; 1st Shock Army was moved up from the West Front area of operations to North-West Front at Staraya Russa, to be ready to take the offensive on 6 February. The North-West Front would also receive two rifle divisions and two brigades to aid the assault east of the town. Kurochkin argued to retain 3rd Shock but failed to change Stalin's mind.

20 January 1942

NORTHERN SECTOR

Soviet forces crossed the Lovat and attacked Staraya Russa. The town held, but German forces east of the Lovat were increasingly exposed to Soviet attacks. Fierce counter-attacks by the 3rd SS *Totenkopf* and 18th Motorised Divisions inflicted heavy losses upon the 11th Army.

To the south, 4th Shock Army attacked Toropets. Bitter fighting ensued as the Soviets forced the Germans out of the town. Huge quantities of munitions and supplies fell to the Soviets, who were in dire need of replenishment.

CENTRAL SECTOR

Mozhaisk fell to 5th Army as West Front pounded the centre of 4th Army. Kubler was dismissed from command of 4th Army following its string of defeats. Heinrici, commanding 43rd Korp, was appointed in his place. The 11th Cavalry Corp resumed its southward attacks. Paratroops again landed in the rear of 4th and 9th Armies but casualties were heavy as terrible weather dispersed the force through the dense forests.

21 January 1942

NORTHERN SECTOR

Second Shock Army increased its attacks on the Volkhov, bringing up additional artillery and infantry units. The Germans responded by also increasing their forces in this sector. The attack by 54th Army had ground to a halt, as had 4th Army. The 52nd Army continued to attack towards Novgorod and Soltsy but with little success.

The Stavka reformed 8th Army from elements of 54th Army fighting east of Leningrad. The new 8th fought on the southern shore of Lake Ladoga, while the old 8th continued its struggle in the Oranienbaum pocket.

Attacks by 3rd and 4th Shock Armies pushed deeper into the northern flank of Army Group Centre. Lead elements of 3rd Shock encircled the Germans at Kholm, threatening to overwhelm the southern wing of 16th Army. A scratch force of 3,500 men under Major Scherer was trapped in the town but held on for the next four months against repeated Soviet attacks.

CENTRAL SECTOR
Yet more paratroops dropped behind the German lines near Vyazma, bringing their number to more than 1,600. Zhukov decided to drop the complete 4th Airborne Corp into battle.

The Stavka began to withdraw forces from the central sector during mid-January. The 1st Shock and 16th Armies were taken out of the line and began to move north and south. As Zhukov predicted, the net result was to bring the attack against 9th and 4th Armies to a halt.

22 January 1942

NORTHERN SECTOR
The 16th Army partially stabilised its southern wing as Group Scherer anchored it at Kholm. Fighting around the town was heavy as 3rd Shock launched fierce attacks in an effort to annihilate the German force.

CENTRAL SECTOR
Fifty-ninth Korp dug in before Velikiye Luki to secure the junction of Army Groups North and Centre. To the east 39th Army launched attacks at Osuga and Sychevka, but 9th Army was able to hold on to both towns. However, the 39th and 29th Armies were themselves brought under attack as 23rd Korp, isolated at Olenino, forced its way out of encirclement and advanced towards 6th Korp west of Rzhev. Attacks by 46th Panzer Korp re-established some stability in other 9th Army sectors.

SOUTHERN SECTOR
The Soviet 6th and 57th Armies punched a twenty-mile deep salient and penetrated to Balakleya and Slavyansk. An infantry division held each town against strong attacks by 6th Army. Stalled, the Soviets introduced 1st and 6th Cavalry Corps into the battle along the Krasny Liman–Slavyansk axis. The 5th Cavalry Corp operated with 57th Army in an effort to take Barvenkovo.

SOVIET COMMAND
The 3rd and 4th Shock Armies transferred to Kalinin Front command as the Stavka redeployed its armies.

23 January 1942

NORTHERN SECTOR
There was heavy fighting along the Volkhov as 2nd Shock Army launched repeated attacks. Bitter fighting also raged in Kholm as hand-to-hand battles swept the ruined streets of the town.

CENTRAL SECTOR
The 6th and 23rd Korps linked up, cutting Kalinin Front in two. The 22nd, 30th, 31st and part of 29th Armies were north of the Volga, while 39th and the remainder of 29th, together with 11th Cavalry Corp were encircled south and south-west of Rzhev, between Chertolino and Sychevka.[11] The 22nd, 30th and 31st Armies launched strong attacks, almost succeeding in isolating Rzhev. To the south, 2nd Panzer Army drew closer to Sukhinichi.

24 January 1942

NORTHERN SECTOR
Second Shock Army broke through the German defences on the Volkhov, pushing towards Lyuban. The 13th Cavalry Corp, with two divisions, supported by a rifle division, surged forward to Yelyine. On the flanks of the half-mile wide penetration, 52nd and 59th Armies launched fierce attacks but were pinned down by accurate counter-fire. Farther south, there was intense fighting at Kholm as 3rd Shock hit Group Scherer repeatedly. Scherer repelled each attack and held on to the town.

CENTRAL SECTOR
Ninth Army began to pound the encircled 29th and 39th Armies but lacked the strength to finish off the isolated units. On the southern wing, 208th Infantry Division linked up with 216th in Sukhinichi, relieving the hard-pressed garrison.

The Soviets raised a new 16th Army to the left of 10th Army, taking five rifle divisions from the latter unit. The 10th was left with just three divisions. The new force was designed to increase the pressure upon the southern wing of 4th Army and advance north-west to link up with the Kalinin Front near Smolensk. The original 16th Army was broken up, being split between other armies.

SOUTHERN SECTOR
Lead units of 38th and 6th Armies and 6th Cavalry Corp crossed the Donets south of Kharkov in an effort to outflank the German defences south of the city. To blast his way through Army Group South, Timoshenko placed 9th Army between 37th and 57th Armies. Barvenkovo fell to 9th Army. Reinforcements were committed, the Stavka allocating more than 300 tanks to strengthen Timoshenko's armies.

25 January 1942

NORTHERN SECTOR
Bitter fighting raged along the Volkhov as 2nd Shock Army tried to widen the breach in the 18th Army line. The 52nd and 59th Armies also attacked on the flanks. German fire pinned the Soviet units, preventing further penetration.
   The 1st and 2nd Guards Rifle Corp of 34th Army and elements of 3rd Shock launched heavy attacks at Staraya Russa but failed to push forward to Soltsy. To the south, Group Scherer was heavily attacked at Kholm by other units of 3rd Shock.

CENTRAL SECTOR
Soviet forces closed in upon Velikiye Luki, but 59th Korp had established blocking positions, albeit with less than adequate forces. Heavy fighting raged on the approaches to the city as the Germans struggled to prevent the disintegration of Army Group Centre's northern wing. The 3rd Panzer Army continued to withdraw from the Rzhev sector as 9th Army took responsibility for the tip of the salient. Third Panzer redeployed onto the left flank to prop up the front between 16th and 9th Armies. Farther south 47th Panzer Korp attacked 10th Army near Sukhinichi but was unable to advance.

26 January 1942

CENTRAL SECTOR
Fourth Shock Army threw screening forces around Velizh, isolating the garrison and increasing the threat to the northern wing of Army Group Centre. The 11th Cavalry Corp reached the Moscow highway north-west of Vyazma but could not take the town and was forced onto the defensive.

SOUTHERN SECTOR
Bock regrouped his forces to hold the line of the Donets and prevent a Soviet penetration to the Dniepr. Command of 17th Army was subordinated to 1st Panzer Army, henceforth referred to as Group Kleist. Kleist

was made responsible for the defence of the line from the Izyum salient to the Azov coast. Group Mackensen was formed around 3rd Panzer Korp to provide 17th Army with its own armoured component and protect its left flank. As the fighting continued Soviet 6th Army and 6th Cavalry Corp cut the Kharkov–Lozovaya road.

27 January 1942

NORTHERN SECTOR
Fourth Shock Army launched heavy attacks upon Velizh while other units moved upon Demidov.

CENTRAL. SECTOR
The Soviets concentrated for an all-out assault upon Vyazma, 11th Cavalry moving from the north, Group Belov from the south-west and 33rd Army from the east. As a prelude to the attack, 4th Airborne Corp began to drop west of Vyazma.

SOUTHERN SECTOR
Soviet 6th Army and 6th Cavalry Corp captured Lozovaya.

28 January 1942

CENTRAL SECTOR
Ninth Army counter-attacked with 46th Panzer Korp, aiming to restore positions in the Rzhev salient. On the extreme left wing, 4th Shock Army attacked Velizh but could not encircle the town, which was held by elements of 59th Korp.

The Luftwaffe attacked Soviet air bases near Kaluga where 4th Airborne Corp assembled for its drop at Vyazma.

SOUTHERN SECTOR
Groups Mackensen and Kleist counter-attacked to prevent further Soviet progress along the road to Dnepropetrovsk, while in the Crimea the Stavka activated a new Crimean Front under General Kozlov. The Stavka was planning to launch a major attack in the Crimea, using 44th Army along the coastal road to push into the rear of the Germans at Sevastopol. A second assault force was to land at Sudak. The attack was scheduled to start on 13 February.

29 January 1942

CENTRAL SECTOR
Soviet forces encircled Velizh. Fierce artillery fire and air strikes pounded

Group Sinzinger, which was cut off inside the town. Sinzinger had 3,000 men to the 30,000 Soviets.

Soviet airdrops around Vyazma were abandoned because of the casualties suffered at Kaluga during the Luftwaffe attacks, in addition to heavy casualties in the drop zone. Sukhinichi was given up as 2nd Panzer Army pulled back to stronger positions. Tenth and 16th Armies moved in as the Germans retreated.

SOUTHERN SECTOR
Following bitter fighting over the previous few days, 3rd Panzer Korp began to move up to the Kramatorsk and Krasnoarmiesk sectors, positioning itself across the line of the Soviet advance, in an effort to prevent any further gains on the road to the Dniepr.

30 January 1942

NORTHERN SECTOR
Heavy fighting raged along the southern shore of Lake Ilmen as 34th Army and 3rd Shock Army attacked the left flank of 16th Army. With the arrival of 1st Shock Army during the first days of February, the Soviet offensive to isolate and destroy 2nd Korp in the Demyansk sector would begin in earnest.

CENTRAL SECTOR
The threat to the northern flank of Army Group Centre grew as Soviet units, having bypassed Velizh, moved towards Demidov. The 59th Korp threw units out along an increasing line in order to shore up the flank of the army group and prevent Soviet forces flooding into the rear. Heavy fighting continued around Velizh as 4th Shock attempted to storm the town. Sinzinger held out against the odds, repulsing each new attack.

31 January 1942

SOUTHERN SECTOR
During the Barvenkovo–Lozovaya Offensive Operation the South and South-West Fronts lost 11,095 killed and missing and 29,786 wounded.[12]

The Germans had by this time largely contained the Soviet offensive around Kharkov.

GERMAN DEPLOYMENT
During January the Germans committed seven infantry and two security divisions to the fighting. No divisions left the line but many were well below their regulation strengths. As an example the 23rd Infantry Division had around 1,000 men, while 106th had just 500 left in the combat line. The

4th Army had just thirty-two field guns and howitzers and twelve assault guns left at its disposal. The Germans had increased their commitment to nineteen panzer, fifteen motorised and one hundred and fifteen infantry divisions.[13]

During January 1942 the Germans lost 48,000 killed in the east.

1 February 1942

CENTRAL SECTOR
The 59th Korp was incorporated into 3rd Panzer Army. Third Panzer Army held Soviet attacks before Vitebsk, while between Rzhev and Vyazma 9th and 4th Armies stabilised their lines. Near Rzhev, 9th Army succeeded in encircling 29th and 39th Armies.

SOVIET COMMAND
The Stavka reactivated Glavkom West under Marshal Zhukov. The new theatre incorporated the West, Kalinin and Bryansk Fronts. Zhukov continued to command the West Front with Golikov as his deputy.

2 February 1942

NORTHERN SECTOR
Heavy fighting raged along the Volkhov as 18th Army pounded 2nd Shock Army. Neither 52nd nor 59th Armies were able to break through on the flanks, leaving 2nd Shock in isolation. Farther south, the fighting around Demyansk and in the Valdai Hills intensified as the Soviets struck the left flank of 16th Army. There was continued fighting around Kholm as Group Scherer repulsed repeated attacks by 3rd Shock Army.

3 February 1942

NORTHERN SECTOR
Lead units of 1st Shock Army entered the line east of Staraya Russa, deploying on the northern base of the exposed Demyansk salient.

CENTRAL SECTOR
Soviet forces encircling Velizh launched strong attacks in an effort to take the town, but Group Sinzinger repelled them each time. Continued Soviet thrusts though also encircled Demidov and began to hit Velikiye Luki and Surazh. Fighting was intense as both sides struggled in the minus forty degree centigrade temperatures. As fighting raged around Velizh, Demidov and Velikiye Luki, 9th Army redeployed its forces in the Rzhev sector. Model planned to strike at the exposed Soviet positions near Rzhev to break up the encircled elements of 29th and 39th Armies.

The 4th Panzer Army launched a ferocious counter-attack and closed the line between itself and 4th Army to the south. The result was the encirclement of Efremov's 33rd Army, together with the paratroops and men of 11th Cavalry Corp around Vyazma.

4 February 1942

CENTRAL SECTOR
As the Soviet situation around Vyazma deteriorated, Zhukov ordered a general attack upon the town in an effort to smash through the German defences. The 11th Cavalry Corp, only six miles to the west, was unable to make any progress, while to the south and south-east, Belov Group and 33rd Army fought in encirclement.

5 February 1942

CENTRAL SECTOR
As heavy attacks pounded Velizh and Demidov, 9th Army launched a concerted counter-attack, units from Olenino and Rzhev attacking and forcing apart the encircled 29th and 39th Armies. The bulk of 29th Army was lost during the fighting, only 5,000 men escaping to the tenuous safety of 39th Army. The Germans also attacked 39th Army, preventing it from lending any support to the hard-pressed 29th. Soviet forces outside the pocket launched a new attack upon Rzhev but could not break through the firmly established German positions. There were also fierce battles around Vyazma.

6 February 1942

CENTRAL SECTOR
The 4th Shock Army launched strong attacks against Velizh, almost succeeding in breaking into the centre, but Group Sinzinger repelled the attack after close quarters fighting. The Germans were hampered by the extreme cold, lack of food and warm clothing, and scarcity of ammunition, Sinzinger's men becoming weaker with each day. Army Group Centre decided that the situation must be restored as quickly as possible and both Demidov and Velizh relieved. The heavy fighting in the Rzhev and Vyazma sectors continued without pause as the Germans piled pressure on the encircled Soviet units.

The 3rd and 4th Shock Armies had lost 10,400 killed and missing and 18,810 wounded during the month long Toropets-Kholm Offensive Operation.[14]

7 February 1942

NORTHERN SECTOR
Soviet forces smashed through the base of the Demyansk salient and penetrated into the rear of 16th Army. Elements of 3rd Shock Army, 11th and 34th Armies drew closer together, and the encirclement of 2nd Korp and part of 10th Korp became imminent.

CENTRAL SECTOR
The 59th Korp attempted to relieve the encircled battle groups at Velizh and Demidov, elements of 4th Shock Army fighting fiercely near Dukhovschina. The 3rd Panzer Army was unable to support 59th Korp. Further bitter fighting raged around Rzhev as the Soviets tried to overrun the town. The 9th Army beat off each attempt, inflicting heavy casualties upon Koniev's tired armies.

GERMAN COMMAND
Minister Todt, in charge of war production and munitions, was killed in a flying accident. Albert Speer was appointed his successor. Formerly Hitler's personal architect, Speer overhauled the German war industry and increased production substantially, particularly in the latter years of the war. It was under his auspices that German industry was placed on a war footing, leading to total war.

8 February 1942

NORTHERN SECTOR
Lead elements of 1st Shock and 11th Armies linked up near Saluchi and Ramushevo on the Lovat, encircling 2nd Korp and part of 10th Korp of 16th Army. Over 90,000 men in 12th, 30th, 32nd, 123rd and 290th Infantry Divisions and part of 3rd SS Motorised Division *Totenkopf* were cut off in the Valdai Hills and became reliant upon Luftwaffe supply drops. It was estimated that the trapped force needed a minimum of 200 tonnes of supplies per day to stay in action. The Luftwaffe would succeed in reaching this figure and on some days exceed it by upwards of 100 tonnes. The surrounding Soviet forces, despite having suffered heavy casualties during the fighting, launched strong attacks upon the German pocket. There was further heavy fighting around Kholm as Group Scherer was pounded by elements of 3rd Shock Army.

The isolation of the 2nd Korp around Demyansk was crucial in a number of respects. Primarily it proved that the Red Army was able to effectively carry out an offensive operation which led to the isolation of sizeable enemy forces. However, at this early stage of the campaign, the Soviet forces lacked both the expertise and the strength needed to destroy the surrounded units.

Secondly, the pocket presented the Germans with a unique problem. A force of nearly 100,000 men had never been supplied solely from the air and the airlift that followed was to lay the foundation for a defeat of catastrophic proportions later in the year. Had Demyansk not occurred, Hitler's decision to accept Goering's assurances over the success of the Stalingrad airlift might never have been taken. Little did the combatants realise the importance of this diversionary battle.

CENTRAL SECTOR
The Soviets pressed 59th Korp hard as the fighting at Velizh, Demidov, Dukhovschina and Velikiye Luki intensified.

9 February 1942

NORTHERN SECTOR
There was heavy fighting along the Volkhov as 18th Army pounded the 2nd Shock Army in its vulnerable salient. The Soviets dug in around the Demyansk pocket and prepared to attack the encircled forces.

10 February 1942

NORTHERN SECTOR
Heavy fighting raged along the road to Staraya Russa as the Soviets attempted to push the remnants of 10th Korp away from the Demyansk group. There were also bitter battles around the pocket as the Soviets attacked the encircled force. General Bockdorff-Ahlenfeldt coordinated the defence of the pocket but was at the mercy of the Luftwaffe. Goering and the OKL (Oberkommando der Luftwaffe) assured Hitler that the Demyansk pocket would be supplied by air transport and that the evacuation of the 2nd and 10th Korps to the west would be averted. Hitler ordered the immediate implementation of supply missions. The 1st Air Fleet mustered 230 aircraft but barely one third were operational. Hitler expected a force of only seventy planes at best to keep a force of almost 100,000 men supplied with food, ammunition and fuel in the middle of the Soviet winter and under heavy attack.

As fighting in the Rzhev sector continued, 9th Army wrenching back the initiative from the Kalinin Front, the 4th Shock Army launched a bloody assault upon Velizh. After furious fighting the Soviets penetrated into the town, but Group Sinzinger counter-attacked and threw them back. The 3rd Panzer Army began its relief attack towards Velizh but progress was slow.

12 February 1942

NORTHERN SECTOR
The Germans began the Demyansk airlift, just as Soviet forces surrounding 16th Army began their artillery bombardment and launched probing attacks upon the perimeter of the pocket. Bitter fighting ensued, but the Germans held their positions in the majority of sectors.

CENTRAL SECTOR
The 4th Shock Army kept Group Sinzinger pinned down in Velizh with repeated infantry and tank assaults. The relief attacks towards the town continued but made slow progress in the deep snow and amid concerted Soviet counter-attacks. Farther east, 9th Army was involved in heavy fighting around Rzhev and Olenino as the German and Soviet forces launched repeated attacks. The Germans pounded 29th and 39th Armies, while the Kalinin Front attempted to smash those German units in the exposed Olenino salient.

13 February 1942

NORTHERN SECTOR
The Soviets threw 1st Shock Army into new attacks west towards the Polist river, the intention being the annihilation of German units deployed on the southern shores of Lake Ilmen, preventing the relief of the Demyansk pocket.

15 February 1942

NORTHERN SECTOR
In a bold attempt to bring about a decisive decision in the Demyansk pocket, the Soviets dropped paratroops behind the German lines. However, the Germans brought heavy fire to bear, inflicting terrible casualties. Virtually the entire force was lost and the few who did survive the landing were captured.

CENTRAL SECTOR
Soviet forces on the Moscow axis had been substantially reinforced during the first half of February. The Kalinin Front received seven new rifle divisions, a guards rifle corp and four air regiments, while West Front took over 60,000 men into its ranks, three rifle divisions, one guards rifle corp and two paracbute brigades. In line with the developing offensive, Zhukov issued a new set of directives to the forces of Glavkom West. The Kalinin Front was to capture the Olenino region with 22nd, 30th and 39th Armies, destroying German 9th Army. West Front was to attack

with its 43rd, 49th and 50th Armies, taking Yukhnow, and 16th and 61st Armies were to capture Bryansk. Simultaneously, 4th Airborne Corp was to complete its drop in the Yukhnow area to threaten the rear of German 4th Army. The 50th Army was to support the airborne forces, attacking towards Yukhnow.

At the front, Group Sinzinger came under fierce attack while new Soviet attacks pushed towards Surazh.

16 February 1942

CENTRAL SECTOR
The 59th Korp repulsed Soviet attacks towards Surazh, but at Demidov 4th Shock Army penetrated into the town.

17 February 1942

CENTRAL SECTOR
The German relief force from Velikiye Luki linked up with Group Sinzinger at Velizh. However, the 4th Shock Army remained at the gates, making an all-out effort to overrun the garrison before it could be reinforced. The 4th Shock also attempted to overcome Demidov, but again the Germans beat off each attack.

Fighting erupted around Rzhev as 30th and 39th Armies attempted to relieve the remnants of 29th Army trapped near the town. A counter-attack by 1st Panzer Division isolated 29th west of Rzhev. The Soviets attacked with 39th Army and 30th Army from the west and north to try to free 29th.

The next phase of Zhukov's attack began as 14th Airborne Brigade dropped west of Yukhnow. Losses were again heavy, many of the men being scattered on landing. Over the next few days, the Soviets would continue to drop paras into the Yukhnow area.

20 February 1942

CENTRAL SECTOR
Since 17 February the Soviets had landed nearly 7,000 paras west of Yukhnow but had been contained by the Germans.

22 February 1942

CENTRAL SECTOR
A relief attack towards Demidov began, while 9th Army attacked with 6th and 23rd Korps, pounding 29th, 30th and 39th Armies around Rzhev.

26 February 1942

NORTHERN SECTOR
The 2nd Shock and 54th Armies launched new attacks to break through to Lyuban, while 59th Army attacked towards Chudovo. Both armies fared badly as the Germans pinned down the attacking forces. The 2nd Shock penetrated the German positions at Krasnaya Gorka but was quickly brought to a halt. Meretskov proposed to strengthen 2nd Shock with 4th Guards Rifle Corp.

CENTRAL SECTOR
Heavy fighting raged at Velizh as 4th Shock Army launched repeated attacks.

27 February 1942

NORTHERN SECTOR
The Stavka ordered the Volkhov Front to form shock groups to break the German lines. The 2nd Shock formed a group of four divisions, 59th Army one of three divisions and 4th Army one of two divisions. Meretskov visited the 2nd Shock Army headquarters and found its command disorganised and demoralised. Vlassov was appointed commander in place of Klykov.

CENTRAL SECTOR
The relief attack towards Demidov succeeded, as the garrison was relieved.

SOUTHERN SECTOR
The Soviets began a new attack in the Crimea aimed at dislodging 11th Army from the Kerch peninsula and relieving Sevastopol. On the Kerch peninsula, 51st Army attacked in unwieldy columns, supported by tanks, but was smashed by German artillery fire and air strikes. The costly attacks continued for the next two weeks. The Sevastopol garrison also attacked but was unable to break through the ring of forces around the city.

28 February 1942

NORTHERN SECTOR
The Stavka ordered 2nd Shock and 54th Armies to link up and encircle the German forces in the Lubansk area.

CENTRAL SECTOR
The Germans launched a fierce counter-attack at Demidov, forcing back
4th Shock Army.

SOUTHERN SECTOR
The 51st Army repeated its attacks on the Kerch peninsula, suffering terrible casualties as 11th Army rained fire down upon it.

THE OSTHEER, FEBRUARY 1942
During February the Germans committed eight infantry divisions to the east,
bringing their strength up to nineteen panzer, fifteen motorised and one hundred and twenty three infantry divisions.[15] A casualty return by the Ostheer
recorded that up to the end of February the war in the east had cost 394,000
killed (44,000 in February), 725,000 wounded, 414,000 captured, 46,000 missing and 112,000 injured through frostbite and illnesses. Army Group Centre
alone had suffered a staggering 357,000 casualties but received only 130,000
replacements. The field armies had also lost 3,240 tanks and assault guns
but received only 840 replacement vehicles. This left the panzer divisions
with fewer than 900 vehicles, of which only 465 were operational. Combined
with the depletion of its offensive capability, the supply and logistic services
had lost 74,000 motor vehicles since October 1941 but replaced only 7,500.
The already inadequate motor pool had been reduced to less then a quarter
of its June 1941 complement. Since the beginning of Operation Typhoon in
October '41, the Ostheer also lost 180,000 horses but replaced only 20,000.

1 March 1942

NORTHERN SECTOR
Vlassov took command of 2nd Shock Army as Klykov reported sick.

3 March 1942

SOUTHERN SECTOR
The 51st Army wore itself out after heavy fighting and terrible casualties.

5 March 1942

CENTRAL SECTOR
West Front captured Yukhnow after a bitter struggle.

7 March 1942

SOUTHERN SECTOR
Elements of Moskalenko's 38th Army attacked German positions north of

Kharkov. After heavy fighting, a bridgehead was secured on the west bank of the Northern Donets.

11 March 1942

SOUTHERN SECTOR
Four days of fierce fighting had seen the 38th Army extend its bridgehead north of Kharkov. Stubborn German resistance had brought the advance to a halt.

13 March 1942

SOUTHERN SECTOR
The 51st Army had regrouped to renew attacks on the Kerch peninsula. In all, eight rifle divisions and two tank brigades struck 11th Army, but again the Germans repelled the waves of tanks and infantry. Casualties continued to mount as the attacks were pressed home repeatedly. In the three days between the 13th and the 15th, the 51st and 44th Armies lost over 130 tanks to the German guns.

15 March 1942

GERMAN CASUALTIES
Since 1 January the Ostheer had suffered 240,000 casualties, an average loss rate of 3,200 men per day.

19 March 1942

NORTHERN SECTOR
The 18th Army launched a furious counter-attack on the Volkhov, closing the net around 2nd Shock Army and encircling 130,000 men.

The Germans prepared to launch a relief attack towards 2nd and 10th Korps at Demyansk from Staraya Russa. A shock group under General Seydlitz-Kurzbach with 5th and 8th Light and 122nd, 127th and 329th Infantry Divisions, aimed to fight their way through the waist-deep snow along the southern shores of Lake Ilmen to effect a junction with the pocket.

20 March 1942

SOUTHERN SECTOR
Manstein committed 22nd Panzer Division to the fighting on the Kerch peninsula but the new and inexperienced division suffered a severe mauling. However, the German counter-attack succeeded in breaking up new Soviet assaults, giving 42nd Korp a brief respite.

SOVIET COMMAND
The Stavka revised its orders to the Kalinin and West Fronts. The objectives were to reach the line Belyi–Dorogobuzh–Elnya–Krasnoye by mid April. By the end of March, the West Front was to establish contact with those units in the German rear, while 5th Army was to capture Gzhatsk. The 5th would then cooperate with 43rd, 49th and 50th Armies to take Vyazma and the 61st and 16th Armies Bryansk. Kalinin Front was to take Rzhev using 29th, 30th, 39th and 31st Armies and then cooperate with 22nd Army to destroy the Germans around Olenino. Group Kolpakchy, a force of five rifle divisions, was to take Belyi.

21 March 1942

NORTHERN SECTOR
Seydlitz-Kurzbach began the relief attack towards Demyansk. The Germans had to overcome the Soviets around Staraya Russa before advancing towards the pocket. Heavy fighting raged around the town over the next few days as the Germans met furious resistance from the firmly dug in 11th and 1st Shock Armies.

24 March 1942

CENTRAL SECTOR
The encircled 33rd Army and Group Belov were ordered to fight their way free and effect a junction with 50th Army.

26 March 1942

SOUTHERN SECTOR
The Soviets renewed their offensive on the Kerch peninsula, but immediately their leading units encountered strong resistance and suffered heavy casualties.

NORTHERN SECTOR
The German counter-attack south-east of Staraya Russa began to make headway as the junction of 11th and 1st Shock Armies was breached.

31 March 1942

NORTHERN SECTOR
The Soviets punched a corridor through to 2nd Shock Army but could not free the starving army. Farther south, the fighting on the road to Demyansk continued as the Germans slowly progressed towards 2nd and 10th Korps.

GERMAN DEPLOYMENT

During March the Ostheer committed two panzer and four infantry divisions to the front, bringing its field strength to twenty-one panzer, fifteen motorised and one hundred and twenty-seven infantry divisions.[16] Since June '41 the Panzerwaffe in the East had lost 3,486 tanks but replaced just 873. The German tank strength stood at 1,503 vehicles.

During March the Ostheer lost 44,000 men killed.

THE SOVIET ARMED FORCES

The Red Army and Navy lost 675,315 killed and missing in action and 1,179,457 wounded during the first quarter of 1942.[17] Soviet tank strength stood at 4,690 vehicles.

Soviet Command raised the ADD (Long-Range Aviation). This was the bomber arm of the Soviet air force and was independent of the combat fronts. It was commanded by Golovanov.[18]

In the north, the Volkhov Front was downgraded to an Operational Group under command of Khozin's Leningrad Front. Meretskov was given command of 33rd Army and made deputy commander of the West Front.

ASSESSMENT: 7 JANUARY–31 MARCH 1942

The fighting in the east between January and March 1942 witnessed a remarkable turn around in the fortunes of the two combatants. It was apparent that the Stalin Offensive had failed to bring about the destruction of the German forces in the east. The dispersal of the Soviet strength from the centre diluted the weight of the blow, which could have resulted in the destruction of Army Group Centre. Combined with this, since the front wide offensive began, the Red Army lost in excess of 330,000 killed, 1,000 tanks and 1,000 artillery pieces destroyed and more importantly, the chance the destroy Army Group Centre.

Since the Soviet counter-offensive before Moscow had begun, the Germans lost 900,000 men, including 110,000 killed and missing and 268,000 wounded but in return received only 450,000 reinforcements.

As spring took its grip on Russia, the opposing armies took the opportunity to reflect and rebuild. The Ostheer, so sure of victory in 1941, had entered 1942 on the back foot, fighting for its very survival in the face of fanatical Soviet attacks. The Red Army meanwhile had begun the long road towards victory. Stalin and the Higher Command were in the very early stages of mastery of the operational art, while the lower units remained unsophisticated, in contrast the German army operated with spirit and élan at its base but was uncoordinated at its head, led by a dictator who increasingly ignored the ability of his commanders. Such trends were to develop on both sides of the combat line as the year and the war progressed, each dictator still tasting defeat and victory in equal measure in the immediate future.

1 April 1942

NORTHERN SECTOR
The Germans resumed their attack towards the Demyansk. The 2nd Korp came under intense Soviet attack.

SOUTHERN SECTOR
The Soviets were building up their forces in the south in preparation for their offensive around Izyum. South-West Front deployed the 21st Army (three rifle and one motorised divisions, one rifle brigade), 38th Army (ten rifle and three cavalry divisions) and 6th Army (seven rifle divisions, one cavalry division and two tank brigades) in the pocket while the headquarters of the 28th Army, together with seven rifle divisions and two tank brigades, were in reserve. Covering the southern face of the pocket were the thirteen rifle divisions of the 57th and 9th Armies and nine cavalry divisions, one rifle and six tank brigades of the 2nd, 5th and 6th Cavalry Corps of the South Front. The 37th, 12th, 18th and 56th Armies, totalling eighteen rifle divisions, six rifle brigades and three tank brigades, completed the line to the Azov Sea.[19]

Covering the Kharkov sector the Germans deployed the 29th, 17th, 51st and 8th Korps of the 6th Army and 4th Rumanian Korp of the 17th Army. In all the 6th had on the Kharkov axis sixteen infantry divisions and two tank divisions. Facing the South Front the Germans fielded twenty-six divisions. These units formed Group Kleist, made up from the 17th Army and 1st Parizer Army. On the Mius was the 14th Panzer Korp (two infantry, two panzer and the 1st and 5th SS Motorised Divisions) while to its north, covering the river line to Dehaltsevo, were three Italian divisions and the 49th Mountain Korp (one infantry, one mountain and one Slovak divisions). From Slavyansk to Debaitsevo were the nine infantry divisions of the 44th, 4th and 52nd Korps, while the 3rd Panzer Korp was against the southern face of the Barvenkovo pocket.[20]

5 April 1942

GERMAN COMMAND
Hitler had made the decision to concentrate the German effort during 1942 on the southern sector of the front. Directive 41 called for rapid advances into the Caucasus and the capture of the Soviet oil refineries and production centres near Maikop and Grozny. Without these supplies secured, Hitler maintained that Germany would not be able to prosecute the war past the end of 1943. As the planning continued, the armies at the front pushed on with their relief attacks.

SOVIET COMMAND
The 40th Army, with five rifle divisions, was allocated to Golikov's Bryansk Front.

9 April 1942

SOUTHERN SECTOR
The Soviets renewed their offensive in the Crimea, attacking on the Kerch peninsula with eight rifle divisions, supported by one hundred and fifty tanks. Yet again the Soviets attacked with waves of infantry. This attack was a prelude to the next phase of the Soviet offensive.

11 April 1942

SOUTHERN SECTOR
In an effort to turn the rear of 11th Army, a new force went ashore at Evpatoriya. The Germans were prepared for such a move and repelled the Soviet landing. But this time the attack at Kerch also failed and was called off.

14 April 1942

CENTRAL SECTOR
There was renewed fighting near Vyazma as 50th Army launched a strong attack to free the encircled 33rd Army and Group Belov. Initial progress was good; by afternoon leading elements of 50th Army were only three miles from Group Belov, having taken the Zaitsevo heights by storm. The Luftwaffe then entered the battle, launching a crushing attack upon the advancing units. Repeated assaults inflicted crippling casualties, forcing 50th Army to fall back.

15 April 1945

CENTRAL SECTOR
The Germans launched a series of furious attacks against Soviet partisans and paratroops trapped in the Dorogobuzh area.

18 April 1942

CENTRAL SECTOR
Bitter fighting saw the destruction of the Paras and partisans at Dorogobuzh, partially clearing the lines of communication to the Rzhev salient. The 33rd Army was brought under heavy attack.

19 April 1942

CENTRAL SECTOR
The remnants of 33rd Army tried to break out east but were trapped, many men being killed in the ensuing fighting. Minor elements did succeed in reaching the 43rd Army, but by far the bulk of the 33rd together with its commanding officer, General Efremov, fell in the battle.

20 April 1942

NORTHERN SECTOR
Lead elements of Seydlitz-Kurzbach's relief force made a tentative link with the Demyansk pocket. The SS *Totenkopf* Division, fighting its way west from inside the pocket, established a bridgehead on the Lovat as the forces inside the pocket attacked to the west.

CENTRAL SECTOR
The Bryansk Front had lost 21,319 killed and missing plus 39,807 wounded since the beginning of January.[21]

21 April 1942

NORTHERN SECTOR
The Demyansk pocket was relieved as elements of the relief force linked up with 2nd Korp.
   Govorov was appointed to command the Leningrad Front, while Khozin was placed in command of the Volkhov Group.

SOUTHERN SECTOR
General Golikov, commanding Bryansk Front, received orders from the Stavka to assemble a new 48th and reinforce 40th Armies in the Kursk and Lgov areas for a counter-attack against the northern flank of Army Group South. The Bryansk Front had 61st, 3rd, 13th and 40th Armies with twenty-three rifle divisions and three tank brigades. Stalin believed the next German offensive would come in the centre.

23 April 1942

CENTRAL SECTOR
Golikov received further orders, ordering him to also concentrate 61st and 48th Armies for a concentric attack upon Orel. Golikov doubted whether he could complete the assembly of his forces in time and requested more time to prepare.

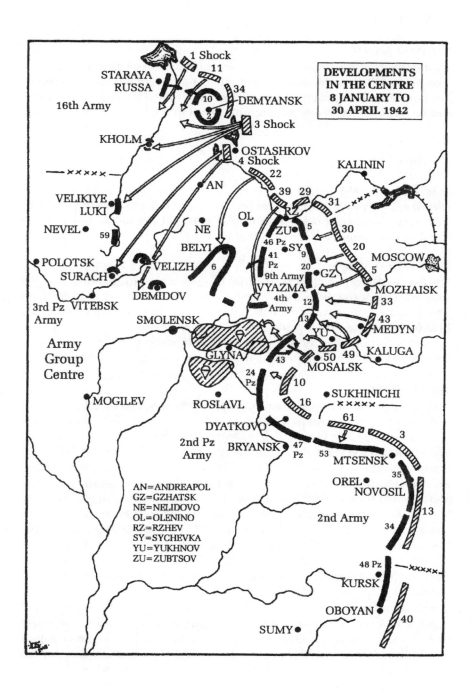

STARAYA
RUSSA

16th Army

KHOLM

VELIKIYE
LUKI

NEVEL

POLOTSK
SURACH

3rd Pz VITEBSK
Army

Army
Group
Centre

MOGILEV

1 Shock
11
34
10
2
DEMYANSK
3 Shock

OSTASHKOV
4 Shock
22

KALININ

AN
OL
NE
BELYI
59
VELIZH
DEMIDOV
SMOLENSK

39 29
RZ
ZU
46 Pz
41
Pz
9th Army
VYAZMA
4th
Army
GLYNA
24
Pz
43

31
5
30
20
SY 9
20
GZ
12
13
YU
50 49
MOSALSK
10

MOSCOW
5
MOZHAISK
33
43
MEDYN
KALUGA

ROSLAVL
16
SUKHINICHI
×××××
61

DYATKOVO
2nd Pz BRYANSK 47
Army   Pz

53

MTSENSK
OREL
NOVOSIL

2nd Army

3
35
13
34

48 Pz ×××××
KURSK

OBOYAN 40

SUMY

AN=ANDREAPOL
GZ=GZHATSK
NE=NELIDOVO
OL=OLENINO
RZ=RZHEV
SY=SYCHEVKA
YU=YUKHNOV
ZU=ZUBTSOV

DEVELOPMENTS
IN THE CENTRE
8 JANUARY TO
30 APRIL 1942

24 April 1942

FINLAND AND NORWAY
After a quiet period, the war on the Finnish front erupted once more as 26th Army launched a fierce attack in the Kastenga area with three rifle divisions. The Finnish 3rd Korp halted the Soviet thrust within three miles of the town and inflicted severe casualties. Fighting continued for the remainder of the month.

30 April 1942

NORTHEN SECTOR
The Volkhov and Leningrad Fronts concluded the Lyuban Offensive Operation, the battle having cost the Soviets 95,064 killed and missing and 213,303 wounded.[22]

CENTRAL SECTOR
The Soviet attacks in the centre since the beginning of January bled the armies on the Moscow axis dry. The Kalinin Front alone lost 123,400 killed and missing plus a further 217,800 wounded, while the West Front lost 149,000 killed and missing and 286,000 wounded.[23]

During April 4th Panzer Army had been withdrawn from the central sector and moved south to deploy on the northern wing of Army Group South.

THE OSTHEER
During April the Germans withdrew one panzer and one infantry division from the east, giving a total deployment of twenty panzer, fifteen motorised and one hundred and twenty-six infantry divisions.[24] The fighting during April had cost the Germans 23,000 killed. The Ostheer was short of 625,000 men, 7,000 anti-tank weapons and 200 artillery pieces. As Germany's allies moved east, the number of forces assembled rose considerably, making good the shortfall of German soldiers among the combat units. The Finns had 300,000 men in service, the bulk of whom were fighting near their homeland, while the Rumanians provided 330,000, the Hungarians 70,000 and the Italians 295,000. Other nations also sent consignments, Slovakia 28,000 men and Spain 14,000. By far the bulk of these forces were deployed on the southern sector to allow the Germans to deploy as great a number of soldiers as possible in the front line.

The German planned their next offensive for the south. Elements of 2nd Army and 4th Panzer Army were to smash the Bryansk Front and push east to Voronezh, where Don crossings were to be secured. The Germans would then swing south along the line of the Don. Simultaneously, 6th Army would begin its advance from the Kharkov area and push east to the Don, where it was to link up with 4th Panzer Army and, encircle the greater part of South West Front. The Germans then planned to push along the Don, 17th Army and 1st Panzer Army joining the offensive. As the Don elbow was cleared the Germans would advance to the Volga and take Stalingrad. The 4th and 1st Panzer Armies were then to push into the Caucasus to take the oilfields at Maikop and Grozny.

SOVIET COMMAND

The Red Army was building up its forces in the centre and south. Those in the centre were preparing to meet the expected renewal of the German thrust towards Moscow, while those in the south prepared to launch their own attack. During the latter half of April the Bryansk Front had received the 1st, 3rd, 4th and 6th Tank Corps, seven rifle divisions, eleven rifle brigades and four tank brigades. Some of these units had been used to form the new 48th Army.

Marshal Timoshenko's South-West Theatre had been substantially reinforced as both the South and South-West Fronts were re-equipped and fleshed out. The South-West Front would lead the offensive from the Izyum salient and crush the German forces around Kharkov before pushing on to the Dniepr. Soviet 6th Army would simultaneously advance towards Kharkov, while Group Bobkin moved from Izyum towards Krasnograd. The northern pincer was also to strike at the left wing of German 6th Army. This group planned to move from Volchansk with 28th, 21st and 38th Armies and envelop Kharkov in conjunction with 6th Army. South-West Front had at its disposal 640,000 men with 1,200 tanks and 13,000 artillery pieces, plus 900 aircraft in support.

Situated to the south was South Front, which was to secure the southern wing of the main offensive and aid the attack from the Izyum pocket. The 57th and 9th Armies planned to attack from the southern face of the salient and press towards the Dniepr, while the remainder of the front remained on its current positions along the Donets and Mius, holding the German forces frontally.

1 May 1942

NORTHERN SECTOR

The 39th Panzer Korp began a counter-attack aimed at relieving the long encircled garrison in Kholm.

The Demyansk Operation had cost the Soviet forces 88,908 killed and 156,603 wounded.[25]

5 May 1942

NORTHERN SECTOR

Lead units of 39th Panzer Korp were in sight of Kholm and, after a furious battle with 3rd Shock Army, broke through to relieve Group Scherer. The 103-day siege was broken, but the struggle had cost Group Scherer dear, over 1,500 men killed and 2,200 wounded. Barely 1,200 men of the original force remained fit for action. The siege had also cost the Luftwaffe significant losses. Some 252 Ju–52 planes were lost, but 65,000 tons of supplies were flown into the pocket together with 30,000 men. 35,000 wounded were also flown out of the battle.

CENTRAL SECTOR
Bryansk Front reported to the Stavka that it was unable to attack towards Orel as scheduled. Golikov requested a postponement until 16 May at the earliest, to which Stalin reluctantly agreed. However, the Stavka maintained that the attack must begin by the 16th, as the South-West Front offensive would be launched as planned on the 12th.

6 May 1942

SOUTHERN SECTOR
In the Crimea, the 11th Army prepared to wipe out the Soviet forces at Kerch and capture Sevastopol. Manstein had decided to deal with the Kerch concentration first, deploying the bulk of his strength here and leaving only thin covering forces to screen Sevastopol. Operation Bustard aimed to strike 44th and 51st Armies in their exposed forward positions, encircling the mass of the two armies on the narrow Isthmus. The Crimean Front deployed 249,800 men.[26] For the operation Manstein assembled 42nd, 7th Rumanian and 30th Korps, a force of five German and two Rumanian infantry divisions, one panzer division and one Rumanian cavalry division. To the west the 54th Korp covered Sevastopol.

8 May 1942

SOUTHERN SECTOR
Operation Bustard began as 30th Korp struck 44th Army frontally. Simultaneously, an assault force landed behind the coastal flank of 44th, unhinging the shaken Soviet defences. In the centre of the line, 42nd Korp also attacked but was held up in strong Soviet defences. After a brief battle the southern wing of 44th Army collapsed, enabling 30th Korp to introduce its mobile units into battle.

9 May 1942

SOUTHERN SECTOR
The 30th Korp pushed deep into the southern flank of 44th Army. The 22nd Panzer Division thrust through the Soviet line to overwhelm 51st

Army to the north. Just as the attack gained momentum, a heavy rain shower brought movement to a halt. This gave the Soviets a chance to pull back, which they took. However, only a fraction of 44th and 51st Armies managed to fight their way out to the Kuban.

10 May 1942

SOUTHERN SECTOR
At noon the weather in the Crimea cleared and the Germans resumed their attack. With its armies crumbling, the Stavka instructed the Crimean Front to pull back its forces to the Tartar Ditch. Manstein quickly overcame this position as he strove to complete the encirclement of 44th and 51st Armies.

GERMAN CASUALTIES
Field Marshal Halder estimated that since June 1941 the Ostheer had suffered 1,183,000 casualties.

11 May 1942

SOUTHERN SECTOR
In the Crimea the Germans pushed rapidly east with mobile forces, while the bulk of 30th Korp thrust into the rear of 51st Army. The 42nd and 7th Rumanian Cavalry Korps pinned the 51st frontally while 30th Korp penetrated into the rear. After just four days of intense fighting, the 44th Army had been virtually destroyed. Late in the day the 22nd Panzer Division reached the northern coast of the Kerch peninsula, isolating the bulk of 51st Army, some eight Soviet divisions.

> As the second summer campaigning season beckoned, Stalin aimed to continue the drive began in the winter. However, Hitler had laid his own plans for the summer, a summer that would see the German army achieve glory once again as it pushed eastward.

NOTES

1   Erickson, *The Road to Stalingrad*, p 285
2   Kirosheev, *Soviet Casualties and Combat Losses in the Twentieth Century*, Table 75
3   Erickson, *The Road to Stalingrad*, p 286
4   Erickson, *The Road to Stalingrad*, p 290
5   Ellis, *The World War Two Databook*, p 175
6   Kirosheev, *Soviet Casualties and Combat Losses in the Twentieth Century*, Table 67
7   Ellis, *The World War Two Databook*, pp 277–8

8   Kirosheev, *Soviet Casualties sod Combat Losses in the Twentieth Century*, Table 75
9   Kirosheev, *Soviet Casualties and Combat Losses in the Twentieth Century*, Table 75
10 Kirosheev, *Soviet Casualties and Combat Losses in the Twentieth Century*, Table 75
11 Erickson, *The Road to Stalingrad*, p 308
12 Kirosheev, *Soviet Casualties and Combat Losses in the Twentieth Century*, Table 75
13 Ellis, *The World War Two Databook*, p 175
14 Kirosheev, *Soviet Casualties and Combat Losses in the Twentieth Century*, Table 75
15 Ellis, *The World War Two Databook*, p 175
16 Ellis, *The World War Two Databook*, p 175
17 Kirosheev, *Soviet Casualties and Combat Losses in the Twentieth Century*, Table 67
18 Ellis, *The World War Two Databook*, p 82
19 Glantz, *Kharkov 1942*, p 41
20 Glantz, *Kharkov 1942*, pp 42–3
21 Kirosheev, *Soviet Casualties and Combat Losses in the Twentieth Century*, Table 75
22 Kirosheev, *Soviet Casualties and Combat Losses in the Twentieth Century*, Table 75
23 Kirosheev, *Soviet Casualties and Combat Losses in the Twentieth Century*, Table 75
24 Ellis, *The World War Two Databook*, p 175
25 Kirosheev, *Soviet Casualties and Combat Losses in the Twentieth Century*, Table 75
26 Kirosheev, *Soviet Casualties and Combat Losses in the Twentieth Century*, Table 75

CHAPTER VI
The March East Resumes

In the sun-drenched Ukraine, Timoshenko prepared to launch the second battle for Kharkov. Having massed more than three quarters of a million men and large quantities of equipment, the Soviet armies were sure of victory. But the Germans lay in wait, replenished and ready to attack. Hard fighting lay ahead before the real business of the summer could begin.

12 May 1942

SOUTHERN SECTOR

The South-West Front began its offensive to liberate Kharkov and throw Army Group South back to the Dniepr and Azov Sea. Over the previous month the Soviet forces around Kharkov had been heavily reinforced. The plan was for 6th Army to push towards Kharkov from the south, while Group Bobkin attacked towards Krasnograd, securing the southern flank of the 6th Army. 28th Army attacked from Volchansk, together with 21st and 38th Armies, flanking Kharkov from the north. While the South-West Front attacked, the South Front was to envelop the Germans from the south with its 9th and 57th Armies. The Soviet forces totalled 765,000 men, 1,200 tanks, 13,000 artillery pieces and 900 aircraft.

At 0630 hours the Soviet offensive north of Kharkov began with an hour-long artillery barrage. After the artillery fire subsided, the infantry and tanks of the 21st, 28th and 38th Armies attacked, only to encounter heavy fire from the infantry of the 17th and 51st Korps. During heavy fighting, the 38th Army managed to advance six miles, while the 21st had also pushed around six miles forwards. The spearhead 28th Army was struggling against fierce German resistance and had only managed to advance about two miles.

Despite their relatively successful defence, the 17th and 51st Korps had been taken by surprise by the Soviet attacks. Bitter fighting had seen the

294th Infantry Division of the 17th Korp suffer extremely high losses. In an effort to offer stability to their defensive positions, the 6th Army command began the movement of the 3rd and 23rd Panzer Divisions up to the Donets bridgehead from their positions around Kharkov.[1] These forces had been earmarked for the planned offensive south of Kharkov against the Izyum pocket.

As with the forces to the north, the Soviet offensive south of Kharkov began at 0630 hours with an hour-long artillery preparation. Following the barrage, elements of Gorodnyansky's 6th Army attacked the 51st and 8th Korps. The 62nd Infantry Division was hard-pressed by the left wing of the 6th Army south of Taranovka. On the southern wing of the Soviet 6th Army, Group Bobkin began its attack. Thrusting the 6th Cavalry Corp into the fighting, Bobkin virtually destroyed the 454th Security Division and reached the Orel river. By dusk the 6th Army and Group Bobkin had advanced up to ten miles on a twenty-five-mile front.

13 May 1942

NORTHERN SECTOR
The 52nd and 59th Armies launched repeated attacks in an effort to free the 2nd Shock Army. The three armies begin the operation with 231,900 men.[2]

SOUTHERN SECTOR
Soviet forces north of Kharkov renewed their attacks. Efforts by the 21st Army to expand its positions met fierce German resistance. However, leading Soviet units by-passed the German defences to advance south of Murom, pushing forward seven miles during the course of the day. The 38th Army also met with success, advancing some three miles by 1300 hours, but were then struck by strong German counter-attacks. Elements of the 3rd and 23rd Panzer Divisions had reached the forward Soviet positions and brought the advance to an abrupt halt. Heavy fighting inflicted severe losses upon the rifle units of the 38th, bringing its offensive to a complete halt. Realising the seriousness of the situation, Timoshenko ordered Moskalenko to place his 38th firmly on the defensive.

Heavy fighting south of Kharkov resumed once again as the Soviets renewed their attacks. 6th Cavalry Corp continued its drive into the defences of the 8th Korp towards Krasnograd, while the Soviet 6th Army established a strong bridgehead over the Orel river. Fierce fighting raged all day as the 8th and 51st Korps threw in repeated counter-attacks. With the success of their offensive towards Krasnograd, South-West Front command decided that it would commit its armour to this axis during the following day.

On the Kerch peninsula, lead elements of 11th Army drew closer to Kerch as 44th and 51st Armies, isolated to the rear, were destroyed.

14 May 1942

SOUTHERN SECTOR

Heavy fighting raged north of Kharkov. With the 38th Army stalled and the 28th struggling to make any gains at all, the Soviet offensive appeared to be on the verge of stalemate. German aviation had flooded the area and swept the Red Air Force from the skies. In turn the rear echelon of the 28th and 38th Armies were heavily attacked. Despite their best efforts, the men of the 28th Army managed only a three-mile advance before they were halted by the efforts of the 51st and 17th Korps. Further strong attacks by the 3rd and 23rd Panzer Divisions around Stary Saltov against the junction of the 28th and 38th Armies forced the southern wing of the Soviet attack back slightly.

After just three days of fighting, the offensive north of Kharkov had been decided. Soviet inaction on the Bryansk Front enabled the Germans to pull forces down from the north to strengthen their infantry units, while the panzers intended for their own offensive quashed the immediate danger.

Ferocious fighting raged along the line south of Kharkov. Soviet 6th Army continued to press the Taranovka axis and the northern wing of the 8th Korp hard, while Group Bobkin pushed along the Krasnograd axis with the 6th Cavalry Corp.

In the Crimea, the 170th Infantry Division entered Kerch, slicing through the Soviet defences. Manstein had comprehensively defeated a numerically superior force, leaving units on the Kerch peninsula to mop up isolated pockets of resistance before the redeployment of the main force to the Sevastopol perimeter.

15 May 1942

SOUTHERN SECTOR

The fighting north of Kharkov intensified as the Germans launched vigorous attacks with their 3rd and 23rd Panzer Divisions and supporting infantry. Heavy fighting compelled the 28th and 38th Armies to use their strength to fend off the German thrusts rather than continuing the offensive.

South of Kharkov, the Soviet 6th Army and Group Bobkin continued their offensive operations. By the end of the day, the 6th Cavalry Corp had closed upon Krasnograd, throwing back the defeated 454th Security Division. With his front advanced, Timoshenko prepared to commit his mobile forces in order to exploit the German rear. The threat of exploitation, coupled with the immediate danger to Krasnograd, placed the 6th and 17th Armies in a difficult situation, their lines of communication being threatened. Paulus continued to assemble infantry forces to bolster his positions.

With the main Soviet effort of the summer seemingly identified, the German High Command decided to bring forward its own offensive to overwhelm the South-West Front in a massive counter-attack. German Command had debated whether to abandon their attack in the south, but it was decided that an even greater victory could he achieved if the South West Theatre was nipped off in the deepening Izyum salient.

Kerch fell after a brisk battle with 170th Infantry Division, German troops attacking the docks to mop up the last pockets of Soviet resistance. The defeat cost the Crimea Front dear, 162,282 being killed or captured, 14,284 wounded and 1,100 artillery pieces, 260 tanks and 3,800 vehicles destroyed or lost to the Germans. Over 300 aircraft were shot down or destroyed, leaving the forces of the Crimean Front utterly shattered. Only 80,000 Soviet soldiers manage to escape across the Kerch straits to the Kuban. Kozlov, Chernyak and Kolganov, the army and front commanders, were recalled to Moscow and degraded in rank. The battle cost 11th Army only 7,500 casualties all told.

FINLAND AND NORWAY
The 36th Korp and Finnish 3rd Korp attacked 26th Army at Kastenga. The Soviets had recently reinforced their forces along the Finnish front and halted the Axis attack after a week of heavy fighting.

16 May 1942

CENTRAL SECTOR
Golikov's Bryansk Front offensive was called off until a later date.

SOUTHERN SECTOR
Despite plans to renew the offensive with 21st Army, the build up of German infantry and armoured forces opposite the Soviet offensive group compelled the 21st, 28th and 38th Armies to remain on the defensive. 21st Army attempted to launch offensive actions, but strong German coun-ter-thrusts forced Gordov to remain firmly on the defensive. Paulus' 6th Army offered stubborn resistance to Group Bobkin and Gorodnyansky's 6th Army in an effort to bring the Soviet advance to a halt. Limited gains continued however, as the Soviet armies brought their armoured forces forward and prepared to commit them to the offensive on the 17th. Fierce fighting raged at Krasnograd where the 6th Cavalry Corp attempted to break into the town. Repeated German counter-attacks in and around Krasnograd sapped the strength of the now over-extended Group Bobkin. Soviet 6th Army attacks towards Taranovka bogged down without any real gains. Once again the German defences thickened and the advance ground to a halt.

Throughout the entire time that South-West Front had been attacking the German lines, the South Front remained largely inactive and offered no assistance to the offensive. This failure to act prevented any release of forces to the main westward thrust, hampering the offensive.

On the flanks of the salient, Army Group South prepared to launch its own counter-offensive, aiming to envelop the bulk of the South-West Front, destroying it in a massive cauldron battle on the western bank of the Donets. The Germans planned to slice through the 9th Army on the southern face of the salient and force their way along the Donets, cutting off the Soviet forces from the river line. The 3rd Panzer Korp was deployed against this southern face of the salient with the 14th Panzer and 60th Motorised Divisions, 20th Rumanian Infantry and 1st Mountain Divisions. To the 3rd's right was the 44th Korp, situated around Slavyansk. This force deployed the 16th Panzer Division together with four infantry divisions. The 52nd Korp was east of Slavyansk with two infantry divisions. Together these three korps formed Group Kleist.

The final pockets of Soviet resistance in Kerch were wiped out as 11th Army consolidated its hold on the peninsula. Manstein immediately began to redeploy his forces for the next phase of operations in the Crimea – the long-planned and awaited attack upon the fortress of Sevastopol. With his rear secured by 42nd and 7th Rumanian Cavalry Korps, Manstein moved the bulk of his army to this battle while also bringing up the heaviest artillery pieces available to the Ostheer.

17 May 1942

CENTRAL SECTOR
Boldin was sent to Bryansk Front to instruct 40th Army to attack in order to aid the South-West Front. The 40th Army reported it was unable to attack.

SOUTHERN SECTOR
With elements of the 3rd Panzer Division deep into the junction of the 28th and 38th Armies, the Soviet assault units north of Kharkov were limited to trying to restore the junction of the two forces. However, even these efforts were disrupted as the Germans unleashed new attacks against the Soviet forces. German attacks pressed the Soviets back to the east, towards the northern Donets. In addition to the panzer forces hitting the front of the 28th Army, the fresh German 168th Infantry Division was now attacking the flank of the 21st Army, compelling it to fall back slowly. By now all the Soviet forces attacking north of Kharkov were on the defensive and many of them were slowly withdrawing under intense German pressure.

South of Kharkov, and facing the thus far quiet southern face of the Izyum salient, Group Kleist erupted into action. Following a ninety-minute artillery and aerial barrage, the Germans attacked between Barvenkovo

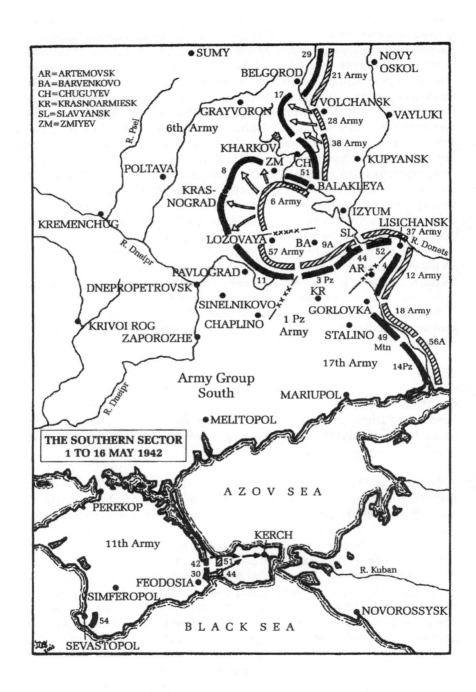

SUMY

AR=ARTEMOVSK
BA=BARVENKOVO
CH=CHUGUYEV
KR=KRASNOARMIESK
SL=SLAVYANSK
ZM=ZMIYEV

29

BELGOROD

NOVY
OSKOL

21 Army

R. Psel

17

VOLCHANSK

GRAYVORON

VAYLUKI

6th Army

28 Army

KHARKOV

38 Army

ZM CH

POLTAVA

8

51

KUPYANSK

KRAS-
NOGRAD

BALAKLEYA

6 Army

IZYUM

KREMENCHUG

LISICHANSK

R. Dneipr

LOZOVAYA

xxxxx

SL

37 Army

BA

9A

R. Donets

57 Army

44

52

PAVLOGRAD

11

AR

4

DNEPROPETROVSK

3 Pz

12 Army

SINELNIKOVO

KR

1 Pz

18 Army

KRIVOI ROG

CHAPLINO

GORLOVKA

ZAPOROZHE

Army

STALINO

49

56A

Mtn

17th Army

14Pz

Army Group
South

MARIUPOL

R. Dneipr

MELITOPOL

**THE SOUTHERN SECTOR
1 TO 16 MAY 1942**

A Z O V   S E A

PEREKOP

11th Army

KERCH

42

51

R. Kuban

30

44

FEODOSIA

SIMFEROPOL

54

B L A C K   S E A

SEVASTOPOL

and Slavyansk. Fierce fighting erupted as the German armour and infantry slammed into the 9th Army, puncturing its front line and pushing six miles into its rear in a few hours. Heavy air raids hit the command facilities of the army hard, compelling Kharitonov to abandon his forward command post. Contact with 57th Army was lost early in the battle. By noon tanks of the 14th Panzer Division had reached Barvenkovo, while the 44th Korp advanced from Slavyansk. As the fighting spread, the 14th Panzer overran the headquarters of the 57th Army. Despite a limited counter-attack by Pliev's 5th Cavalry Corp, the Germans scattered the Soviet officers. By evening Barvenkovo had fallen and the Germans prepared to push north to Izyum. A twelve-mile hole had been ripped in the Soviet line between the 57th and 9th Armies and German forces were up to twenty miles inside the Soviet lines.

While the German counter-attack ripped the Soviet line apart, the Soviet assault forces to the west continued their attacks. Gorodnyansky committed the 21st and 23rd Tank Corps through his 6th Army early in the day in an effort to develop the attack further while Bobkin continued to fight at Krasnograd. After heavy fighting, Taranovka fell to 21st Tank Corp, while 23rd Tank Corp pushed forward on its left.

Timoshenko called Stalin to detail the situation. Stalin and Stavka instructed the Bryansk Front to hand over the majority of its armour and aircraft to South-West Front.

18 May 1942

SOUTHERN SECTOR
North of Kharkov, the 38th Army launched a limited action, but was soon under heavy German counter-attack and forced to pull back to its start lines. Later in the morning, the 28th Army also attempted an attack but achieved only limited success.

Throughout the day, Group Kleist continued to pound the 57th and 9th Armies. Forward units of the 44th Korp closed upon Izyum, but strong resistance by the 5th Cavalry Corp prevented the early capture of the town.

The Soviet 6th Army continued to attack, but its 23rd and 21st Tank Corps were, during the day, ordered to disengage and march east to deal with the threat to the 57th and 9th Armies. Bobkin's advance was now fully stalled around Krasnograd, the Soviet force no longer having the strength to overcome the increasingly strong German forces in the town. Timoshenko resisted requests by his army commanders to abandon the offensive and ordered them to press on.

19 May 1942

SOUTHERN SECTOR

The 28th and 38th Armies again attempted to renew the offensive, but were struck by fierce German counter-fire. Fierce fighting raged close to Murom as the 168th infantry Division pushed into the southern wing of the 21st Army. This threatening German advance compelled 28th Army to move forces as a precaution to cover its rear.

Forces of the 44th Korp were close to Izyum and cut off the escape route of the 5th Cavalry Corp and the right wing of the 9th Army from the Donets. Isolated elements of the 5th managed to escape into the loop of the river, while the bulk of the 9th Army established defensive positions on the east bank south of Izyurn.

The 57th Army sector remained relatively quiet as the Germans concentrated on enveloping the forces around it. Units of the 23rd Tank Corp deployed on the left wing of the army to reinforce its positions, while the 21st Tank Corp moved up to the rear. As the Soviets attempted to build a defensive position, Kleist concentrated his 14th and 16th Panzer and 60th Motorised Divisions together with the 389th and 384th Infantry Divisions for a renewed strike into the Soviet rear from the area north of Barvenkovo.

The Soviet 6th Army attacks continued, forward forces fighting their way into the outskirts of Zmiyev. However, the withdrawal of the tank corps effectively brought the attacks to a standstill.

With the threat of South-West Front encirclement apparent, Timoshenko reluctantly called Stalin and requested permission to go onto the defensive and draw his attacking units away to deal with the threat posed to the 9th Army. Kostenko, deputy commander of the South-West Front, formed a new army detachment around Bobkin's force to counter the German attack. Timoshenko had reacted too late to the German threat.

During the evening Hitler ordered Bock to push Group Kleist north to Balakleya and isolate the entire Soviet grouping inside the now perilous Izyum pocket.

20 May 1942

SOUTHERN SECTOR

The Soviet forces north of Kharkov went onto the defensive once more as the Germans piled on the pressure. The hard-won positions from the early days of the offensive were rapidly lost as the 3rd Panzer Division launched a fierce attack against the junction of the 21st and 28th Armies. By the end of the day, these forces were back to their 12 May start lines. This success enabled the rapid transfer of the 3rd and 23rd Panzer Divisions to the south, to strike into the northern wing of the Izyum pocket.

The Soviet forces south of Kharkov hastily attempted to regroup in order to meet Kleist's attack. However, the Germans plunged forward once again, smashing the extreme right wing of the 57th Army, bending it back upon itself towards Lozovaya. Now not only was the 9th Army in danger of disintegration and the rear of the 6th Army and Group Kostenko exposed, the 57th Army faced a separate encirclement. The 23rd Tank Corp attempted to bolster the now detached right wing of the 57th but was held back by the 44th Korp. The gap between the 44th Korp to the south and 51st Korp to the north of the salient was now just twelve miles.

21 May 1942

SOUTHERN SECTOR
Throughout the day the 57th Army fought a fierce defensive battle, preventing its isolation by the German armour. However, 3rd Panzer Korp had unexpectedly turned north, away from the smaller encirclement of the 57th to the larger isolation of the entire Izyum grouping. Meanwhile, the 3rd and 23rd Panzer Divisions prepared to attack from Balakleya in order to link up with 3rd Panzer Korp. By the end of the day, the corridor to the east had been halved. The fate of the Soviet troops in the Izyum salient appeared bleak.

22 May 1942

SOUTHERN SECTOR
The 23rd and 3rd Panzer Divisions attacked from Andreyevka and Balakleya, while the 3rd Panzer pushed up from the south. By the end of the day, the pocket had been sealed. Timoshenko tried to counter-attack immediately with 38th Army in an effort to relieve the pocket, but his forces were unable to move in time. Simultaneously he ordered the 6th and 57th Armies and Group Kostenko to break out.

23 May 1942

SOUTHERN SECTOR
Heavy fighting raged between Barvenkovo and Balakleya as the Germans widened their corridor. The destruction of the pocket began. Kostenko took control of 6th and 57th Armies inside the pocket. Amid confused and heavy fighting, the 57th Army abandoned Lozovaya while the limited relief attacks by the 38th and 9th Armies were easily repelled.

FINLAND AND NORWAY
The Finns abandoned their attacks at Kastenga after a lack of success. Bitter fighting with 26th Army had exacted a high price upon the attacking Finns.

24 May 1942

SOUTHERN SECTOR
Group Kleist began the destruction of the Izyum pocket. Massive attacks pounded the disintegrating Soviet armies, constricting the pocket considerably. The 57th Army was virtually spent as it ran out of munitions, while the 6th Army desperately attempted to fight its way east.

25 May 1942

SOUTHERN SECTOR
The Soviet forces in the Izyum pocket attempted to bulldoze their way to the east. Bitter fighting with the 3rd Panzer and 51st Korps on the eastern face of the pocket proved fruitless as the German lines held last.

26 May 1942

SOUTHERN SECTOR
Repeated futile attacks failed to provide an exit for the Soviet forces from the Izyum pocket. Heaps of killed and wounded littered the battlefield while the pocket was reduced further, the Soviet troops being hemmed into a space ten miles deep by two miles long. Masses of Soviets soldiers were by this time surrendering to the German troops. During the bitter fighting, General Gorodnyansky of the 6th Army was killed.

27 May 1942

SOUTHERN SECTOR
The shocked remnants of the Izyum grouping continued their vain attempts to escape. Bloodied and defeated, few managed to escape the German defensive fire and air attacks.

28 May 1942

SOUTHERN SECTOR
Only the last stubborn units of the Soviet armies in the Izyum pocket fought on. The bulk of the Soviet force had now either been destroyed or was surrendering.

29 May 1942

SOUTHERN SECTOR
The Izyum battle was largely over as the Soviets surrendered. Barely 22,000 men had escaped. The battle since the 12th had cost the Soviets

170,958 killed or captured and 106,232 wounded,[4] 1,250 tanks and 2,000 artillery pieces destroyed or captured. Generals Kostenko, Podlas, Bobkin and Gorodnyanski all fell in the fighting.

The disastrous offensive left the South-West Front with barely two thirds of its original strength, while the German 6th Army had suffered only 20,000 casualties during the operation.

> *The débâcle at Kharkov proved once again the inability of the Soviet Command to master a rapidly-developing situation. Sticking rigidly to predetermined goals in spite of a significant change in combat conditions had cost the Red Army a quarter of a million men. Stalin's refusal to heed the advice of his generals had had the same results as in the summer of '41. However, the defeat at Kharkov had been an outstanding achievement for the Germans. A seemingly desperate situation had been turned to their advantage, and a considerable force, which would have presented real problems had it been intact at the time of the impending offensive, had been disposed of relatively easily. This victory went a long way towards rebuilding German confidence, so badly shaken during the winter.*

30 May 1942

NORTHERN SECTOR

The Germans counter-attacked along the Volkhov, isolating 2nd Shock Army. Vlassov's men had been fighting in virtual encirclement for nearly three months. Nine divisions and six brigades were cut off, all short of food and ammunition. Repeated attacks by 59th and 52nd Armies failed to break through and create an escape corridor for 2nd Shock.

GERMAN DEPLOYMENT, MAY 1942

The Ostheer had been extensively reinforced and rebuilt for the summer campaigning season, the Panzerwaffe numbering 3,981 vehicles, of which nearly 1,000 were operational while the Luftwaffe had 3,400 aircraft.

The Luftwaffe had taken time to restructure its forces, deploying a number of new formations with the army groups. In Finland, 5th Air Fleet had been strengthened to 260 aircraft, Keller's 1st Air Fleet with Army Group North had 375 aircraft, while Army Group Centre had Greim's Luftwaffe Kommando Ost with 600 aircraft. By far the greatest Luftwaffe commitment was in the Ukraine and the Crimea. Army Group South could call upon Lohr's 4th Air Fleet, comprising 4th and 8th Air Korps and 1st Flak Korp with nearly 1,600 aircraft.

The Ostheer began to redeploy its forces for the next phase of operations during June. The 11th Army was to destroy the Soviet forces at Sevastopol, concentrating 1,300 artillery pieces around the port and the

8th Air Korp with 720 aircraft. The Soviets had 101,000 men in seven infantry and three marine divisions and three marine brigades, 600 artillery pieces, 2,000 motor vehicles, forty tanks and, sixty aircraft. The city was ringed by three lines of defence, the first consisting of a belt of trenches and minefields, supported by divisional artillery, while to the rear was the second, stronger defensive position. This line had a series of strongly built forts sited between the Belbek Valley and Severnaya Gulf that were designed to hold up any forces attacking towards the port. The final line of defence consisted of another belt of trenches on the outer limits of the city, again supported by minefields and artillery. To overcome this formidable array, Manstein had redeployed his army, leaving 42nd Korp and 7th Rumanian Korp at Kerch to deal with any Soviet threat from the Kuban. The bulk of the German strength was massed around the Sevastopol perimeter, 54th Korp against the northern flank and 30th to the south, with the Rumanian Mountain Korp in between. The 54th Korp (22nd, 24th, 50th and 132nd infantry Divisions) had been reinforced with fifty-six heavy and medium artillery batteries and forty-one light gun batteries, eighteen mortar batteries and two assault gun battalions,[5] while 30th Korp (72nd and 170th infantry and 28th Light Divisions) had twenty-five heavy and medium batteries, five light artillery batteries, six mortar batteries and one assault gun battalion.[6] The Rumanian corp had twelve medium batteries and twenty-two light artillery batteries.[7] Many of the heavy artillery pieces were the super-heavies of the German army. Among these was the Gamma mortar, a huge 427mm weapon with a range of nearly nine miles, the Karl 61.5mm artillery piece and the Gustav 800mm gun. The Gustav was so large it took a crew of 2,500 to operate it, but could fire its massive projectile twenty-eight miles. Its fire was so powerful that it could disable a fortress with one shot. Around the city perimeter the Germans had seven infantry divisions, with two Rumanian divisions in support. A five-day artillery barrage was to soften the Soviet defences before the main assault began. As 11th Army lacked panzer forces, a number of assault gun battalions operated in conjunction with the infantry.

During May the Germans had brought six infantry divisions into the line, but one panzer and three infantry left. This gave the Ostheer a combat force of nineteen panzer, fifteen motorised and one hundred and twenty-nine infantry divisions.[8]

GERMAN CASUALTIES
During May 1942 the Germans lost 38,000 men killed on the Eastern Front.

SOVIET DEPLOYMENT, MAY 1942
Despite their disastrous defeats at Kerch and Kharkov, May had been spent rebuilding the combat units, armoured and air forces. At the end of

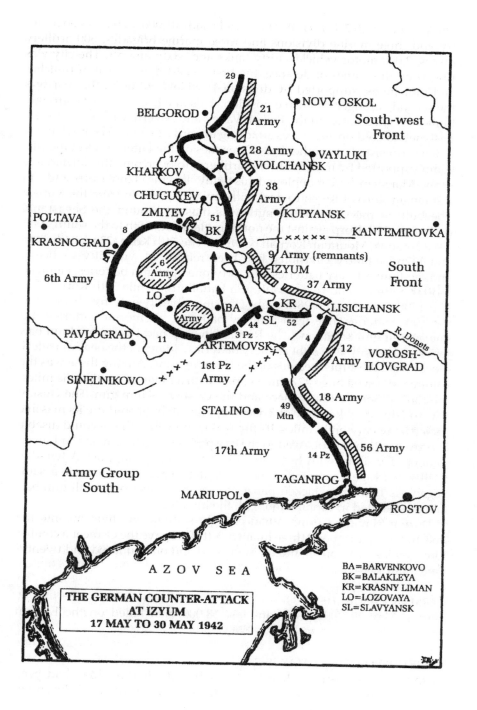

THE GERMAN COUNTER-ATTACK
AT IZYUM
17 MAY TO 30 MAY 1942

the month, the Red Army had 6,190 tanks and the air force 3,160 aircraft. New air armies had begun to form, being allocated to specific fronts, providing aerial support whenever and wherever it was required. The 1st to 5th Air Armies were raised, 1st going to West Front, 2nd to South-West Front, 3rd to Kalinin Front, 4th to South Front and 5th to North Caucasus Front.

1 June 1942

GERMAN COMMAND
General Hoth was appointed to command 4th Panzer Army, which was completing its redeployment onto the northern flank of Army Group South. Ruoff took over the 17th Army. In Germany the SS Panzer Korp was created. It comprised the 1st, 2nd and 3rd SS Panzer Grenadier Divisions and was intended for deployment on the Eastern Front towards the end of the year.

2 June 1942

SOUTHERN SECTOR
The thunderous detonation of 1,300 artillery pieces broke the Crimean dawn. By the end of the battle 11th Army and 8th Air Korp had dropped more than half a million rounds on Sevastopol port. Manstein committed the full weight of his artillery to smashing the strongly built Soviet defences, easing the difficult task for the infantry in the coming battle. The 8th Air Korp was heavily committed on the first day of the battle, flying hundreds of sorties over the burning city. Fierce artillery fire continued for a week before the main attack was launched.

7 June 1942

SOUTHERN SECTOR
After five days of artillery fire, 11th Army began its offensive against Sevastopol. At 0350 hours the four infantry divisions of the 54th Korp attacked the strongly defended Belbek Valley and heavily fortified Mackenzie Heights, while 30th Korp launched preliminary attacks aimed at gaining ground on the main road into Sevastopol from the south. The Germans met ferocious resistance from the well dug in Soviets, suffering heavy casualties. The ground units called upon Luftwaffe support as they were pinned down by accurate Soviet counter-fire. By the end of the day, 54th Korp had managed to advance a short distance but suffered considerable casualties.

8 June 1942

SOUTHERN SECTOR
The 54th Korp renewed its attack upon Sevastopol, supported by 8th Air Korp and massive artillery fire. The Soviet defences were literally blasted out of the ground by the crushing bombardment, but still progress was disappointingly slow. The first line of Soviet defences continued to hold up 30th Korp. Attacks continued over the next few days, the German slowly nibbling at the Soviet positions, taking one strong point after another in bloody close-quarters fighting.

SOVIET COMMAND
At a Stavka session Stalin admitted that it had been a mistake to downgrade the Volkhov Front and proposed to reform the front under Meretskov.

9 June 1942

NORTHERN SECTOR
The Volkhov Front became operational once again, its primary aim being the relief of 2nd Shock Army.

10 June 1942

NORTHERN SECTOR
The Volkhov Front resumed its relief attacks in an effort to free 2nd Shock Army. After a day of fighting, the 52nd Army punched a narrow corridor through to 2nd Shock but was then fiercely attacked by the Luftwaffe and forced to withdraw. Again 2nd Shock had come painfully close to escape, only to be beaten back.

CENTRAL SECTOR
West Front attacked 2nd Panzer Army, but only managed a slow advance in the face of well coordinated German defence.

SOUTHERN SECTOR
German 6th Army launched Operation Wilhelm, a limited operation aimed at destroying the 28th Army around Volchansk before the offensive towards the Don. Initial attacks made good progress and succeeded in penetrating the Soviet line.

Bitter fighting continued in the Crimea as 11th Army pounded the Soviet defences by day and night. Both 54th and 30th Korps were increasingly exhausted in the close-quarters fighting and needed to achieve a breakthrough soon before their strength was spent.

GERMAN CASUALTIES

In the month since Halder's last casualty return German losses on the Eastern Front rose by 85,000 to 1,268,000 killed, wounded or missing.

THE WESTERN THEATRE

In the Balkans the US air force launched a long-range raid upon the Ploesti oil refineries in Rumania. In later years these raids would cause the Germans real difficulties as their fuel resources became scarce. At present though it was yet another propaganda blow against the Reich as the Allies proved their ability to strike German territory even as far east as the Balkans.

13 June 1942

SOUTHERN SECTOR

The slow German advance at Sevastopol began to make headway as Fort Stalin fell to 22nd Infantry Division of 54th Korp after a furious battle.

15 June 1942

SOUTHERN SECTOR

The 6th Army completed its attack in the Volchansk area. The 28th Army had been comprehensively defeated and retreated across the Donets. The fighting attracted the attention of Bryansk Front, which reported to the Stavka that it was detecting a significant build up of German forces in the Kolpina, Shchigra and Kursk areas. The Stavka accepted this information but interpreted it as a German attempt to draw attention away from the main attack that they expected in the Yukhnow and Orel sectors.

17 June 1942

NORTHERN SECTOR

The 29th Tank Brigade punched a four hundred-yard corridor through the 2nd Shock Army at Myasnoi Bor. The men of 2nd Shock rushed for the slender lifeline in a desperate bid to escape the pocket. German fire inflicted massive casualties upon the tightly massed ranks of Soviets.

SOUTHERN SECTOR

The 54th Korp took Fort Siberia after a fierce battle. German troops had to wipe out each pocket of resistance with artillery fire and flame-throwers, the Soviets fighting to the last man. 54th Korp had driven a deep wedge into the Soviet secondary defence line. 30th Korps' 72nd Infantry Division captured the heavily defended North Nose, Chapel Mount and Ruin Hill strong points, and its 170th Infantry Division took Kamary. The

28th Division encountered particularly strong resistance as it attempted to advance along the Crimean coast.[9]

Vessels of the Black Sea Fleet tried to bring reinforcements in, landing 3,000 soldiers together with ammunition, but this was not enough to replace the heavy losses of the past few days.

18 June 1942

NORTHERN SECTOR
The disaster on the Volkhov ran its course as the Germans counter attacked and isolated 2nd Shock again.

SOUTHERN SECTOR
Fortress Maxim Gorki fell to 54th Korp as the Sevastopol defences crumbled. During the day the Germans also took the Gepau, Molotov, Cheka, Volga and Ural fortresses.

19 June 1942

SOUTHERN SECTOR
Major Reichel, operations officer of 23rd Panzer Division, was flying over the Soviet lines near Nezhegol when his plane was forced down. Inside the aircraft, carefully stored in Reichel's briefcase, was a complete set of plans for the attack by 40th Panzer Korp as part of Case Blue. The plans were forwarded to the South-West Front headquarters and from there to the Stavka, but the Soviet command believed the plans were a plant, a German attempt to draw attention away from the expected attack towards Moscow. With Army Group Centre still close to the capital, the Stavka believed the Germans would resume their attack in the centre. Hitler though was the one factor that the Soviets could not account for.

20 June 1942

SOUTHERN SECTOR
The 54th Korp captured Fort Lenin in Sevastopol.

21 June 1942

SOUTHERN SECTOR
With the defeat of the last defenders of the Maxim Gorki fort, the 24th Infantry Division of 54th Korp secured the Severnaya Bay area. The battle then entered its final stage as the Germans prepared to attack the final ring of defences before the city itself.

22 June 1942

SOUTHERN SECTOR
Sixth Army and 1st Panzer Army began another limited operation to destroy 38th and 9th Armies around Kupyansk.

THE AXIS FORCES AFTER ONE YEAR OF CONFLICT
One year on, the Germans found themselves massively committed to the fighting in Russia. The Ostheer deployed five divisions, a force of 150,000 men, in Finland alongside the sixteen divisions of the 300,000-strong Finnish army. On the main combat front, Army Group North had thirty-six divisions, Centre had sixty-three and South sixty-eight. Army Group Centre shortly gave up a number of its divisions to Army Group South for Case Blue. To the rear the Germans had five divisions with a total of 80,000 men in the Balkans and three divisions totalling 54,000 men in Germany. The number of allied units committed to the fighting in the east had also risen, the Finns, as already noted, had sixteen divisions in action, while the Rumanians had thirteen, the Hungarians nine divisions *en route* or deployed with the German armies, the Italians three divisions and one brigade committed and the Slovakians one division. In addition, the Spanish provided the *Azul* Division around Leningrad with 18th Army.

Army Group South completed its deployment for Case Blue. Paulus' 6th Army was by far the strongest formation of the entire group, having 330,000 men and 300 panzers or assault guns in two panzer, one motorised and fifteen infantry divisions, while the 2nd Army had one motorised and four infantry divisions, a total of 95,000 men; the 17th Army had 150,000 men and 180 panzers or assault guns in one panzer, one motorised and six infantry divisions; the 1st Panzer Army three panzer, two motorised and seven infantry divisions with 220,000 men and 480 panzers or assault guns, and the 4th Panzer Army had three' panzer, two motorised one) six infantry divisions with some 200,000 men and 480 panzers. The 2nd Hungarian and 8th Italian Armies were both *en route*. Manstein's 11th Army remained committed to the fighting in the Crimea with the 3rd Rumanian Army in support. This gave the Germans a formidable array of 1,000,000 men with nearly 1,500 panzers and assault guns. With German commitment on the Eastern Front standing at 2,847,000, a sizeable proportion of the field army was earmarked for the offensive in the south.

The Ostheer managed to concentrate such a large force in the Ukraine through the ruthless stripping of resources from Army Groups North and Centre. Many of the two group's infantry divisions were reduced to six battalions from their regulation nine. Despite this reinforcement of the southern armies, their divisions remained short of mechanised support. Many motorised divisions had been reinforced at the expense of their neighbours to the north, but there were still not enough vehicles to go round. Increasing numbers of civilian vehicles were pressed into service, the loss of more than half a million transport vehicles during the first year of fighting proving too much for the German war industry to make good.

23 June 1942

NORTHERN SECTOR
The Germans compressed 2nd Shock Army into a smaller area, bringing it under heavy artillery fire.

24 June 1942

NORTHERN SECTOR
Vlassov ordered the break out of his army. Small bands of men tried to fight their way east but 2nd Shock had shot its bolt and organised resistance ended. During the confused fighting, Vlassov surrendered. In later years Vlassov would be the main impetus behind the formation of a free Soviet army to fight for the overthrow of Stalin and his regime.

25 June 1942

NORTHERN SECTOR
The final pockets of resistance on the Volkhov were snuffed out as 2nd Shock Army was destroyed. The 52nd and 59th Armies abandoned their attacks to free 2nd Shock Army as the latter force had disintegrated under German attack. The fighting had cost the three armies 54,774 killed and missing and 39,977 wounded.[10]

> *The destruction of Vlassov's army on the Volkhov, and its abandonment by the Soviet High Commmand were to lead a loyal Soviet general into collaboration with the Nazis. Stalin's disregard for his fellow countrymen bred in Vlassov and thousands of Soviet prisoners a desire to see the end of Communism in Russia. Had Hitler recognised the real value of men such as Vlassov at this stage of the conflict, the shortages and difficulties of later years might to a large degree have been overcome.*

SOUTHERN SECTOR
The 6th Army pounded 38th and 9th Armies, capturing Kupyansk.

26 June 1942

SOUTHERN SECTOR
Operation Fridericus II was brought to a successful conclusion, 38th and

9th Armies having lost more than 40,000 captured. This defeat combined with Fridericus and the Izyum debacle left the South-West Front a mere shell.

At Sevastopol, 11th Army began to attack the inner defence ring. Manstein planned to launch an attack across Severnaya Bay with elements of 54th Korp, placing units in the Soviet rear and bringing about the collapse of the final defences without the need for large-scale frontal assaults. Simultaneously, 30th Korp would attack the Soviets holding the Sapun Heights. The fighting had inflicted heavy casualties upon the Black Sea Fleet as it tried to reinforce the garrison. The last supply vessels left the port, loaded with wounded soldiers, for the Kuban. No more supplies or reinforcements would arrive in Sevastopol as the Stavka finally wrote the garrison off.

SOVIET COMMAND
The Stavka summoned Golikov to Moscow to inform him that his front would begin its offensive towards Orel on 5 July. Golikov considered his forces inadequate for the task, the bulk of his armour having been lost in the fighting at Izyum.

27 June 1942

SOUTHERN SECTOR
The 8th Air Korp was removed from the Crimea and moved north to aid the offensive in the Ukraine. With Case Blue due to begin on 28 June an eerie lull settled over the southern sectors.

To ward off the German attack, the Soviets deployed Bryansk Front with 169,000 men in twelve rifle divisions, four rifle brigades, two tank corps and four independent tank brigades. South-West Front, even after its defeat at Kharkov, had 610,000 men between thirty-three rifle and six cavalry divisions, six rifle brigades, four tank corps, three motor rifle brigades and ten tank brigades, while South Front had 522,500 men in its twenty-three rifle divisions, four rifle brigades and six tank brigades. The fronts also deployed a combined total of 3,470 tanks, over 2,300 being T-34 and Kv models that could out-perform and out-gun their German opponents.

28 June 1942

SOUTHERN SECTOR
At 0215 hours 4th Panzer Army, with 2nd Army in support, attacked the junction of the 13th and 40th Armies. Fierce fighting developed as 24th Panzer Korp crushed two divisions of Bryansk Front and pushed towards the Kshen river. Golikov committed his 16th and 1st Tank Corps to seal

off the wound, while Stavka ordered 4th and 24th Tank Corps of South-West Front to help and 17th Tank Corp to move from operational reserve at Kastornoye.

By evening 24th Panzer Korp had punched its way through the junction of the 13th and 40th Armies and attacked the headquarters of 40th Army, throwing it into disarray. Recognising this as the beginning of the German summer offensive, but mistakenly believing it to be aimed at Moscow, the Stavka instructed Golikov to commit 5th Tank Army with its 2nd and 11th Tank Corps.

In the Crimea, Inkerman fell to 50th Infantry Division. Manstein was preparing to launch an attack across Severnaya Bay in order to outflank the rear of the Sapun position that was holding up the 30th Korp.

29 June 1942

SOUTHERN SECTOR
Fourth Panzer Army continued to attack, widening the hole in the Soviet line. Bryansk Front reeled under the German attacks as artillery, armour and aircraft pounded its forward units while it tried to bring up armour.

The 11th Army attacked Sevastopol, 54th Korp sending an assault force of 22nd and 24th Infantry Divisions across Severnaya Bay to land in the Soviet rear. The Soviet defences were breached with little cost, undermining the inner defence zone. As Manstein successfully turned the Soviet northern flank, 30th Korp penetrated the Sapun Heights with its 170th Infantry Division, while the Inkerman Heights fell to 50th and 132nd Infantry Divisions. The English Cemetery south of Sevastopol fell to the 28th Light Division.

30 June 1942

GERMAN DEPLOYMENT: NORTHERN SECTOR
Army Group North deployed its 16th and 18th Armies across its sector of the front. The 18th Army comprised the 1st Korp (five infantry divisions) on the Volkhov, 26th Korp (two infantry divisions) south of Leningrad, the 28th Korp (one panzer and six infantry divisions) south of Lake Ladoga, the 38th Korp (five infantry divisions) on the southern Volkhov and 50th Korp (five infantry divisions) around the Leningrad perimeter.

The 16th Army comprised the 2nd Korp (seven infantry and two motorised divisions) in the exposed Demyansk salient, the 10th Korp (three infantry and one motorised divisions) also in the salient and the 39th Panzer Korp (a panzer and infantry division) holding the long southern wing of the army.

GERMAN DEPLOYMENT: CENTRAL SECTOR
Army Group Centre deployed the 4th, 9th, 2nd Panzer and 3rd Panzer Armies. The 3rd Panzer Army, holding the eastern face of the Rzhev salient, comprised the 9th Korp (four infantry divisions) near Gzhatsk and 20th Korp (four infantry divisions) north-east of Vyazma.

The 9th Army held the long left wing of the army group with the 6th Korp (three infantry divisions) on the long Velizh sector, 23rd Korp (two panzer, four infantry divisions) west of Rzhev, the 27th Korp (three infantry divisions) between Rzhev and Sychevka, the 41st Korp (one motorised and two infantry divisions) near Belyi and the 46th Panzer Korp (a panzer and infantry divisions) between Sychevka and Gzhatsk.

The 4th Army held its 12th Korp (four infantry divisions) south of Vyazma, the 43rd Korp (three infantry divisions) and 56th Panzer Korp (one motorised and three infantry divisions) to its south. The southern wing of the army group was secured by the 2nd Panzer Army which comprised the 35th Korp (one panzer and three infantry divisions), 47th Panzer Korp (two panzer and five infantry divisions) and 53rd Korp (one motorised and four inlantry divisions).

SOUTHERN SECTOR
The 13th and 40th Armies fought desperately to hold off the German attacks that continued to develop on the road to Voronezh. Fortieth Army was in difficulties as the armoured support it expected floundered. The 17th Tank Corp was running on virtually dry tanks, while 4th and 24th rank Corps lost touch with front headquarters. With 4th Panzer Army and 2nd Army pushing towards Voronezh, sweeping aside the shattered Bryansk Front, 6th Army joined the offensive. Fierce artillery fire and air support accompanied the attack, breaking the junction of 21st and 28th Armies. German forces immediately exploited their gains and pushed towards Novy Oskol.

The 11th Army was embroiled in heavy fighting in Sevastopol. With Germans in their rear, the fall of Sevastopol was not far off. The Stavka ordered the evacuation of the garrison, but the Black Sea Fleet was unable to mount an effective evacuation, leaving the majority of the garrison to its fate. Stalin ordered the evacuation by air of Admiral Oktybrski and General Petrov.

GERMAN DEPLOYMENT
German commitment continued to increase, with one panzer, one motorised and seven infantry divisions joining the line. Only one division left the combat zone, leaving the Ostheer with a force of twenty panzer, sixteen motorised and one hundred and thirty-five infantry divisions, plus allied divisions. The allies accounted for thirteen Rumanian divisions,

nine Hungarian divisions, three italian divisions and one brigade, one Slovak and one Spanish divisions and sixteen Finnish divisions.[11]

CASUALTIES

Halder noted that the Ostheer had lost 1,362,000 men since June 1941, the army in the field being reduced to 2,847,000 men. In June 1942 alone the field armies lost 29,000 killed. In just the last twenty days the Ostheer had lost 94,000 men. A report issued by Fremde Heer Ost claimed that between 22 June 1941 and 1 May 1942 the Soviet armed forces lost 7,300,000 killed, wounded, missing or captured. An appreciation of Soviet potential estimated, that the Soviet armed forces had a further 9,700,000 men available for combat, of whom 7,800,000 had already been called up. Of these, 6,000,000 were serving with the Red Army, 4,500,000 of them in the front line, while 1,500,000 were with the Air Force. Another 500,000 were in the Navy. The appreciation was surprisingly accurate and gave a realistic idea of Soviet potential. However, Soviet industrial potential was massively underestimated and would be for the remainder of the war.

THE SOVIET ARMED FORCES

The Red Army and Navy lost 842,898 killed and missing in action and 706,647 wounded during the second quarter of 1942.[12]

The Soviets pressed ahead with the reorganisation of their Air Force, raising 6th, 8th and 14th Air Armies. These new units were distributed throughout the war zone, 6th going to North-West Front, 8th to the Stalingrad sector and 14th to Volkhov Front.

1 July 1942

CENTRAL SECTOR

Left-wing units of the West Front began to attack 2nd Panzer Army. The fighting would rage for a week without any appreciable Soviet success.

SOUTHERN SECTOR

The 21st and 40th Armies began to abandon their positions and fall back towards the Don. Both 4th Panzer and 6th Armies, not realising that the Soviet forces were withdrawing, and under direct orders from the Führer, turned their attacks in to envelop the Soviet forces on the west bank of the Don.

In the Crimea, the Germans pounded the Soviets around Sevastopol. Fierce Luftwaffe and artillery attacks soffened the Soviet positions around the city in preparation for the infantry assault. However, a large part of the garrison had abandoned Sevastopol and fallen back to the Khersonnes peninsula.

2 July 1942

SOUTHERN SECTOR
Leading elements of 4th Panzer and 6th Armies linked up at Stary Oskol, but the Soviets had evaded their trap. The 40th Army, 17th, 4th and 24th Tank Corps retreated towards Voronezh. To halt the expected German thrust towards Moscow, which the Stavka still believed was the German intention, 6th and 60th Armies were allocated from Stavka reserve to Golikov's Bryansk Front. Both armies were to deploy north and south of Voronezh and prevent the Germans from gaining a staging post for the attack towards Moscow.

On the Khersonnes peninsula, 11th Army began the task of destroying the remnants of the Sevastopol garrison. Fighting was severe as the Soviets fought to the bitter end.

3 July 1942

SOUTHERN SECTOR
The 48th Panzer Korp reached the Don west of Voronezh and crossed with strong armoured units. Stalin immediately ordered 5th Tank Army to counter-attack and seal the gap between Bryansk and South-West Fronts, the army being ordered to concentrate south of Yelets.

4 July 1942

SOUTHERN SECTOR
The 5th Tank Army moved into battle under Stavka direction. Over six hundred tanks, many of them the modern T-34 and Kv models, were committed piecemeal over the next five days, blunting the effectiveness of this powerful unit. Luftwaffe attacks also took a heavy toll of the Soviet armour. The 48th Panzer Korp crossed the Don after a severe Baltic with 7th Tank Corp.

In the Crimea, the remnants of the Soviet Coastal Army surrendered on the Khersonnes peninsula, ending the epic siege of Sevastopol. More than 30,000 men laid down their arms, bringing the tally of prisoners taken during the battle to more than 90,000. Material losses were also considerable, the Red Army losing 460 artillery pieces, 760 mortars and 155 anti-tank guns. Since October 1941 the fighting around the port had cost the Soviets 156,880 killed and missing and 43,601 wounded.[13] German casualties during the June attack were 24,000 killed, wounded and missing.

The fall of Sevastopol effectively left the Ostheer with a spare army, which should have been committed to supporting 17th Army in the Caucasus. Hitler would squander 11th Army though, breaking up along the whole front. The 42nd Korp remained in the Crimea and later crossed the Kerch strait into the Kuban to join Ruoff's 17th Army, but the headquarters of the army, together with elements of 54th and 30th Korps headed north to Leningrad. Barely four divisions of the army remained together.

The epic siege and battle for Sevastopol had shown the true measure of Manstein's ability. Using limited forces against a well dug in enemy, he had fought a costly, but ultimately successful action. Only the sheer fanaticism of the Soviet defenders had prevented the early capture of the fortress city, yet Manstein had used all the forces at his disposal to break the Soviet defences brick by brick. However, opportunities that arose unexpectedly, such as the crossing of Severnaya Bay, were seized upon and exploited. These skills would be put to the test later in the year as Manstein fought to prevent the destruction of the German southern wing.

GERMAN DEPLOYMENT: SOUTHERN SECTOR

With its offensive underway, the Germans reorganised the structure of Army Group South, splitting it into Groups A and B. Army Group B was commanded by Field-Marshal von Bock. Its forces comprised 6th, 2nd, 4th Panzer and 2nd Hungarian Armies. Paulus' 6th Army had the 8th Korp (three infantry divisions), 17th Korp (three infantry divisions), 29th Korp (three infantry divisions), 40th Panzer Korp (two panzer, one motorised and two infantry divisions) and 51st Korp (four infantry divisions); Group Weichs, based upon the German 2nd Army, had the 55th Korp (four infantry divisions) and Jany's 2nd Hungarian Army. The Hungarian force comprised the German 7th Korp (one German and one Hungarian infantry division) and 3rd Hungarian Korp (two Hungarian infantry divisions). Hoth's 4th Panzer Army had the 13th Korp (three infantry divisions), 24th Panzer Korp (two panzer, one motorised and one infantry division) and 48th Panzer Korp (one panzer and two motorised divisions). The army group also included the assembling 8th Italian Army with its 2nd Italian Korp (three Italian infantry divisions). Army Group B was tasked with the destruction of Soviet forces between the upper Donets and middle Don, securing a crossing of the Don near Voronezh. During the next few days this would be achieved, but 4th Panzer Army, instead of releasing its forces to the south, remained around the city to deal with the threat posed by 5th Tank Army. It would then push 4th Panzer and 6th Armies into the Don Elbow, while allied units and 2nd Army arrayed themselves along the Don to cover the long left flank. From the Don 4th Panzer and 6th Armies were to press east and reach Stalingrad before the Red Army could prepare its defences. From Stalingrad the 4th Panzer and part of 6th Army would turn south to support Army Group A in the Caucasus.

Field-Marshal List's Army Group A comprised three armies, Kleist's 1st
Panzer Army had 3rd Panzer Korp (two panzer and one motorised divisions), 14th Panzer Korp (one panzer and one motorised divisions), 44th
Korp (four infantry divisions) and Group Strecker with 11th Korp and 4th
Rumanian Korp. The 17th Army deployed the 4th Korp (three infantry
divisions), 49th Mountain Korp (two divisions) and 52nd Korp (two infantry divisions) and also attached a Rumanian motorised korp. Manstein's
11th Army had the 42nd Korp (a single infantry division), 7th Rumanian
Korp (two Rumanian infantry divisions and a Rumanian cavalry division),
30th Korp (a Rumanian mountain division and three German infantry
divisions) and 54th Korp (a Rumanian mountain division and our German
infantry divisions). In reserve the army group held the 5th Korp headquarters and 57th Panzer Korp (one panzer and two infantry divisions).

Air support was provided to both army groups by 4th Air Fleet,
4th Air Korp allocated to Army Group A and 8th Air Korp to Army
Group B. Richthofen had taken command of the air fleet following
Lohr's appointment as commander of the German forces in Greece and
Yugoslavia. The primary objective of Army Group A was the defeat
of the Soviet forces on the Mius line followed by a rapid advance
into the Caucasus after the successful capture of Stalingrad by Army
Group B.

5 July 1942

CENTRAL SECTOR
West Front began a new operation aimed at tying down 2nd Panzer Army
near Sukhinichi.

SOUTHERN SECTOR
Soviet armies fighting around Voronezh were pounded on the banks of the
Don by 4th Panzer Army and smashed by the Luftwaffe. Hoth crossed the
Don and entered the outskirls of Voronezh, while 2nd Army moved up to
protect the exposed left flank.

SOVIET COMMAND
Stalin ordered the formation of a new Voronezh Front. Golikov assumed
temporary command until the arrival of Vatutin. The front comprised the
40th, 3rd and 6th Armies. Chibisov took over at Bryansk Front.

6 July 1942

SOUTHERN SECTOR
The Germans had captured the greater part of Voronezh but were bogged
down in bitter fighting with Soviet rearguards. The Stavka was preparing

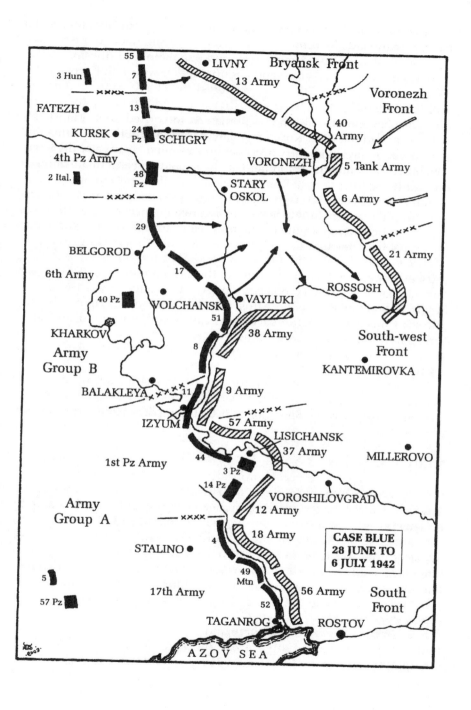

55
3 Hun
7
LIVNY
Bryansk Front
13 Army
Voronezh
Front
FATEZH
13
KURSK
24
Pz
SCHIGRY
40
Army
4th Pz Army
48
Pz
VORONEZH
5 Tank Army
2 Ital.
STARY
OSKOL
6 Army
29
21 Army
BELGOROD
17
6th Army
ROSSOSH
40 Pz
VOLCHANSK
VAYLUKI
51
KHARKOV
8
38 Army
South-west
Front
Army
Group B
KANTEMIROVKA
BALAKLEYA
11
9 Army
IZYUM
57 Army
LISICHANSK
37 Army
MILLEROVO
1st Pz Army
44
3 Pz
14 Pz
VOROSHILOVGRAD
12 Army
Army
Group A
18 Army
STALINO
4
CASE BLUE
28 JUNE TO
6 JULY 1942
5
49
Mtn
56 Army
South
Front
57 Pz
17th Army
52
TAGANROG
ROSTOV
AZOV SEA

to move additional forces up to prevent the movement of German armour north-east towards Moscow.

7 July 1942

SOUTHERN SECTOR
The final pockets of resistance in Voronezh were quelled as 4th Panzer Army completed the conquest of the city. Farther south the 6th Army and 4th Panzer Army linked up near Vayluki as another encirclement was concluded. The tally of prisoners was low following the withdrawal of the South-West Front.

The 1st Panzer and 17th Armies began their offensives, striking Malinovsky's South Front. Soviet forces again gave ground to avoid encirclement, prompting the Germans to believe the Soviets had reached the end of their resources.

8 July 1942

SOUTHERN SECTOR
The 4th Panzer Army began to release units from Voronezh for the drive south along the western bank of the Don. However, Bock was reluctant to send the entire strength of 4th Panzer south, as he believed there remained a threat posed by Bryansk and Voronezh Fronts.

Farther south, the Soviets withdrew from Oskol as 6th Army advanced. The 1st Panzer Army crossed the Donets after meeting negligible resistance, the South Front falling back a little too rapidly before the German attacks.

9 July 1942

SOUTHERN SECTOR
The 4th Panzer Army reached Tikhnaya Sosna but was brought to an unexpected halt as it ran out of fuel. Hoth had still not released his full strength from Voronezh and was ordered to quit the area and move all his armour south, upon Kantemirovka, where 40th Panzer Korp, with 6th Army, would be allocated to 4th Panzer. Elements of Paulus' 6th Army reached the Rossosh river.

GERMAN COMMAND
Army Groups A and B took command of their forces. Army Group B, under von Bock, fielded 4th Panzer, 2nd and 6th Armies, while Army Group A, under List, had 1st Panzer, 11th and 17th Armies.

10 July 1942

SOUTHERN SECTOR
With the arrival of supplies, 4th Panzer Army resumed its advance along the Don, both 4th Panzer and 6th Armies attacking the few Soviet units left on the west bank. On the Azov coast and in the Donbas, 1st Panzer and 17th Armies pushed towards Rostov and the Don, meeting only scattered resistance from the rearguards of South Front.

11 July 1942

SOUTHERN SECTOR
Lisichansk fell to 1st Panzer Army while other elements reached the Aidar river at Starobelsk. Group Ruoff, with 17th Army and Rumanian forces, launched strong attacks against rearguards of South Front. Heavy fighting raged on the road from Taganrog as the Soviets fought on the approaches to Rostov.

Hitler, believing the Soviets defeated on the west bank of the Don, ordered 1st and 4th Panzer Armies to converge at Kamensk and Millerovo to destroy the remainder of South and South-West Fronts before attacking in conjunction into the Caucasus. Believing the Red Army to have been vanquished, Hitler left 6th Army to advance alone towards Stalingrad and seize the city. The 1st and 4th Panzer Armies and 17th Army pushed towards the oilfields. This was a break from the original plan, the German forces being sent simultaneously along separate axes of advance instead of securing the Volga before their southward drive. Hitler issued Directive 43, confirming the transfer of 4th Panzer to Army Group A and also ordering 11th Army, which had been reduced to nothing more than 42nd Korp, to cross the Kerch strait.

12 July 1942

SOUTHERN SECTOR
Expecting a German thrust in strength to the Volga, the Stavka created a new Stalingrad Front, allocating 62nd, 63rd and 64th Armies. In all the Stalingrad Front comprised thirty-four rifle divisions, three cavalry divisions, three tank and eight rifle brigades, fourteen independent tank brigades and 540,000 men. The 63rd Army was to hold the east bank of the Don, while 21st Army regrouped on the north bank between 63rd and 62nd Armies.

South-West Front retained command of the 38th, 28th, 57th and 21st Armies. The 38th and 28th Armies would soon be taken out of the line to reform as 1st and 4th Tank Armies. Timoshenko was given command of Stalingrad Front. In the fighting since 28 June the old South-West Front lost 161,400 killed and missing and 71,000 wounded.

13 July 1942

SOUTHERN SECTOR
Fourth Panzer Army reached Boguchar, linking up with 40th Panzer Korp, encircling minor Soviet forces. The pocket yielded just 14,000 prisoners, taking the total captured so far in the campaign to 50,000. Hitler took this to be an indication that the Soviets were finished. The 4th Panzer Army was instructed to cross the Don at Konstantinovka and from there to head west towards Rostov to encircle the Soviet force that Hitler mistakenly believed was massed there. Simultaneously, 1st Panzer Army was to move west along the Don to link up with 4th Panzer. What remained of Army Group B's spearhead was left immobile in the Don Elbow, supplies having been redirected to the panzer armies. Paulus' 6th Army was left stranded in the Don Elbow, giving the Soviets the opportunity to build up their defences on the approaches to Stalingrad. Had Hitler carried the advance into the Don Elbow, it is likely that 6th Army would have taken Stalingrad in mid-July. By the time the advance was resumed, the Soviets had had time to deploy 62nd and 64th Armies.

14 July 1942

SOUTHERN SECTOR
Bryansk Front pinned down the German 2nd Army. To shorten the extremely long left flank of 6th Army, the 2nd Hungarian Army deployed south of 2nd Army.

15 July 1942

SOUTHERN SECTOR
Kamensk and Millerovo were given up as South Front pulled back.

GERMAN COMMAND
Interfering in the operations of the field armies, Hitler sacked von Bock from command of Army Group B, charging him with not attacking with enough vigour and failing to ensure the adequate supply of his units. Weichs took command of the army group, leaving 2nd Army under General Salmuth.

17 July 1942

NORTHERN SECTOR
The Soviets began a series of attacks against the neck of the Demyansk salient. Bitter fighting raged for the remainder of the month.

18 July 1942

SOUTHERN SECTOR
With yet another change of mind, Hitler ordered Army Group B to resume the advance upon Stalingrad. The 6th Army, already involved in fighting the Stalingrad Front in the Don Elbow, could not comply with this directive as it lacked the resources to push into the river bend. Voroshilovgrad fell to 1st Panzer Army after heavy fighting, while 4th Panzer Army reached the Don near Tsimlyansk.

19 July 1942

SOUTHERN SECTOR
To carry out the attack in the Don Elbow the 6th Army was substantially reinforced and replenished with one panzer and one infantry korp. The objectives of 1st and 4th Panzer Armies were again amended. Instead of advancing towards Rostov from the east, the armies would cross the Don between Tsimlyansk and Rostov and advance on a broad front directly into the Caucasus.

20 July 1942

NORTHERN SECTOR
On the southern perimeter of Leningrad, Nikolayev's 42nd Army attacked 18th Army in an effort to wear down and disperse the strong forces near the city. Bitter fighting continued until 26 August.

SOUTHERN SECTOR
Sixth Army launched strong envelopment attacks against the northern and southern flanks of the Don Elbow. Both 62nd and 64th Armies were heavily attacked and suffered severe casualties. The 63rd and 64th Armies combined numbered 160,000 men, 400 tanks and 2,200 artillery pieces.

The Stavka disbanded South-West Front and allocated its forces to Stalingrad Front. The 38th Army, with ten divisions and 28th Army with six divisions began their transformation into 4th and 1st Tank Armies.

Twenty-first Army with another six divisions also joined the Stalingrad Front.

21 July 1942

SOUTHERN SECTOR
Gordov took command of Stalingrad Front as Timoshenko was relieved. Chuikov took over at 64th Army. On the Stalingrad axis, the concentration of forces increased as the Germans prepared their thrust towards

Stalingrad and the Volga. At this stage of the battle there were eighteen German divisions on this axis, totalling 250,000 men with 7,500 artillery pieces, 740 panzers and 1,200 aircraft of 4th Air Korp. To face this force the Soviets had 187,000 men with 7,900 artillery pieces and 360 tanks.

22 July 1942

SOUTHERN SECTOR
The Soviets fought desperate battles in the Don Elbow as 6th Army crashed into the flanks of 62nd and 64th Armies. After a bloody struggle, the northern flank of 62nd Army was pierced and elements encircled. To the south, 64th Army started to crumble under the weight of the German attack.

Fighting at Rostov intensified as the 13th Panzer and 5th SS *Wiking* Motorised Divisions drew a ring around the city, pressing the Soviets back into the Caucasus. Heavy fighting raged between Rostov and Tsimlyansk as 1st Panzer and 17th Armies attacked, Novocherkassk falling to 17th Army.

With Rostov on the verge of capture and the Soviet forces in the Don Elbow being crushed, Hitler issued Directive No 45. This called for the advance into the Caucasus by 17th Army, while 1st Panzer Army secured the Maikop oilfields and pressed south to Grozny, where the oilfields would be secured. Army Group B was to destroy Soviet forces on the Stalingrad axis and capture the city. In the Crimea, 11th Army was to march to the Leningrad sector, leaving 42nd Korp to carry on the offensive into the Caucasus. The 4th Panzer Army was again allocated to Army Group B, being instructed to push along the south bank of the Don from Kotetnikovo to the Volga, where it was to link up with 6th Army and capture Stalingrad. After the fall of Stalingrad, 6th Army and 4th Panzer were to push along the Volga and take Astrakhan. By ordering both objectives to be seized simultaneously, Hitler was sending his armies on very separate courses. As if this was not bad enough, the secondary objective of securing Stalingrad in order to protect the exposed rear of the forces advancing into the Caucasus had become a primary objective.

To oppose the Germans in the Caucasus, the Soviets had South Front and North Caucasus Front to the rear. Malinovsky's South Front was worn out, 56th and 9th Armies fighting to save Rostov. The 18th and 37th Armies fought on the line of the Don and the 12th and 51st Armies were on the extreme right flank.

To the rear, Budenny's North Caucasus Front deployed 47th Army near Tikhoretsk and 44th Army in the Kuban. On the Russo–Turkish border there was Trans Caucasus Front under Tyulenev.

23 July 1942

NORTHERN SECTOR
With 42nd Army pinning down 18th Army, Sviridov's 55th Army also attacked.

SOUTHERN SECTOR
Elements of 6th Army broke into the right wing of 62nd Army, out-flanking the Soviet unit from the north. A rapid German thrust then reached the Don at Kamensk. Stavka immediately ordered the situation to be restored and the Germans forced back to the Chir. However, the Germans isolated two rifle divisions and one tank brigade of 62nd while the 64th Army also began to crumble.

24 July 1942

SOUTHERN SECTOR
Vasilevsky proposed a counter-attack to defeat the Germans in the Don Elbow. Moskalenko's 1st Tank Army, with two tank corps, one tank brigade and one rifle division, was to attack from Kalach towards Verkhne Buzinovka from where it would strike at Kletskaya. Fourth Tank Army, under Kryuchenkin, was to cross the Don at Kachalinskaya with its two tanks corps, tank brigade and rifle division during 28 July, push west of Verkhne Golubaya and then link up with 1st Tank Army. Danilov's 21st Army would also attack from Serafimovich and Kletskaya at 0300 hours on 27 July to break into the rear of the Germans forces facing 62nd Army. 1st and 4th Tank Armies assembled 550 tanks for the attack, many being new T-34 and Kv models, but neither army was up to full strength.

Fighting in Rostov intensified as the NKVD tried to hold on to the Taganrog road bridge. The sheer weight and ferocity of German attacks forced the Soviets to give ground.

The fighting since the start of the German offensive at the end of June had been costly to the Soviets. Bryansk Front's 13th, 40th and 5th Tank Armies lost 37,000 killed and missing and 29,000 wounded, while South Front lost 128,000 killed and missing and 65,000 wounded. The new Voronezh Front suffered 43,000 killed and missing and 32,000 wounded in the short period from 9 July. The three units also lost 2,400 tanks, 13,700 artillery pieces and 780 aircraft.

25 July 1942

SOUTHERN SECTOR
The Germans pounded the 64th Army, its junction with 62nd Army crumbling. Chuikov attempted to restore the situation by moving armour and

artillery up to the confluence of the Don and Chir rivers. Further German attacks panicked the 64th, its rear area personnel running for the bridges only to be cut down by the Luftwaffe.

Army Group A began its offensive from the Don as 1st Panzer and 17th Armies pushed into the Caucasus and 4th Panzer Army advanced towards Stalingrad. Heavy fighting erupted as 1st Panzer forced back 37th and 12th Armies, leaving 51st vulnerable and at risk of being enveloped on its left flank by 4th Panzer Army. In Rostov 56th and 9th Armies abandoned their positions north of the Don, falling back across the river.

When the German attack began, the 51st, 37th, 12th and 18th Armies mustered 112,000 men, 121 tanks and 2160 artillery pieces supported by the 130 aircraft of the 4th Air Fleet.[14]

26 July 1942

SOUTHERN SECTOR
Chuikov's 64th continued to fight on around the confluence of the Don and Chir. Desperate fighting raged as the men at the front tried to halt the German attacks, while the men in the rear made every effort to escape. With the front crumbling, the 64th was ordered to fall back over the Don. As they withdrew, the bridge at Nizhne Chirskaya was prematurely destroyed, trapping substantial elements of the army on the west bank.

Fighting to the south intensified as 1st Panzer smashed 12th and 37th Armies aside and thrust south. Inside Rostov the Soviets withdrew under heavy attack and by nightfall had given up the city.

27 July 1942

SOUTHERN SECTOR
Leading elements of the 4th Tank Army crossed the Don but came under intense aerial attack. The 1st Tank Army was similarly hard-pressed as it attempted to move into action. While the Soviets attempted to coordinate their counter-attack the Germans broke through south of the Don, punching a forty mile hole in the Soviet line. In the Caucasus, Bataisk fell to 17th Army.

28 July 1942

SOUTHERN SECTOR
The German attack in the Don Elbow ground to a halt as the 6th Army ran out of fuel. This allowed 62nd and 64th to build a thin defence line west of Stalingrad. However, the bulk of 64th was withdrawn via Kalach to the eastern bank of the Don.

In the Caucasus the German attack from the Don had torn apart South Front, leaving a one hundred-mile hole in the Soviet line. The Stavka disbanded South Front and absorbed its units into North Caucasus Front. In just three days of heavy fighting, the South Front lost 15,000 killed and missing and 1,500 wounded. Marshal Budenny became overall commander in this sector but his front was split into two distinct groups. Don Group, under General Malinovsky comprised 37th, 51st and 12th Armies and was instructed to halt the advance of 1st Panzer Army towards the Maikop oilfields, while Coastal Group, under General Cherevichenko, with 18th, 56th and 47th Armies and 17th Cossack Cavalry Corp, was ordered to halt 17th Army and protect the Kuban and the approaches to Krasnodar. Tyulenev was ordered to fortify the line of the Terek and Urukh rivers and the Caucasus mountain passes.

SOVIET COMMAND
With the southern axis crumbling as the Germans pushed deeper into the Caucasus and the Stalingrad Front reeling on the road to Stalingrad, Stalin issued his infamous Order No 227, the 'no step back' order. This forbade any more withdrawal east by the combat forces. The Red Army was rapidly running out of space to manœuvre as the Wehrmacht pressed east and south. Draconian punishments were extended to prevent any retreat from the front, combat units being backed up by NKVD security patrols, which had the authority to open fire on anyone or any unit that retreated before the Germans.

29 July 1942

SOUTHERN SECTOR
The Germans reached Proletarskaya which fell to 1st Panzer Army. Elements then crossed the Manych river and struck south towards Maikop.

30 July 1942

CENTRAL SECTOR
The Kalinin Front with the 29th, 30th and 3rd Air Armies, and the Western Front with its 20th, 31st and 1st Air Armies, launched the Rzhev–Sychevka Offensive Operation with an initial force of 345,100 men.[15]

SOUTHERN SECTOR
Stalingrad Front began its counter-attack in the Don Elbow. The 4th Tank Army finally attacked, striking the northern flank of 6th Army, while 1st Tank Army also began its attack. Both forces were struck by the Luftwaffe and suffered heavy casualties. Despite this, 4th Tank hit 14th Panzer Korp,

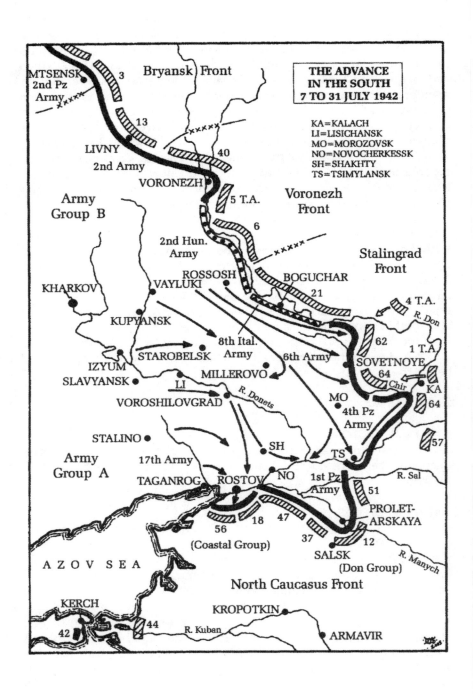

THE ADVANCE
IN THE SOUTH
7 TO 31 JULY 1942

KA=KALACH
LI=LISICHANSK
MO=MOROZOVSK
NO=NOVOCHERKESSK
SH=SHAKHTY
TS=TSIMYLANSK

MTSENSK
2nd Pz
Army
3

Bryansk Front

13

LIVNY
2nd Army
40

VORONEZH

Army
Group B

5 T.A.

Voronezh
Front

2nd Hun.
Army

6

ROSSOSH
VAYLUKI

BOGUCHAR

Stalingrad
Front

KHARKOV

21

4 T.A.
R. Don

KUPYANSK

8th Ital.
Army

6th Army

62

1 T.A.

STAROBELSK

SOVETNOYE

IZYUM
SLAVYANSK

MILLEROVO

LI

R. Donets

64

Chir

KA

VOROSHILOVGRAD

MO

64

4th Pz
Army

STALINO

SH

TS

57

Army
Group A

17th Army

NO

1st Pz
Army

R. Sal

TAGANROG

ROSTOV

51

56

18

47

37

PROLET-
ARSKAYA

(Coastal Group)

12

SALSK

R. Manych

A Z O V   S E A

(Don Group)

North Caucasus Front

KERCH

KROPOTKIN

42

44

R. Kuban

ARMAVIR

resulting in a furious tank battle. The 62nd Army was pressed back while 64th Army was pounded at Kalach. In direct response to the beating the 64th Army was receiving, Gordov began to move 57th Army up to the Don.

31 July 1942

SOUTHERN SECTOR

German attacks halted the 4th and list Tank Armies, inflicting crippling losses. Hoth's 4th Panzer struck Kolomit's 51st Army, pushing its five weak divisions back upon Kotelnikovo. To meet this new threat, Gordov had to try to redeploy his skeletal forces. Lopatin took over 62nd Army while Shumilov took over 64th, Chuikov going to command an operational group on the southern wing of 64th. The 57th Army was to be pushed into the line from the reserve.

GERMAN DEPLOYMENT

The Germans were increasingly relying on their allies to protect the long exposed Don flank, having introduced 2nd Hungarian and 8th Italian Armies between 2nd and 6th Armies. Across the front as a whole, the Germans had moved two infantry divisions into the line but one panzer, one motorised and two infantry divisions left, leaving nineteen panzer, fifteen motorised and one hundred and thirty-five infantry divisions in the line. During July the German motorised divisions were re-designated panzer-grenadier divisions.[16]

GERMAN CASUALTIES

During July the Germans lost 38,000 men killed in the east.

SOVIET COMMAND

The 15th Air Army, under Pyatykhin, was raised and attached to Bryansk Front.[17]

1 August 1942

CENTRAL SECTOR

The Kalinin Front, using 30th and 29th Armies, began a series of attacks aimed at clearing the Germans from the north bank of the Volga around Rzhev and taking the town. The 31st and 20th Armies of the West Front were to punch their way through the south face of the salient, taking Pogoreloye, Gorodische and Karmanovo. The attack continued during August, placing great pressure upon the 9th Army but failing to make any territorial gain.

SOUTHERN SECTOR
In the Don Elbow fierce battles raged as Stalingrad Fronts 1st and 4th Tank Armies tried to gain time for the shattered 62nd and 64th Armies to fall back across the Don. There was heavy fighting around Kalach where 64th Army crossed to the east bank.

First Panzer Army pushed deeper into the Caucasus, 13th Panzer Division reaching the Kuban at Kropotkin and threatening the rear of 44th Army in the Kuban peninsula.

2 August 1942

SOUTHERN SECTOR
German mobile units entered Kotelnikovo as they pushed towards Stalingrad.

SOVIET COMMAND
The Stalingrad Front was dismembered, being split up into two new formations. A smaller Stalingrad Front was created and a new South-East Front formed. The Stalingrad Front, with 63rd, 21st, 62nd, 1st Guards, 4th Tank and 16th Air Armies, was placed under the command of General Gordov, while General Eremenko took over South-East Front, which deployed 64th, 57th and 51st Armies and 8th Air Army. Tolbukhin's 57th Army had only recently deployed on the southern approaches to Stalingrad. The boundary of the two fronts was along the Tsaritsyn river in Stalingrad and on to Kalach.

3 August 1942

SOUTHERN SECTOR
Attacks by the 6th Army broke the right wing of 62nd Army and reached the Don on a broad front near Malogolubaya. Gordov aimed to counter-attack with 21st Army and 1st and 4th Tank Armies to isolate the German spearhead. Lopatin asked permission to pull his embattled 62nd back but was refused.

The 4th Panzer Army threw 51st Army back along the road to Stalingrad. In the Caucasus, Stavropol fell to Kleist's panzers. Malinovsky's Don Group was pushed farther away from the Coastal Group as the German attack gained momentum.

4 August 1942

SOVIET COMMAND
Attacks by the 21st, 1st and 4th Tank Armies failed to push the Germans away from the Don. Stalin appointed Trufanov to command 51st Army.

5 August 1942

SOUTHERN SECTOR
The 21st, 1st and 4th Tank Armies halted their attacks after a total lack of success.

Hoth breached the Soviet outer defences around Stalingrad as 64th and 57th Armies were attacked South-West of the city. Fierce fighting erupted at Tinguta station as panzers bogged down in extensive Soviet minefields. Fourth Panzer suffered heavy casualties, its attack coming to a costly halt. With the Germans stalled, the Soviets launched a furious counter-attack, forcing 4th Panzer onto the defensive. As 4th Panzer approached from the south-west, 6th Army hit 64th Army.

Farther south, 1st Panzer Army crossed the Kuban. Voroshilovsk fell but the Soviets evaded encirclement by advancing German panzers. In an effort to catch the rapidly withdrawing Soviets the 1st Panzer pushed south-west towards Armavir, Maikop and Tuapse. The 17th Army planned to destroy the Soviets in the Novorossysk, Krasnodar and Tuapse area. To accomplish this, Army Group A split into two groups. Group Ruoff, with 17th Army (five German and three Rumanian divisions) was tasked with the destruction of the Coastal Group, securing the mountain passes and the Black Sea coast. Group Kleist comprised 1st Panzer Army with three panzer, two motorised and four infantry divisions and one Slovak division. Kleist had four hundred panzers at his disposal but was at the end of a long supply line that stretched two thousand miles to the west. His target was the capture of Baku and its oilfields.

6 August 1942

NORTHERN SECTOR
Heavy attacks were unleashed against the Demyansk salient. The 11th Army launched strong attacks aimed at nipping off the salient and isolating the Germans.

Hitler had begun to lay down plans for the capture of Leningrad. Operation Nordlicht would throw the 11th Army into a concerted attack into the city environs. It was planned for mid-September.

CENTRAL SECTOR
The Soviets committed 6th and 8th Tank Corps and 2nd Guards Cavalry Corp to support 31st and 20th Armies attacks around Rzhev. Fierce tank battles erupted as the Germans committed their armoured reserves.

SOUTHERN SECTOR
After a bitter battle around Armavir the Germans smashed 1st Independent Rifle Corp, the town falling to 1st Panzer Army, which then forced the

Kuban river. Both 18th and 12th Armies retreated before Group Kleist, falling back to cover the Maikop oilfields. Tikhoretsk fell to 17th Army as Group Ruoff reached the Chelbas.

To prevent the loss of the Maikop–Tuapse line, Budenny deployed the 12th and 18th Armies, together with 17th Cavalry Corp. Tyulenev started the fortification of defensive positions along the Terek.

7 August 1942

CENTRAL SECTOR
Fierce fighting continued around Rzhev as the Soviet and German armoured units struggled to gain headway. Losses to both combatants were very heavy.

SOUTHERN SECTOR
The Germans launched a massive effort to crush 62nd Army in the Don Elbow. The 24th and 16th Panzer Divisions hit both flanks of the 62nd.

8 August 1942

CENTRAL SECTOR
Zubtsov fell to the Soviets after a costly battle. The Germans restored their lines east of Sychevka, having repelled the massed Soviet armoured forces.

SOUTHERN SECTOR
The German attacks in the Don Elbow took Surovniko as 14th and 24th Panzer Korps penetrated into the flanks of 62nd Army and 1st Tank Army. Soviet armoured losses were crippling as the Luftwaffe pounded Soviet movement.

9 August 1942

SOUTHERN SECTOR
The 24th and 16th Panzer Divisions met behind 62nd Army, cutting off eight divisions and elements of the 1st Tank Army. Fighting inside the pocket was intense as 6th Army immediately began the destruction of the encircled units. First Guards Army threw three divisions into an attack to relieve the trapped force.

SOVIET COMMAND
The Stavka subordinated the Stalingrad Front to Eremenko's South-East Front. Gordov became deputy commander of Stalingrad Front as Eremenko took senior command. Golikov became deputy for South-

East Front. Moskalenko was given command of the newly forming 1st Guards Army. To assess the deteriorating situation in the south, Stalin ordered Zhukov to join Vasilevsky.

10 August 1942

SOUTHERN SECTOR
The Maikop oilfields fell to 13th Panzer Division of 1st Panzer Army, but the retreating Red Army sabotaged the oil production installations. 17th Army attacked Krasnodar, while 1st Panzer was involved in heavy fighting near Stavropol.

The Soviet High Command ordered North Caucasus Front to cover the approaches to the Black Sea, using Kamkov's 18th Army and 17th Cavalry Corp to cover the mountain passes and Grechko's 12th Army to defend the junction of 18th and 56th Armies. Kotov's 47th Army was to protect Novorossysk.

11 August 1942

SOUTHERN SECTOR
The Soviet forces trapped in the Don bend were destroyed, 62nd Army losing 35,000 men killed and captured. Kalach fell to 6th Army as its pincers again met up behind the remnants of 62nd Army. The Soviets were retreating across the river in force, destroying the Don bridges as they went.

GERMAN COMMAND
The acrimonious relationship between Hitler and Field Marshal Halder hit rock bottom as Halder argued that the primary objective of the campaign remained the capture of Moscow. Hitler countered that it was oil that was vital to Germany and pinned his planning upon the capture of the Caucasus oilfields. However, as the fighting around Stalingrad intensified, Hitler became obsessed with the capture of the city, throwing more and more forces into the exposed salient that would jut out to the Volga.

12 August 1942

NORTHERN SECTOR
A sudden change in the weather saved the Germans at the neck of the Demyansk salient from being overrun. Lashing rain halted Soviet attacks as their air forces were grounded and the ground turned to swamp.

SOUTHERN SECTOR

Slavyansk fell to 17th Army. The fighting in the Kuban intensified as Coastal Group fought to prevent the Germans from reaching the Black Sea coast.

GERMAN COMMAND

The German 11th Army received orders from OKH instructing the army headquarters, together with headquarters of 54th and 30th Korps, to proceed to the Leningrad sector. Only four divisions were to remain with 11th Army, the remainder being dispersed along the eastern front or held in the Crimea.

14 August 1942

SOUTHERN SECTOR

Sixth Army cleared the Don Elbow. The 1st Tank Army had been comprehensively defeated alongside the 62nd Army and was disbanded within a few weeks.

Fourth Panzer Army pushed its 16th Motorised Division out to the south, capturing Elitsa. The 16th Motorised protected the floating junction of Army Groups A and B and patrolled a vast sector stretching from the Sarpa Lakes south of Stalingrad to the Kuma river in the Caucasus. Leading scouts of this division would push the farthest east of any Germans, coming to within twenty miles of Astrakhan. Only the lack of Soviet units prevented a deep penetration into the junction of the two army groups.

Mineralnye Vody fell to 1st Panzer Army as it closed upon Grozny. Supplies were increasingly short as the lines of communication stretched to breaking point. 13th Panzer Division was instructed to join with 3rd and 23rd Panzer Divisions of 3rd Panzer Korp.

15 August 1942

SOUTHERN SECTOR

At 0430 hours the 6th Army unleashed another offensive in the Don Elbow, striking the 4th Tank Army in the small loop of the Don. Already weakened, the 4th Tank struggled against the massive German hammer blows. German forces crossed the river at Trekhostrovskoya and also at the junction with 62nd Army at Perepolnyi.[18]

The Germans consolidated in the Don Elbow as 6th Army attacked Soviet concentrations at Sirotinskaya. First Guards and 4th Tank Armies were severely mauled, over 13,000 prisoners being taken as the Soviets abandoned their positions and fell back across the Don. A Soviet bridgehead at Kamensk remained to threaten the German flank.

The build up of forces on the Stalingrad axis continued as both combat-ants committed increasing numbers to the fighting. Against Stalingrad Front's forty-two divisions between 63rd, 24th, 66th, 21st, 1st Guards and 4th Tank Armies, with 414,000 men, 200 tanks and 2,000 artillery pieces and South-East Front with 62nd, 64th, 57th and 51st Armies with 160,000 men, 70 tanks and 1,400 artillery pieces the Germans deployed Paulus' 6th Army with 430,000 men, 440 panzers and 5,300 artillery pieces and Hoth's 4th Panzer Army with 158,000 men and 2,100 artillery pieces. Fourth Panzer Army was a shadow of its former self though, having lost 14th and 24th Panzer Korps to 6th Army and 40th Panzer Korp to Army Group A. This left Hoth with 48th Panzer Korp of one panzer and one motorised division, 4th Korp with three infantry divisions and 6th Rumanian Korp with four divisions. Later in the campaign even 48th Panzer Korp was detached to bolster 3rd Rumanian Army to the north and 16th Motorised Division was unavailable, being situated far out on the Kalmyuk Steppe.

Farther south, 1st Panzer Army pushed into the Caucasus, captur-ing Georgievsk. With the continuing success of the German attacks, the Stavka ordered the establishment of Maslennikov's Northern Group with 44th, 37th and 9th Armies. Maslennikov's group was to cover the approaches to Grozny. Budenny was to block the approaches to the Black Sea with 18th Army and 17th Cavalry Corp, while 12th Army secured the junction of the 18th and 56th Armies. The 47th Army was to defend Novorossysk.

16 August 1942

CENTRAL SECTOR
After two weeks of bitter fighting in the Rzhev region, 20th, 31st, 29th and 30th Armies had made only minor gains in salient, but inflicted over 20,000 casualties upon 9th Army. Army Group Centre requested permis-sion to evacuate the salient to shorten the line and create an operational reserve but Hitler categorically refused.

SOUTHERN SECTOR
The Germans conquered the Kuban, inflicting heavy losses upon North Caucasus Front. The divergent axes of the German advance in the Caucasus had stretched Army Group A to breaking point, Groups Rouff and Kleist operating as two widely separate forces. With the fall of the Kuban, Army Group A began to regroup to undertake the second phase of its offensive. First Panzer Army was to push east from Voroshilovsk towards Grozny, Makhatchkala and Baku, securing the Caucasus and cutting off the Soviet forces against the Turkish border. Group Ruoff was to attack from Krasnodar, take Novorossiysk and roll up Soviet defences on the

Black Sea coast and reach the Turkish border near Batumi. The high mountain ranges separating the two German axes were to be conquered by 49th
Mountain Korp, attacking from Cherkessk. In an effort to strengthen his
defences in the mountains, Tyulenev raised Sergatskov's 46th Army and
moved it north to block the German advance.

17 August 1942

SOUTHERN SECTOR
After heavy losses, the 1st Tank Army was disbanded, its skeletal divisions being incorporated into 62nd Army. The Soviets attempted to
rebuild their broken units, reinforcing 62nd, 1st Guards, 21st, 63rd and
4th Tank Armies.

With the Soviet forces in disarray, 6th Army captured bridgeheads
over the Don at Vertyachi and Luchinskoy with 76th and 295th Infantry
Divisions. Sixty-second and 4th Tank Armies launched repeated counter
attacks in an effort to destroy the bridgehead but failed.

Army Group A resumed its attacks, Yessentuki, Kislovodsk and
Pyatigorsk falling to Group Kleist.

18 August 1942

SOUTHERN SECTOR
The 1st Guards Army crossed the Don with five divisions and established
a bridgehead at Kremenskaya, brushing aside the Italian 8th Army with
ease.

In the Caucasus the Germans opened the battle for the mountain
passes, Konrad's 49th Mountain Korp striking 46th Army. Maslennikov's
Northern Group came under heavy attack along the Kuma river, the
Germans forcing the Soviets away from the river line as they pushed
towards Mozdok. The retreat to the Terek began.

19 August 1942

NORTHERN SECTOR
The Neva Group and 13th Air Army of the Leningrad Front, together with
the reformed 2nd Shock, 8th and 14th Air Armies of the Volkhov Front,
mounted the Sinyavino Offensive Operation. Some 190,000 men were
committed to the attack.[19]

20 August 1942

SOUTHERN SECTOR
The Soviets launched a new attack from the Kremensk bridgehead in an

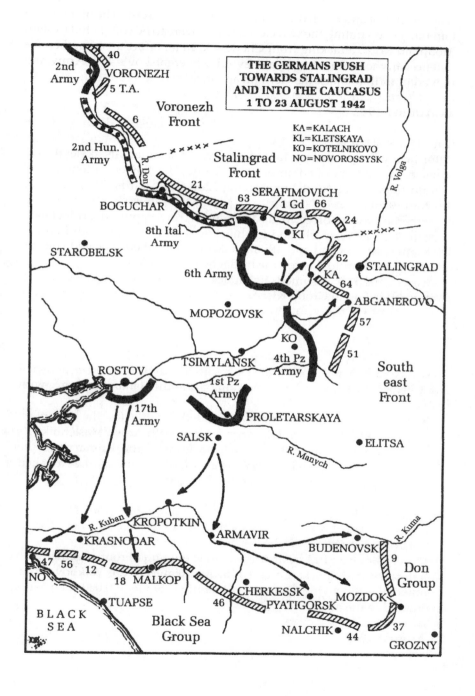

THE GERMANS PUSH
TOWARDS STALINGRAD
AND INTO THE CAUCASUS
1 TO 23 AUGUST 1942

KA=KALACH
KL=KLETSKAYA
KO=KOTELNIKOVO
NO=NOVOROSSYSK

2nd
Army
VORONEZH
5 T.A.

Voronezh
Front

2nd Hun.
Army

R. Don

Stalingrad
Front

R. Volga

21

BOGUCHAR

SERAFIMOVICH
63
1 Gd   66

24

8th Ital.
Army

KI

STAROBELSK

6th Army

62

KA
64

STALINGRAD

MOPOZOVSK

ABGANEROVO

57

KO
4th Pz
Army

51

ROSTOV

TSIMYLANSK

1st Pz
Army

South
east
Front

17th
Army

PROLETARSKAYA

SALSK

R. Manych

ELITSA

R. Kuban

KROPOTKIN

ARMAVIR

R. Kuma

KRASNODAR

BUDENOVSK

9

Don
Group

47 56

NO

12

18 MALKOP

TUAPSE

CHERKESSK

MOZDOK

46   PYATIGORSK

37

BLACK
SEA

Black Sea
Group

NALCHIK   44

GROZNY

effort to pin the flank of 6th Army and prevent the transfer of troops or the assault upon Stalingrad. Garibaldi's 8th Italian Army had deployed here, releasing German forces. The Soviet attack succeeded in forcing the Italians back but failed to prevent the 6th Army offensive. Fourth Panzer Army began its attack from Abganerovo with Kempf's 48th Panzer Korp. Committing 24th and 14th Panzer and 29th Motorised Divisions, the Germans ran into strong Soviet defences, many tanks being lost in mine-fields at Tundutovo. The three infantry divisions of Schwedler's 4th Korp (94th, 371st, 297th) were also bogged down in heavy fighting with 64th Army and failed to push away from their start lines, being strung out on a line from Tinguta to Abganerovo.

With heavy fighting at the gates of Stalingrad, in the Caucasus 17th Army pressed closer to Novorossysk. Krymsk fell after a bitter struggle as the Soviet defences crumbled.

21 August 1942

SOUTHERN SECTOR
Bitter fighting continued around Abganerovo and Tinguta as the Germans repeated their unsuccessful attacks.

22 August 1942

SOUTHERN SECTOR
The 64th Army stalled both 48th Panzer and 4th Korps south-west of Stalingrad.

> *Hitler's continual interference and redirection of forces had impacted heavily upon the course of offensive to the Don. Wasted time and lost opportunities meant the Red Army had evaded destruction in the fashion of '41. Despite this, Hitler jumped to the conclusion that a lack of prisoners meant a lack enemy forces. Nothing could be further from the truth. Truly the Soviet conduct of the campaign had been appalling, Hitler's own meddling having been their saving grace, but the field armies were still largely intact, if demoralised. Stalin though had changed everything with his 'Not one more step back' order. No longer would the Red Army retreat. Soviet space was no longer limitless. Germany had reached the peak of its success.*

NOTES

1   Invaluable detail has been offered by Glantz, *Kharkov 1942*, on the course of this little documented offensive.
2   Kirosheev, *Soviet Casualties and Combat Losses in the Twentieth Century*, Table 75
3   Kirosheev, *Soviet Casualties and Combat Losses in the Twentieth Century*, Table 75
4   Kirosheev, *Soviet Casualties and Combat Losses in the Twentieth Century*, Table 75
5   Manstein, *Lost Victories*, p 245
6   Manstein, *Lost Victories*, p 245
7   Manstein, *Lost Victories*, p 245
8   Ellis, *The World War Two Databook*, p 175
9   Manstein, *Lost Victories*, p 250
10 Kirosheev, *Soviet Casualties and Combat Losses in the Twentieth Century*, Table 75
11 Ellis, *The World War Two Databook*, p 175
12 Kirosheev, *Soviet Casualties and Combat Losses in the Twentieth Century*, Table 67
13 Kirosheev, *Soviet Casualties and Combat Losses in the Twentieth Century*, Table 75
14 Erickson, *The Road to Stalingrad*, p 376
15 Kirosheev, *Soviet Casualties and Combat Losses in the Twentieth Century*, Table 75
16 Ellis, *The World War Two Databook*, p 175
17 Ellis, *The World War Two Datatbook*, p 81
18 Erickson, *The Road to Stalingrad*, p 369
19 Kirosheev, *Soviet Casualties and Combat Losses in the Twentieth Century*, Table 75
20 Tarrant, *Stalingrad*, p 55

CHAPTER VII

Bloodbath on the Volga

With Paulus poised on the Don, ready to strike east to the Volga and Kleist forcing his way deeper into the Caucasus, the German armies on the southern wing found themselves advancing on broadly separate axes. Hitler's decision to alter his own plan to achieve both of the campaign objectives simultaneously would fundamentally affect the outcome of the 1942 summer offensive. The Ostheer would find itself fighting a battle it was entirely unsuited for in the city on the banks of the Volga river.

23 August 1942

CENTRAL SECTOR

During the Rzhev–Sychevka Operation, the armies of the Kalinin and Western Fronts suffered 51,482 killed and missing and 142,201 wounded.[1]

SOUTHERN SECTOR

At 0430 hours Weitersheim's 14th Panzer Korp, with one panzer and two motorised divisions, crossed the Don at Vertyachi. After a brief battle, 16th Panzer Division broke through 98th Rifle Division of 62nd Army and forced 214th Rifle Division on its right back to the north. By 0800 hours the Soviets had collapsed and the Germans rushed across the narrow Don–Volga land bridge. The 16th Panzer Division pushed rapidly east, disregarding the threat to its open flanks. By 1815 hours its leading panzer grenadier regiment reached the west bank of the Volga at Rynok and secured Spartakovka to the north of Stalingrad The Germans then tried to push additional forces across the Don, 71st Infantry Division crossing at Kalach. The alerted Soviets put up fierce resistance, slowing 71st Infantry while counter-attacks by 87th Rifle Division threatened to isolate 16th Panzer Division. Bitter fighting raged as the panzers rushed from one sector to another, repelling numerous Soviet attacks. The two motorised divisions of 14th Panzer Korp struggled to close up to 16th Panzer, being held up by continual Soviet counter-attacks. By nightfall the 3rd Motorised was twelve miles behind 16th Panzer and 60th Motorised a further ten miles behind 3rd.

A massive Luftwaffe raid by 600 bombers struck the city during the day, killing over 40,000 civilians and wrecking many buildings. Oil tanks on the west bank of the Volga were set alight and the docks burned.

24 August 1942

SOUTHERN SECTOR
The Luftwaffe appeared over Stalingrad again, bombing the city and reducing its buildings to rubble. Fires raged out of control along the western bank of the Volga as oil tanks in the northern industrial suburbs burned. Whole stretches of the river seemed to be on fire as burning oil flowed onto the water, blanketing the city with a pall of choking, black smoke. In the southern suburbs, Tsaritsyn and Dar Gova were largely destroyed, the majority of their wooden buildings burning to the ground.

The 3rd and 60th Motorised Divisions, of 14th Panzer Korp, struggled to hold off Soviet attacks along the Don–Volga land bridge while launching attacks with 16th Panzer into the northern suburbs of Stalingrad. With the infantry of the 6th Army pounding the 62nd Army west of the city, Lopatin requested permission to pull his army back to the middle defence line. Eremenko was planning to counter-attack around Vertyachi.

The advance of 4th Panzer Army again bogged down at Tundutovo, Hoth's panzers suffering further heavy losses.

25 August 1942

NORTHERN SECTOR
The Soviets opened fierce attacks at the neck of the Demyansk salient, pounding the weakened German units.

SOUTHERN SECTOR
With 62nd Army under heavy attack along its positions west of Stalingrad, at 0515 hours Stalin ordered Lopatin end 64th Army back to the final defence line. Later in the day Stalin changed his mind and ordered the 64th and 62nd Armies to counter-attack at Vertyachi. The Soviets duly attacked and were repulsed.

The 71st Infantry Division smashed its way out of the Kalach bridgehead, pushing towards Karpovka. Soviet resistance continued to be fierce, with the 71st taking the next seven days to push the Soviets back twenty miles.

Fourth Panzer Army broke off its attacks at Tundutovo after a complete lack of success. Hoth began to redeploy his forces west of Abganerovo to skirt around the flank of 64th Army and roll it up upon Stalingrad. The 64th Army was unaware of the German plan.

To the south, Group Kleist was involved in heavy fighting along the Terek, 9th Army resisting fiercely at Mozdok. After a bitter battle, the town fell to the Germans. In an effort to halt the German advance the Soviets began to move 58th Army up from Makhachkala to the Terek.

26 August 1942

SOUTHERN SECTOR

Heavy fighting raged as the 16th Panzer Division fought on the bank of the Volga. The 6th Army was fully committed to the battle for Stalingrad but only managed a slow advance, pushing the Soviet forces closer to the city. The advance actually forced the Soviets out of the danger of encirclement, the Soviet pocket to the west and south-west of the city being flattened by Paulus' uninspired frontal assaults. Hoth's failed attack at Tundutovo compounded the German failure to isolate the Soviets west of the city. With the defence of Stalingrad a priority, Stalin appointed General Zhukov as his deputy.

27 August 1942

NORTHERN SECTOR

Following a quiet period, the Leningrad sector erupted into life as the Soviets began a new offensive aimed at relieving the siege. Meretskov's Volkhov Front led the assault with the reformed 2nd Shock Army, smashing the 18th Army near Gaitolovo with ease and advancing rapidly into the German rear. The 2nd Shock aimed to link up with the Neva Operational Group inside Leningrad, breaking the year-long siege. However, the arrival on the Volkhov of what was left of the German 11th Army altered the situation. Manstein, originally tasked with the reduction of Leningrad, was immediately ordered to halt the Soviet attack and destroy the revitalised Volkhov Front.

SOUTHERN SECTOR

North of Stalingrad 16th Panzer Division was in danger of annihilation as it ran low on ammunition. The division was exhausted and could not hold out much longer. Sixth Army continued its slow advance towards the Volga, while Hoth's 4th Panzer Army redeployed around Abganerovo.

As the situation at Stalingrad deteriorated, with 62nd Army falling back towards the city, the Stavka began to concentrate 24th, 1st Guards and 66th Armies along the Don–Volga land bridge to bring pressure to bear upon the over-extended 14th Panzer Korp. The attack was to begin on 2 September, but all three armies needed to redeploy into their new sectors.

28 August 1942

SOUTHERN SECTOR
The 48th Panzer Korp had completed its redeployment around Abganerovo and prepared to strike 64th Army in its flank. The 14th Panzer Korp fought its way across the land bridge, 3rd Motorised Division securing communications with 16th Panzer. Sixtieth Motorised Division still lagged behind, being out of touch with the 3rd and 16th Divisions. Soviet attacks against 16th Panzer Division relented as 66th Army wore itself out. The pressure that had been brought to bear upon 14th Panzer Korp had prevented the Germans from attacking straight into Stalingrad after they reached the Volga, giving the Soviets a chance to construct their defences. In the Caucasus, 17th Army captured Anapa as it drew closer to Novorossysk.

29 August 1942

SOUTHERN SECTOR
With supporting artillery fire, 48th Panzer Korp launched its attack south west of Stalingrad. Shumilov's 64th Army was surprised by the new attack and broke, Hoth's panzers advancing twenty miles to Gavrilovka at the end, of the day. The 4th Korp attempted to pin 64th Army frontally, but Shumilov extricated his army, withdrawing towards Stalingrad to avoid isolation south of the city.

As the battle on the approaches intensified, Zhukov arrived to coordinate the attacks of the armies on the Don–Volga land bridge. After consultation with the Stalingrad Front command, Zhukov informed Stalin that 66th, 1st Guards and 24th Armies would be unable to counter-attack until 6 September. Stalin ordered Zhukov to begin the offensive as soon as possible but accepted 6 September.

30 August 1942

SOUTHERN SECTOR
The 60th Motorised Division linked up with 3rd Motorised and 16th Panzer Divisions, while the six infantry divisions of 51st and 8th Korps secured the Don–Volga land bridge. Kempf's 48th Panzer Korp crossed the Karpovka river, just thirty miles from Stalingrad. With their lines of communication under threat, 62nd and 64th Armies abandoned their salient west of the city and fell back to the final defensive position. Hoth concentrated his forces for a rapid advance directly into Stalingrad, cutting 62nd and 64th Armies off from the Volgo. However, the sluggishness of Paulus' attack allowed the Soviets to slip into the city first.

The 1st Panzer Army renewed the attack towards Grozny as 40th Panzer

Korp launched a ferocious attack and 52nd Korp moved upon Malgobek and Ordzhonikidze. Third Panzer Korp was ordered to cut the Batumi to Tflis road. The 9th and 37th Armies put up fierce resistance. Heavy fighting raged around Mozdok as Kleist attempted to break the Soviet forward defences. After bitter fighting, elements of 13th Panzer Division forced a crossing of the Terek at Ishcherskaya, securing a small bridgehead.

With the Germans once more on the move, Tyulenev's Trans–Caucasus Front was made responsible for the defence of the mountain passes which led to the Black Sea, while Cherevichenko's Coastal Group was renamed Black Sea Group. Maslennikov's Northern Group incorporated the Don Group into its strength, deploying 44th, 9th and 37th Armies on the line of the Kuma and Terek rivers.

31 August 1942

SOUTHERN SECTOR

The 1st Guards Army concentrated north of Stalingrad to bring pressure to bear upon 14th Panzer Korp. Twenty-fourth and 66th Armies began to move into their attack sectors but remained weak, lacking personnel and weapons. The advance of 48th Panzer Korp drove into the rear of 62nd and 64th Armies, penetrating close to Pitomnik. Paulus reacted too slowly to effect the isolation of the Soviet armies. As a preventive measure, the headquarters of Stalingrad Front was moved to Malaya Ivanovka.

In the Caucasus, heavy fighting along the Terek river saw 1st Panzer Army attempt to break the defences of Northern Group. The Soviets resisted fiercely but were unable to prevent the Germans from consolidating their bridgeheads across the river.

The heavy fighting in the Caucasus had cost the Soviets dear. Since the end of July the North Caucasus Front had lost 35,000 killed and missing and 8,800 wounded, while Trans–Caucasus Front lost 7,300 killed and missing and 5,000 wounded since 10 August.

SOVIET DEPLOYMENT

The Soviet raised the 9th Air Army but was not attached to a combat front. The 10th Air Army, 11th and 12th were also raised and held in reserve with the 9th. The 16th was attached to Don Front.[2]

GERMAN DEPLOYMENT

During August the 257th Infantry Division left the east, no other new units entering the combat area to replace it, giving a strength of nineteen panzer, fifteen motorised and one hundred and thirty-four infantry divisions.[3] The commitment of Germany's allies increased, 3rd Rumanian Army becoming fully operational. This new force began to deploy onto

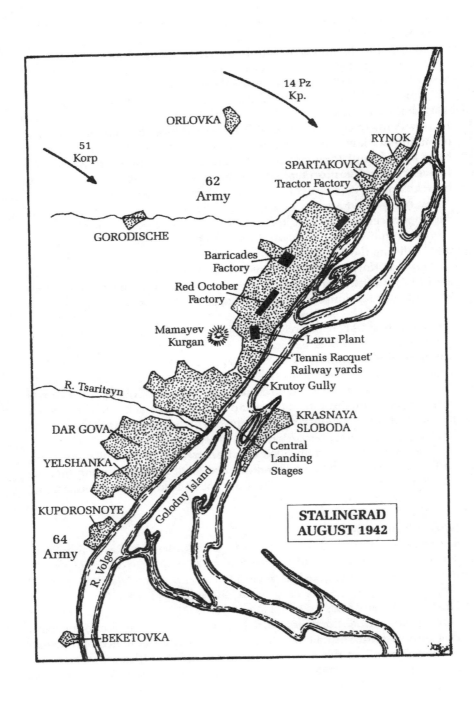

14 Pz Kp.

ORLOVKA

RYNOK

51 Korp

SPARTAKOVKA

62 Army

Tractor Factory

GORODISCHE

Barricades Factory

Red October Factory

Mamayev Kurgan

Lazur Plant

'Tennis Racquet' Railway yards

R. Tsaritsyn

Krutoy Gully

KRASNAYA SLOBODA

DAR GOVA

YELSHANKA

Central Landing Stages

Golodny Island

KUPOROSNOYE

64 Army

R. Volga

STALINGRAD AUGUST 1942

BEKETOVKA

the northern flank of 6th Army, releasing German units for the assault into Stalingrad.

The fighting during the month had cost the Germans 62,000 killed.

1 September 1942

SOUTHERN SECTOR

Fourth Panzer Army pushed 64th Army back to the southern suburbs of Stalingrad and was close to linking up with 6th Army near Pitomnik, 14th Panzer and 29th Motorised Divisions launching strong attacks. However, 62nd Army escaped encirclement at Pitomnik and fell back into Stalingrad. As the fighting around Stalingrad intensified, 1st Guards Army redeployed around Lozenoye to strike at the northern flank of 6th Army between the Don and the Volga. The Soviets were short of weapons and ammunition, but Stalin would not grant any further time for preparation, ordering the attack to begin as planned.

The 42nd Korp, all that remained of 11th Army in the Crimea, crossed the Kerch strait to land in the Kuban. The 42nd then joined Group Ruoff in its efforts to conquer the Black Sea coast.

2 September 1942

SOUTHERN SECTOR

The 51st Korp and 48th Panzer Korp pushed into the Pitomnik area but found the bulk of the 62nd and 64th Armies had pulled out. German pressure at Stalingrad forced 62nd and 64th Armies back closer to the city. Paulus had acted too slowly to trap the Soviet forces on the steppe.

In the Caucasus, the 17th Army entered the northern suburbs of Novorossiysk but was embroiled in bitter street fighting with 47th Army. Ott's 52nd Korp crossed the Terek in force as it advanced upon Grozny, supporting 3rd Panzer Korp. A substantial bridgehead was secured, threatening Maslennikov's left flank.

3 September 1942

SOUTHERN SECTOR

North of Stalingrad, Moskalenko's 1st Guards Army attacked at 0700 hours, hitting 14th Panzer Korp with 24th and 116th Rifle Divisions and 7th and 16th Tank Corps. The 1st launched its attacks earlier than 66th and 24th Armies at Stalin's orders for action to relieve the pressure upon 62nd and 64th Armies. Moskalenko's attack was badly coordinated and visible to the Germans on the high ground to the south, 14th Panzer bringing down concentrated artillery fire and aerial attacks upon the tightly packed Soviet forces. After just a few thousand yards, the attack ground to a halt.

Stalin pressed Zhukov to continue the attacks. Zhukov reported that the armies were not yet ready to attack in force and wanted to wait until 5 September. Stalin agreed reluctantly.

Leading elements of 4th Panzer and 6th Armies linked up at Pitomnik but failed to isolate 64th or 62nd Armies outside Stalingrad, the Soviets having withdrawn closer to the city. German attacks pressed towards Stalingrad on a broad front, pushing the Soviets into the suburbs rather than encircling them on the steppe. In a massive show of strength, the Luftwaffe again bombed Stalingrad, reducing more buildings to rubble. All this achieved though was the formation of ready-made barricades across the streets running to tile Volga, which 6th Army would later have to fight bloody battles to overcome.

Heavy fighting raged to the south as 17th Army pressed 47th Army back into Novorossiysk. Meanwhile, 1st Panzer Army clawed its way closer to Grozny but was reaching the end of its strength.

> *Paulus' failure to isolate the 64th and 62nd Armies west of Stalingrad was a basic error. His uninspired leadership enabled the Red Army to escape an obvious trap. Had the Germans isolated Soviet defenders on the steppe west of the city, it is doubtful Stalingrad would have held and German forces would have dominated the lower Volga, securing the rear of their forces in the Caucasus.*

4 September 1942

NORTHERN SECTOR
The German 11th Army redeployed into the Gaitolovo sector to destroy the salient jutting into the line between Leningrad and the Volkhov. Quickly manoeuvring their forces, the Germans committed 26th Korp (121st Infantry, 5th Mountain and 28th Light Divisions) to their northern wing and the newly arrived 30th Korp (24th, 132nd, 170th Infantry and 3rd Mountain Divisions) to the south. Manstein aimed to crush the flanks of the salient and encircle the Soviet force.

SOUTHERN SECTOR
First Guards Army renewed its attack at 0630 hours after a thirty-minute artillery barrage, but suffered heavy casualties under the fire of 14th Panzer Korp. At 0900 hours 66th Army joined the attack, followed by 24th in 1500 hours. Both armies were also pounded by German artillery and small arms fire and brought to an abrupt halt. Strong German counter-attacks threw the 24th and 66th Armies back to their start lines.

The Germans launched yet more air raids upon Stalingrad. Over one thousand aircraft operated at will, inflicting massive destruction upon the already damaged city. As the air attacks continued, the ground forces drew closer, 6th and 4th Panzer Armies slowly pushing 62nd and 64th Armies back to the inner defence zone.

5 September 1942

SOUTHERN SECTOR
The 1st Guards launched more attacks but again suffered heavy casualties with no real gain. Attacks by 66th and 24th Armies were beaten off. Concentrated and well directed artillery fire smashed 66th Army on its start line, while 24th was beaten off by a combination of artillery and small arms fire. Both armies tried to provide support on the flanks of the 1st Guards but failed miserably. However, they were successful in preventing the release of German forces into Stalingrad from the north.

6 September 1942

SOUTHERN SECTOR
The 1st Guards had worn itself out, having suffered crippling casualties. Farther south, 62nd and 64th Armies dug into their final defensive positions before Stalingrad and prepared to fight a last ditch battle to prevent the Germans from taking the city

In the Caucasus, the 17th Army completed the capture of Novorossysk after a bitter struggle with 47th Army.

7 September 1942

SOUTHERN SECTOR
With 62nd Army in the suburbs of Stalingrad, 51st Korp of 6th Army launched a strong attack with two infantry divisions. Launched from Gumrak, the attack was designed to break into the city centre. After intense fighting the Germans almost reached the Mamayev Kurgan but at great cost against stubborn Soviet resistance. The Mamayev Kurgan was to become the scene of ferocious battles over the coming weeks as both armies fought for control of the commanding height.

To the south, there was heavy fighting around Novorossysk as 47th Army launched a series of punishing counter-attacks, putting 17th Army under severe pressure.

9 September 1942

SOUTHERN SECTOR
The 51st Korp closed up to the Mamayev Kurgan, putting the centre of 62nd Army under pressure. The Soviets were in real danger of disintegra-

tion as the Germans delivered hammering blows upon the length of the front before the Volga. On its northern flank, 62nd was assailed by 14th Panzer Korp, in the centre it was under pressure from 51st Korp and to the south was being heavily attacked by 48th Panzer Korp. Paulus decided to commit his main strength to the battle for the city, while to the north 14th Panzer Korp protected the exposed Don–Volga land bridge and 8th and 11th Korps protected the junction with 3rd Rumanian Army in the Don Elbow. Later in the battle, the Rumanian force would take over a larger sector of the line so that 8th could defend the sector between the Volga and the Don and 14th Panzer and 11th Korps could be fully committed to the fighting inside the city. Farther south, 4th Panzer Army had drawn closer to the southern suburbs, pounding the 64th Army.

With Army Group A bogged down, Hitler relieved Field Marshal List from command of the army group. Instead of appointing a successor, Hitler took over personal command of the army group, the day-to-day running of the German offensive in this region being added to his responsibilities as head of state, leader of the party and commander in chief of the armed forces.

10 September 1942

SOUTHERN SECTOR

North of the city, 1st Guards, 66th and 24th Armies attacked but remained unable to break through the German screen and suffered further heavy casualties. Zhukov reported to Stalin that it was clear the Soviets would not break through to relieve 62nd Army, the Germans having strengthened their northern flank. Stalin ordered Zhukov to report to Moscow. Before he left, he ordered 1st Guards to hand over its forces to the 24th and 66th Armies and move sectors, taking on five rifle divisions and three tank corps from the Stavka reserve. The new 1st Guards was to attack on 17 September.

Following the attack by 6th Army, the 4th Panzer Army struck 62nd Army with 48th Panzer Korp, pounding the junction of 62nd and 64th Armies. Furious fighting ensued, the likes of which had not been seen before on the eastern front. With the front in danger of disintegration, the Stavka replaced Lopatin as commander of 62nd Army, General Chuikov being appointed instead. Until Chuikov arrived Krylov deputised.

GERMAN CASUALTIES

As the fighting on the eastern front intensified, Field Marshal Halder estimated that the campaign since 22 June 1941 had cost the Ostheer 1,637,000 men killed, wounded and missing.

11 September 1942

SOUTHERN SECTOR

The attacks by 6th Army and 4th Panzer Army pressed 62nd and 64th Armies back into Stalingrad. Heavy fighting raged in the Mnina suburb where 48th Panzer Korp was punching its way through to the Volga. Already to the north in the Rynok and Spartakovka suburbs, the Germans held a five-mile stretch of the Volga river bank, bringing artillery fire to bear upon Soviet river traffic.

In the Caucasus, 17th Army was fighting inside Novorossysk, while elements of 47th Army continued to resist in the cement factory.

12 September 1942

SOUTHERN SECTOR

Chuikov arrived in Stalingrad to take command of the battered 62nd Army. Since 23 August 6th Army had suffered 7,700 killed and 31,000 wounded.[4] With the battle for Stalingrad barely underway, Zhukov left for Moscow, where Stalin informed him that he and Vasilevsky must come up with a solution to relieve the pressure on 62nd Army.

THE OPPOSING FORCES AT STALINGRAD

The build up of German forces clearly indicated that the Ostheer was pinning its hopes on the capture of Stalingrad. As the Germans prepared to launch their offensive, both 6th Army and 4th Panzer Army were heavily committed in and around Stalingrad, a total of 590,000 men with 10,000 artillery pieces and nearly 1,000 panzers facing the 590,000 Soviets of Stalingrad and South-East Fronts, who had 7,000 artillery pieces, 600 tanks and 389 aircraft between sixty-five rifle divisions, four cavalry divisions, seven rifle brigades, thirty-four tank brigades and six motorised brigades.[5] Stalingrad Front deployed 21st and 4th Tank Armies on the northern bank of the Don, facing 11th Korp's four infantry divisions, while 8th Korp's two infantry divisions confronted 66th, 1st Guards and 24th Armies on the forty-mile sector between the Volga and the Don. The 14th Panzer Korp's 3rd Motorised Division faced north, 60th Motorised was split between the northern wing and Stalingrad and 16th Panzer faced Stalingrad. Inside Stalingrad and to the south, South-East Front deployed 62nd and 64th Armies inside the city, and 57th and 51st Armies on the left flank between the Sarpa lakes. From Rynok to Kuporosnoye 62nd Army had 54,000 men with 900 artillery pieces and 110 tanks while 64th Army held the line from lvanovka with 40,000 men, 1,100 artillery pieces and a handful of tanks.[6] This sector saw the commitment of the bulk of 6th Army and 4th Panzer Army. From Orlovka to the Tsaritza river were the 71st, 76th, 295th, 100th and 389th Infantry Divisions of 51st Korp, while south of the Tsaritza was 94th infantry, 29th Motorised and 14th and 24th Panzer Divisions of 48th Panzer Korp. With the increasing commitment of 48th Panzer to the fighting inside the city, 4th Panzer Army relinquished control of Kempf's korp to 6th Army. This left Hoth with only the 287th and 371st Infantry Divisions of 4th Korp and 6th Rumanian Korp. These weak forces faced 64th and 57th Armies.

13 September 1942

SOUTHERN SECTOR
The 51st and 48th Panzer Korps attacked at Stalingrad. Paulus aimed to break into the city centre, having massed 71st, 76th, 295th and 94th Infantry Divisions, 29th Motorised and 14th and 24th Panzer Divisions. Supported by 8th Air Korp and overwhelming artillery fire, 71st, 76th and 295th Infantry Divisions attacked at 0630 hours from Gumrak, hitting the centre of 62nd Army. To the south 94th Infantry, 29th Motorised and 14th and 24th Panzer Divisions crashed into the Yelshanka and Dar Gova suburbs to reach the Volga. Furious fighting raged as the Soviets offered fierce resistance and considerable counter-artillery fire. Despite ferocious fighting, the Soviet line remained intact, but the Sadovaya railway station had fallen. The Mnina suburb was the scene of bitter fighting, as were Dar Gova and Yelshanka. German attacks continued throughout the night.

During the night, Chuikov was forced to move his headquarters from the Mamayev Kurgan, which was under German artillery and mortar fire, to the Tsaritsyn bunker. Eremenko reported to Stalin at the end of the day, stating that new German attacks were expected on 14 September. Stalin ordered Rodimtsev's 13th Guards Rifle Division to cross the Volga into Stalingrad to reinforce the hard-pressed 62nd Army.

SOVIET COMMAND
Zhukov and Vasilevsky spent the whole day planning a counter-blow around Stalingrad. Late in the day, they reported to Stalin and the nucleus of Operation Uranus was born.

14 September 1942

SOUTHERN SECTOR
Soviet forces north of Stalingrad began to redeploy. Over the next few days, 1st Guards Army and 24th Army switched sectors, 1st Guards deploying on the extreme right flank to face 8th Korp. First Guards was also reinforced with nine new rifle divisions,

At Stalingrad, the day opened with a series of spoiling attacks by 62nd Army. Under massive German counter-fire, the Soviet units failed to make any headway and were then struck by the renewed German attacks. By early afternoon, the Tzaritsyn quarter had fallen to 48th Panzer Korp, which linked up with 51st Korp, penetrating to the Volga at Kuporosnoye. The central landing stages were brought under heavy mortar and machine-gun fire. Furious battles raged around the central hospital as 76th infantry Division smashed through the Soviet line south of Mamayev Kurgan. The central railway station fell to 76th, while heavy fighting raged in the engineers' housing near by Soviet counter-attacks retook the central station later in the day, but then the Germans launched another attack that recaptured the station once more. By the end of the day the railway station had changed hands four times. During this bitter fighting, units of 76th Infantry punched a corridor through to the Volga. The 295th Infantry Division reached the base of the Mamayev Kurgan and after a furious assault took the hill by the end of the day.

With the success of the German attacks towards the Volga, 62nd Army had been severed. The larger northern group, isolated in the factory district and central portions of the city, fought against the attacks of 51st Korp, leading units of which were only eight hundred yards from Chuikov's headquarters. To the south, the southern group remained in contact with 64th Army in the Beketovka area but was under intense pressure. Repeated counter-attacks failed to close the gap between 64th and 62nd Armies.

After nightfall, Rodimtsev's 13th Guards began to cross the Volga. Lead elements crossed under heavy German fire from the central landing stages and immediately counter-attacked when they reached the west bank. Furious fighting erupted as the Guards clawed a small bridgehead on the banks of the Volga.

15 September 1942

SOUTHERN SECTOR

The newly committed 13th Guards attacked from its small bridgehead, crashing into the 71st Infantry Division. Bitter battles raged for control of the central railway station, which changed hands frequently. Other elements of 13th Guards launched a fierce attack upon the Mamayev Kurgan, hitting 295th infantry Division. While the 13th Guards launched its attacks, 71st and 295th Infantry Divisions again tried to push into the city centre. To the south, 94th Infantry, 24th and 14th Panzer Divisions fought their way through Dar Gova, Mnin and Yelshanka as they tried to smash open the junction of the 64th and 62nd Armies at Kuporosnoye. During the night, Chuikov brought more units of 13th Guards across the Volga into Stalingrad.

16 September 1942

SOUTHERN SECTOR
After bitter fighting, the 13th Guards Division cleared the central landing stage ol German troops and retook the railway station, it having changed hands fifteen times in just three days' fighting. One regiment of the 13th Guards and another of the 112th Rifle Division counter-attacked at dawn, storming the 295th Infantry Divisions positions on the Mamayev Kurgan. Bloody fighting eventually saw the Soviets retake the summit, but the Germans immediately counter-attacked with tanks and infantry. Despite heavy losses, the Soviets clung on to the hill.

17 September 1942

SOUTHERN SECTOR
Men of the 92nd Rifle Brigade, newly committed to the battle, took up positions in the grain elevator, opening a savage three-day battle for the building. Repeated German attacks were repulsed by the small band of Soviet defenders.

Chuikov signalled the Front headquarters that he needed reinforcements, requesting two or three divisions. High Command committed the 92nd Rifle and 137th Tank Brigades, elements of the former having already started to cross the Volga and enter the battle. The 92nd began to take up positions to the left of the 13th Guards, while the 137th rank was to the right, in the Tennis Racquet railway yards.

Under heavy German fire, Chuikov was again forced to relocate his headquarters, moving from the Tsaritsyn bunker to the north of Krasnyi Oktyabr factory. Unbeknownst to the Soviets, the oil storage tanks on the hills over the headquarters were still full of fuel.

18 September 1942

SOUTHERN SECTOR
At 0530 hours 1st Guards Army launched new attacks north of Stalingrad with five rifle divisions supported by one tank corp and three tank brigades. Heavy German counter-fire brought the attack to an immediate halt, and the arrival of the Luftwafle smashed the Soviet units. A fierce German counter-attack then threw 1st Guards back to its start lines. In an effort to reverse the flow of the battle, the Soviets committed two tank corps but to no effect. Bitter fighting raged all day without any success.

In Stalingrad the fighting raged unabated. Ten attacks on the grain elevator failed to dislodge 92nd Rifle Brigades. Heavy fighting also erupted on the Mamayev Kurgan and in the central railway station as

51st Korp launched repeated attacks against 13th Guards Division. The Luftwaffe was particularly active against both these targets, blanket-bombing the Soviet positions as German infantry wrestled the Soviets out of the ruins.

Towards the end of the day 62nd Army was ordered to prepare a counter-attack on its right wing to link up with the 1st Guards, 66th and 24th Armies. The attack was to strike out from Mamayev Kurgan to the north-east.

19 September 1942

SOUTHERN SECTOR
Chuikov counter-attacked with 112th Rifle Division from the Mamayev Kurgan to the north-east, but was halted by fierce German fire. The attacks by 1st Guards, 66th and 24th Armies were equally unsuccessful. Inside Stalingrad, the battle continued.

20 September 1942

SOUTHERN SECTOR
Attacks by 1st Guards and 24th Armies failed to break through to 62nd Army. The 66th Army joined the attack with an equal lack of success.

At first light the Luftwaffe arrived over Stalingrad, bombing the central railway station in force. Heavy artillery fire then joined the attack, closely followed by infantry and armour. Under ferocious fire, a single battalion of 13th Guards Rifle Division attempted to hold out but was forced to give ground. Fighting as they fell back, the Soviet troops made a stand in the Nail Factory. German attacks rapidly enveloped this position, hitting the Soviets from three sides as fighting raged on through the night. Fierce battles also continued in the grain elevator as elements of 92nd Rifle Brigade fought on.

21 September 1942

NORTHERN SECTOR
The 11th Army began its counter-attack at Gaitolovo. Soviet forces in the salient were attacked on both flanks, 26th and 30th Korps slicing through to isolate virtually the entire force. The constricted forces inside the pocket were subjected to ferocious artillery and air attack, suffering terrible casualties.

SOUTHERN SECTOR
Sixth Army beat off more attacks by 1st Guards, 24th and 66th Armies, keeping the German forces north of Stalingrad fully occupied.

Inside the city, the battle for the Nail Factory continued. The Soviet battalion was cut in two as hand-to-hand fighting raged among the ruined machinery and buildings. Under fierce attack, the Soviets abandoned the factory. Elements fought to the end in the Univermaag store, while others fell back to the Volga, establishing strong positions on the corner of Krasnopiterskaya and Komsomolskaya streets.[7] The fighting here raged for five bloody days. Further heavy fighting also raged on the slopes of the Mamayev Kurgan and in the grain elevator.

After protracted fighting, the 48th Panzer Korp cleared the bed of the Tsaritsyn stream, isolating the 92nd and 42nd Rifle Brigades on the southern wing of 62nd Army. The 14th and 24th Panzer, 29th Motorised and 94th Infantry Divisions were attacking the Soviet brigades.

22 September 1942

SOUTHERN SECTOR
The Luftwaffe was again active over Stalingrad, while the ground forces fought for every yard of the rubble-strewn city.

23 September 1942

SOUTHERN SECTOR
In the small hours of the morning, Batyuk's 284th Rifle Division began ferrying across the Volga into Stalingrad, while the hard-pressed 13th Guards took 2,000 reinforcements into its ranks. Chuikov planned to use these new troops to clear the central landing stages. Luftwaffe attacks on the oil storage tanks near the landing stages started a ferocious blaze, sending burning oil flowing into the Volga. Under heavy fire, the 284th fought its way ashore, breaking through the German line and penetrating into the Metiz Factory and onto the south-eastern slopes of the Mamayev Kurgan. The 95th Rifle Division joined the attacks, driving the Germans back towards the central railway station.

To the south, 42nd and 92nd Rifle Brigades struggled under intense German attacks. The commander of 42nd Brigade was wounded during a Luftwaffe attack and his force amalgamated with 92nd. Shortly afterwards the headquarters of the now combined brigades evacuated to the Golodnyi Island, leaving the men of the brigade to fight on without direction. From the island the commander submitted false battle reports to Chuikov.

In the Caucasus, Group Ruoff began Operation Attica, a last bid to break the Soviet defences in the Caucasus Mountains. Two korps of 17th Army struck 56th and 8th Armies. However, the Germans only managed to advance around a mile across the front, fighting for every yard of ground.

24 September 1942

SOUTHERN SECTOR

Fighting inside Stalingrad eased as Paulus regrouped his bloodied divisions for the next phase of the offensive. With 62nd Army defences crumbling in the southern suburbs, the new assault would concentrate upon the factory district and Orlovka salient jutting out on the left wing of 6th Army's positions on the Volga.

Paulus moved 16th Panzer Division opposite the right wing of 62nd Army, while the fresh 389th Infantry Division moved out of reserve to deploy at Gorodische. The 295th Infantry Division, still around the Mamayev Kurgan, was reinforced with armour and 71st and 76th Infantry Divisions grouped in the central railway station and central landing stages areas. The 71st was to attack the Red October factory, while 100th Jaeger Division reinforced the attack on the Mamayev Kurgan. The 14th and 24th Panzer, 29th Motorised and 94th Infantry Divisions remained in the south. Sixth Army also assumed control of 48th Panzer Korps divisions in the southern suburbs as the korp headquarters was withdrawn to redeploy in the rear of 3rd Rumanian Army. This army took over a large section of the Don line on the left wing of 6th Army.

GERMAN COMMAND

Hitler dismissed Halder as Chief of the General Staff. Zeitzler was appointed to the post.

> Paulus' second attack upon Stalingrad, this time through the streets of the city, had again been uninspired and fatally flawed. Rather than using his established positions on the Volga to strike along the line of the river into the rear of the Soviet defences, he had attacked directly from the west, channelling the 62nd Army into hedgehogs of defence. Chuikov, an expert in the art of street fighting, conducted small-scale actions throughout the city, breaking up the force of the German offensive into countless fire fights. Thus was set the pattern at Stalingrad, of bludgeoning German attacks breaking against a wall of small, expertly-led combat teams in the ruins of the city. The Verdun of the East had begun.

25 September 1942

SOUTHERN SECTOR

Chuikov learned of the desertion of the command of 92nd Rifle Brigade but was unable to help the men of the brigade, who were still under heavy German attack.

Taking advantage of the lull, Chuikov regrouped his army in preparation for the expected German attacks. The Mechetka river and Mamayev

Kurgan sectors were reinforced and the defences around the factories strengthened.

Between the Sarpa Lakes, the 51st and 57th Armies began a series of limited attacks aimed at gaining control of the high ground around the lakes in order to observe the movement of 4th Rumanian Army. The capture of the hills was largely achieved by 4 October as Rumanian 6th Korp relinquished ground readily, the Rumanians proving no match for the combat hardened Red Army.

26 September 1942

SOUTHERN SECTOR
On the corner of Krasnopiterskaya and Komsomolskayn Streets, the remnants of the 13th Guards Rifle's battalion fell back after a harrowing five-day struggle. Of the forty men who began the battle only six survived to fall back to the Volga. To the south, the forlorn men of 92nd Rifle Brigade collapsed under the attacks of the 94th Infantry and 24th Panzer Divisions.

SOVIET COMMAND
Stalin ordered the planning of the Rzhev and Stalingrad offensive operations. Zhukov was to coordinate the central thrust while Vasilevsky led the Stalingrad offensive. The Rzhev offensive was codenamed Operation Mars, while the Stalingrad operation took the name Uranus. Mars was due to begin in mid-October and Uranus in early to mid-November.

27 September 1942

SOUTHERN SECTOR
Expecting the renewal of the German attack on the factory district, at 0600 hours Chuikov began a spoiling attack in order to disrupt the German assault. While 62nd Army tried to pin the Germans down, 36th Guards Rifle Division of 64th Army attempted to retake Kuporosnoye. After heavy fighting at 0800 hours, the Luftwaffe arrived over the city and began to pound the Soviets, pinning down the 62nd Army. The 64th Army also failed to break the German positions. Furious attacks with aircraft and artillery struck the Mamayev Kurgan followed by an armoured attack with 150 panzers upon the factory district. Throughout the morning, 95th Rifle Division was almost wiped out on the Mamayev Kurgan, the Germans flailing away with 100th Jaeger, 295th Infantry and 24th Panzer Divisions. By mid-afternoon, panzers penetrated to the western walls of the Red October factory, reaching the Banny Gully and south-western corner of the Barrikady factory, where they were involved in heavy fighting. At dusk 95th Rifle had been forced off the summit of Mamayev Kurgan and only held the northern and eastern slopes.

The remnants of 92nd Rifle Brigade disintegrated, allowing the Germans to reach the Volga on a five-mile front south of the river. The 10th NKVD Division continued to fight on in the German rear south of the Tsaritsyn.

By the end of the day the 6th Army had bludgeoned its way a few hundred yards forward at a cost of 2,000 killed and fifty panzers destroyed. Chuikov called upon South-East Front to support his hard-pressed army. During the night of 27–28 September the 193rd Rifle Division began to cross the Volga, taking up positions in the Red October coke houses.

In the Caucasus, 13th Panzer Division, 370th Infantry and 5th SS *Wiking* Motorised Divisions fought their way into Elchetovo and captured the town. The Germans lacked the strength to punch their way forward to Ordzhonikidzhe.

28 September 1942

SOUTHERN SECTOR

The Germans resumed their attacks in Stalingrad with massed infantry and armour supported by artillery and air strikes. The Luftwaffe was active, trying to locate Chuikov's headquarters. Heavy raids were launched against the Volga ferries, incurring heavy losses upon the barges bringing reinforcements and supplies to 62nd Army.

In the factory district, the Germans attacked the Red October and Silikat factories, penetrating the south-eastern edge of the Silikat. In the centre, the 95th and 284th Rifle Divisions counter-attacked on the Mamayev Kurgan but were stopped short of the summit.

SOVIET COMMAND

With the battle for Stalingrad at its height, the Stavka re-designated its forces in the Stalingrad sector. Eremenko's South-East Front became the new Stalingrad Front, while the old Stalingrad Front was renamed the Don Front, commanded by Rokossovsky. The two fronts numbered 771,000 men, 8,100 artillery pieces, 525 tanks and 448 aircraft deployed between seventy-eight rifle and six cavalry divisions, five tank corps and eighteen tank brigades. Stalingrad Front was allocated the 8th and 16th Air Armies to provide increased cover against the 8th Air Korp. The new Don Front comprised thirty-nine rifle divisions, three cavalry divisions and three tank corps, nine tank brigades and two rifle brigades. Its 63rd Army held a 100-mile sector on the right wing, 21st Army held a seventy mile sector around Serafimovich and 4th Tank Army, 24th Army and 66th Army were between the Volga and the Don.[8] The 1st Guards Army was pulled out of the line and transferred to reserve.

Since 7 August the 'old' South-East Front had lost 110,000 killed and missing and 62,000 wounded.

29 September 1942

SOUTHERN SECTOR
Fighting at Stalingrad spread to the Orlovka salient. The five-mile long and two-mile wide salient was held by the remnants of 112th Rifle Division and 115th Rifle Brigade. This small force was struck by 16th Panzer, 60th Motorised and 389th and 100th Infantry Divisions from the north and south. Furious battles developed as the Soviets put up a stiff defence. Two battalions of the 115th were hit from the north and south and fell back, one battalion retreating into Orlovka itself. The penetrating German attacks threatened to isolate the Soviet units.

Farther south, the fighting on the Mamayev Kurgan continued, while the 193rd Rifle Division was forced back into the western edge of the Red October factory. During the afternoon a large air attack hit the Tractor factory, setting the factory buildings alight.

Even farther south, 57th and 51st Armies gained ground around the Sarpa lakes as Rumanian 6th Korp fell back.

> *Once again Paulus made the same mistake, herding the defenders of Orlovka back towards the river rather than prising them away from it.*

30 September 1942

SOUTHERN SECTOR
The Germans launched strong attacks into the Orlovka salient, the Luftwaffe striking 115th Brigade in Orlovka. While units tackled the Soviets in the village, others pushed along the Orlovka gully in the direction of the Tractor and Barrikady factories. To support the developing attacks, the Germans brought 94th Infantry and 14th Panzer Divisions up from the south to support their attacks.

Chuikov brought more forces across the Volga to reinforce his shattered front units. The reformed 42nd Rifle Brigade was moved into the north-western sector of the city to re-enter the fighting in the factories, while 92nd Brigade was sent up to relieve 23rd Tank Corp. Thirty-ninth Guards Division was also committed, with 4,000 men, to take up positions just west of the Red October factory to support the 193rd Rifle Division.

SOVIET COMMAND AND CASUALTIES
The Stavka planned to form a new South-West Front based upon the headquarters of the 1st Guards in the Kletskaya and Verkhnaya Maman sectors, but kept its existence secret until the counter-offensive was due. In the Stavka reserve, and destined for the south, were 3rd and 5th Tank Armies and 43rd Army from the Central Sector.

During the third quarter of 1942, the Red Army and Navy lost 1,224,495 killed and missing and 1,283,062 wounded.[9]

ASSESSMENT: THE OSTHEER AT THE END OF SEPTEMBER 1942

From December 1941 to the end of September 1942, Army Group North had suffered 375,000 casualties but replaced only 270,000, while Army Group Centre lost 765,000 men and replaced 480,000. The 'old' Army Group South, Army Groups A and B, lost more than 547,000 men but received only 415,000 reinforcements. Despite the fall in strength, the Ostheer committed two more divisions during September, one panzer and one mountain division, bringing their strength up to twenty panzer, fifteen motorised and one hundred and thirty-five infantry divisions. During September the Germans had lost 45,000 men killed.

1 October 1942

NORTHERN SECTOR

The Germans completed the destruction of 2nd Shock Army encircled in the Gaitolovo pocket.

SOUTHERN SECTOR

German pincers closed at Orlovka, trapping a battalion of 115th Rifle Brigade. Two other brigade battalions attempted a relief attack from the east but were pinned down by massive German artillery fire and air strikes. Under intense fire, the isolated battalion continued to hold for another week in the Orlovka gully.

In the factories district, the Germans hammered at the Soviet defences. Heavy attacks struck the 193rd Rifle Division before the Red October factory throughout the day, the 284th Rifle and 13th Guards also being hard-pressed as the Germans tried to push on to the Volga. German efforts to reach the river through the Krutoy and Dolgi gullies failed as the 13th Guards wiped out the attackers. During the night 295th Infantry Division sent an assault force of 300 men into the Krutoy Gully and onto the banks of the Volga. Once they reached the river, the group turned south, into the rear of the 13th Guards, and then waited for dawn when they would attack from both front and rear.

As his defences crumbled, Chuikov ordered the 39th Guards to fortify and hold the Red October workshops.

The fighting in Stalingrad cost both sides dear. Since 13 September Paulus had suffered over 40,000 casualties, while 62nd Army lost 78,000 men. However, the Soviets were constantly reinforced, maintaining a combat strength of around 55,000 men. Inside the city, the Soviets had 950 artillery pieces, 500 mortars and eighty tanks.[10]

SOVIET COMMAND
The Stavka disbanded 4th Tank Army, absorbing its remnants into 65th Army. The 17th and 18th Tank Corps were pulled out of the Voronezh sector and moved behind Don Front to refit, together with 3rd and 5th Tank Armies, which went into Stavka reserve. Fourth Tank Corp, already with the Don Front, was also pulled out of the line to refit.

2 October 1942

NORTHERN SECTOR
The remnants of 2nd Shock Army was destroyed, Volkhov Front losing 12,000 men captured along with as many killed, and 300 artillery pieces, 500 mortars and 240 tanks lost.

SOUTHERN SECTOR
At 0600 hours 295th Infantry Division launched a frontal and surprise rear attack on the right wing of 13th Guards Division. Ferocious fighting erupted as the Soviets fought to prevent their annihilation, instead destroying to a man the German infiltration force.

Further heavy attacks continued to smash the divisions in the factories. The 112th Rifle was hard-pressed, suffering heavy losses as the Germans attacked with overwhelming force. Fighting intensified as the Germans penetrated into the Barrikady, Tractor and Red October complexes. The 193rd Rifle Division fought in the Red October kitchens, bathhouse and workers' houses, while 39th Guards held the factory itself.

On the southern wing, the 64th Army counter-attacked with four rifle divisions south-west of Yelshanka in an effort to link up with 62nd Army. After a day of bitter fighting the attack failed.

To reinforce 62nd Army, 308th Rifle Division was ferried across the Volga during the night of 2–3 October. The division was ordered to take up positions in the Barrikady factory. Forward elements of 37th Guards Division also crossed the Volga and deployed in the Tractor factory, close to the north-western edge of the Barrikady estate. The 37th Guards deployed between the 112th and 308th Divisions.

3 October 1942

SOUTHERN SECTOR
The bitter battle for Orlovka reached its climax as 115th Rifle Brigade struggled to hold off the attacks of 14th Panzer Korp. The isolated battalion in the village suffered heavy casualties under the constant German artillery fire and planned a break out through the Orlovka Gully to the factories. Around the factories, the 308th Rifle Division launched a furious counter-attack and pushed the Germans back into the Silikat factory.

4 October 1942

SOUTHERN SECTOR
Paulus continued his attack to smash through the Soviet defences to the river. Gains were made in the factory district as 51st Korp pressed into the Tractor, Barrikady and Red October complexes. Chuikov threw in yet more reserves, 84th Tank Brigade entering the battle.

5 October 1942

SOUTHERN SECTOR
Early in the day, the Soviets launched an artillery barrage with more than 300 guns sited on the east bank of the Volga. Heavy losses were inflicted upon the fightly packed German units close to the factories. Shortly afterwards, 8th Air Korp pounded the Soviet defences in the factory district, two thousand sorties being launched against the Soviets. Heavy fighting erupted as the Germans recaptured the Silikat factory and isolated the 42nd and 92nd Rifle Brigades and 6th Guards Tank Brigade.

The Germans brought the entrance to Chuikov's command bunker under accurate and sustained mortar and machine-gun fire.

6 October 1942

SOUTHERN SECTOR
The Luftwaffe was back over Stalingrad in force, bombing Soviet positions. With his bunker under heavy fire, Chuikov moved his headquarters to the Tractor factory, itself threatened by German attacks. The 10th NKVD Division was pulled out of the line, having been reduced to a handful of men.

As the struggle for Stalingrad dragged on, Weichs stressed to Paulus that 62nd Army must be overcome as soon as possible to enable 6th Army to transfer forces to its exposed flanks. It was just as apparent to the German High Command as it was to the Stavka that the forces of Army Group B were stretched too thin and 6th Army was in an extremely exposed position.

7 October 1942

SOUTHERN SECTOR
The fighting in the Orlovka sector ended as the survivors of the isolated battalion broke out through the Orlovka Gully and rejoined the northern wing of 62nd Army, linking up with the 112th Rifle Division.

A heavy attack with two infantry division struck the Tractor Factory. The 37th Guards was hard-pressed and struggled to hold the Germans in the workers' houses. Other German thrusts penetrated into the sports stadium, while 193rd Rifle Division fought a day-long battle in the Red October bathhouse.

8 October 1942

SOUTHERN SECTOR
There was further fighting in the factories, 193rd Rifle Division suffering heavy casualties as German infantry penetrated into the Red October bathhouse. Near the Tractor factory, 14th Panzer Korp conquered the workers' houses after a bitter struggle with 37th Guards. The guards fell back to the sports stadium, already the scene of heavy fighting.

In the Caucasus, Group Ruoff ground to a halt in the face of strong resistance from the Coastal Group.

9 October 1942

SOUTHERN SECTOR
An eerie lull began to settle over Stalingrad as the Germans wore themselves out. Both armies took the opportunity to rest and recuperate their exhausted units after the furious fighting of the previous month. Fighting continued in various sectors of the city but without the ferocity of the last few days.

Chuikov redeployed his battered divisions to face what he expected would be the next phase of German attacks. The 95th Rifle Division, with 3,000 men, was moved from the Mamayev Kurgan north-west into the factories, taking up positions between 37th Guards and 308th Rifle Divisions in the Red October. The 42nd Rifle Brigade, down to 900 men, was subordinated to 95th Rifle Division. Chuikov also moved 112th Rifle Division, with 2,300 men, into the Tractor factory.[11]

SOVIET COMMAND
Order No 307 restored unitary authority to the Red Army. Party representatives remained part of divisional and army staffs for the rest of the war but were used to extol the party line rather than directly command military operations.

> Yet again Paulus had failed to smash the 62nd Army. Despite massive losses in men, material and crucially territory, the Soviet defenders refused to give in to the German juggernaut. Chuikov's task now was to hold German attention while the Stavka assembled its forces in secret against the exposed flanks of the Stalingrad salient.

10 October 1942

NORTHERN SECTOR
The Sinyavino battle, raging since 19 August, cost the Soviet armies around Leningrad 40,085 killed and missing and 73,589 wounded.[12]

10–12 October 1942

SOUTHERN SECTOR
The lull in Stalingrad continued, Paulus massing his forces for another hammer blow. New, fresh divisions were released from the left flank of 6th Army as 3rd Rumanian Army took over the positions of 8th Korp, allowing Paulus to use these units as the spearhead for his attack. In exchange many of the burnt-out divisions that suffered badly in the recent battles in the city were sent to the flanks to rest. By moving his fresh units into Stalingrad, Paulus succeeded in bleeding dry the remaining strong divisions in the army.

The Stalingrad Front received 4th Cavalry Corp as reinforcement, 7th Rifle Corp as front reserve and 93rd, 96th and 97th Rifle Brigades, which deployed at Dubrovka.

12 October 1942

CENTRAL SECTOR
Operation Mars, the planned Soviet offensive against the Rzhev salient, was postponed until the end of October due to bad weather. The plan called for the right wing of West Front and the left wing of Kalinin Front to encircle the Germans at Rzhev and free the Moscow to Velikiye Luki railway. West Front's 20th and 31st Armies, supported by 29th Army, were to attack along the Osuga and Vazuza rivers towards Sychevka and link up with 41st Army of Kalinin Front which had attacked from Belyi. The 31st and 20th Armies would then mop up the German salient and strike towards Vyazma.

The Kalinin Front was to attack with one grouping (41st Army and attached corps) from Belyi towards Sychevka, while 22nd Army encircled the Germans at Olenino. Thirty-ninth Army was to attack along the Molodi–Tud to push the Germans back into the arms of the 22nd and 39th Armies.[13]

13 October 1942

SOUTHERN SECTOR
Fighting flared in Stalingrad as the Germans brought the power station, still producing electricity for the factories to the north, under heavy artillery and air attack.

The Red Army continued its preparations for the counter-offensive from the Don and Sarpa lakes. South-West Front, still not publicly in existence, received 1st and 26th Tank Corps and 8th Cavalry Corp plus a tank brigade, three rifle divisions and sixteen artillery regiments. Stalingrad Front had received 13th Tank, 4th Mechanised and 4th Cavalry Corps, two rifle divisions, six rifle and three tank brigades, six anti-aircraft and two anti-tank artillery regiments, while the Don Front had taken in three new rifle divisions. Movement of reinforcements was carried out at night and elaborate measures were taken to hide the build-up from the Germans. During the day, the new forces were skilfully hidden and radio traffic forbidden so as not to alert the enemy. Even so, hiding a force of half a million men was a difficult task.

14 October 1942

SOUTHERN SECTOR
Chuikov, expecting a renewal of the German offensive, launched a spoiling attack with 37th Guards from the Tractor factory. However, at 0800 hours the German assault began, 90,000 men and 300 panzer ol 94th and 389th Infantry, 100th Jaeger and 14th and 24th Panzer Divisions striking the Soviets defending the factories with the aim of crushing the final pockets of resistance. The 37th Guards and 95th Rifle Divisions were hit hard but fought back with determination, the area between the Barrikady and Tractor factories changing hands several times during the day. At noon a force of two hundred tanks smashed through 37th Guards Division and reached the Tractor factory, where the Germans then turned to strike at the rear of 112th Rifle Division. Fierce battles raged, but by late afternoon 112th Rifle and 37th Guards were fighting in encirclement. Further German attacks blew apart the right wing of the 308th Rifle Division, bringing Chuikov's headquarters under intense lire. Despite their losses, the Soviet units fought to the bitter end, each isolated section refusing to yield to the overwhelming German attacks.

The battle continued into the night as the Germans reached the Tractor factory on three sides. Repeated infantry and armoured assaults struck the Soviets and during the course of the fighting the Germans were able to reach the Volga on a two thousand-yard front, splitting the 62nd Army apart. The 112th Rifle Division, 2nd Motorised Brigade, 115th, 124th and 149th Rifle Brigades all fought on in isolation on the right wing of the army, 37th Guards having been virtually wiped out. However, the few remaining men of the guards division continued to fight on.

During the bloody night Chuikov began to bring 138th Rifle Division across the Volga into the city, intending to reinforce the Barrikady factory.

Group Ruoff renewed its attacks in the Caucasus in an effort to reach the Black Sea. Initial gains were promising, but Soviet defences soon stiffened.

The Stavka relieved Cherevichenko as commander of the Black Sea Group, appointing Petrov in his place.

15 October 1942

CENTRAL SECTOR

The West Front had been heavily reinforced in preparation for Operation Mars. In mid-October it comprised 30th, 29th, 31st, 20th, 5th, 33rd, 49th, 50th, 10th, 16th and 61st Armies, 3rd Tank Army under Rybalko, 5th and 8th Guards Rifle Corps, 3rd, 5th, 6th, 8th, 9th and 10th Tank Corps, 1st and 2nd Guards Cavalry Corps.[14]

Model's 9th Army, the target of Operation Mars, deployed 39th Panzer Korp along the Vazuza and Osuga rivers with three infantry divisions (102nd, 337th and 78th) and 5th Panzer Division in reserve. The 9th Panzer Division was in operational reserve at Sychevka. Ninth Army also deployed 27th Korp west of Rzhev to the Osuga with six infantry divisions (256th, 87th, 129th, 254th, 72nd and 95th) and 14th Motorised in reserve, 23rd Korp west of Rzhev to the south-west of Olenino with three infantry divisions (110th, 253rd and 206th) and *Grossdeutschland* Division in reserve at Belyi, while 41st Panzer Korp held the line from Belyi to Olenino with one Luftwaffe (2nd) and two infantry divisions (246th and 86th). Model's extended left wing was held by 59th Korp at Velikiye Luki, named Group von der Chevallerie, while 2nd Luftwaffe Korp with two Luftwaffe divisions (2nd and 3rd) and 6th Korp with two infantry (205th and 330th) and one Luftwaffe (7th) divisions held the long line from Velikiye Luki to the Rzhev salient.

The 1st Panzer Division was in army reserve while 12th, 20th and 19th Panzer were in army group reserve.[15]

SOUTHERN SECTOR

As the Germans continued their attacks, the 138th Rifle Division entered the battle for the Barrikady factory. Heavy German fire prevented any Soviet river traffic from crossing the Volga during the day. Fierce battles raged in the Tractor factory as 37th Guards and 112th Rifle Divisions fought on, but by evening the isolated forces had been almost annihilated, a few surviving men continuing to resist.

With his headquarters under heavy fire, Chuikov requested permission to move part of his staff to the east bank. Eremenko refused. The Stavka ordered the armies between the Volga and the Don to begin new relief attacks to take some of the pressure of 62nd Army. To the north 66th and 24th Armies resumed their attacks but were unable to draw sizeable German forces away from the city. On the southern wing, 51st and 57th

Armies attacked at Tundutovo and around the Tsatsa lakes.

SOUTHERN SECTOR
The 1st Guards Army was disbanded, its headquarters forming the command centre for the South-West Front. A new 1st Guards was raised in time for the counter-offensive.

16 October 1942

SOUTHERN SECTOR
Fighting in the factories reached a peak as the Luftwaffe launched a massive raid. Heavy fighting followed as German infantry attacked south from the Tractor factory towards the Barrikady, striking 84th Tank Brigade hard. Amid furious fighting, the brigade held the Germans on Tramvaynaya Street. In the Tractor factory, 37th Guards was down to just 200 men but fought on.

17 October 1942

SOUTHERN SECTOR
Chuikov ferried the rest of Lyudnikov's 138th Division into Stalingrad during the night of 16–17 October as German attacks continued.

German attacks south from the Tractor factory along the bank of the Volga drove the 138th Rifle Division back. The 84th Tank Brigade also attempted to hold back the Germans. New attacks also broke into the southern part of Spartakovka. An attack on Red October was repulsed, but an assault along the railway lines and upon the Barrikady penetrated the junction of 138th and 308th Rifle Divisions. The Germans then entered the north-west corner of the Barrikady complex where fierce battles erupted. Heavy fighting also saw the fall of the Tractor factory, the remnants of the 37th Guards being destroyed.

With losses among his command staff mounting, Chuikov moved his headquarters back to the south, near the Mamayev Kurgan.

18 October 1942

SOUTHERN SECTOR
Soviet attacks regained the northern outskirts of Rynok and forced the Germans out of Spartakovka. During the afternoon, the Germans broke through 84th Tank Brigade on Tramvaynaya Street, attacking the Barrikady factory as they advanced. Bloody battles raged across the railway lines as the Soviets fought to hold every yard. Again the Luftwaffe operated in force but was unable to influence the battle, the Soviet units bugging the German front line closely in order to negate the German air superiority.

19 October 1942

GERMAN COMMAND
With 6th Army bogged down in Stalingrad and Army Group A rendered immobile in the Caucasus, Hitler issued Operational Order No 1, closing the German summer offensive. As he was confirming his order, rain began to fall at Stalingrad, heralding the onset of the autumn mud.

20 October 1942

SOUTHERN SECTOR
The fighting in Stalingrad had settled down into stable positions, 62nd Army having broken up the German attack despite considerable losses. The fresh divisions of 8th Korp had been bloodied in the bitter street fighting as Paulus pressed home his attack without skill, using sheer firepower and weight of numbers to blast a way through to the Volga.

The condition of the Luftwaffe in the south began to cause concern. The 4th Air Fleet had been operating along an extensive sector from the Don and the Caucasus. Combined, the 4th and 8th Air Korps numbered only 970 aircraft at the end of October, of which barely 590 were operational.

The newly-created 4th Mechanised Corp under General Volskii, with 36th, 59th and 60th Tank Corps, began to deploy in the Beketovka salient.

21 October 1942

SOUTHERN SECTOR
The 79th Infantry Division launched strong attacks against the Barrikady and Red October factories. Luftwaffe support aided the attack but the Soviets repelled each assault. Minor gains were made in the Red October area as the workers' houses fell.

22 October 1942

SOUTHERN SECTOR
As the first winter snows fell at Stalingrad, Shumilov's 64th Army attacked from the Beketovka salient to link up with the southern wing of Chuikov's force. However, the attack was disrupted by massed German counter artillery fire, the 64th suffering heavy casualties under the protracted bombardment.

SOVIET COMMAND
The Stavka activated South-West Front, Vatutin taking command. The front deployed 63rd and 21st Armies, Romanenko's 5th Tank Army, the latter formation having 1st and 26th Tank Corps, six rifle divi-

sions, one tank brigade and one cavalry corp and Krasovsky's 17th Air Army. The 63rd Army, with six rifle divisions, was in the process of re-forming, shortly being re-designated 1st Guards Army under Lelyushenko. Chistyakov's 21st Army deployed six rifle divisions, 4th Tank and 3rd guards Cavalry Corps.

As the date for the planned counter-offensive grew close, South-West Front was also allocated 2nd Air Army to overwhelm the thinly stretched German air forces and gain air superiority over the battlefield. The 4th Tank Army, recently disbanded, was taken over by General Batov and renamed 65th Army (nine rifle divisions and 91st and. 121st Tank Brigades). It was allocated to Rokossovsky's Don Front. Galanin's 24th (nine rifle divisions and 16th Tank Corp) and Zhadov's 66th (six rifle divisions) Armies were already with Don Front, involved in fighting between the Volga and the Don.

To the rear, the Stavka raised 2nd Guards Army, this unit later being used in the offensive against Rumanian 4th Army, shortly to deploy south 6th Army.

23 October 1942

SOUTHERN SECTOR
German attacks reached the north-western corner of the Red October factory. Paulus had committed the bulk of his reserve and was close to the end of his resources. To the north and south, the attacks by 66th and 24th Armies between the Don and the Volga and 64th Army at Beketovka continued. The Germans moved elements of 295th, 71st, 100th Infantry and 29th Motorised Divisions south to ward off the 64th Army

24 October 1942

SOUTHERN SECTOR
The Germans smashed their way through to the south-western and central areas of the Barrikady factory. Repeated attacks tore holes in the 138th and 308th Rifle Divisions. However, 39th Guards Division regained control of the Voentarg building after a bloody battle.

25 October 1942

SOUTHERN SECTOR
At 1000 hours the 64th Army launched another attack towards Stalingrad. Fierce fighting erupted as the Soviets clawed their way towards Kuporosnoye. Inside Stalingrad, the fighting in the factories intensified as the Germans launched repeated attacks upon the Red October and Barrikady plants.

In the Caucasus, 3rd Panzer Korp launched a surprise attack towards Ordzhonikidzhe, taking 37th Army off guard. 13th Panzer, 23rd Panzer and 2nd Rumanian Mountain Divisions attacke along the road to Nalchik. As the Germans advanced, the Soviet defences disintegrated, Luftwaffe intervention proving decisive as it pinned the Soviets down.

SOVIET COMMAND

Preparations for Operation Uranus entered their final stages. The operation called for South-West and Stalingrad Fronts to launch deep envelopment attacks against Rumanian forces on each flank of 6th Army, cutting off the German units attacking 62nd Army inside the city. South West Front was to attack 3rd Rumanian Army from Serafimovich and press south-east to secure the Don at Kalach. It would establish a secure front on the line of the Chir and Kriv to repel any German relief attacks. The Don Front was to attack north of Stalingrad from the Kletskaya bridgehead and push into the left flank of 6th Army near Vertyachi. Stalingrad Front would strike 6th and 7th Rumanian Korps south of 4th Panzer Army. Once the Rumanian positions had been pierced, Soviet mechanised forces would move west to Sovetski and Kalach, effecting a junction with South-West Front. The operation planned to isolate 90,000 German soldiers inside Stalingrad. The outer wing of the Stalingrad Front was also to strike South-West upon Kotelnikovo to threaten the lines of communication with Army Group A. On the Kalmuyk Steppe, 28th Army was to move up from Astrakhan to attack 16th Motorised Division. The offensive was to begin on 9 and 10 November with the South West Front jumping off first. South-West Front numbered 340,000 men, Don Front 292,000 and Stalingrad Front 383,000.

The Stavka required considerable nerve to carry out its lengthy preparations for Uranus. With Stalingrad and the 62nd Army on the verge of destruction, the Stavka had to tread a fine line between feeding in enough troops to prolong the battle but no so many as to arouse German suspicions. It was a strategy they carried out remarkably well considermg their failures in the earlier campaigns.

26 October 1942

SOUTHERN SECTOR

Chuikov ferried 45th Rifle Division over the Volga to deploy between the Red October and Barrikady factories.

Nalchik fell to elements of 13th Panzer and 2nd Rumanian Mountain Divisions.

27 October 1942

SOUTHERN SECTOR
The Germans made minor gains in the Red October and Barrikady factories, bringing the landing stages on the west bank under direct fire. Reinforcements coming into the city had to run the gauntlet of sustained artillery, mortar and machine-gun fire all the way across the river and on the western bank as they tried to disembark. Many units suffered heavy casualties even before they entered the battle.

Chuikov counter-attacked along Samarkandskaya Street after scraping together three repaired tanks and a handful of infantry. Sixth Army was nearing the end of its stiength, Paulus having nothing more to throw into the battle.

The German advance in the Caucasus drew closer to Ordzhonikidze as 37th Army fell back. German air strikes plagued the Soviet withdrawal, causing heavy casualties.

28 October 1942

SOUTHERN SECTOR
The 14th Panzer and 51st Korps struck the Soviet forces in the Red October and Barrikady factories. Despite heavy fighting, the Germans failed to make any progress.

SOVIET COMMAND
Operations Mars was postponed to the end November, after Operation Uranus had begun around Stalingrad.

29 October 1942

SOUTHERN SECTOR
Rumanian 4th Army became operational as Constantinescu's headquarters took command of 6th and 7th Rumanian Korps from 4th Panzer Army. Hoth was left with 4th Korp and 16th Motorised Division.

30 October 1942

SOUTHERN SECTOR
A lull settled over Stalingrad, both 62nd and 6th Armies having fought themselves to a standstill. Paulus intended to reinforce and regroup during the lull for what he expected would be the final attack that would break 62nd Army.

The Red Army hastened to complete its preparations for Operation Uranus. The plan was revised slightly as South-West Front's attack from

Serafimovich with 5th Tank and 21st Armies was altered so that these forces moved on the Chir and Kalach while 1st Guards supported the attacks on the Chir line. Stalingrad Front was to attack with 64th, 57th and 51st Armies from the Sarpa lakes to Sovetski and Kalach. The 57th Army (two rifle divisions, 13th Tank Corp and two tank brigades) was to attack an eight-mile front south-west of Kundutovo, enabling 13th Tank Corp to penetrate into the Rumanian rear while 51st Army (four rifle divisions, 4th Mechanised Corp and 4th Cavalry Corp) attacked between Lakes Tsatsa and Barmantsak on a six-mile front. The 4th Mechanised Corp was to exploit these gains. The 64th Army (five rifle divisions) was to attack from the Beketovka salient, while 62nd pinned 6th Army inside Stalingrad.

31 October 1942

SOVIET DEPLOYMENT
The Red Army deployed 6,124,000 men with 77,000 artillery pieces and mortars, nearly 7,000 tanks and over 3,200 aircraft between 391 divisions, 247 rifle, tank and mechanised brigades, fifteen tank and mechanised corps. The Stavka reserve had grown to twenty-five divisions, seven rifle and tank brigades and thirteen mechanised and tank corps.[16]

During October the Stavka reinforced the Stalingrad axis with ten rifle divisions, six rifle brigades, three tank, one mechanised and two cavalry corps, one tank and twenty artillery regiments.[17]

Soviet forces were deployed along two main axes, the central Smolensk axis and the southern Stalingrad axis. In the centre, Soviet forces with Kalinin and West Fronts and the Moscow Defence zone, numbered 1,900,000 men, 24,000 artillery pieces, 3,300 tanks and 1,100 aircraft, while on the Stalingrad axis the Don, South-West and Stalingrad Fronts comprised 1,000,000 men, 15,000 artillery pieces, 1,400 tanks and 900 aircraft. This diverse concentration clearly demonstrated that, despite the ferocity of the fighting in the south, the Soviet High Command still saw the central axis as their main theatre of operations.[18]

GERMAN DEPLOYMENT
The Germans activated four Luftwaffe field divisions during October. While the Luftwaffe divisions were numerically strong, they lacked the training and combat experience and fared badly in action. At the end of the month the Germans deployed twenty panzer, fifteen panzer-grenadier and 139 infantry divisions, the 3rd SS Motorised Division leaving the east.[19] The Ostheer was short of 800,000 men. It lost a further 25,000 killed during October.

Allied strength on the Eastern Front stood at twenty-seven Rumanian divisions, twelve Hungarian, ten Italian divisions and three brigades, one Slovak, one Spanish and sixteen Finnish divisions.[20]

1 November 1942

SOUTHERN SECTOR
Elements of 64th Army penetrated into Kuporosnoye but were brought to a halt by withering German fire.

2 November 1942

SOUTHERN SECTOR
Fighting was renewed in the Caucasus as 1st Panzer Army launched an attack towards Ordzhonikidze. Lead units of 3rd Panzer Korp were only five miles from the town but faced stiffening Soviet resistance. The first winter snows began to fall, heralding the onset of another dreaded Soviet winter.

4 November 1942

SOUTHERN SECTOR
The reformed 1st Guards Army became operational.

SOVIET COMMAND
With preparations for operation Uranus well advanced, the Stavka also began to lay plans for the destruction of Italian 8th Army by South-West and Voronezh Fronts. This operation, designated Saturn, planned to smash the German southern wing and take the Red Army across the Dniepr, threatening the forces of Army Groups A and B with encirclement against the Black and Azov Sea coasts. 6th Army and 1st Guards Army would lead the attack.

6 November 1942

GERMAN COMMAND
A Fremde Heer Ost report stated that the most likely location for a Soviet counter-attack was the central sector, most probably against 2nd Panzer Army.

9 November 1942

GERMAN COMMAND
As feverish activity continued behind the Soviet lines, the Fremde Heer Ost department of the German High Command issued a statement which maintained that a limited offensive against Army Group Centre was likely and, that while a build up of forces against the positions of 3rd Rumanian Army was recognised they were not thought to constitute a

major threat. To stiffen the Rumanian defences, 48th Panzer Korp, with one German and one Rumanian armoured divisions, was moved behind the Rumanian front.

Lead units of 13th Panzer Division reached the western outskirts of Ordzhonikidze. The 23rd Panzer Division was unable to provide support, being strung out along the flank of 13th Panzer.

11 November 1942

SOUTHERN SECTOR
The German 6th Army began its last offensive in Stalingrad. At 0630 hours artillery and aircraft began the systematic bombardment of the front line. Following closely on the heels of the barrage came panzers and infantry, moving up and striking 62nd Army a fearsome blow. After heavy fighting, most of the Red October factory fell, 138th Division being isolated south of the Barrikady factory against the Volga, which had begun to freeze over. In fierce fighting 13th Guards was reduced to 1,500 men but was the 62nd Army's strongest unit.

By the end of the day 62nd Army had been reduced to three small pockets along the Volga. The northern pocket, held by 1,000 men at Rynok and Spartakovka was under heavy attack by 14th Panzer Korp, while the central pocket, comprising 138th Rifle Division with just 500 men, was near the Barrikady factory. Farther south were the remnants of the 95th, 45th, 39th Guards, 284th and 13th Guards Divisions plus various scratch units, some 45,000 men with fewer than twenty tanks. The 51st Korp pounded the two southern pockets.

As the battle reached its climax, Zhukov informed Stalin that all was ready and the counter-offensive could begin on 19 November to the north and 20 November to the south.

The 13th Panzer Division retreated from Ordzhonikidze, its flanks having been threatened by Soviet attacks. 5th SS *Wiking* Motorised Division attacked towards the hard-pressed 13th.

12 November 1942

SOUTHERN SECTOR
Fighting raged unabated as 6th Army pounded 62nd Army. The Germans were already bogged down in costly, close-quarters fighting with the small and aggressive combat groups that simply refused to give up. Luftwaffe reconnaissance over the Rumanian 3rd Army sector detected a build up of Soviet forces, which Fremde Heer Ost believed would be used for a limited counter-offensive against the Rumanian lines.

13–17 November 1942

SOUTHERN SECTOR
The battle for Stalingrad raged as the German attacks began to overwhelm 62nd Army. With floating ice on the Volga, the Soviets had difficulty sending supplies across the river and 62nd began to run short of food and ammunition. The men cut off at Rynok and Spartakovka suffered badly, coming under sustained attack from 16th Panzer Division. This group, commanded by Gorokhov, was down to just 300 men but continued to fight on. Chuikov was forced to admit that the end was in sight for 62nd Army.

18 November 1942

SOUTHERN SECTOR
The Red Army prepared to launch its biggest and most ambitious offensive of the war so far. The deployment of strike forces was completed during the night of 18–19 November.

On the right wing of the offensive, South-West Front deployed 1st Guards, 21st Armies and 5th Tank Army together with 3rd Guards Cavalry and 4th Tank Corps Vatutin's force numbered 398,000 men with 6,500 artillery pieces, nearly 150 Katyushas and 730 tanks. Supporting the front was a fleet of 14,000 transport vehicles and 69,000 horses. 17th Air Army provided aerial support with 380 aircraft and 2nd Air Army with 150 planes. In all the front had eighteen rifle divisions, eight artillery regiments, three tank corps, two cavalry corps, one tank brigade and one motorised brigade.

To the left were the forces of Rokossovsky's Don Front. This formation had 66th Army, 24th Army and 65th Army and 16th Air Army with 260 aircraft. Total deployment amounted to twenty-four rifle divisions, one tank corp, six tank brigades and forty-two artillery regiments, a force of 307,000 men, 5,300 artillery pieces and mortars and 150 Katyushas, 180 tanks, 12,000 motor transport vehicles and 45,000 horses.

The Stalingrad Front, commanded by Eremenko, formed the southern pincer. This force had 62nd Army fighting inside Stalingrad, 64th Army, Trufanov's 51st and Tolbukhin's 57th Armies. In support were 4th and 13th Mechanised Corps, 4th Cavalry Corp and 8th Air Army, the latter having more than 530 aircraft at its disposal. In all the Stalingrad Front committed twenty-four rifle divisions, seventeen rifle brigades, two mechanised corps, one cavalry corp and sixty-seven artillery regiments, 429,000 men, 5,800 artillery pieces and mortars, 145 Katyusha, 650 tanks, 15,000 motor vehicles and 55,000 horses.

Against the strike sectors lay 3rd and 4th Rumanian Armies. Third Rumanian Army, commanded by General Dumitrescu, faced South-West and Don Fronts and deployed 1st Korp with 7th and 11th Divisions, 2nd Korp with 9th and 14th Divisions, 5th Korp with 5th and 6th Divisions and 4th Korp with 13th and 15th Divisions. The 1st Cavalry Division protected the army's right-wing junction with 11th Korp of 6th Army, while 7th Cavalry division was in reserve. The army totalled 100,000 men dug in on the southern bank of the Don. To the rear stood Heim's 48th Panzer Korp with 22nd Panzer and a Rumanian armoured division. Facing 51st and 57th Armies on the southern flank was 4th Rumanian Army under Constantinescu. Only recently activated, this army had 6th Rumanian Korp with 2nd, 18th, 20th, 1st and 4th Infantry Divisions and 4th Rumanian Cavalry Corp with 5th and 8th Cavalry Divisions, some 70,000 men.[22] Bogged down inside Stalingrad, facing 62nd Army and 64th Army, were 6th Army and 4th Panzer Army. Sixth Army deployed 51st, 11th and 8th Korps and 14th Panzer Korp, while 4th Panzer Army had 4th Korp.

Deep in the Caucasus were 1st Panzer and 17th Armies. The 17th Army had de Angelis' 44th Korp near Maikop, and 49th Mountain and 5th Korp near Novorossysk. First Panzer deployed 3rd Panzer Korp at Ordzhonikidze, and 52nd Korp and 40th Panzer Korp at Mozdok.

THE OSTHEER

Germany's allies deployed significant forces on the eve of the Soviet offensive. Rumania had twenty-seven divisions, Hungary twelve divisions, Italy ten divisions and three brigades, while Slovakia had one division, the Spanish one division and the Finns sixteen divisions.

SOVIET CASUALTIES

Since the defence of Stalingrad had begun in July, the Stalingrad Front had lost 194,600 killed and missing and 215,000 wounded, while the Don Front, in action since the end of September, lost 18,000 killed and missing and 42,000 wounded. The Soviet forces on the Stalingrad axis lost 1,400 tanks, 12,000 artillery pieces and 2,000 aircraft.

> On the eve of the Soviet counter-offensive, with winter closing in, the Germans were faced with the prospect of fighting another bloody battle against an enemy who was equipped for the rigours of winter war. The 6th Army was woefully short of winter clothing and equipment. Paulus himself was demoralised, his attention fixed on the capture of the city to the detriment of his flanks. Having encountered Soviet forces in the Crimea and western Ukraine, the Rumanians had proved unable to stand up to the Red Army and such a burden of responsibility should never have been placed upon their shoulders. The 170,000 men of 3rd and 4th Rumanian Armies held the fate of Paulus' 6th Army in their hands. The Red Army stood prepared to take the war back to the Germans, to begin the long battle for the re-conquest of Russia.

NOTES

1 Kirosheev, *Soviet Casualties and Combat Losses in the Twentieth Century*, Table 75
2 Ellis, *The World War Two Databook*, p 175
3 Ellis, *The World War Two Databook*, p 175
4 Tarrant, *Stalingrad*, p 69
5 Tarrant, *Stalingrad*, p 72
6 Erickson, *The Road to Stalingrad*, p 403
7 Erickson, *The Road to Stalingrad*, p 408
8 Erickson, *The Road to Stalingrad*, p 427
9 Kirosheev, *Soviet Casualties and Combat Losses in the Twentieth Century*, Table 67
10 Tarrant, *Stalingrad*, p 83
11 Erickson, *The Road to Stalingrad*, pp 421–2
12 Kirosheev, *Soviet Casualties and Combat Losses in the Twentieth Century*, Table 75
13 Glantz, *Zhukov's Greatest Defeat*, p 22
14 Glantz, *Zhukov's Greatest Defeat*, p 25
15 Glantz, *Zhukov's Greatest Defeat*, pp 34–5
16 Erickson, *The Road to Stalingrad*, p 453
17 Erickson, *The Road to Stalingrad*, p 446
18 Glantz, *Zhukov's Greatest Defeat*, p 19
19 Ellis, *The World War Two Databook*, p 175
20 Ellis, *The World War Two Databook*, p 178
21 Erickson, *The Road to Stalingrad*, p 462
22 Rumanian deployments from Tarrant, *Stalingrad*, pp 98–9

Bibliography

Ailsby, C, SS: *Hell on the Eastern Front*, Spellmount, 1998

Barr, N and Hart, R (eds), *Panzer*, Aurum Press, 1999
Buchner, A, *Ostfront 1944*, Schiffer Military, 1991
_____*The German Infantry Handbook*, Schiffer Military, 1991

Carell, P, *Hitler's War on Russia, Vol 1*, Corgi, 1967
_____*Scorched Earth, Hitler's War on Russia Vol II*, Harrap, 1970
Carruthers, R and Erickson, J, *The Russian Front, 1941–1945*, Cassell, 1999
Cross, R, *Citadel*, BCA (Michael O'Mara), 1993
Chuikov, V I, *The Beginning of the Road*, MacGibbon & Kee, 1963
_____*The End of the Third Reich*, MacGibbon & Kee, 1967
Clark, Alan, *Barbarossa*, Cassell, 2000

Duffy, Christopher, *Red Storm on the Reich*, Routledge, 2001

Ellis, John, *Brute Force*, Deutsch, 1990
_____*The World War Two Databook*, Aurum Press, 1993
Erickson, John, *The Road to Stalingrad*, Weidenfeld & Nicolson, 1983
_____*The Road to Berlin*, Weidenfeld & Nicolson, 1993

Glantz, David M, *From the Don to the Dnepr*, Frank Cass, 1991
_____*Zhukov's Greatest Defeat*, University Press of Kansas, 1999.
_____*Barbarossa 1941*, Tempus 2001.
Glantz, David M and House, Jonathan, *When Titans Clashed*, Birlinn, 2000
Gorbatov, A, *Years of My Life*, Constable, 1964
Gilbert, Marlin, *The Second World War*, Fontana, 1990
Guderian, Heinz, *Panzer Leader*, Arrow, 1990

Halder, F, *Hitler as Warlord*, Putnam, 1950
Healy, Mark, *Kursk 1943* (Osprey Combat Series), Osprey, 1992

Hughes, Matthew and Mann, Chris, *The T-34, Weapons of War*, Spellmount, 1999

Lederrey, E, *Germany's Defeat in the East*, War Office, 1959
Liddell-Hart, B H, *The Other Side of the Hill*, Cassell, 1948
Lucas, James, *Last Days of the Reich*, Guild, 1986
_____*Storming Eagles*, Guild, 1988
_____*War on the Eastern Front*, Greenhill, 1991
_____*The Last Year of the German Army*, BCA (Arms & Armour), 1994
_____*German Army Handbook 1939–1945*, Sutton, 1998

Macksey, Kenneth, *Tank versus Tank*, Guild, 1988
Manstein, Erich von, *Last Victories*, Greenhill, 1987
Meilenthin, F W von, *Panzer Battles*, University of Oklahoma Press, 1989
Minasyan, M M, *The Great Patriotic War of the Soviet Union*, 1974.
Mitcham, S W, *Hitler's Legions: the German Army Order of Battle, World War II*, Leo   Cooper/Secker & Warburg, 1985

Perrett, Bryan, *Knights of the Black Cross*, Hale, 1986

Quarrie, Bruce, *Hitler's Samurai*, Guild, 1985
_____*Hitler's Teutonic Knights*, Patrick Stephens, 1987
_____*Weapons of the Waffen SS*, Patrick Stephens, 1988
Rauss, Erhard and Njatzmer, Oldwig Von, *The Anvil of War*, Greenhill, 1994

Salisbury, Harrison E, *The 900 Days*, Pan, 2000
Seaton, Albert, *The Russo–German War 1941–45*, Presidio, 1990
Shirer, William L, *The Rise and Fall of the Third Reich*, Secker & Warburg, 1984
Speer, Albert, *Inside the Third Reich*, Phoenix, 1995

Tarrant, V B, *Stalingrad*, Leo Cooper, 1992
Trevor-Roper, H R (ed), *Hitler's War Directives*, 1939–1945, Pan, 1973

Werth, A, *Russia at War 1941–45*, Corgi, 1965

Young, Peter, *The Almanac of World War II*, Hamlyn Bison, 1981

Zaloga, Steven J and Grandsen, James, *Soviet Tanks and Combat Vehicles of World War II*, Arms & Armour Press, 1984
Ziemke, E F, *Stalingrad to Berlin: the German Defeat in the East*, GPO, Washington, 1968
Zhukov, Georgi K, *Marshal Zhukov's Greatest Battles*, Macdonald, 1965

Index – Places

Index – People

Pavlov 20, 35, 36, 39, 40, 44, 45, 48, 49, 51, 52, 57
Petrov 94, 252, 305
Pliev 237
Podlas 97, 241
Ponedelin 24, 86, 88, 91
Popov 25, 27, 44, 61, 79, 100, 101,113, 188, 189, 190, 191
Potapov 24, 37, 45, 33, 56, 57, 71, 86, 88, 89, 95, 97, 100, 103, 115, 119, 124
Pshennikov 27, 85, 88
Pyadyshev 44, 64, 74, 79

Raeder 4
Rakutin 96,99
Reichenau 21, 36, 42, 47, 49, 53, 56, 57, 77, 97, 100, 107, 126, 150, 153, 154, 174, 176, 203, 204
Reinhardt 14, 33, 34, 38, 41, 46, 48, 52, 55, 58, 64, 66, 68, 69, 71, 74, 84, 98, 104, 141, 169
Remezov 63, 71, 79, 184
Ribbentrop 3, 6, 8
Richthofen 20, 256
Rodimtimv 290, 291
Rokosiovsky 24, 77, 142, 147, 166, 168, 169, 84, 186, 193, 297, 308, 314
Rominenko 308
Rundstedt 21, 23, 36, 62, 104, 113,128, 144, 160, 166, 169, 170, 173, 174
Ruoff 18, 244, 255, 259, 269, 270, 273, 274, 285, 287, 294, 302, 305
Ryabyshev 81, 103
Rybalko 305

Salmuth 23, 260
Scherer 206, 217, 211, 214, 228
Schmidt 19, 39, 46, 101, 117, 191
Schobert 22, 59, 60, 92
Schwedler 21, 83, 276
Schweppenburg 19, 35, 57, 63, 65, 86, 107, 112, 117, 119, 146, 160
Seydlitz-Kurzbach 219, 220, 224
Shaposhnikov 32, 32, 85, 113, 117, 120, 138, 158
Shchebakov 120
Shumilov 267, 282, 307
Sinzinger 210, 212, 215, 216
Smirnov 43, 60, 63
Sobennikov 16, 43, 44, 55, 57, 67, 100
Sokolov 145, 200

Sorge 12, 13
Speer 213
Sponek 192, 203
Stalin, Josef 6, 7, 8, 9, 11, 12, 13, 14, 31, 32, 33, 37, 40, 51, 52, 60, 61, 75, 77, 85, 94, 95, 111, 114, 117,118, 119, 120, 122, 124, 128, 138, 141, 143, 152, 159, 183, 193, 196, 203, 221, 224, 228, 229, 237, 238, 241, 245, 249, 232, 254, 236, 265, 268, 271, 276, 280, 281, 282, 285, 286, 288, 289, 290, 296, 313
Strauss 17, 34, 45, 47, 71, 28, 139, 203
Strecker 256
Stuplnagel 21, 40, 49, 53, 59, 63, 65, 92, 126, 141

Timoshenko 5, 7, 12, 32, 38, 44, 45, 47, 4.8, 49, 52, 58, 62, 70, 94, 119, 130, 152, 159, 161, 170, 178, 183, 185, 194, 195, 196, 208, 227, 232, 233, 237, 238, 239, 239, 261
Tolbukhinl 268, 314
Trufanov 269, 314
Tukhachevski 6
Tyulenev 24, 43, 58, 64, 77, 81, 84, 88, 98, 100, 103, 141, 262, 265, 270, 274, 283

Vasilevsky 263, 271, 289, 290
Vatutin 73, 150, 151, 256, 308, 314
Vietinghoff 19
Vlassov 24, 72, 95, 97, 107,119, 217, 218, 241, 249
Volskii 307
Voroshilov 5, 6, 32, 52, 56, 70, 93, 100, 103, 113, 118, 124

Weichs 255, 260, 301
Weitersheim 21, 49, 279

Yakovlev 119, 160

Zeitzler 295
Zhadov 308
Zhakharov 24, 147, 167
Zhukov 31, 32, 52, 84, 85, 107, 118, 120, 124, 133, 143, 144, 145, 152, 160, 163, 167, 169, 171, 173, 175, 178, 179, 184, 185, 188, 196, 204, 206, 211, 212, 215, 216, 271, 281, 282, 286, 288, 289, 290, 296, 313